PUBLIC POLICY
AND PRIVATE
HIGHER EDUCATION

STUDIES IN HIGHER EDUCATION POLICY

PUBLIC POLICY AND PRIVATE HIGHER EDUCATION

EDITED BY

David W. Breneman and Chester E. Finn, Jr.

WITH THE ASSISTANCE OF

Susan C. Nelson

AND WITH CONTRIBUTIONS BY

*Robert O. Berdahl, Colin C. Blaydon, David W. Breneman,
David G. Brown, Chester E. Finn, Jr., Lawrence E. Gladieux,
Robert W. Hartman, Michael S. McPherson, Susan C. Nelson,
Emil M. Sunley, Jr., Thomas E. Wenzlau,
and Thomas R. Wolanin*

THE BROOKINGS INSTITUTION
Washington, D.C.

Copyright © 1978 by
THE BROOKINGS INSTITUTION
1775 Massachusetts Avenue, N.W., Washington, D.C. 20036

Library of Congress Cataloging in Publication Data:
Main entry under title:
Public policy and private higher education.
Includes bibliographical references and index.
1. Higher education and state—United States.
I. Breneman, David W. II. Finn, Chester E., Jr.,
1944– III. Nelson, Susan C.
LC173.P82   379'.344'0973   77-91798
ISBN 0-8157-1066-6
ISBN 0-8157-1065-8 pbk.

9 8 7 6 5 4 3 2 1

THE BROOKINGS INSTITUTION is an independent organization devoted to nonpartisan research, education, and publication in economics, government, foreign policy, and the social sciences generally. Its principal purposes are to aid in the development of sound public policies and to promote public understanding of issues of national importance.

The Institution was founded on December 8, 1927, to merge the activities of the Institute for Government Research, founded in 1916, the Institute of Economics, founded in 1922, and the Robert Brookings Graduate School of Economics and Government, founded in 1924.

The Board of Trustees is responsible for the general administration of the Institution, while the immediate direction of the policies, program, and staff is vested in the President, assisted by an advisory committee of the officers and staff. The by-laws of the Institution state: "It is the function of the Trustees to make possible the conduct of scientific research, and publication, under the most favorable conditions, and to safeguard the independence of the research staff in the pursuit of their studies and in the publication of the results of such studies. It is not a part of their function to determine, control, or influence the conduct of particular investigations or the conclusions reached."

The President bears final responsibility for the decision to publish a manuscript as a Brookings book. In reaching his judgment on the competence, accuracy, and objectivity of each study, the President is advised by the director of the appropriate research program and weighs the views of a panel of expert outside readers who report to him in confidence on the quality of the work. Publication of a work signifies that it is deemed a competent treatment worthy of public consideration but does not imply endorsement of conclusions or recommendations.

The Institution maintains its position of neutrality on issues of public policy in order to safeguard the intellectual freedom of the staff. Hence interpretations or conclusions in Brookings publications should be understood to be solely those of the authors and should not be attributed to the Institution, to its trustees, officers, or other staff members, or to the organizations that support its research.

Foreword

OVER HALF the 3,000 colleges and universities in the United States are private institutions. Theirs is a unique heritage whose emphasis on independence, diversity, and individuality has helped mold the American character. And from the late 1950s until recently they enjoyed an unprecedented boom. By the mid-1970s private colleges employed more professors and taught more students than ever before, and many of them enjoyed well-deserved reputations for educational excellence. Yet the picture is clearly changing, not only for the private colleges but for all of higher education. The strong demand for postsecondary schooling that marked the past quarter-century will abate in the 1980s. Population trends, social attitudes, and high prices are among the causes. The number of eighteen-year-olds will decline sharply, and if recent trends persist fewer of them will continue their education beyond high school. For most of those who do, the ability to choose a private college may be foreclosed if the price difference between public and private institutions for a bachelor's degree (currently around $8,000) continues to grow.

Leaders of private higher education fear that retrenchment will take place at their expense as they compete with state-subsidized institutions in a shrinking marketplace. Government—state and federal—will strongly influence the outcome of this competition, since both public and private sectors of higher education are highly dependent on the government for financial support, both direct and indirect.

Concern for such policy issues in the field of higher education prompted Roger W. Heyns, a distinguished scholar-administrator and former president of the American Council on Education, to urge the late Kermit Gordon to bring to Brookings more researchers interested in higher education issues. This book on the politics and economics of private higher education is the first of the new Brookings series of Studies in Higher Education Policy.

Despite the manifest complexity of the issues, the authors conclude with two straightforward propositions. First, anyone seeking to solve the

vii

dilemmas facing private higher education in the 1980s cannot avoid a fundamental policy choice between making private colleges financially more like public ones, or public colleges more like private ones. Either is possible, but the choice must be made before other serious issues are addressed. Second, federal and state education policies have to be consciously coordinated (as they rarely have been in the past), if a strong and balanced system of higher education is to be preserved.

In preparing this book, the editors developed its outline and distributed an early version of the first chapter to the authors, who met as a group in April 1976 to discuss and amend the editors' conception. Drafts of the first nine chapters served as background papers for a Brookings conference in November 1976, whose participants are listed on pages 459–60. While this book is not intended in any way to reflect their views, the conferees made valuable comments and offered suggestions that led to substantial revision of all chapters. The conference discussion and subsequent correspondence were also helpful to the editors as they wrote the concluding chapter.

Those primarily interested in the recent history of public-private issues, policy options, and the editors' recommendations can gain such an overview from the first and last chapters. The intervening, more specialized, chapters include two that provide analytical background on the financing of private higher education (Susan C. Nelson) and the demand for it (Michael S. McPherson); three on federal policy, dealing with the Washington political arena (Lawrence E. Gladieux and Thomas R. Wolanin), student aid (Robert W. Hartman), and tax matters (Emil M. Sunley, Jr.); two on state policy, covering political relationships (Robert O. Berdahl) and financing options (Colin C. Blaydon); and one written from the private college president's point of view (David G. Brown and Thomas E. Wenzlau).

The editors, for themselves and on behalf of the authors, thank the conferees for their comments and criticisms; Susan C. Nelson, who in addition to her own chapter, assisted in all aspects of editorial and project management; John M. Jefferies, Mara P. O'Neill, Nancy J. Osher, Ellen W. Smith, and Ellie Winninghoff, who provided research assistance; and Annette Hartling, Radmila Nikolić, Celia B. Rich, and Gail L. Zirkel, who provided secretarial support.

The factual content of this book was verified by Evelyn P. Fisher. The manuscript was edited by Barbara P. Haskins, and the index was prepared by Diana H. Regenthal.

Financial support for the project was provided by the Andrew W. Mellon Foundation and the Exxon Education Foundation, and for certain chapters by the Cleveland Foundation and the U.S. Steel Foundation.

The views expressed in this book are solely those of the authors, and should not be attributed to the trustees, officers, or staff of the Brookings Institution or to the foundations that contributed to the financing of the project.

BRUCE K. MACLAURY

President

February 1978
Washington, D.C.

Contents

Chapter One

An Uncertain Future

David W. Breneman and Chester E. Finn, Jr.

DAVID W. BRENEMAN is a senior fellow in the Brookings Economic Studies program. CHESTER E. FINN, JR., senior legislative assistant to Senator Daniel P. Moynihan, is a former research associate in the Brookings Governmental Studies program.

Tables

Figures

The private colleges and universities of the United States are, individually and collectively, in extreme danger.

NEW YORK TIMES

One of the central questions facing higher education today is whether small private colleges, and the educational pluralism they offer to the nation, have any future.

WALL STREET JOURNAL

I think the institution of private colleges and universities will survive but I'm afraid that I don't believe that all the present examples of those institutions will survive. I have predicted if present terms continue about half of them are going to go out of business. One way or another they will no longer be private colleges in the sense in which they exist now.

JOHN G. KEMENY[1]

THE GROWTH of private higher education is one of the most durable and impressive success stories in the history of American domestic institutions. In the mid-1970s the private sector boasts more colleges and universities, more students and more professors than ever before, and many of its campuses enjoy well-deserved reputations for educational excellence. Why, then, do serious and responsible observers believe that it is imperiled? Why do reasonable people suggest that if private higher education endures at all it will be so diminished and altered as to bring to an end its singular contribution to American society? Is there actually a problem and, if so, what is its relevance for public policy at the state and federal levels?

Such questions concern many thoughtful observers of—and participants in—U.S. higher education, but answers grounded on careful study are hard to find. What is needed, therefore, is an examination of these issues, including the conflicting forces that affect public policy; the options facing federal, state, and institutional decisionmakers; and recommendations based on sound analysis for action in the years ahead.

That is what this book sets out to do. Part one of this chapter defines the problems and explains the purpose of this study; part two presents in broad perspective the issues covered in the following chapters.

---

1. The quotations are from: *New York Times*, editorial, March 11, 1975; *Wall Street Journal*, editorial, December 4, 1975; and *Washington Star*, interview with President John G. Kemeny of Dartmouth College, April 24, 1975.

Figure 1-1. *Number of Eighteen-year-olds in the U.S. Population, 1970–93*[a]

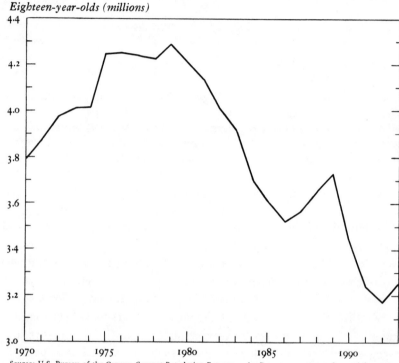

Eighteen-year-olds (millions)

Source: U.S. Bureau of the Census, *Current Population Reports,* series P-25, nos. 511, 529, 601, and 643.
a. Based on actual births. Changes in data caused by deaths and net migration would be relatively minor.

PART ONE: THE PROBLEMS

Simple demographic trends explain much of the malaise in higher education generally and in the private sector particularly. Figure 1-1 charts the size of the eighteen-year-old age group in the U.S. population for the years 1970 through 1993. This age group, representing the traditional source of entering college freshmen, peaks in 1979 at 4.3 million, and declines markedly to a low of 3.2 million in 1992, a drop of more than 25 percent from the peak. Census statistics cannot be easily translated into enrollment projections, however, since there are so many additional variables.[2] If other age groups were to matriculate in unprecedented

2. Detailed discussions of enrollment projections to the year 2000 are found in Carnegie Foundation for the Advancement of Teaching, *More Than Survival: Prospects for Higher Education in a Period of Uncertainty* (Jossey-Bass, 1975),

numbers, postsecondary enrollments could still grow. So would they if larger percentages of any particular group were to apply. Yet demographic trends alone are ample cause for concern about higher education in the United States. And the mounting evidence of falling economic returns to a college degree exacerbates the problem, so that gloomy enrollment projections both symbolize and contribute to widespread fears that an industry, which in the past quarter-century has grown in an unprecedented fashion, is heading for a period of retrenchment and decline.[3]

Spokesmen for the private sector fear that their institutions may absorb much of that retrenchment. A greatly expanded public sector, nurtured and maintained by the state, competes with them for students, revenue, and status. The existing structure of public subsidies greatly influences the nature of that competition. In an era of spiraling costs in higher education, public colleges and universities receive subventions that help them to keep down prices, whereas private institutions are forced to pass much of their rising costs on to those who purchase their services. A student endeavoring to choose between public and private schools must anticipate paying substantially more—an average of $7,000 to $8,000 in the course of a bachelor's degree—if he or she elects a private institution. If there are too few students to fill the classrooms of both sectors, the private colleges reason, how can the high-priced schools expect to survive?

Not surprisingly, worried leaders of private institutions have turned to the state and federal governments for policies—and dollars—that would stave off this prospect of decline. Arguments have been made for new forms of support through the tax system (such as tuition tax credits), through direct institutional aid, and through tuition-sensitive student aid policies. The recent shift in self-designation from "private" to "independent" common among the colleges and universities is intended to buttress the case for increased public support, since the new label stresses the independent governance of institutions serving *public* purposes. Before becoming enmeshed in the details of specific forms that public aid to the private sector could take, however, there is a basic question to be considered.

---

pp. 39–49; and Allan M. Cartter, *Ph.D.'s and the Academic Labor Market* (McGraw-Hill, 1976), pp. 41–71.

3. See, for example, Richard B. Freeman, *The Overeducated American* (Academic Press, 1976), and chapter 3 of this book.

Is There a Case for Increased Public Support of the Private Sector?

In our judgment, any case for increased public support cannot—and should not—be made in the abstract or by relying on existing social science knowledge. At issue is the optimal allocation of resources to higher education, for which economic analysis has provided no clear solution.[4] Indeed, some analysts would reverse the question: is there any economic justification for continued subsidy of *public* higher education?[5] Other analysts argue that the subject cannot properly be considered without taking into account the entire range of programs supporting human development, including activities such as employment and training assistance and military programs that are not part of higher education. Still others insist that a solution must be deferred until more is known about the effects of higher education, and how particular programs and types of institutions influence individual development. Although policy would no doubt be improved if there were answers to the research questions implied by these lines of reasoning, immediate choices still have to be made.

Supporters of private higher education have not generally advanced sophisticated economic arguments to bolster their case, but have instead maintained that private institutions contribute in important and unique ways to diversity, independence, quality, efficiency, and innovation within U.S. higher education.[6] While such arguments are generally persuasive, their acceptance (and few would deny them, at least as historically accurate) does not lead directly or unambiguously to clear public policies. Consequently, it is not a fruitful exercise to try to "prove" the

4. We pose here the basic questions underlying the theme of this book, but we defer our answers until chapter 10, in which we make explicit policy recommendations designed for the projected conditions of the 1980s.

5. See "Investment in Education: The Equity-Efficiency Quandary," a Supplement to the *Journal of Political Economy*, vol. 80, no. 3, pt. 2 (May/June 1972).

6. Representative samples from the vast literature extolling the merits of private higher education are Edward Shils, "The American Private University," *Minerva*, vol. 11 (January 1973), pp. 6–29; David Riesman, "The Future of Diversity in a Time of Retrenchment," *Higher Education*, vol. 4 (Amsterdam: Elsevier, November 1975), pp. 461–82; Gerard Piel, "Public Support for Autonomous Universities," and Richard W. Lyman, "In Defense of the Private Sector," both in *Daedalus*, vol. 104 (Winter 1975), pp. 148–55 and 156–59, respectively; Christopher Jencks and David Riesman, *The Academic Revolution* (Doubleday, 1968); Paul C. Reinert, *To Turn the Tide* (Prentice-Hall, 1972); and National Council of Independent Colleges and Universities, *A National Policy for Private Higher Education* (Association of American Colleges, 1974).

case for increased public support for private colleges and universities by extended analysis of the merits of such institutions.

There are, however, cogent reasons for developing a study of public policy toward private higher education:

1. The prospect of severe retrenchment faces higher education for the next decade or more,[7] and the public interest would be poorly served indeed if all of the shrinkage or deterioration were concentrated in the private sector; far better to strive for a fair and honestly competitive situation in which the fate of specific institutions depends on their performance.

2. The impersonal working of the existing higher education marketplace cannot be relied upon to direct resources in a socially optimal manner because of the crazy-quilt of subsidies and prices that characterizes this industry. Tuition prices do not reflect resource costs accurately; consequently, there would be no reason to accept the market's verdict as optimal if the heavily subsidized state institutions managed to drive large numbers of private colleges from the field.

3. Given the existing investment in physical plant and personnel within the private college sector, it would be foolish for a state to contemplate further expansion of its public campuses without exploring what might be more cost-effective options of partially subsidizing additional enrollment in independent institutions.

4. The fact that over forty states have developed some form of financial support for private colleges or their students[8] indicates widening acceptance of the principle of public subsidy for private higher education. What is needed, therefore, is not further debate on the principle, but rather careful analysis of the social costs and benefits of the different forms of aid, both state and federal.

How Critical Is the Need for Support?

In the seven years since the publication of Earl Cheit's *New Depression in Higher Education*,[9] there have been many assertions that colleges

7. The Carnegie Council on Policy Studies in Higher Education has suggested that as many as 10 percent of current institutions of higher education will not survive into the early 1980s in their current form; see Carnegie Foundation for the Advancement of Teaching, *More Than Survival*, p. 4.

8. *Higher Education in the States*, vol. 5, no. 1 (Education Commission of the States, 1975).

9. Earl F. Cheit, *The New Depression in Higher Education: A Study of Financial Conditions at 41 Colleges and Universities* (McGraw-Hill, 1971).

Table 1-1. *Closings of Private Four-Year Institutions,*
Spring 1970 to Fall 1976

Institution and State	Enroll- ment	Institution and State	Enroll- ment
Alaska		*New Jersey*	
Alaska Methodist		Shelton College[b]	153
University[a]	878	*New Mexico*	
Arizona		College of Artesia[b]	544
College Del Ray[b]	54		
Prescott College	455	*New York*	
California		Finch College	379
Arizona Bible College of		Verrazzano College[b]	45
Biola College[b]	190	*Ohio*	
Tahoe College[b]	253	College of the Dayton	
Connecticut		Art Institute[b]	298
College of Notre Dame		Mary Manse College	509
of Wilton[b]	118	St. John College of	
District of Columbia		Cleveland	732
Dunbarton College of		*Oregon*	
Holy Cross	345	Mount Angel College[b]	280
Illinois		*Rhode Island*	
St. Dominic College[b]	212	Catholic Teachers College[b]	119
Iowa		Roger Williams College,	
Midwestern College[b]	800	Providence Branch[b]	2,059
Parsons College	1,270		
Kansas		*Tennessee*	
College of Emporia	510	Siena College	239
Maryland		*Texas*	
St. Joseph College	403	Dominican College	307
Massachusetts		University of Corpus Christi	560
Cardinal Cushing College	390	University of Plano[b]	135
Michigan		*Virginia*	
Mackinac College[b]	311	Stratford College	562
Minnesota			
Lea College[b]	367	*Wisconsin*	
Nebraska		College of Racine	817
Hiram Scott College[b]	1,600	Layton School of Art	
John F. Kennedy College[b]	266	and Design[b]	276
John J. Pershing College[b]	521	Mount St. Paul College[b]	218
New Hampshire		*Puerto Rico*	
Belknap College[b]	411	Caribbean Center for	
Canaan College[b]	92	Advanced Studies	121

Source: Virginia Fadil, "Openings, Closings, Mergers and Accreditation Status of Independent Colleges and Universities," Occasional Research Report (National Association of Independent Colleges and Universities, November 1977; processed), tables 8, 9.

Note: A total of thirty-nine four-year institutions closed during this period with an enrollment of 17,799

and universities are in financial difficulty, a point buttressed by periodic feature stories on the closing of yet another small campus. But the actual number of four-year college closings in the 1970–76 period has been insignificant, as table 1-1, from a report of the National Association of Independent Colleges and Universities, shows.[10]

Bowen and Minter had already commented on this fact in 1975:

Most of the four-year institutions that have disappeared as separate entities were extremely small and obscure. Many were new institutions that had never taken root. It may be said emphatically that there have as yet been no Penn Centrals in higher education. It may also be said that in the course of American history hundreds of small struggling colleges have disappeared. One of the results of the free enterprise system in higher education is that not every venture will succeed, and that failure is sometimes a concomitant of independence and innovation. The main stream of private higher education is far from defunct. Reports of the demise of the private sector are, like Mark Twain's death, greatly exaggerated. However, as this report indicates, there are signs of strain, and there are no guarantees against future casualties.[11]

An accurate assessment of either the current or prospective financial situation of colleges and universities has thus far eluded those who have investigated the subject. The reasons have been well documented in reports by the National Commission on the Financing of Postsecondary Education and by Hans Jenny.[12] The ensuing uncertainty makes it difficult to develop public policy since no one knows for sure whether, as the

10. Virginia Fadil, "Openings, Closings, Mergers and Accreditation Status of Independent Colleges and Universities," Occasional Research Report (National Association of Independent Colleges and Universities, November 1977; processed), tables 8, 9.

11. Howard R. Bowen and W. John Minter, *Private Higher Education: First Annual Report on Financial and Educational Trends in the Private Sector of American Higher Education* (Association of American Colleges, 1975), p. 101.

12. National Commission on the Financing of Postsecondary Education, *Financing Postsecondary Education in the United States* (Government Printing Office, 1973), pp. 185–226; and Hans H. Jenny, *Higher Education and the Economy*, ERIC Higher Education Research Report 2 (American Association for Higher Education, Educational Resources Information Center, 1976).

Table 1-1 (*continued*)

students, divided between accredited and unaccredited institutions as follows:

Type of institution	Number	Enrollment	
		Number	Percent
Accredited	16	8,477	47.6
Unaccredited	23	9,322	52.4
Total	39	17,799	100.0

In addition, thirty-seven two-year colleges and thirty-seven specialized institutions (primarily seminaries or religious schools) closed.

a. Reopened fall 1977.

b. Unaccredited institutions.

dire warnings predict, x percent of the private colleges in the country will close in the next several years if no action is taken. What can be stated with certainty is that the number of college closings to date does not, of itself, make the case for sudden public intervention to "save" the private sector.

Nonetheless, the increasing pressure for federal and state policies of support for private colleges and universities is clear evidence of the growing financial distress felt within the private institutions. However, as in the case of college closings, anyone who attempts to review recent studies that purport to document the nature, causes, and severity of the financial problem is left confused and frustrated. Recent federal higher education policymaking provides an excellent example. Reports during the late 1960s and early 1970s proclaiming the growing financing problems of colleges and universities set the stage for one of the most hotly contested and divisive attempts to develop federal higher education legislation in recent years—the Education Amendments of 1972.[13] The Washington-based higher education associations chose that moment to press for direct federal institutional aid, allocated on a formula basis and tied to enrollments. In the ensuing debate, several members of Congress grew impatient with the absence of hard data and analysis to support such a case, and hence a provision was added to the law establishing a National Commission on the Financing of Postsecondary Education, charged with the task of thoroughly reviewing the nature and causes of financial distress, with developing an analytical framework for the evaluation of alternative financing schemes, and with presenting recommendations for financing policies that would best serve the national interest. The seventeen-member commission reported in December 1973, and included the following appraisal of recent studies on the subject of financial distress:

Those who have studied the matter are far from unanimous, however, about the seriousness of the problem and the necessity for governmental intervention. Of special significance is the fact that the literature provides clear evidence that there is no agreement on a uniform definition regarding the nature of financial distress among postsecondary institutions, nor are there generally accepted standards or uniform criteria to ascertain its existence or extent.[14]

13. 86 Stat. 235. For an excellent discussion of the development of this legislation, see Lawrence E. Gladieux and Thomas R. Wolanin, *Congress and the Colleges* (Heath, 1976). Chapters 4 and 5 give further information about this act and its effect on public policy. See also Glossary.

14. National Commission on the Financing of Postsecondary Education, *Financing Postsecondary Education in the United States* (GPO, 1973), p. 193.

This thoroughly agnostic conclusion regarding the significance of earlier reports was followed by the observation:

Currently, there is no working consensus about the basic requirements for distress analysis or the key indicators, financial and nonfinancial, of serious financial distress in postsecondary education. Thus, if distress analysis is to become a useful tool for policy making, it is necessary to attempt to identify those indicators and develop the analytical requirements.[15]

The commission's findings reflect several analytical problems, not unique to higher education, but certainly well represented there: the lack of uniform accounting procedures, the difficulty of interpreting reported deficits, and the problems of identifying and evaluating quality deterioration. Although work is proceeding on these fronts, the essential "facts" seem likely to remain uncertain and in dispute for the immediate future. Were another national commission to be named in 1978, it would probably reach much the same inconclusive and frustrating judgments about the state of the art and the health of the academic community.[16]

It is not our intention in this book to second-guess past studies or to add to the debate on the current financial condition of the private sector

15. Ibid, p. 219.

16. The highly publicized special report in the September 1976 issue of *Change* is an example of continuing efforts to assess institutional health. This report relied heavily on the judgments of eight panelists who reviewed and ranked on a one-to-five scale the financial "health" of fifty-five representative institutions, based on 1972–74 financial data. Discriminant analysis was then used to identify the key ratios that "explain" the rankings, and these indicators were applied to data from over 2,100 institutions to combine colleges into categories of differing financial health. On this basis, approximately half of all institutions were reported to be in an "unhealthy" condition, but the percentage for private institutions alone was over 86 percent.

These findings appear more definitive than most but we question them for several reasons. First, the procedure involved comparative ratings by the panel, but the final results were presented as if absolute, rather than relative, criteria were involved. Thus the authors say that the *relatively unhealthy* institutions ". . . might be turned around by good management," but that ". . . long-term survival [for the *unhealthy* institutions] is problematic unless some major external intervention occurs" (Andrew H. Lupton, John Augenblick, and Joseph Heyison, "The Financial State of Higher Education," *Change*, vol. 8 [September 1976], p. 23). Unfortunately, they do not say how the panel's relative ratings on a one-to-five basis (where the labels "healthy" and "unhealthy" were not defined) were converted into these absolute meanings. The inability to make that type of judgment on the basis of existing data has been widely noted and has given rise to several projects to develop better measures of financial condition.

A further problem with the *Change* report is that it is based on only three years of data, and, in fact, several of the key indicators are only single-year operating ratios. Snapshot studies are very unreliable; a dynamic concept such as financial condition must be assessed by time series analysis.

of higher education. In our judgment, the recent Bowen-Minter reports are the best available guide to the current financial and educational status of a large segment of private higher education,[17] and their interpretation of the past half-decade is convincing:

> When the fortunes of higher education changed in the late 1960s and when many institutions were experiencing deficits while adjusting to new and less expansive conditions, dire predictions were made about the future of the private sector. Partly because of these predictions, the institutions quickly set about putting their houses in order. Five or six years have elapsed since the onset of depressed conditions. During that time, no major private institutions have failed and most private colleges and universities are still solvent even though not highly prosperous. This achievement occurred despite adverse reactions of donors to student unrest, despite depression in the economy and in the stock market, despite galloping inflation, despite a widening of the public-private tuition gap, despite the growing competition of new and expanded public institutions, despite demographic changes, and despite the constant and possibly self-fulfilling allegation that most private institutions would soon be defunct.
>
> Some of the credit for the staying power of the private sector goes to the state and federal governments which have helped through student aid programs and in other ways. Some of the credit goes to improved management of the private institutions. Some of the credit is due the trustees, donors, and faculties who have been steadfast in their efforts on behalf of their particular institutions.[18]

The Continuing Debate: What Are the Solutions?

In 1973, an argument first advanced by economists[19] reappeared in the policy recommendations of several national commissions. This was the assertion that heavy institutional subsidies leading to low tuition charges in state colleges and universities are both inefficient and inequitable. In their place, it was contended, public institutions should—as their private-sector counterparts do—charge their students a larger portion

17. Bowen and Minter base their findings on a sample of 100 accredited four-year institutions, representing a universe of 866 colleges and universities. Their reports have not covered two-year colleges, major research universities, or autonomous professional schools, but plans are being made to expand survey coverage.

18. Howard R. Bowen and W. John Minter, *Private Higher Education: First Annual Report*, p. 78.

19. See, for example, W. Lee Hansen and Burton A. Weisbrod, *Benefits, Costs, and Finance of Public Higher Education* (Markham, 1969).

of the cost of instruction, so that public subsidies could be given directly to low-income students.[20]

Defenders of public higher education were outraged. The proposals plainly violated a principle they hold dear: that higher education, like elementary and secondary schooling, should be provided by society at little or no tuition cost to all who want it and are qualified. The ensuing saga was fascinating, but the immediate outcome was straightforward: no state embraced as a matter of explicit policy the notion of sharply increased public tuitions.[21]

Those concerned with the competitive posture of private colleges and universities then reversed their strategy: if subsidies to public institutions were not to be curbed and prices hiked, much the same result could be obtained by securing new subsidies for private institutions that would have the effect of lowering *their* prices. Generally dubbed "tuition offsets," this proposition enjoyed some currency in 1974 and 1975 and, indeed, several states have adopted programs of this nature.[22]

20. The argument was advanced most forcefully by the Committee for Economic Development in *The Management and Financing of Colleges* (CED, 1973), chap. 6, and in a less radical way by the report of the Carnegie Commission on Higher Education, *Higher Education: Who Pays? Who Benefits? Who Should Pay?* (McGraw-Hill, 1973). The resulting furor prompted the commission to prepare a supplement in 1974 entitled *Tuition*, in which the commission, among other things, pointed out that more recent data "show a much closer correspondence between current practice and the Commission recommendation for 1983 than did the earlier report" (Carnegie Commission on Higher Education, *Tuition: A Supplemental Statement to the Report of the Carnegie Commission on Higher Education on "Who Pays? Who Benefits? Who Should Pay?"* [Carnegie Foundation for the Advancement of Teaching, 1974].)

21. Average in-state tuition in public colleges and universities has increased very little in real terms in recent years. Converted to 1974 dollars, average tuition in all public institutions in 1969–70 was $436; in 1975–76, $470 (table 1-8). In universities, comparable figures are $575 in 1969–70, and $601 in 1975–76, and in other four-year institutions, $413 in 1969–70 and $482 in 1975–76 (derived from data in the sources of table 1-8). Averages, of course, conceal variations within states; information on tuition charges by institution for the academic years 1971–72 to 1973–74 is presented in the report of the Carnegie Commission on Higher Education, *Tuition*, pp. 53–60. The battle for significant increases in public tuition is far from ended, however, as the experience of the New Jersey Commission on Financing Postsecondary Education attests. (See Commission on Financing Postsecondary Education, State of New Jersey, "Financing in an Era of Uncertainty" [March 1977; processed].)

22. For a description of the tuition offset proposal, see NCICU, *A National Policy for Private Higher Education*. The Carnegie Council on Policy Studies in Higher Education advanced a similar recommendation for tuition equalization grants in its report, *The Federal Role in Postsecondary Education: Unfinished Business 1975–1980* (Jossey-Bass, 1975), pp. 35–39.

One does well to pause and consider the implications of this sudden shift in strategy between 1973 and 1974 on the part of those in the vanguard of national concern for private higher education. From every perspective save one there is a world of difference between "making the public sector more like the private," which was the implication of the proposals in 1973 for high tuition with subsidies confined to student aid, and "making the private sector more like the public," which is the main outcome of a tuition offset scheme. The costs, the political alignments, the redistributive effects, and the latent impacts on campus autonomy of these two approaches are wholly dissimilar. Yet both are plausible means to one end, that of reducing the disparity between the prices charged by public and private colleges. As the numerous complexities of this subject are explored in the following chapters, one fundamental question continually crops up: when the difference in price between the two sectors is identified as the problem, and when shrinking that difference is perceived as the objective, is there a better case to be made for trimming the "public" character of the one or compromising the "private" features of the other?

None too comfortable with either, public higher education struck back in late 1975 when one of its major national organizations, the American Association of State Colleges and Universities (AASCU), declared itself opposed to any substantial new programs of assistance to private institutions and challenged the analysis on which such proposals were based. This effort was followed in May 1976 by publication and widespread distribution of a "low-tuition fact book," arguing that increases in tuition had been responsible for an alleged decline in higher educational opportunity in recent years.[23]

As the rhetoric heated up, the fragile ties holding the higher education community together began to fray. Sides were taken, positions hardened, and attempts at compromise were scorned. In early 1976, the institutions of the private sector, fearing that no national organization adequately represented their interests, formed a new association as a spin-off of the Association of American Colleges—the National Association of Independent Colleges and Universities—to advance their case in the arenas of public policy and public opinion.

At the federal level, this escalating conflict between the public and

23. American Association of State Colleges and Universities, *Low Tuition Fact Book: Eight Basic Facts about Tuition and Educational Opportunity* (AASCU, 1976).

private sectors broke out into open clashes in 1975 and 1976 over the subject of student aid policies. A line was drawn between "access" and "choice," and federal officials were advised that policies aimed at the former were damaging to private colleges while programs geared to the latter were a menace to the principle of public higher education. In the Education Amendments of 1976, Congress sidestepped the issue altogether by abandoning efforts to overhaul student assistance, and, for want of a consensus, retained the existing programs with minor changes, notwithstanding the deficiencies widely ascribed to them.[24]

At the state level, word circulated that in a time of heavy pressure on budgets, any further subsidies for private colleges or their students were dollars subtracted from the operating funds of public higher education. The private institutions—now increasingly well organized in the state capitals as well—responded with the charge that further heedless subsidization of public higher education would lead to their own deterioration or even bankruptcy, which would then have costly and damaging consequences for the states and society.

The result is confusion: many different state responses, often ill-considered and incomplete, and a Washington incapable of solving the problem. Federal and state policies toward private higher education are frequently incompatible and almost wholly uncoordinated. Differing interests within the academic community itself defeat efforts to explain the condition of higher education as a whole, and policymakers trying to grasp what is happening and what should be done have no ready source of reliable facts and serviceable options.

What Does This Book Contribute?

In this book, we display and examine the facts and issues, and appraise the salient policy choices available to state and federal governments. In seeking a coherent overview of the principal concerns and major options, the book slights a number of narrower and more specific considerations. The singular concerns of many subdivisions within the private sector, for example, are not examined in detail, nor are the unique histories and educational patterns of the fifty states. Neither do we probe the entire corpus of federal activities bearing on private higher education. The following chapters do, however, present a reasonably comprehen-

24. 90 Stat. 2081. See Glossary for definitions of "access" and "choice."

sive overview of the subject, emphasizing both the economics and politics of federal and state policies.

Chapters 2 and 3, written by Susan Nelson and Michael McPherson, respectively, provide basic economic information about the circumstances of higher education in general and its private sector in particular. Nelson examines in detail the financing of private colleges and universities, focusing on the changing pattern of support over time, while McPherson discusses the determinants of demand for higher education, and weighs the importance of the differences in prices charged by public and private colleges.

The next three chapters are concerned primarily with the politics and economics of federal policy. Chapter 4, by Lawrence Gladieux and Thomas Wolanin, examines the Washington political environment facing the higher education associations, concentrating primarily on events since 1972. Their assessment of the political feasibility of various policies toward the private sector is a sobering prelude to chapters 5 and 6, by Robert Hartman and Emil Sunley, which examine the effects of current policies and offer alternatives. Hartman concentrates on the federal student aid programs and advocates a shift in policy that would alter the relationship between private and public tuition charges, whereas Sunley focuses on tax policy, examining in particular detail the effects of the deduction for charitable contributions and the proposal for a tuition tax credit.

In chapters 7 and 8, by Robert Berdahl and Colin Blaydon, the focus shifts to state policy options. Berdahl examines the political forces at work between public and private sectors through case studies in New York, Ohio, and California; he draws several conclusions about the types of policies most likely to be accepted by both higher education factions as well as by state officials. Blaydon concentrates on changes in state financing policy that would put the public and private sectors on a more equal financial footing, whether politically feasible or not. He also provides estimates of regional differences in student financial need, based on average college costs and family incomes.

The "view from the campus" is the subject of chapter 9 by David Brown and Thomas Wenzlau. Its purpose is to remind all those concerned that federal and state policies influence the conduct and nature of higher education in diverse and often unanticipated ways. The authors evaluate existing and proposed governmental policies by several criteria that they believe accurately reflect the values inherent in private higher education.

Chapter 10, written by the editors after a Brookings invitational conference to discuss chapter drafts, contains an analysis of the key points presented in the more specialized chapters and a set of policy recommendations distilled from the individual chapters and conference discussion.

PART TWO: AN OVERVIEW

An overview of private higher education in the United States is essential background for the chapters that follow. Below is a survey of the current structure of higher education; some indications of its growth since 1950; some aspects of demand, including the much-discussed "tuition gap" between public and private institutions; a review of federal and state programs, and a discussion of their respective roles in higher education policy.

A Statistical Summary[25]

Of the 2,827 colleges and universities included in the 1970 classification system of the Carnegie Commission on Higher Education,[26] over half (1,514) are private, but their distribution by category is hardly uniform, as table 1-2 shows. Although each grouping has both public and private members, the four-year liberal arts college categories are dominated by the private sector, whereas public institutions tend to be either universi-

25. Higher education data are slippery, with the numbers one uses depending on the subjective definitions employed, on the choice of sources, and on the selection of years. This book has been carefully checked to ensure that statistics are true to their sources and appropriate for their contexts, but no attempt has been made to relate data from different sources. Hence, there may be minor discrepancies in numbers in this chapter and those that follow.

26. The classification system for institutions of higher education developed by the commission is very helpful in policy analysis. We follow that system wherever possible in this book. As the use of this system suggests, this book is generally limited to established, degree-granting, nonprofit colleges and universities. (*A Classification of Institutions of Higher Education*, A Technical Report Sponsored by the Carnegie Commission on Higher Education [Carnegie Foundation for the Advancement of Teaching, 1973]. See Glossary for a description of the various categories.)

Table 1-2. *Number of Public and Private Institutions of Higher Education, by Carnegie Classification, 1970*

Classification[a]	Number			Percent by type		Percent of total
	Public	Private	Total	Public	Private	
Doctoral-granting institutions						
Research universities I	30	22	52	57.7	42.3	1.8
Research universities II	27	13	40	67.5	32.5	1.4
Doctoral-granting universities I	34	19	53	64.2	35.8	1.9
Doctoral-granting universities II	17	11	28	60.7	39.3	1.0
Comprehensive institutions						
Comprehensive universities and colleges I	223	98	321	69.5	30.5	11.4
Comprehensive universities and colleges II	85	47	132	64.4	35.6	4.7
Liberal arts institutions						
Liberal arts colleges I	2	144	146	1.4	98.6	5.2
Liberal arts colleges II	26	547	573	4.5	95.5	20.3
Other						
Two-year institutions	805	256	1,061	75.9	24.1	37.5
Specialized institutions	64	357	421	15.2	84.8	14.9
Total	1,313	1,514	2,827	46.4	53.6	100.0

Source: *A Classification of Institutions of Higher Education*, A Technical Report Sponsored by the Carnegie Commission on Higher Education (Carnegie Foundation for the Advancement of Teaching, 1973), p. 7. Percentages are rounded.

a. For explanation of the classification system, see Glossary.

ties or two-year colleges. (The private sector also leads in the category of specialized institutions, such as theological schools, medical schools, and schools of art, music, and design.)

Growth in the Last Quarter-Century

As table 1-3 indicates, higher education has been a growth industry since the middle 1950s. From 1950 to 1955 there was little overall change in the number of institutions, although there were compositional shifts as colleges granting bachelor's degrees added graduate programs. The years after 1955, however, witnessed a steady net increase in the number of colleges and universities, with the system expanding approximately 65 percent by 1975. The bulk of this growth occurred in the two-year college sector, in which the number of institutions more than doubled:

from 510 to 1,141. Universities awarding doctorates also increased from 180 to 405 although much of this growth reflected the conversion of institutions that previously granted only bachelor's or master's degrees, rather than the creation of new campuses. A quarter of a century of growth in higher education also produced a changing distribution of public and private institutions, as table 1-4 shows; while private colleges and universities accounted for 66 percent of the institutions in 1950, by 1975 this figure had fallen to 52 percent, primarily because of the remarkable expansion of public two-year colleges.

Student Enrollments

The fact that private colleges and universities are still in a slight majority among institutions is misleading, however, in terms of student enrollments, since the typical private campus is much smaller than its public counterpart. Although enrollments in the private sector roughly doubled from 1950 to 1976 (increasing from 1.14 million to 2.39 million), as a percentage of the total this represented a drop from 50 to 24 percent. Over the same period, enrollments in the public sector increased more than sixfold, from 1.15 million to 7.44 million (table 1-5). Not surprisingly, the two-year colleges also account for much of the enrollment growth over this period, increasing from 218,000 degree-credit students in 1950 to an estimated 2.65 million in 1976.[27]

In much of the popular discussion of the "plight" of private higher education, great stress is laid on the declining percentage of students in the private sector; table 1-5, however, helps to place this trend in proper perspective. In fact, the private sector has experienced steady (though slow) growth over the past quarter of a century (only between 1970 and 1971 was there a slight decline), whereas much of the rapid growth occurred in the two-year public colleges, institutions that tend to serve different clienteles from those found in most private colleges. Given the remarkable increase in college enrollments that occurred from the late 1950s through the 1960s (the postwar baby boom cohorts), it is virtually certain that the private sector of higher education could not (and would not) have expanded sufficiently—either through growth of existing institutions or through the creation of new ones—to have maintained its 1950 share of total enrollments.

27. American Council on Education, *A Fact Book on Higher Education: Enrollment Data*, issue 2 (ACE, 1976), p. 76.98. An additional 1.4 million nondegree-credit students were enrolled in two-year colleges in 1976.

Table 1-3. *Number of Institutions of Higher Education,*
by Highest Level of Offering, Academic Years 1950–51
to 1960–61 and Fall 1962–Fall 1975

	Number of institutions[a]				
		Highest level of offering			
Period	All institutions	Two but less than four years beyond the twelfth grade	Bachelor's and/or first professional degree	Master's and beyond, but less than doctorate[b]	Doctor of philosophy and equivalent	Other[c]
1950–51	1,859	527	800	360	155	17
1951–52	1,889	529	806	379	159	16
1952–53	1,851	517	768	390	163	13
1953–54	1,857	518	747	406	171	15
1954–55	1,855	510	732	415	180	18
1955–56	1,886	525	714	426	191	30
1956–57	1,937	548	723	442	193	31
1957–58	1,957	557	720	449	197	34
1958–59	2,011	585	718	462	205	41
1959–60	2,028	593	739	455	210	31
1960–61	2,040	593	741	455	219	32
Fall 1962	2,100	628	766	458	223	25
Fall 1963	2,139	644	792	455	223	25
Fall 1964	2,168	656	801	464	224	23
Fall 1965	2,207	664	823	472	227	21
Fall 1966	2,252	685	828	483	235	21
Fall 1967	2,489	866	828	511	263	21
Fall 1968[d]	2,537	867	833	509	278	12
Fall 1969[e]	2,551	903	835	517	296	f
Fall 1970[e]	2,573	897	850	528	298	f
Fall 1971[e]	2,626	943	828	543	312	f
Fall 1972[e]	2,686	970	843	546	327	f
Fall 1973[e]	2,738	1,008	847	547	336	f
Fall 1974	3,038	1,152	903	599	384	g
Fall 1975	3,055	1,141	872	637	405	h

Source: American Council on Education, *A Fact Book on Higher Education: Institutions, Faculty and Staff, Students,* issue 3 (ACE, 1976), p. 76.142.

a. Institutions are those in the United States and outlying parts included in the annual directories of higher education issued by the U.S. Office of Education and, recently, by the National Center for Education Statistics (NCES). Before the 1967–68 academic year, an institution was listed in the directory if it (1) offered at least a two-year program of college-level studies in residence, (2) submitted the necessary information for a listing, and (3) met certain accreditation criteria. The latter required that an institution either be accredited or approved by a nationally recognized accrediting agency, by a state department of education, or by a state university; or have its credits accepted as if coming from an accredited institution by at least three accredited institutions. The 1967–68 list included, in addition, those institutions that attained a preaccredited status with designated nationally recognized accrediting agencies. The 1968–69 list included all institutions providing the information required for a listing. Directories for years after 1968–69 use the 1967–68 criteria. See U.S. Office of Education, *Education Directory, 1966–67, Part 3: Higher Education* (Government Printing Office, 1967); National Center for Education Statistics, *Education Directory, 1975–76:*

Table 1-4. *Number and Percentage Distribution of Public and Private Institutions of Higher Education, Academic Years 1950–51 to 1960–61 and Fall 1962–Fall 1976*

		Number[a]		Percent	
Period	Total	Public	Private	Public	Private
1950–51	1,859	638	1,221	34	66
1951–52	1,889	643	1,246	34	66
1952–53	1,851	646	1,205	35	65
1953–54	1,857	653	1,204	35	65
1954–55	1,855	652	1,203	35	65
1955–56	1,886	661	1,225	35	65
1956–57	1,937	669	1,268	35	65
1957–58	1,957	677	1,280	35	65
1958–59	2,011	698	1,313	35	65
1959–60	2,028	703	1,325	35	65
1960–61	2,040	721	1,319	35	65
Fall 1962	2,100	743	1,357	35	65
Fall 1963	2,139	762	1,377	36	64
Fall 1964	2,168	784	1,384	36	64
Fall 1965	2,207	790	1,417	36	64
Fall 1966	2,252	806	1,446	36	64
Fall 1967	2,489	1,000	1,489	41	59
Fall 1968	2,537	1,037	1,500	41	59
Fall 1969[b]	2,551	1,079	1,472	42	58
Fall 1969[b]	2,836	1,312	1,524	46	54
Fall 1970	2,855	1,335	1,520	47	53
Fall 1971	2,902	1,381	1,521	48	52
Fall 1972	2,951	1,414	1,537	48	52
Fall 1973	3,018	1,445	1,573	48	52
Fall 1974	3,038	1,453	1,585	48	52
Fall 1975	3,055	1,454	1,601	48	52
Fall 1976	3,075	1,467	1,608	48	52

Sources: American Council on Education, *A Fact Book on Higher Education: Institutions, Faculty and Staff, Students*, issue 3 (ACE, 1976), p. 76.141; Arthur Podolsky and Carolyn R. Smith, *Education Directory, 1975–76: Colleges and Universities*, National Center for Education Statistics (GPO, 1976).

a. See table 1-3, note e.

b. Beginning in 1969, each part of a multicampus institution is counted as a separate institution. In previous years they are shown as part of their parent institutions. The data are reported both ways for 1969 for comparison purposes.

Table 1-3 *(continued)*

Higher Education (GPO, 1976) and previous issues for academic years 1967–68 to 1974–75.

b. Data prior to 1968 are for "master's and/or 2nd professional degree."

c. Includes nondegree-granting institutions and institutions with accelerated programs.

d. Fall 1968 figures do not add to total.

e. Totals do not correspond to those in table 1-4 because of a difference in reporting. Here, branches are included as part of the main institution through 1973, rather than counted separately as in 1974 and 1975.

f. Not separately identified in source; included in other categories.

g. Four institutions classified as nondegree-granting have been distributed among the four study levels; two to the lowest level and two to the master's level and beyond.

h. Forty-nine institutions classified as nondegree-granting have been distributed between the lowest level and those granting master's degrees and above; fifteen undergraduate nondegree-granting institutions have been added to the lowest level; thirty-four graduate nondegree-granting institutions have been added to the master's-and-above level. Most of these institutions are rabbinical seminaries.

Table 1-5. *Number and Percentage Distribution*
of Higher Education Degree-Credit Enrollments
in Public and Private Institutions, 1950, 1955, and 1960–76

	Number			Percent	
Year	*Total*	*Public*	*Private*	*Public*	*Private*
1950	2,296,592	1,154,456	1,142,136	50	50
1955	2,678,623	1,498,510	1,180,113	56	44
1960	3,610,007	2,135,690	1,474,317	59	41
1961	3,891,230	2,351,719	1,539,511	60	40
1962	4,206,672	2,596,904	1,609,768	62	38
1963	4,528,516	2,872,823	1,655,693	63	37
1964	4,987,867	3,205,783	1,782,084	64	36
1965	5,570,271	3,654,578	1,915,693	66	34
1966	5,928,000	3,940,000	1,988,000	66	34
1967	6,406,000	4,360,000	2,046,000	68	32
1968	6,983,093	4,928,320	2,054,773	71	29
1969	7,542,992	5,454,990	2,087,993	72	28
1970	7,985,532	5,845,032	2,140,500	73	27
1971	8,188,169	6,059,989	2,128,180	74	26
1972	8,341,919	6,207,134	2,134,785	74	26
1973	8,602,153	6,442,084	2,160,069	75	25
1974	9,109,883	6,891,422	2,218,461	76	24
1975	9,830,224	7,480,524	2,349,700	76	24
1976[a]	9,830,000	7,440,000	2,390,000	76	24

Sources: American Council on Education, *A Fact Book on Higher Education: Enrollment Data*, issue 2 (ACE, 1976), p. 76.81, and ibid., issue 2 (1975), p. 75.65.
a. Preliminary.

Location

The geographic distribution of private colleges and universities among states is very uneven. Eight states (California, Illinois, Massachusetts, Michigan, Missouri, New York, Ohio, and Pennsylvania) account for nearly 50 percent, whereas eleven (Alaska, Arizona, Delaware, Hawaii, Idaho, Montana, Nevada, New Mexico, North Dakota, Utah, and Wyoming) each have five or fewer private colleges and universities (see table 1-6). When the states are organized into regions, the proportion of private to total institutions is as follows: New England, 66 percent; Mid-East, 64 percent; Great Lakes, 56 percent; Plains, 55 percent; Southeast, 47 percent; Southwest, 34 percent; Rocky Mountain, 28 percent;

and Far West, 43 percent.[28] Because of the wide disparity in the role of the private sector in each state's system of higher education, it is not surprising that the states differ markedly in their policies toward private higher education. And this disparity complicates the attempt to link federal and state policies into a sensible and mutually supportive pattern. A further complicating factor is that private colleges differ significantly in the proportions of out-of-state students enrolled; some private institutions are essentially national in character, whereas others draw primarily from the local population.

Religious Affiliation

The 1975–76 *Education Directory* identifies 786 private colleges and universities as religiously affiliated, nearly 50 percent of all private institutions. A majority of them (501) are associated with Protestant sects, while 247 are affiliated with the Catholic church.[29] Table 1-7 shows the percentage distribution of religiously affiliated private institutions by Carnegie Commission category. The majority of doctoral-granting private universities are nonsectarian, and the category with the highest percentage of church-related colleges is Liberal Arts Colleges II, the less selective four-year campuses.

Revenue by Source

An understanding of the sources of revenue by institutional type is essential to evaluation of policy options. The principal sources are familiar: tuition, endowment income, annual private giving, sponsored research (primarily federal), and state and local appropriations. But their importance differs significantly for particular types of institutions. In a recent paper, Patricia Smith and Cathy Henderson present financial profiles of institutions that were developed from an analysis of data

28. The regions are those defined by the National Center for Education Statistics.

29. Arthur Podolsky and Carolyn R. Smith, *Education Directory, 1975–76: Colleges and Universities*, National Center for Education Statistics (GPO, 1976), p. xxix. For a good, although brief, treatment of the legal issues involving federal and state aid to religiously affiliated colleges, see William H. McFarlane, A. E. Dick Howard, and Jay L. Chronister, *State Financial Measures Involving the Private Sector of Higher Education*, A Report to the National Council of Independent Colleges and Universities (Association of American Colleges, 1974).

Table 1-6. *Geographic Distribution of Public and Private Institutions of Higher Education, Academic Year 1975–76*

State	Number			Percent private
	Total	Public	Private	
United States[a]	*3,018*	*1,434*	*1,584*	*52*
Alabama	56	34	22	39
Alaska	9	7	2	22
Arizona	22	17	5	23
Arkansas	29	16	13	45
California	247	131	116	47
Colorado	39	27	12	31
Connecticut	46	22	24	52
Delaware	10	6	4	40
District of Columbia	18	3	15	83
Florida	74	37	37	50
Georgia	66	33	33	50
Hawaii	12	9	3	25
Idaho	9	6	3	33
Illinois	147	60	87	59
Indiana	64	23	41	64
Iowa	63	24	39	64
Kansas	52	29	23	44
Kentucky	38	9	29	76
Louisiana	30	19	11	37
Maine	25	10	15	60
Maryland	52	30	22	42
Massachusetts	119	34	85	71
Michigan	93	45	48	52
Minnesota	66	31	35	53
Mississippi	45	27	18	40
Missouri	81	27	54	66
Montana	12	9	3	25
Nebraska	30	17	13	43
Nevada	6	5	1	16
New Hampshire	24	10	14	58
New Jersey	64	30	34	53
New Mexico	17	14	3	18
New York	285	84	201	71
North Carolina	114	72	42	37
North Dakota	15	11	4	27
Ohio	129	59	70	54
Oklahoma	44	29	15	34
Oregon	43	21	22	51
Pennsylvania	175	62	113	65
Rhode Island	13	3	10	77

Table 1-6 (Continued)

State	Number			Percent private
	Total	Public	Private	
South Carolina	55	31	24	44
South Dakota	17	7	10	59
Tennessee	67	23	44	66
Texas	145	90	55	38
Utah	14	9	5	36
Vermont	23	6	17	74
Virginia	73	39	34	47
Washington	47	33	14	30
West Virginia	28	16	12	43
Wisconsin	58	30	28	48
Wyoming	8	8	0	0

Source: Podolsky and Smith, *Education Directory, 1975–76: Colleges and Universities.*
a. Numbers for the United States differ from those in tables 1-3 and 1-4 because territories and outlying areas are not included.

from the higher education general information survey (HEGIS).[30] Their study documents considerable variation in financing patterns within both public and private sectors, although the greatest variation occurs among private institutions; it is clear from their work that no specific public policy will have a uniform impact on private institutions. In chapter 2 Susan Nelson examines in detail these trends in revenue sources. Contrary to expectation, she finds that the greatest shift in recent years toward increased tuition dependence occurred not within the private liberal arts colleges, but in the private research universities. In the liberal arts colleges, there has been no general increase in tuition's share of total revenues in the last decade.

Nelson reviews the experience of states that have introduced programs of support for private institutions or their students and finds (again, contrary to conventional wisdom) little evidence to support the view that state expenditures on private institutions have come at the expense of the public campus budgets. She also highlights the numerous ways in which current federal, state, and local policies directly and indirectly benefit private higher education; it is ironic that the private sector has recently chosen to rename itself the "independent" sector

30. Patricia Smith and Cathy Henderson, "A Financial Taxonomy of Institutions of Higher Education," Policy Analysis Service (American Council on Education, April 1976; processed). The annual HEGIS reports are prepared by the National Center for Education Statistics of the U.S. Department of Health, Education, and Welfare.

Table 1-7. *Percentage Distribution of Private Institutions of Higher Education, by Religious Affiliation, Carnegie Classification, Academic Year 1972–73*

Type of institution	Protestant	Roman Catholic	Non-sectarian
All institutions	33.9	18.8	47.3
Doctoral-granting universities	9.3	14.1	76.6
Comprehensive universities and colleges	31.9	20.8	47.2
Liberal arts colleges I[a]	27.5	17.6	54.9
Liberal arts colleges II[a]	39.2	27.8	33.0
Two-year institutions[b]	34.5	13.0	52.5
Specialized institutions	33.1	10.0	56.9

Source: Adapted from Elaine H. El-Khawas, *Public and Private Higher Education: Differences in Role, Character, and Clientele*, Policy Analysis Service Reports, vol. 2, no. 3 (American Council on Education, December 1976), p. 55.

a. For definitions of liberal arts colleges I and II, see Glossary.

b. Percentages for the two-year colleges are based on 200 of the 256 institutions from the Carnegie classification that were listed in Arthur Podolsky, *Education Directory, 1974–75: Higher Education*, National Center for Education Statistics (GPO, 1975).

when the data show that *financially* these institutions are anything but independent of government.

The Tuition Gap

Recent evidence of the declining financial value of a college education, an apparently related drop in attendance rates of white males in the early 1970s, and a demographic decline in the traditional college-going age groups beginning in the early 1980s all point toward excess capacity in the higher education industry in the not-too-distant future. If enrollments do drop significantly, colleges and universities may be forced to close or retrench in major ways, and it is not unreasonable for administrators in private institutions charging high tuition rates to fear that their institutions will bear the brunt of this shrinkage. It is essential, therefore, to review what is known about the determinants of demand for higher education, including price and income effects, labor market effects, the influence of particular types of student aid, and the effects that altered institutional behavior might have (such as changes in scheduling, enrollment policies, curricula, and the like). In recent years numerous studies have chipped away at pieces of this central question, and

Table 1-8. *Average Tuition in Public and Private Institutions of Higher Education, in Current and 1974 Dollars, Selected Academic Years, 1956–57 to 1975–76*

| Academic year | Current dollars | | | 1974 dollars | | | Ratio, private to public |
	Public	Private	Dollar gap	Public	Private	Dollar gap	
1956–57	173	589	416	314	1,069	755	3.4
1961–62	218	906	688	359	1,493	1,134	4.2
1964–65	243	1,088	845	386	1,730	1,344	4.5
1966–67	275	1,233	958	418	1,874	1,456	4.5
1967–68	283	1,297	1,014	418	1,916	1,498	4.6
1968–69	295	1,383	1,088	418	1,962	1,544	4.7
1969–70	324	1,534	1,210	436	2,065	1,629	4.7
1971–72	376	1,820	1,444	458	2,217	1,759	4.8
1972–73	407	1,898	1,491	480	2,238	1,758	4.7
1974–75	470	2,131	1,661	470	2,131	1,661	4.5
1975–76	513	2,333	1,820	470	2,138	1,668	4.5

Sources: Current dollars, Martin M. Frankel and Forrest W. Harrison, *Projections of Education Statistics to 1985–86*, National Center for Education Statistics (GPO, 1977), table 41, and relevant preceding issues of *Projections;* 1974 dollars, calculated from the current-dollar data by application of the consumer price index from U.S. Bureau of Labor Statistics, converted to 1974 = 100.

Michael McPherson in chapter 3 provides a thorough survey of what is known (and not known) about the demand for higher education. As preface to that review, we describe below a few key indicators relating to the tuition gap between public and private colleges. Much ink has been spilled in discussing the subject since students and their families are undoubtedly influenced in their choice of college by price. Table 1-8 gives average public and private tuition rates in current and constant 1974 dollars for selected academic years from 1956–57 to 1975–76. It shows that average private tuition was 3.4 times higher than average public tuition in 1956–57 and that the ratio jumped to 4.2 in 1961–62, moving slowly upward since the early 1960s until it reached a maximum of 4.8 by 1971–72. The dollar gap between the two averages, however, had increased from $755 (in 1974 dollars) in 1956–57 to $1,668 by 1975–76.

Tuition charges, of course, form just one component of the cost of going to college. Room and board, transportation, books, and miscellaneous fees are substantial out-of-pocket expenses, while forgone earnings add appreciably to the true economic costs of a decision to attend college. But tuition is important in policy debates because all other out-

Table 1-9. *Average Tuition and Required Fees at Public and Private Institutions of Higher Education, by Carnegie Classification, Academic Year 1973–74*

Dollars

Classification[a]	Public	Private	Dollar gap
Doctoral-granting institutions			
Research universities I	627	3,050	2,423
Research universities II	496	2,580	2,084
Doctoral-granting universities I	558	1,956	1,398
Doctoral-granting universities II	485	2,350	1,865
Comprehensive institutions			
Comprehensive universities and colleges I	411	2,015	1,604
Comprehensive universities and colleges II	412	1,740	1,328
Liberal arts institutions			
Liberal arts colleges I	[b]	2,510	...
Liberal arts colleges II	420	1,728	1,308
Other			
Two-year institutions	302	1,382	1,080

Source: Carnegie Commission on Higher Education, *Tuition: A Supplemental Statement to the Report of the Carnegie Commission on Higher Education on "Who Pays? Who Benefits? Who Should Pay?"* (Carnegie Foundation for the Advancement of Teaching, 1974), pp. 70–73.

a. For explanation of the classification system, see Glossary.

b. Data not supplied; there are only two institutions in this category.

lays tend to be relatively constant across institutions, whether public or private; it is the only substantial cost that the student can affect through his or her choice of institution. (For full-time students, the economic cost of forgone earnings clearly does not depend on the choice of institution; room and board expenses can be reduced somewhat by living at home, but where the choice lies between residential attendance at a public or a private college, nontuition cost differences are inconsequential.)

There are two other important points to consider in this regard. First, the above statistics are put in terms of average tuition charges, but averages conceal substantial variation in stated prices within both the public and private sectors. As shown in table 1-9, average charges within each sector vary by more than a factor of two, and the average tuition gap between public and private institutions within each Carnegie Commission category ranges from approximately $1,100 in the two-year college sector to over $2,400 for the major research universities. Tuition charges (and increases in rates) in a handful of highly selective (and high-priced) institutions tend to receive the most publicity, but the range of stated prices is really quite wide.

Second, the stated tuition price is not the actual price paid by many students who attend private (and public) institutions. Federal, state, and institutional grants drive a wedge between stated price and net price for a substantial number; it is presumably the net price that influences student choice. Each college and university, therefore, offers its education not at a single price but at a wide range of prices, a factor that severely complicates analysis of demand.

Also affecting the debate on tuition differentials is the widely held belief that the cost of college attendance has soared in recent years relative to a family's ability to pay, a situation that, if true, would diminish demand for higher education. In figure 1-2, the ratio of tuition and room and board charges to income are measured in two ways: first as median income of families whose head is between forty-five and sixty-four years of age, a group that is likely to have children in college, and then as per capita disposable income.[31] The figure clearly shows that the ratio of cost to income has not risen over the 1961–75 period, indicating that increases in median family income and in per capita disposable income have kept pace with increases in college costs.[32] Indeed, the more comprehensive cost figure of tuition plus room and board in both sectors has actually fallen consistently as a fraction of either measure of income. Although it may not have become much easier in the last fifteen years for the typical family to send a son or daughter to a private college, these data do not support the claim that the burden has increased dramatically.[33]

McPherson argues in chapter 3 that during the years of rapid enrollment growth, nonprice factors, such as geographic accessibility, diversity of curriculum offerings, and the vast expansion of community colleges, played a more important role than the widening tuition gap in determining the distribution of students between the two sectors.

31. Disposable family income would have been a more appropriate measure of a family's ability to pay for higher education than per capita income, but such data are not available in a reliable form over time.

32. Similar findings are reported in Congressional Budget Office, *Postsecondary Education: The Current Federal Role and Alternative Approaches* (GPO, 1977), p. 24. Several universities have also reported similar findings with reference to their own charges; see, for example, William G. Bowen, "Report of the President," *University*, no. 67 (Winter 1976), p. 24, for data on Princeton University.

33. See chapter appendix and chapter 3 for further discussion.

Figure 1-2. *Relationship between Income and College Costs,
Academic Years 1961–62 to 1975–76*

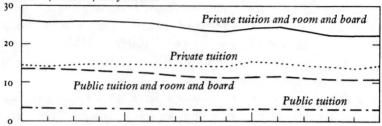

COSTS RELATIVE TO MEDIAN FAMILY INCOME [a]

Percent of median family income

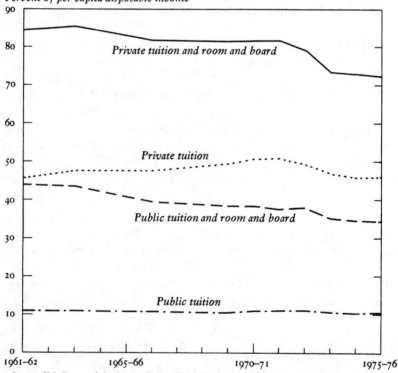

COSTS RELATIVE TO PER CAPITA DISPOSABLE INCOME

Percent of per capita disposable income

Sources: U.S. Bureau of the Census, *Current Population Reports,* series P-60, nos. 39, 41, 43, 47, 53, 64, 66, 75, 80, 85, 90, 97, 101, and 105; Martin M. Frankel and Forrest W. Harrison, *Projections of Education Statistics to 1985–86,* National Center for Education Statistics (GPO, 1977), and relevant preceding issues of *Projections; Economic Report of the President, January 1977,* p. 213.

a. The median family income is for those families with heads aged forty-five to sixty-four. From 1961 through 1966 the Census Bureau category of age of head was divided into two decades, forty-five to fifty-four and fifty-five to sixty-four. A weighted average based on the size of the two groups was used to calculate median family income for those families with heads aged forty-five to sixty-four.

While such factors will continue to be important, the tuition gap is likely to be of greater significance in an era of stable or declining enrollments. The literature on demand for higher education suggests that, although the decision to enroll in college is relatively insensitive to modest price changes, the decision *where* to enroll is quite sensitive to changes in relative charges of competing institutions. At a minimum, therefore, policies designed to prevent the public-private tuition gap from further widening are important to the welfare of most private institutions.

Characteristics of Students and Faculty[34]

Many regard the private sector as consisting entirely of highly selective institutions, populated with the intelligent and privileged children of wealthy families. While there is some truth to this stereotype in some institutions, highly selective admissions policies prevail primarily in just two Carnegie Commission categories—research universities I and liberal arts colleges I—and these two groups represent less than 12 percent of all private campuses. In terms of family income, a 1974 survey of freshmen reports that for two of the Carnegie categories—the less selective private liberal arts colleges and private two-year colleges— the income profiles of entering freshmen were virtually the same as those of entering freshmen in public two-year colleges and comprehensive universities (those with few or no doctoral programs).[35] The percentage distribution of 1974 college freshmen who came from families with incomes less than $10,000 was as follows:

Public two-year colleges	30.0
Private two-year colleges	29.6
Public comprehensive universities and colleges	27.9
Private liberal arts colleges II	27.6

Students from wealthier families were enrolled in larger proportions in several categories of private institutions, although over one-third of the

34. A comprehensive discussion of students and faculty by institutional type is inappropriate in a study of public policy, but a few key features are helpful background for this and the following chapters. This section draws heavily on Elaine H. El-Khawas, "Public and Private Higher Education: Differences in Role, Character, and Clientele," Policy Analysis Service Reports, vol. 2, no. 3 (American Council on Education, December 1976).

35. Alexander W. Astin and others, *The American Freshman: National Norms for Fall 1974* (Los Angeles: University of California and American Council on Education, Cooperative Institutional Research Program, Graduate School of Education, n.d.).

freshmen enrolled in public doctoral-granting institutions were also from high-income families. The percentage distribution of 1974 college freshmen from families with incomes above $20,000 was as follows:

Private doctoral-granting universities   55.0
Private liberal arts colleges I   49.1
Private comprehensive colleges
  and universities   41.4
Public doctoral-granting universities   35.3

There were, however, consistent differences in career orientation depending on the category of institution. Over half the students enrolling in two-year colleges, both public and private, planned to major in such career-related fields as agriculture and forestry, business, education, engineering, health professions, and other technical fields, whereas the percentages of freshmen with similar plans in the private doctoral-granting universities and the leading private liberal arts colleges were only 34 and 23 percent, respectively. But much higher proportions of students in these latter two groups of institutions did plan to follow their undergraduate liberal arts education with graduate or professional study.

After a careful analysis of faculty characteristics in the various Carnegie groups, El-Khawas concludes that faculty differences by *type* of institution (that is, two-year college, research university, and the like) are far more significant than differences associated with public or private control. This pattern is particularly true of faculty credentials, of attitudes toward research, and of various measures of scholarly activity.

Of striking significance, according to El-Khawas, is the strong emphasis that private liberal arts faculty place on the college's role in furthering the emotional and moral development of the students. The nurturing (or cultivation) of the whole person, in fact, takes precedence over job training. Thus her analysis of survey findings tends to confirm the widely held view that four-year liberal arts colleges do have a distinctive focus that is not duplicated in the two-year college, the comprehensive campus, or the research university, whether public or private. Virtually all four-year liberal arts colleges are privately controlled and they constitute nearly half of the private institutions in the United States.

The Federal Role

American colleges and universities and their students received some $12 billion in fiscal 1976 from the federal government. Even this large sum—the equivalent of roughly $1,200 for every student in the nation—fails to account for all the monies channeled circuitously into the higher education system by practically every agency in Washington.

The sheer number and variety of programs undertaken by the national government to support the higher education industry—the Library of Congress recently tallied 439 separate federal statutory authorities bearing on postsecondary education—indicates that Washington has never made a straightforward commitment to support higher education per se and has refrained from adopting individual universities as national responsibilities. Aside from the military academies and a handful of other exceptions, federal support has stopped short of general-purpose subsidies such as those the states provide for their public campuses. Instead, one categorical program has followed another, each purchasing a particular service. Although these purchases range from the schooling of low-income students to the conduct of research in particle physics, and although individual institutions may amass tens of millions of dollars a year from divers federal sources, Washington's stated purposes remain limited and discrete.

Public and private colleges generally have equal access to these federal programs, and the public-private distinction that looms so large at the state level holds little interest for federal officials. Yet equal access does not guarantee equal treatment. Because of their distinctive features, public and private colleges are affected by federal policies in quite different ways, so that, even with the well-established principle of federal neutrality, federal policies have some results that are less than evenhanded. These may be inadvertent, but they are not always inconsequential.

Federal involvement with higher education can be briefly summarized as follows: (a) payments to colleges and universities; (b) payments to students; (c) payments to states and other intermediate bodies; (d) tax provisions, either for the individual or the institution, that benefit higher education; and (e) regulatory activities.

Direct Institutional Payments

Federal obligations to colleges and universities amounted to $4.46 billion in fiscal 1974 (academic year 1973–74). Of these funds 60.8 percent and 39.2 percent went to public and private institutions, respectively; 2,512 institutions received funds, including all but 210 of the nation's private colleges and all but 16 of the public institutions.[36]

Nearly half of these monies supported scientific research and development activities; private institutions received 42 percent of these funds and public institutions 58 percent. Since, in 1973–74, the private sector accounted for 25 percent of all enrollments and for 56 percent of all the institutions, federal research outlays may be said to favor the private sector on a per-student basis and the public sector on a per-institution gauge. What is most noteworthy, however, is the heavy concentration of research funds in a small number of major universities, both public and private, and the correspondingly large number of institutions in both sectors that obtain little or nothing from this source. One hundred universities regularly absorb about 85 percent of the entire federal research and development allocation. Of those institutions, thirty-four were private in 1973–74 and sixty-six were public or quasi-public (state-related).[37]

Other federal obligations to colleges and universities amounted to $2.3 billion in fiscal 1974. These included certain student aid programs (the so-called campus-based programs), construction, fellowships and traineeships, agricultural extension, and assorted categorical programs run by various Washington agencies. Because these activities touch most colleges and universities, the number of participating institutions is much higher than it is in scientific research, and the funds are less concentrated. Overall, some 2,500 colleges and universities (37 percent of them private) benefited.[38]

These hundreds of programs are, for the most part, unaffected by the public or private character of a particular college or university. Most of them give some latitude to government program officers—and the networks of peer review panels, regional boards, and advisory committees that share their responsibility—to parcel out the available funds to institutions deemed competent to undertake the work the agency wants done. A few programs—such as the land-grant college annual subventions and enrollment-based capitation grants to medical schools—work by formula, but in most instances a college has to submit a proposal that federal officials have some discretion in deciding whether to fund

36. National Science Foundation, *Federal Support to Universities, Colleges and Selected Nonprofit Institutions, Fiscal Year 1974*, NSF 76-305 (GPO, 1976), and NSF, *Detailed Statistical Tables, Appendix B*, NSF 75-325 (NSF, 1975).
37. Ibid.
38. Ibid.

and at what level. Some programs, by their very nature, favor the private or public sector. The land grant payments, for example, go almost exclusively to state universities, as do most of the postsecondary outlays of the Department of Agriculture. The U.S. Office of Education's program to strengthen developing institutions, by contrast, tips toward private colleges; this is not surprising, since its barely concealed mission is assistance to traditionally black colleges, most of which are private. In general, however, public and private institutions are both eligible to compete for these funds and recent history indicates that the private sector fares at least as well as its "share" of the industry would warrant.

Payments to Students

Washington has steadily been channeling more of its postsecondary outlays into student financial aid, and for at least the past five years the lion's share of such expenditures has flowed via programs that effectively bypass the colleges and universities, putting federal dollars directly into student hands whence they can only be retrieved by the institutions through tuitions, fees, and other charges.

MAJOR STUDENT PROGRAMS

The most conspicuous examples, and the three largest federal student aid programs, are veterans' education benefits (the GI bill), student stipends paid through the social security system, and basic educational opportunity grants administered by the Office of Education. In fiscal 1976, their appropriations were approximately $5.23 billion, $1.3 billion, and $0.9 billion, respectively.[39]

Student beneficiaries of these programs are free to attend public or private colleges. The relevant policy question is whether such aid is equally serviceable to students at both types of colleges, and thus whether the terms of the aid may affect the choices of those receiving it. It stands to reason that this depends on the fit between the costs of attending particular colleges and the levels of assistance provided by particular federal programs.

In the 1975–76 academic year, tuition and room and board averaged

39. The higher education portions of outlays made under the veterans' and social security programs were approximately $4.3 billion and $1.0 billion. Technically, of course, the social security payouts are not appropriated funds. (See *Special Analyses, Budget of the United States Government, Fiscal Year 1978*, tables I-1, I-2, and I-3, pp. 172, 175, and 177.)

$1,748 in the public sector and $3,667 in the private sector (see table 1-A1).[10] The GI bill provided $270 monthly at that time to an unmarried veteran pursuing a full-time course of study: $2,430 for a nine-month school year. Student benefits are paid under the social security program to eligible members of families already on social security. They are more difficult to cast in dollar terms, but the *average* annual payment for fiscal 1976 was $1,700. The basic grants program had a ceiling of $1,400 a year in 1975–76, although Congress raised the ceiling to $1,800 in the Education Amendments of 1976.[41]

Clearly, none of these programs supplies enough money for a student lacking other resources to meet the cost of attending the average private college. Indeed, only the GI bill program gives a stipend sufficient to pay for the average *public* college. Although the basic grants program is the only one of the three to employ a means test, pegging the size of the grant to financial ability (and in part to college charges), most recipients of all three lack sufficient current income to pay private college prices without assistance, or even to make up the difference between those prices and the federal stipend. At the same time, many additional sources of funds are available: other federal aid programs, state assistance schemes, the earnings from summer or term-time jobs, loans, savings, and the college's own aid offerings. Hence, beneficiaries of the large federal grant programs *are* found in private as well as public colleges. For recent years, the percentage distribution of grant recipients between private and public higher education was approximately as follows:[42]

Academic year	Program	Institutions Private	Public
1974–75	GI bill	17.1	82.9
1972–73	Social security	29.0	71.0
1974–75	Basic educational opportunity grants	22.7	77.3

40. It may be noted that out-of-state tuition in public institutions is about midway between the private and the public rates charged students in their home states.

41. Congress enacted the Veterans' Education and Employment Assistance Act of 1976 (90 Stat. 2383) to amend the so-called Vietnam Era GI bill; veterans who enlisted after January 1, 1977, are to be eligible for a contributory program with federal matching funds. (See Glossary for changes in veterans' education benefits.) Social security education benefits are outlined in Congressional Budget Office, *Social Security Benefits for Students* (GPO, May 1977).

42. The data were compiled from Karen J. Winkler, "Mustering Out the GI Bill," *Chronicle of Higher Education*, vol. 11, no. 5 (October 14, 1975), p. 11; Frank J. Atelsek and Irene L. Gomberg, *Student Assistance: Participants and Programs, 1974–*

The essential point is that the stipend levels for these federal programs are unresponsive to the wide price range found within American higher education—a range that generally locates private institutions at the upper end. A program designed to afford a student access to postsecondary education may be far less helpful in providing him with choice—the ability to select a college without undue concern for its tuition level. Two distinctive characteristics of private higher education are its heavy dependence on student payments as a source of institutional revenue and its correspondingly high prices; federal aid programs that fail to heed these features are clearly unhelpful to the private sector.

OTHER PROGRAMS

This trio of grant programs accounts for the largest federal expenditure, but Washington sponsors others as well. The three campus-based student aid programs—college work-study, national direct student loans, and supplemental educational opportunity grants (described elsewhere in this book)—channel their funds through the colleges and universities, rather than directly to individuals, and afford the skillful financial aid officer some flexibility in packaging multiple sources of assistance. Moreover, these programs employ a fully developed needs-analysis system, subtracting from the estimated cost of a student's education the amount his family is thought able to contribute. Funds are allocated to each institution in large part according to the aggregate "need" of its students.[43] Hence, these stipends are somewhat responsive to the higher prices of private colleges, as well as to the poverty of individual students. For this reason, they have been especially popular among private college spokesmen, who have stubbornly resisted attempts by recent administrations to eliminate or reduce them.

The guaranteed student loan program (GSL) insures and subsidizes loans made to students by banks, other commercial lenders, and the colleges themselves. Although it has come under scrutiny because of the seemingly high rate of default by student borrowers, this program affords a welcome source of cash to private college students, the prosper-

---

75, Higher Education Panel Reports 27 (American Council on Education, December 1975), p. 16; and Philip Springer, "Characteristics of Student OASDI Beneficiaries in 1973: An Overview," *Social Security Bulletin*, vol. 39 (November 1976), p. 14. In reviewing the percentage distribution, it must be remembered that 75 percent of all enrollments are in the public sector.

43. But, as mentioned below and in chapter 5, this distribution is also strongly affected by formulas allotting specific funds to each of the fifty states.

ous as well as the impoverished, and has helped many to narrow the gap between outright subsidy and the actual cost of attendance. But such arrangements also have their critics. Some leaders of public higher education, for example, fear that readily available loans and a heavy emphasis on borrowing as the means of paying for college will erode the doctrine that society should pay for higher education and that it should be "free"—or nearly so—to all students.

To some extent, that concern underlies the public sector's overall attitude toward student aid. If state and federal governments increase their spending on student aid, these funds may come at the expense of direct institutional support and may lead to upward pressure on tuition charges. Neither of these is a welcome development for public higher education. Yet most spokesmen for the public sector also understand that even free tuition—a rarely achieved goal—does not afford postsecondary access to low-income persons who cannot pay the other costs of college attendance. Some student aid is therefore necessary to assure equal opportunity. But, in their view, it ought not to be overly generous—as stipend levels pegged to private college prices would be—it ought not to absorb funds, especially state funds, that would otherwise provide institutional subsidies, and it most certainly ought not to postulate that students *should* pay for higher education themselves.[44]

Payments to States

To a degree rarely found in other realms of domestic policy, federal higher education programs ignore state boundaries. Most financial and regulatory relationships are between the appropriate Washington agency and the individual or institution affected. Even though, under the Tenth Amendment, the states and their subdivisions bear primary responsibility for education at every level, the growing federal involvement in post-secondary education tends to disregard governors, legislatures, and state education agencies.

There are a handful of exceptions. Some federal programs, such as facilities construction and campus-based student aid, allot the national appropriation via a state-by-state formula. Others require the approval of some state agency before the federal funds are forthcoming. Still

44. See John P. Mallan, "The Case for Low Tuition," *Change*, vol. 8, no 8 (September 1976), pp. 48–49.

others require state matching funds. But in few cases do the federal dollars flow to the state's general-purpose government in ways that allow it much discretion over their use, and the most prominent of these—general revenue sharing—is not a higher education program at all, nor is there any obligation for the states to use its funds for that purpose.[45]

A prominent—although quite new and still small—example of a federal-state program geared to higher education is the state student incentive grant (SSIG) program enacted in 1972. This is another scholarship scheme, affording need-based grants to individual students. The Office of Education matches state outlays used for this purpose, but modest appropriations—$44 million in 1976—limit the extent of federal matching, even though the state response has been substantial. The program exemplifies a clear federal attempt to stimulate purposeful state behavior in the postsecondary realm, and private college students are prominent beneficiaries of this particular partnership. (Not surprisingly, the SSIG strategy figures prominently in the recommendations offered in chapters 5 and 10.)

Tax Provisions

Several provisions of the federal tax code benefit higher education and, in so doing, cost the Treasury approximately $3 billion to $4 billion a year in lost revenues ($3.84 billion in fiscal 1977).[46] For example:

1. Scholarships, fellowships, and similar payments such as veterans' and social security benefits are not taxed as income. The revenue lost is approximately $500 million.

2. Parents supplying more than half the support of students beyond the age of eighteen may claim them as dependents and take the personal exemption of $750, even if the student's own earnings would otherwise disqualify him. The revenue loss is $715 million.

3. Contributions by individuals and corporations to nonprofit institutions such as colleges and universities are deductible from income, within certain limits. The revenue loss (for all education, including a

45. There is some evidence, however, that state governments have used the lion's share of their general revenue sharing receipts for education, and one can reasonably assume that some portion of it therefore supports higher education. Whether it augments or replaces state revenues previously used for that purpose is less clear. (See Richard P. Nathan, Allen D. Manvel, and Susannah E. Calkins, *Monitoring Revenue Sharing* [Brookings Institution, 1975], pp. 237–44.)

46. The source of this and the following statistics is table 6-1.

small portion for private elementary and secondary schools) is $780 million. This tax benefit holds special importance for the private sector since private institutions presently receive three-fourths of all philanthropy directed to higher education[47] and since for some of them such gifts account for a large portion of overall income. Nevertheless, this provision is viewed by some tax reformers as an undesirable loophole.

Regulatory Activities

Washington intrudes itself with growing frequency into college and university affairs that were once left to the faculty, the administration, or the trustees. From civil rights to employee pensions, from laboratory safety standards to ethical controls on human and animal research, from the management of student records to the admission practices of medical schools, federal actions of a regulatory nature (including actions of the judicial branch) are invading unfamiliar campus domains, affecting, with few exceptions, private and public institutions alike. Perhaps because independence from government interference is a cherished attribute of private higher education, such regulation seems especially vexing to its leaders.[48]

In any event, the conflicting pressures of growing reliance on federal funds, fear of government control, and Washington's aversion to unrestricted funding make the current federal intrusions extremely uncomfortable, particularly for these private educators.[49]

Options

Robert Hartman examines in chapter 5 some of the issues and alternatives in the realm of federal direct expenditures affecting undergraduate educational finance. There are three general options open to federal policymakers: direct student aid, direct institutional aid, and programs

47. See Council for Financial Aid to Education, *Voluntary Support of Education, 1974-75* (CFAE, n.d.), p. 58. (The survey covered 986 institutions.)

48. Collective bargaining, for example, is presently subject to supervision by the National Labor Relations Board on private, but not on public, campuses. In several areas—retirement benefits, wage and hour controls, occupational safety and health—the state government is primarily responsible for enforcement with respect to public institutions, whereas private colleges and universities are answerable directly to the cognizant federal agencies.

49. While this book does not dwell on government regulation, the issue is discussed in chapter 9. See also Chester E. Finn, Jr., *Scholars, Dollars, and Bureaucrats* (Brookings, 1978).

to stimulate state action. A different type of option lies in alternative tax policies discussed in depth by Emil Sunley in chapter 6.

STUDENT AID

Given that federal funds for student subsidies are not limitless, the trade-off between access and choice will continue. If large sums are given to individual students to enable them to enter a private college, fewer students will be helped. If, on the other hand, federal subsidy programs adhere to the goal of access, the private sector will find itself harmed—at the very least, not helped—by such federal efforts. Aid would be pegged to low public tuition at a time when the average public-private tuition gap would exceed $2,000 a year and when falling enrollments would accelerate the competition for students. However, any serious attempt to promote both access and choice will be extremely expensive if a sizable grant to large numbers of students is the chosen route.

A cheaper alternative to such large stipends is to structure aid programs in ways that blunt the competitive edge that public institutions would otherwise enjoy in the undergraduate marketplace. The half-cost limitation in the current basic grants program is an example discussed by Hartman, but the controversy raised by that provision illustrates its hazards. By limiting individual basic grants to half the cost of attending a college, the maximum stipend otherwise available to needy students does not function as such a potent economic lure favoring low-priced public colleges. Unfortunately, this provision affects only students in the most impoverished circumstances, and it is therefore rightly accused of promoting choice by curbing the postsecondary access of those very students for whom federal aid is intended.

The projected shrinkage of GI bill outlays may unlock funds for such need-based programs as basic grants. The prospect has encouraged analysts and interest groups to explore variations of the basic grants program that might better serve the goal of choice without inhibiting access. One such possibility is a two-tier program in which a low-income student would be entitled to x percent of his costs of access and to y percent of the additional costs incurred if he or she elects a higher-priced institution.[50]

50. See American Council on Education, Policy Analysis Service, "Proposal for a Two-Level Basic Educational Opportunity Grant" (ACE, November 25, 1975; processed); and Consortium on Financing Higher Education, "Federal Student Assistance: A Review of Title IV of the Higher Education Act" (Hanover, N.H.: COFHE, April 1975; processed).

Grants and scholarships constitute but one set of federal student aid strategies. Other issues arise in connection with loans. The notion of a national educational opportunity bank reappears from time to time and, although nothing quite like it has been enacted, Washington is heavily engaged in loan programs carrying with them subsidies, forgiveness features, guarantees, and the like. Seen through one set of lens, loans present a satisfactory middle ground between costly scholarship schemes and skimpy measures that do little for the private college student. To opt for loans is to say that a student, poor or not, choosing a higher-priced college must pay the difference, but that he does not have to do so out of past or present income. Viewed through a different philosophical prism, however, loans allow society to abrogate what many consider to be its responsibility for providing low-priced higher education. Colleges are not inhibited in raising their tuition rates; young graduates are saddled with heavy debts; the disadvantaged are discouraged from entering college; and, by doing little about the net price differential between public and private colleges, loans fail to establish genuine choice for the uncertain student and thus fail to improve the competitive position of private higher education.

INSTITUTIONAL AID

Despite the billions of dollars that flow each year from Washington agencies to American colleges and universities, no general institutional aid program has ever been funded, and in the eyes of many educators that failure is the principal deficiency in federal postsecondary policy.

In 1971–72, when Congress faced what was seen at the time as a historic choice between student aid and institutional assistance, it favored the former. A program of federal cost-of-education allowances for the colleges was also authorized, with the amounts for each to be based on its enrollment of federally aided students, but no funds to energize that program have yet been appropriated. In recent years, both the Carnegie Council on Policy Studies in Higher Education and the National Council of Independent Colleges and Universities have urged a different approach: tuition offsets, or formula payments, exclusively for students attending private institutions to enable those colleges and universities to remain competitive with state-subsidized public institutions.[51] Whether

51. See Carnegie Council on Policy Studies in Higher Education, *Federal Role in Postsecondary Education: Unfinished Business, 1975–1980*, pp. 35–39, and National Council of Independent Colleges and Universities, *A National Policy for Private Higher Education*, Report of a Task Force, chap. 5.

such a scheme constitutes institutional or student aid is open to debate and, ultimately, is not very important. Notwithstanding Washington's reluctance thus far to subsidize colleges and universities as institutions, this idea and other plans for formula payments retain special allure for higher education's private sector.

STATE STIMULI

During a time of generalized growth for American higher education, federal and state postsecondary policies could afford to be oblivious of one another, leaving it to the colleges and universities to avail themselves of both. But in a time of lessened growth and impending retrenchment, a continuation of this practice may be especially troublesome for private higher education, seemingly entrusted by each level of government to the care of the other. Hartman argues that providing incentives to change state behavior in financing undergraduate education is the appropriate focus for federal policymakers troubled by the competitive disadvantage of private colleges and universities. He reasons that the best way to straighten out a skewed marketplace is to attack the source of the distortion, that is, the uneven patterns of state subsidies, and he contends that national objectives of access and choice can be served by suitable federal encouragement of the states to rationalize their practices.

TAX POLICY

A few perplexing tax issues arise at the state and local level and Emil Sunley, in chapter 6, touches on these, but the tax issues of greatest moment to private higher education are those embedded in the federal tax code and in amendments that are proposed from time to time. Is the charitable deduction, in all its complexity, an equitable, efficient, and precise form of support for private higher education? Which institutions does it benefit? Can it be improved? What can be learned about the desirability, from the private college's perspective, of modifications and alternatives periodically offered by tax reformers?

Beyond the charitable deduction, is there a case for continued exemption of fellowships, scholarships, and similar benefits? For the dependents' exemption? Is there a compelling case for the recurring idea of a tuition tax deduction or credit such as the Senate passed in 1976? Sunley doubts such reforms would particularly benefit private colleges and universities and finds little other analytic justification for them, although he acknowledges their political appeal.

Political Realities

How effectively does the private sector of American higher education prosecute its interests in Washington? The question has no easy answer, for the 1,500 private colleges and universities have many different interests, some of them shared with their public-sector counterparts, others common to a wide range of organizations and activities, still others of singular concern to the private sector or parts of it. On many issues, all of higher education strives to speak with a single voice. On a few, notably those associated with tuition and student aid, the rift between public and private seems unbridgeable.

As mentioned earlier, no national organization represented private higher education as such until 1976, although several Washington-based associations have long spoken for parts of the private sector. As federal postsecondary policy came more and more to stress student aid, as particular formulas were seen to favor public or private institutions rather than higher education in general, and as colleges and universities came to realize that they had a proper and important role to play in looking after their interests at the national level, the need for an unabashed private-sector lobby became more apparent—hence, the formation of the National Association of Independent Colleges and Universities.

Lawrence Gladieux and Thomas Wolanin, in examining these issues in chapter 4, find that in many national policy domains the interests of the private sector harmonize with those of the public, but that in a few areas the independent institutions have distinctive and definite objectives of their own. The federal government's historic reluctance to differentiate its policies by type of institution is belied in part by its efforts to accommodate rival interests in the structure of its programs, most notably in the complex and fractious realm of student aid. There is little basis for confidence that Washington will adopt explicitly "pro-private" policies, but there is hope that a united private sector can continue to safeguard its major interests.

The State Role

State policies toward private higher education are inherently awkward, often ambivalent, and frequently unclear. Unlike the federal government, the states bear primary operating responsibility for their own networks of public campuses, institutions that often compete directly with private colleges. The states must simultaneously assume the roles of regulator, licensing agent, and central planner for their respective postsecondary systems that embody both public and private elements. At the same time, they are a source of funds, besieged with requests from their private colleges and universities.

Four developments in the mid-twentieth century have revived state awareness of the plight of private higher education.

First, when the soaring cost of education forced many private colleges to seek new sources of revenue, their states seemed the logical recourse, particularly for those institutions enrolling predominantly local residents. Why, it was asked, should one group of universities receive subsidies for educating the youth of the state while another group performing a similar service gets no such help?

Second, as higher education changed from an elite to a mass phenomenon, and as access for the low-income individual became an explicit goal of public policy in many states, legislatures authorized programs of scholarships, loans, and other forms of need-based student aid. Unlike institutional subsidies, where the "public-private" distinction held sway, it was more difficult to deny state student aid to otherwise eligible individuals simply because they matriculated in private rather than public universities. In fact, it *was* denied them in a few jurisdictions.[52] But for the most part, state entry into the field of student aid meant state funds for public and private higher education alike.

Third, burgeoning systems of public colleges and universities began to compete directly with established private institutions. The clearest expression of this rivalry was the battle for students as private universities found their accustomed hegemony in particular academic fields and geographic areas menaced by new public institutions offering much the same program in much the same place at a far lower price. But subtler forms of competition also arose in such realms as public service, faculty hiring, and, more generally, stature in the community. Private colleges petitioned state governments to curb the proliferation of public institutions, to limit campus growth plans, and to contract with existing schools rather than build new ones. Occasionally a private campus would find itself unable to withstand the economic pressures and would

52. As of fiscal 1974, Colorado, Nebraska, and Utah confined the use of their state scholarships to public-sector students (and Maine, South Carolina, and Texas limited theirs to private-college matriculants).

ask the state for a straightforward subsidy or, in some instances, would allow itself to be taken over and turned into a state institution.

Fourth, the movement toward statewide planning and coordination of higher education often encompassed private as well as public institutions. Washington encouraged the states to establish broadly based commissions to harmonize postsecondary planning for public, private, and proprietary institutions alike. Consortium-building and other efforts to parcel out educational tasks frequently found state officials closeted with leaders of private and public colleges trying to hammer out mutually agreeable arrangements. Private institutions organized themselves in new statewide associations to bring political pressure to bear on these and other decisions.

By January 1, 1976, forty-two states had authorized programs of direct or indirect assistance to private higher education.[53] These arrangements followed many patterns—in keeping with the unique educational, fiscal, and political circumstances of each state—but as with federal policy they can be roughly divided into institutional support programs and student aid programs. Some states boast both and several have multiple forms of one or the other.

Institutional Support

By late 1974, nineteen states had one or more types of institutional support for private postsecondary institutions. The most common forms of aid were the service contract, with the state hiring a private university to perform a particular function for it; assistance for facilities, typically help with the financing of new buildings; and the formula grant providing subsidies on the basis of enrollments, degrees awarded, or other student-linked measures.

The range and size of such programs is impressive. In New York State, for example, $57 million of "Bundy aid" was allotted to private colleges and universities in the 1975–76 academic year using a formula keyed to the number of degrees awarded.[54] Pennsylvania has a well-established tradition of direct aid to a dozen "private" institutions, al-

53. See *Higher Education in the States*, vol. 5, no. 3 (Education Commission of the States, 1976), pp. 121, 148.

54. In 1968 the New York State legislature passed a bill authorizing such grants based on the recommendation of the Select Committee on the Future of Private and Independent Higher Education, chaired by McGeorge Bundy—hence, the term "Bundy aid." New York has several other forms of aid as well.

though the strings tied to the funds have effectively transformed several of them into quasi-public (state-related) schools. Minnesota, New Jersey, North Carolina, Ohio, and others have begun to award annual contracts to certain private campuses for the performance of particular functions, although sometimes the function appears to be simply staying in existence and continuing to educate state residents.

Student Assistance

In part because constitutional barriers in some jurisdictions prohibit direct aid to private institutions, and in part because political lineups frequently make it easier to enact assistance programs for individuals, student aid has emerged as the most widespread means of channeling state dollars into private higher education. By 1976, thirty-nine states had one or more such programs, including, in nearly every instance, a need-based grant scheme.[55]

These programs differ in size and impact. In the 1976-77 academic year, for example, with state need-based undergraduate student aid programs amounting to $645 million for the nation as a whole, three states (New York, Pennsylvania, and Illinois) accounted for more than 52 percent of that total, whereas other jurisdictions—including some with large private enrollments—boasted extremely modest efforts.[56] In some cases stipends are quite generous; California allots up to $2,700 a student under a single program (with other programs piggybacked, the individual sums could be still higher), and Ohio grants up to $1,500 for each private college student. Elsewhere, aid is limited to a few hundred dollars per student per year, regardless of income level or cost of attendance. In addition, some states apply student aid only to tuition and fees, not to room, board, or other costs of attendance. Recipients in many jurisdictions must be bona fide residents, and they often remain eligible only if they matriculate within the state. This lack of "portability," as it is known, while an understandable stricture from the state's perspective, erodes the usefulness of such aid schemes for private institutions accustomed to drawing many of their students from other states. For example, a Massachusetts program of student aid to residents who attend Massachusetts private colleges may provide little help for Harvard and great

55. *Higher Education in the States*, vol. 5, no. 3 (1976), p. 148.
56. See Joseph D. Boyd, *National Association of State Scholarship and Grant Programs: 8th Annual Survey, 1976-77 Academic Year* (Deerfield, Ill.: Illinois State Scholarship Commission, n.d.).

help to Northeastern while indirectly hurting Cornell University in neighboring New York State.

Issues Facing the States

In chapters 7 and 8 Robert Berdahl and Colin Blaydon examine state policies affecting private higher education. As a preface to their more detailed discussion, several of the issues and options facing the states are sketched below.

THE LEGAL QUANDARY

State laws and constitutions interact with the church-state prohibition of the federal constitution to weave a web of legal impediments to actions that would benefit private higher education. At the same time, state governments bear a basic responsibility for providing education and for licensing and regulating educational institutions. The attempt to use licensing (or degree-awarding) authority to constrain reckless growth and duplication of resources has been an interesting development in recent years, and not one that always redounds to the benefit of the private sector. Several states have initiated moves to amend their constitutions or statutes to permit new forms of assistance to private higher education. Elsewhere, private colleges have loosened their sectarian ties—and in some instances compromised their independence—in order to comply with the terms under which the state is able to aid them. Underlying such developments is always the perplexing question of whether the price of survival—at least the price of state succor—is the sacrifice of distinctive institutional features that helped to justify that survival. A companion question is whether the states should be expected to furnish aid to colleges and universities not fundamentally accountable to elected officials for their use of tax dollars.

THE TUITION–STUDENT AID NEXUS

An idea, already mentioned, that attracted much interest a few years ago was the proposal to hike tuition rates on public campuses and allocate more money for need-based student aid that would be available to public and private enrollees alike. The rationale for this scheme was that it would, first, narrow the tuition gap, second, improve the efficiency of the postsecondary marketplace, and, third, provide public subsidies for those in most need.

While increased student aid commands broad assent from most persons concerned with higher education, the notion of willfully boosting the charges of public colleges and universities met with considerable resistance. Low—preferably zero—tuition is a matter of dogma with many public college leaders, and they found eager allies among students, their bill-paying parents, and elected officials. Moreover, it was asked why one group of students should be obliged to pay more in order to bolster colleges attended by an altogether different group of students. If the private universities could not justify assistance on their own merits, why should public colleges penalize students in order to channel funds indirectly to the private sector?

For all these reasons, no state has explicitly embraced such a plan, although study commissions keep coming back to it as a possibility. Yet in partial and half-concealed ways, much the same outcome may be achieved through the simultaneous expansion of state (and federal) student aid programs on the one hand, and the steady upward drift of public-sector tuition rates on the other. That threat, in any case, seemed real enough to public college spokesmen in 1975 that a number of them joined with other national organizations to form a National Coalition for Lower Tuition. But the slow upward trend of public tuition continues, occasionally dramatized by heated conflicts such as that surrounding the elimination of free tuition at the financially pressed City University of New York. And the growth of student aid programs continues apace. How much do these moves actually benefit private higher education? Is it either realistic or desirable to attempt once again to forge a purposeful link between them? These remain sensitive and important questions for the states.

TUITION OFFSET GRANTS

From the private sector's perspective, a more appealing alternative is simply to obtain for itself the same sorts of subsidies enjoyed by its public counterparts. If the states provide grants for private colleges and universities so that they can reduce their prices, the gap between private and public tuition rates can be narrowed and, presumably, competition encouraged. That is the logic and appeal of "tuition offsets," an approach that attracted attention in 1975. Such payments can elude the hostility of public-sector leaders—unless the funds come from their own appropriations—and they are more predictable than aid channeled through needy students. Moreover, such programs have already been enacted in several states.

But tuition offsets pose their own problems. If it is planned to subsidize every private institution and every student without regard to need, tuition offsets simply duplicate in the private sector what many analysts deem a costly and inequitable feature of public higher education: public assistance to those who can afford to pay for high-priced schooling as well as to those who cannot. There are many other issues. Should offsets be available for all private college students, regardless of residence? Or must private institutions, like most of their public counterparts, establish different rates for home-state and out-of-state students? If the latter route is chosen, will the dual price structure not discriminate against private universities with regional, national, or international clienteles? Will it not tend to inhibit one form of student choice while possibly encouraging another? Is there any way of ensuring that such offsets actually constrain tuition levels, or do they simply function as an unrestricted subsidy to private institutions? Coupled with high tuition, do they boost resources per student and remove the incentive for economy and productivity? The states that have experimented with tuition offsets and kindred schemes have answered—or sidestepped—such questions in different ways, and it is important for them and other jurisdictions considering similar action to examine both the concept itself and its practical effects.

VOUCHER PLANS

President John Silber of Boston University captured notice in early 1975 with a proposal that would virtually eliminate the public-private distinction. (In the belief that all higher education serves the public, he favors the terms "state" and "independent" to distinguish the two types of institutions.) He suggested converting all state postsecondary outlays into sizable vouchers that individual students could use at the college of their choice. As with voucher plans at the elementary school level, the rationale was that students should have the widest possible latitude in selecting educational institutions, that the state's responsibility is to aid students rather than to maintain a particular group of schools, and that true educational diversity and pluralism cannot flourish under a government monopoly. Such a plan would disregard the individual's ability to pay and it would probably also ignore true differences in the cost of education at various institutions. Public-sector opposition is certain to be strong, and the idea, at least in its pure form, seems radical in relation to the current debate, but it may warrant further attention.

INSTITUTIONAL AID

The variety of extant institutional aid schemes illustrates the range of possibilities. Tuition offsets and other formula-based subsidies represent one genre. Perhaps the opposite extreme is an unabashed state take-over of a previously independent college. In between are innumerable options. Whether billed as a form of "aid" to private institutions, or as a purchase of services needed by the state, such schemes raise common policy issues. Is direct funding a reasonable, efficient, and economical use of state resources? Do the terms of such aid seriously limit the independence of private institutions? Are measures that appear sensible in an expansionary phase equally so in a period of retrenchment? Is there reason to assume that a dollar for private higher education is a dollar lost to public higher education? Can the state match its allocation of funds with a judicious parceling-out of educational responsibilities so that its own needs are met and it satisfies all parties? Does analysis sustain the argument that partial institutional subsidies now will save the state money over the long run?

COORDINATION OF RETRENCHMENT PLANS

When both the demand for higher education and the resources available to it are expanding, the essential task of the state agency charged with coordination and planning is to avoid overexpansion and duplication and to assure fair allocation of institutional roles without slighting the educational needs of the state. When curves point downward, however, and cutbacks appear inevitable, the job of coordination becomes far more difficult. It can be reasonably assumed that no college or university will voluntarily shrink, eliminate programs, slash its budget, or curb its enrollment in the interests of rational planning or some abstract notion of fairness toward other institutions. The decentralized nature of university decisionmaking, the high proportion of tenured personnel, and slow academic responses simply exacerbate the situation. Yet the possibility must seriously be entertained that if substantial overall contraction does occur in a state's postsecondary system, and if the state does not forcefully intervene in that process, then (1) the "wrong" programs and institutions will survive through their skill at political manipulation, (2) the private sector will suffer a disproportionate and possibly undesirable retrenchment, and (3) randomized, piecemeal erosion will occur, resulting in a large number of crippled institutions rather than a smaller complement of healthy ones. Yet the resistance to such coordination is sure to be strong, for most institutions will fight retrenchment moves ordered from above, and they will certainly fight decisions to close them down altogether, preferring to continue taking their chances in the political arena. If the state agency's efforts are perceived as an attempt to sustain the private sector at the expense of the public (or vice versa), resistance will be even stronger and better organized.

The Uncertainties Ahead

A number of questions come to mind when one considers the range of policy options touched upon in this chapter and examined in detail later in the book. How crucial are the various financing proposals to the future of specific types of private colleges and universities, and what priority ranking would campus leaders assign to different programs? How much agreement exists within the private sector? Are the disparate interests of private institutions within a state as pronounced as those between public and private institutions? And what are the prospects for détente between the two sectors as higher education approaches a decade or more of limited growth?

Certainly one of the ironies of the dual system of control in higher education is that the private sector has been forced in part by the presence of the public sector to request public aid; and yet if the private sector succeeds too well in this quest, it may cease to be private, independent, and unique. One may have to deal with second-best policy options, but surely it will be possible to avoid those that may do more harm than good.

It is easy to get lost in the welter of program options and to look at the issues from the narrow perspectives of institutional welfare, governmental efficiency, and political feasibility. The leaders of private higher education, like so many others who find their well-being more and more dependent on government action, favor policies that preserve their independence, augment their revenues, and treat them "fairly" in relation to their competitors. What is difficult for private college and university spokesmen (and for so many others) is to devise a way of making their case persuasively and distinctively.

Policies and programs cannot be fairly evaluated without suitable criteria, and in this book the major criterion is in some ways the simplest:

what sort of higher education system will best serve the needs and honor the values of American society in the 1980s and beyond? Our over-riding objective is to help the interested reader ponder possible answers to that question, think about the private sector's place in a sensibly conceived educational system, and weigh the major choices facing public policy in the next decade.

APPENDIX: INCOME AND COLLEGE COSTS

Figure 1-2 compares average college costs over time with two measures of ability to pay; this appendix contains the data underlying that figure, and discusses briefly the limitations of the various time series available for assessing the changing financial burden of sending children to college. None of the available measures of ability to pay is ideal, for a complete analysis would require (among other things) data on family wealth and saving rates as well as income; our main purpose, however, is simply to show that, contrary to popular belief, increases in college costs have not generally outpaced increases in family income.

Income Series

The best income series to help assess parents' ability to pay for college would be after-tax income of families with college-age children,[57] but unfortunately such a series does not exist. Among the existing substitutes are (1) disposable personal income per capita (from the gross national product accounts of the U.S. Bureau of Economic Analysis), (2) median income for families with household heads aged forty-five to sixty-four, (3) median income for families with dependents aged eighteen to twenty-four, and (4) median income for families with dependents aged eighteen to twenty-four in college. The first measure takes into account taxes but is available only on a per capita basis. The three family income series are collected by the Bureau of the Census, which does not define personal income in precisely the same way as in the gross national product accounts. Measure 2 is an appropriate series because parents of most children of college age would fall in the forty-five to sixty-four age bracket, and the size of this group depends only on demographic factors. Measure 3 is probably biased upward because children from high-income families are more likely to go to college and remain in dependent status longer. (Three-fourths of college students aged eighteen to twenty-four were

57. A different measure would be required for independent students.

54

in their parents' households in 1975, compared with less than half the noncollege youth.[58]) Measure 4 clearly has an upward bias since it includes only those families who are paying for college.[59]

Although disposable income per capita and income for families headed by persons aged from forty-five to sixty-four are not ideal for measuring ability to pay, their main advantage is that they are not affected in any way by the decision to attend (or not attend) college. If the need-based student aid programs of recent years have been successful in inducing an ever-growing percentage of low-income students to attend college, measures 3 and 4 would be increasingly biased downward over time. To the extent that student aid programs have encouraged students to become independent of their parents (particularly students from less affluent families), the upward bias of these two series would have increased. The relative magnitudes of these forces is unclear, but their presence causes these time series of income to be less reliable for the present purpose.

College Costs

The appropriate college cost series is either tuition or tuition plus room and board.[60] We chose tuition plus room and board charges as reported by the National Center for Education Statistics as the more comprehensive measure.

Time Period

A final issue arises because none of the income series covers the same twelve months as college costs. Disposable per capita income and income

(Text continues on page 61.)

58. U.S. Bureau of the Census, *Current Population Reports*, series P-20, no. 303, "School Enrollment—Social and Economic Characteristics of Students, October 1975" (GPO, 1976), p. 5.

59. A further technical problem with these last two series is that, compared to income for the middle-aged families, the income for the families with 18–24-year-old dependents is understated, probably by about 20 percent. Measure 2 is collected in each March Current Population Survey (CPS) when Census asks eight questions that identify fourteen separate sources of income. Measures 3 and 4 come from the annual October CPS in which a single estimate of family income is reported for the preceding twelve months, with evidence suggesting that this results in substantial underreporting. (*Current Population Reports*, series P-20, no. 303, p. 67.)

60. Forgone earnings are also an important economic cost of attending college, but are not relevant to the present comparison.

Table 1-A1. *Median Income for All Families and Those with Household Head Aged Forty-five to Sixty-four (March Series), Disposable Income, and College Costs at Public and Private Institutions, 1961-75*

| | Median income (March series) | | Per capita disposable personal income | College costs per student per academic year | | | |
| | | | | Tuition only | | Tuition and room and board | |
Period[a]	All families	Head aged forty-five to sixty-four[b]		Public	Private	Public	Private
			Dollars				
1961	5,735	6,332	1,976	218	906	869	1,666
1962	5,956	6,692	2,058	222	944	901	1,724
1963	6,249	7,018	2,128	234	1,012	926	1,815
1964	6,569	7,306	2,278	243	1,088	950	1,907
1965	6,957	7,673	2,430	257	1,154	983	2,005
1966	7,532	8,326	2,597	275	1,233	1,026	2,124
1967	7,974	8,935	2,740	283	1,297	1,064	2,204
1968	8,632	9,754	2,930	295	1,383	1,117	2,321
1969	9,433	10,808	3,111	324	1,534	1,205	2,533
1970	9,867	11,355	3,348	352	1,685	1,288	2,740
1971	10,285	11,985	3,588	376	1,820	1,357	2,917
1972	11,116	13,036	3,837	407	1,898	1,458	3,038
1973	12,051	14,106	4,285	438	1,989	1,517	3,164
1974	12,836	15,151	4,639	470	2,131	1,617	3,386
1975	13,719	16,320	5,062	513	2,333	1,748	3,667

Index (1967 = 100)[c]

1961	71.9	70.9	72.1	77.0	69.9	81.7	75.6
1962	74.7	74.9	75.1	78.4	72.8	84.7	78.2
1963	78.4	78.5	77.7	82.7	78.0	87.0	82.4
1964	82.4	81.8	83.1	85.9	83.9	89.3	86.5
1965	87.2	85.9	88.7	90.8	89.0	92.4	91.0
1966	94.5	93.2	94.8	97.2	95.1	96.4	96.4
1967	100.0	100.0	100.0	100.0	100.0	100.0	100.0
1968	108.3	109.2	106.9	104.2	106.6	105.0	105.3
1969	118.3	121.0	113.5	114.5	118.3	113.3	114.9
1970	123.7	127.1	122.2	124.4	129.9	121.1	124.3
1971	129.0	134.1	130.9	132.9	140.3	127.5	132.4
1972	139.4	145.9	140.0	143.8	146.3	137.0	137.8
1973	151.1	157.9	156.4	154.8	153.4	142.6	143.6
1974	161.0	169.6	169.3	166.1	164.3	152.0	153.6
1975	172.0	182.7	184.7	181.3	179.9	164.3	166.4
Percent increase							
1961–1967	39.1	41.0	38.7	29.9	43.1	22.4	32.3
1967–1970	23.7	27.1	22.2	24.4	29.9	21.1	24.3
1967–1975	72.0	82.7	84.7	81.3	79.9	64.3	66.4
1970–1975	39.0	43.7	51.2	45.7	38.5	35.7	33.9

Sources: Median income, U.S. Bureau of the Census, *Current Population Reports*, series P-60, no. 105, "Money Income in 1975 of Families and Persons in the United States" (GPO, 1977), and issues for preceding years; per capita disposable income, *Economic Report of the President, January 1977*, p. 213; college costs, Martin M. Frankel and Forrest W. Harrison, Projections: *Education Statistics to 1985–86*, National Center for Education Statistics 77–402 (GPO, 1977), p. 86, and Kenneth A. Simon and Martin M. Frankel, *Projections of Educational Statistics to 1981–82*, DHEW (OE) 73-11105 (GPO, 1973), p. 114.

a. Median and disposable incomes are for the year indicated, on a calendar basis. Per student costs are for the academic year beginning in the year indicated.

b. Median family income applies to those families where the head was between forty-five and sixty-four years of age. For 1961 through 1966 the Census Bureau category of age of head was divided into two decades, forty-five to fifty-four and fifty-five to sixty-four. A weighted average based on the size of the two groups was used to calculate median family income for those families where the head was aged forty-five to sixty-four.

c. Academic year 1967–68 = 100 for student costs.

Table 1-A2. *Median Income for All Families and Those with Dependents Aged Eighteen to Twenty-four (October Series) and College Costs at Public and Private Institutions, 1966–75*

Period[a]	Median income (October series)			College costs per student per academic year			
				Tuition only		Tuition and room and board	
	All families	Families with dependents aged eighteen to twenty-four	Families with dependents in college aged eighteen to twenty-four	Public	Private	Public	Private
	Dollars						
1966–67	6,575	7,809	9,753	275	1,233	1,026	2,124
1967–68	7,060	8,276	10,280	283	1,297	1,064	2,204
1968–69	7,692	8,936	10,832	295	1,383	1,117	2,321
1969–70	8,093	9,519	11,457	324	1,534	1,205	2,533
1970–71	8,479	10,051	12,100	352	1,685	1,288	2,740
1971–72	9,115	10,563	12,817	376	1,820	1,357	2,917
1972–73	10,156	11,342	14,525	407	1,898	1,458	3,038
1973–74	10,650	11,991	15,755	438	1,989	1,517	3,164
1974–75	11,031	12,680	16,389	470	2,131	1,617	3,386

Index (1966–67 = 100)[b]

1966–67	100.0	100.0	100.0	100.0	100.0	100.0	100.0
1967–68	107.4	106.0	105.4	102.9	105.2	103.7	103.8
1968–69	117.0	114.4	111.1	107.3	112.2	108.9	109.3
1969–70	123.1	121.9	117.5	117.8	124.4	117.4	119.3
1970–71	129.0	128.7	124.1	128.0	136.7	125.5	129.0
1971–72	138.6	135.3	131.4	136.7	147.6	132.3	137.3
1972–73	154.5	145.2	148.9	148.0	153.9	142.1	143.0
1973–74	162.0	153.6	161.5	159.3	161.3	147.9	149.0
1974–75	167.8	162.4	168.0	170.9	172.8	157.6	159.4
Percent increase							
1966–67 to 1969–70	23.1	21.9	17.5	17.8	24.4	17.4	19.3
1969–70 to 1974–75	36.3	33.2	43.0	45.1	38.9	34.2	33.6
1966–67 to 1974–75	67.8	62.4	68.0	70.9	72.8	57.6	59.4

Sources: Median income, all families, U.S. Bureau of the Census, *Current Population Reports*, series P-20, no. 303, "School Enrollment—Social and Economic Characteristics of Students, October 1975" (GPO, 1976), p. 67; median income, families with dependents aged eighteen to twenty-four, obtained directly from the Bureau of the Census; college costs, same as table 1-A1.

a. Median income data cover the period October to October. Per student costs are for the academic year.

b. October 1966–October 1967 = 100 for median income data; academic year 1966–67 = 100 for student costs.

Table 1-A3. *Cost Relative to Income of Attending Public and Private Institutions of Higher Education, 1961–75*

	Tuition per student per academic year		Tuition and room and board per student per academic year	
Year[a]	Public	Private	Public	Private
	Percent of disposable personal income per capita			
1961	11.0	45.9	44.0	84.3
1962	10.8	45.9	43.8	83.8
1963	11.0	47.6	43.5	85.3
1964	10.7	47.8	41.7	83.7
1965	10.6	47.5	40.5	82.5
1966	10.6	47.5	39.5	81.8
1967	10.3	47.3	38.8	80.4
1968	10.1	47.2	38.1	79.2
1969	10.4	49.3	38.7	81.4
1970	10.5	50.3	38.5	81.8
1971	10.5	50.7	37.8	81.3
1972	10.6	49.5	38.0	79.2
1973	10.2	46.4	35.4	73.8
1974	10.1	45.9	34.9	73.0
1975	10.1	46.1	34.5	72.4
	Percent of median income per capita of families with head aged forty-five to sixty-four			
1961	3.4	14.3	13.7	26.3
1962	3.3	14.1	13.5	25.8
1963	3.3	14.4	13.2	25.9
1964	3.3	14.9	13.0	26.1
1965	3.3	15.0	12.8	26.1
1966	3.3	14.8	12.3	25.5
1967	3.2	14.5	11.9	24.7
1968	3.0	14.2	11.5	23.8
1969	3.0	14.2	11.1	23.4
1970	3.1	14.8	11.3	24.1
1971	3.1	15.2	11.3	24.3
1972	3.1	14.6	11.2	23.3
1973	3.1	14.1	10.8	22.4
1974	3.1	14.1	10.7	22.3
1975	3.1	14.3	10.7	22.5

Source: Table 1-A1.

a. Disposable and median incomes are for the year indicated, on a calendar basis. Per-student costs are for the academic year beginning with the year indicated.

of middle-aged families follow calendar years, while the two series for families with dependents apply to the twelve months starting in October and tuition, room, and board costs cover the academic year. The October income series present little problem since they nearly correspond with academic years; income for the twelve months preceding October 1975 should be compared with college costs for the 1974–75 academic year. Whether 1974–75 college costs should be compared to calendar-year income for 1974 or 1975 is an open question. We chose 1974 since income for that year probably has more effect on the decision to attend in 1974–75.

Tables 1-A1 and 1-A2 present the data for these four income series (plus median income for all families from both the March and October series), for tuition and total college costs, and for indexes of each series with 1967 as the base year. Table 1-A3 gives the ratios of college costs to income from which figure 1-2 was derived. Tables 1-A1 and 1-A2 show that total college costs (tuition and room and board) in both sectors have generally risen a little more slowly than each of the income series. Over some periods, tuition alone grew faster than income (particularly income of families with dependents aged eighteen to twenty-four and families with dependents in college). Overall, though, tables 1-A1, 1-A2, and 1-A3 do not support the assertion that the costs of college attendance have been outpacing family income in recent years.

Chapter Two

Financial Trends and Issues

Susan C. Nelson

EDITED BY DAVID W. BRENEMAN AND CHESTER E. FINN, JR.

SUSAN C. NELSON is a research associate in the Brookings Economic Studies program.

Tables

WHILE heated debate continues on the financial health of higher education, there is little doubt that the public policies examined in this book might substantially change the situation of private colleges and universities. Adoption or rejection of those policies will not await a conclusive pronouncement on the health of the industry. Decisions should be made, however, with an objective understanding of the financial structure of higher education. This chapter attempts to analyze some of the patterns in sources of revenue for private higher education that would be affected by changes in public policy.

A brief survey of the long-run trends in financing both public and private institutions is followed by a detailed analysis of the private sector during the past decade. This analysis reviews such issues as the stability of tuition as a source of revenue, the destabilizing effects of past federal policies, the determinants of state aid to private institutions, the vulnerability of various types of institutions to changes in the tax treatment of charitable giving, and the dependence of private higher education on public sources of support.

From examining these issues, a number of findings emerge that are either unexpected or run counter to the conventional wisdom.

—Over the last few decades, the private sector's dependence on most of its sources of support has remained fairly stable, except for earnings from endowments, which play a diminishing role, and funds from the federal government, which have been erratic.

—Since the mid-sixties, the financial situation of private universities has differed in important respects from that of private colleges, seemingly because of the fluctuations of federal support. For instance, while the private sector as a whole has become only slightly more dependent on tuition, many universities have, apparently in order to offset sluggish growth in federal research and development funds. Private colleges generally have been spending more of their income from all sources on student aid, while universities have been spending less because of a reduction in federal support for graduate students.

—More expensive institutions generally provide more student aid than their similar but less expensive counterparts. At one extreme, aid per student rises with tuition more sharply among selective Catholic liberal arts colleges than among any other group of private institutions. At the other extreme, an exception to the general pattern occurs among nonselective liberal arts colleges that are not religiously affiliated, where more expensive institutions offer slightly *less* student assistance than their lower-priced counterparts.

—Institutional student aid deficits (see Glossary) have generally been growing, relative to income, but no evidence can be found that this trend has contributed to an increasing reliance on tuition. Indeed, these deficits may even indicate financial strength, rather than weakness.

—Total government assistance to students at public colleges and universities actually exceeds total tuition payments from all students attending those institutions by 24 percent. This is largely due to substantial GI bill benefits and to other assistance that can be used for individual living costs as well as instructional charges.

—Federal funds for research and development have become increasingly concentrated in the public sector, more so than can be explained by the differential growth rates of the two sectors in terms of institutional revenues or researchers.

—Among states, the amount of support for private higher education is unrelated to the subsidies provided for public students. The states that support their private sectors most generously are those with high public tuition, a high budget priority for higher education, or a large percentage of their students enrolled in private institutions.

—Within individual states, there is no evidence that trade-offs between state aid to public and private higher education are widespread. Of eleven states studied, only in New York did the analysis suggest that the private sector benefited at the expense of the public, perhaps on account of New York's programs of substantial direct aid to private institutions. In California, Ohio, and South Carolina, the sectors appeared to prosper together, whereas in the other states the evidence was inconclusive.

—Charitable giving contributes substantially to the financing of private higher education. Eliminating the personal income tax deduction for charitable contributions, however, would reduce institutional income only slightly (about 3 percent of general revenues) because most voluntary support would still be given without the tax incentive. Indeed, the income tax deduction generates less new income for private higher education—induces less additional giving—than the private sector receives in direct support from state governments.

—Voluntary support comes mainly from a few large donations: fewer than 1 percent of the gifts accounted for 72 percent of the amount given by individuals to private institutions.

—The private sector is by no means financially independent of government. The value of current public programs amounts to nearly half of the educational income of private colleges and universities.

The analysis that produced these findings relies heavily on the Higher Education General Information Survey (HEGIS) and its predecessors. These surveys, now conducted by the National Center for Education Statistics, provide financial data on institutions of higher education. HEGIS data are frequently used in analysis because they are the most comprehensive set of statistics available. They attempt to cover all institutions of higher education and can be linked to data extending back to the 1920s. They have rightly been criticized on a number of grounds, however: accounting practices differ among institutions; the response to a number of items is low; definitions change frequently. Also, it is questionable whether information on the most important aspects of any institution's financial situation is provided. Nonetheless, these problems are reduced, though not eliminated, when data for many institutions are aggregated and when changes rather than levels of income are examined; several other sources are also used to supplement the HEGIS data.

Long-Run Trends in Institutional Revenues

Over the past several decades, most funding sources have contributed fairly constant shares to total current-fund income (see table 2-1).[1] In the private sector, tuition accounted for 40 percent of total current revenue in 1939–40 and was only 4 percentage points lower in 1973–74 (though it had reached a low of 33 percent in 1959–60, as shown in table 2-1). During the same period, private giving ranged between 9 and 12 percent with no apparent trend. State support for public institutions hovered around 40 percent during the whole period and aid from all levels of government around 60 percent (with the single exception of 1949–50 when the GI bill temporarily expanded tuition receipts).

The most striking changes that did occur appeared in the private sector, even though the phenomenal expansion of higher education in recent decades was concentrated in the public sector. For private institutions, the share of total current revenues coming from endowment earnings has declined continually, dropping sharply from 18 to 8 percent during the

1. Capital-account revenues are also crucial for the long-term financial health of educational institutions. But because the problems they raise are sufficiently complex to require a separate chapter and because data are even more inadequate than for current-account funds, this chapter focuses on current operating revenues, except in the voluntary support section.

Table 2-1. *Distribution of Current-Fund Income of Private and Public Institutions of Higher Education, by Source, Selected Academic Years, 1939–40 to 1973–74*[a]

Description	1939–40	1949–50	1955–56	1959–60	1965–66	1969–70	1971–72	1973–74[b]
Private institutions								
Source of income				Percent of total income				
Governments, total[c]	2.9	11.2	15.3	21.0	25.7	22.8	22.0	21.4
Federal[d]	0.7	8.6	13.5	19.4	24.0	20.7	19.8	18.6
State	2.1	2.4	1.7	1.4	1.6	1.3	1.6	2.0
Tuition and fees[e]	40.4	41.6	33.4	32.8	34.0	34.7	35.7	35.9
Gifts[f]	9.8	8.7	12.3	11.7	9.1	9.5	9.6	9.5
Endowment earnings	17.9	7.7	8.1	7.4	5.3	5.0	4.6	4.7
Sales, services, and related activities[g]	3.5	4.2	5.1	4.8	3.6	6.3	7.7	8.4
Other educational and general revenue[h]	2.1	2.3	2.9	2.0	2.5	2.2	2.3	2.7
Student aid grants	i	1.0	1.8	2.1	2.6	4.0	3.8	3.7
Auxiliary enterprises	23.6	23.3	21.1	18.2	17.7	15.1	14.0	13.3
				Millions of dollars				
Amount of income	360.9	1,135.7	1,597.8	2,536.1	5,398.5	7,767.6	9,189.9	10,551.5
Public institutions								
Source of income				Percent of total income				
Governments, total[c]	57.6	51.9	60.6	62.3	62.6	62.4	61.9	62.7
Federal	10.3	9.6	12.9	16.6	18.6	15.8	15.4	14.6
State	40.5	37.4	42.6	41.3	39.8	41.3	40.9	42.4

Tuition and fees[e]	15.5	18.5	10.2	10.2	11.7	12.5	13.6	12.8
Gifts[f]	1.4	1.6	2.4	2.6	2.2	1.9	1.8	2.0
Endowment earnings	1.9	0.7	0.8	0.6	0.4	0.4	0.3	0.3
Sales, services, and related activities[g]	5.7	5.2	5.5	5.1	2.8	5.3	6.0	6.4
Other educational and general revenue[h]	1.1	1.8	1.7	1.1	2.7	1.8	2.0	2.4
Student aid grants	[i]	0.4	1.2	1.3	1.7	2.5	2.4	2.3
Auxiliary enterprises	16.6	19.9	17.6	16.6	15.9	12.7	11.7	10.8
				Millions of dollars				
Amount of income	354.3	1,238.9	2,030.9	3,276.7	7,397.7	13,870.9	17,211.0	21,375.7

Sources: Data to 1969–70, June A. O'Neill, Sources of Funds to Colleges and Universities (Carnegie Foundation for the Advancement of Teaching, 1973); data for 1969–70 and 1971–72, Paul F. Mertins and Norman J. Brandt, Financial Statistics of Institutions of Higher Education: Current Funds Revenues and Expenditures—1969–70, DHEW Pub. OE 74-11419 (Government Printing Office, 1973), and ibid., 1971–72 (GPO, 1973); and data for 1973–74, see note b. Figures are rounded.

a. Before 1955–56, data refer to the continental United States, beginning in 1955–56 to the aggregate United States. Current-fund income is primarily composed of educational and general revenue plus revenues from hospitals, from auxiliary enterprises, and for student aid.

b. Starting in 1972–73, the National Center for Education Statistics used a new method of aggregating institutions into university, other four-year, and two-year categories that, among other changes, substantially reduced the number of universities, particularly public. In 1973–74, information was published only by the new method. To make the figures here consistent with previous years, unpublished data from NCES were used.

c. Includes receipts from federal, state, and local governments for all purposes except student aid and hospitals.

d. Includes revenues for federally funded research and development centers. In 1971–72 to 1973–74, NCES grouped these projects with "other major service programs." Since the centers account for approximately 95 percent of that category, for these two years "federal" includes "other major service programs." Before 1969–70, indirect costs recovered were included with the program for which they were incurred; in 1969–70 to 1973–74, they were reported separately though not by source. Here, they are all included as "federal."

e. Includes tuition and fees paid by the federal government under the GI bill for veterans of World War II.

f. Includes private gifts and grants plus nongovernmental sponsored research and nongovernmental other sponsored programs.

g. Through 1955–56 and again in 1965–66 reflects sales and services (of educational departments only; 1959–60 reflects sales and services (of educational departments) plus related activities (of educational departments); 1969–70 (or 1967–68 for appendix tables 2-A1 through 2-A3) to 1973–74 includes major service programs-hospitals.

h. The components of this category changed frequently. For example, in 1965–66, sales and services of educational departments may be reflected here since they were not reported separately; 1969–70 to 1973–74 includes other separately budgeted research.

i. Data not reported separately.

1940s and then falling gradually but consistently to less than 5 percent in 1971–72 and 1973–74. The federal government was probably the least predictable supporter, especially of the private institutions. Federal funds for all types of aid other than that for students rose from virtually nothing in 1939 to nearly one-fourth of total income in 1965–66 and then dropped back to 21 percent of revenues by 1969–70. Income from auxiliary enterprises (such as dormitories and food services) steadily declined in importance for both public and private institutions after World War II. The probable causes were the more rapid inflation in the costs of general educational services than in the costs of housing and food production, the latter's decreasing profitability on campus, and the trend away from the old model of a residential college.

Another interesting characteristic of the financial structure of higher education is the diversity within each sector. Among private institutions, tuition and federal funds are the sources of support that show the most systematic variation by level of institution. In the 1973–74 academic year, for example, tuition and federal payments each accounted for 27 percent of total income for universities. In other four-year institutions, tuition accounted for 44 percent and federal payments 11 percent of total income, whereas the shares were 51 percent and 4 percent, respectively, for the two-year colleges (see tables 2-A1, 2-A2, and 2-A3). In the public sector, the primary variation appears in support from the three levels of government. The state is the major contributor to all types of public institutions, but universities in particular receive substantial help from the federal government—nearly half as much as from the state—and local governments contribute heavily to two-year colleges, though the local share is much less important than it was twenty years ago. The four-year state colleges are caught in the middle, neither sufficiently national nor sufficiently local to attract much federal or local aid, so nearly half of their total current income comes from state governments. The strong positions taken by the American Association of State Colleges and Universities (AASCU)—which represents most of these colleges—in opposition to sharing state funds with private institutions and in support of low public tuition are therefore not surprising.

These broad categories of universities, four-year colleges, and two-year colleges obscure numerous other differences in financial structure that a more detailed breakdown by institutional type would reveal. Hence, in the analyses of particular revenue sources that follow, the universe of private institutions is categorized according to Carnegie Commission classifications.[2] In addition, the liberal arts colleges have been further disaggregated into subsets of institutions with common religious and racial characteristics.

Tuition and Student Aid

The fraction of income derived from tuition indicates institutional vulnerability to drops in enrollment. Within the private sector, reliance on tuition varies considerably by Carnegie classification: in 1973–74, tuition and fees accounted for only 27 percent of all educational and general revenue of the leading research universities, whereas the proportion was 77 percent for comprehensive I institutions (table 2-A4).[3] The common notion that tuition has become a much more important source of income for private institutions in recent years is incorrect. As a whole, the private sector depended only slightly more on tuition in 1973–74 than it did in 1966–67, an increase largely caused by higher rates among the research and doctoral-granting universities.

Gross tuition revenue reported by institutions in the HEGIS surveys, however, overstates the real financial resources transferred from students and their parents to colleges and universities because it includes transfer payments in the form of student assistance. Indirect student aid flows first to the institutions—from private donors, the government, or other sources—before being disbursed among the student body, largely at the school's discretion, while direct student aid goes directly to students from the various levels of government. Both direct and indirect student aid affect the choice between higher education and other goods, encouraging the purchase of the former. Indirect student aid (and direct aid that varies with cost of attendance) also affect the net price difference between two institutions and, in particular, the effective tuition gap between public and private colleges.[4]

2. Carnegie Commission on Higher Education, *A Classification of Institutions of Higher Education* (Carnegie Foundation for the Advancement of Teaching, 1973). See Glossary for definitions.

3. "Educational and general revenue" includes income from most sources related to the educational mission of the institution such as tuition and fees, sponsored research, general government appropriations, private gifts and endowment income, and the like. It excludes, among other items, revenue designated for student aid, income related to hospitals, dormitories and food services, and other auxiliary enterprises.

4. The effects of tuition price differences on demand for higher education are discussed in chapter 3.

Direct student aid does not appear on HEGIS accounts while indirect aid generally does, with revenues from outside the institution identified by source. Hence, federal funds earmarked for student assistance, such as supplementary educational opportunity grants and graduate fellowships, are generally included on the accounts under student aid revenues, as are private giving and endowment income restricted to student aid and some state student assistance. Neither loans, such as those of the national direct student loan program, nor payments to students in exchange for work (for example, through the college work-study program) are counted as student aid; the former does not appear at all on the accounts whereas the latter is reported under "other sponsored programs." An institution's unrestricted funds devoted to student assistance can be inferred as the difference between reported student aid expenditures and revenues—the so-called student aid gap or deficit.

Although funds for basic educational opportunity grants nominally flow through institutions to students, the government selects the recipients and determines the size of the grant. Institutions are not supposed to report basic grants either as student aid revenues or expenditures on the HEGIS surveys. Hence, they qualify as direct student aid. Other programs of direct student assistance include GI bill benefits, the additional benefits that a family on social security receives because it has a child aged eighteen to twenty-one in college, state scholarships that go directly to the student, and the present value of interest subsidies on guaranteed student loans.

Below, several issues relating to indirect student aid and tuition are discussed from the institutional perspective. Next, estimates of direct student aid to the various types of institutions in the public and private sectors are presented (chapters 5 and 8 discuss at length federal and state involvement in such aid programs). And, finally, by combining direct and indirect student aid and taking living expenses into account, estimates are made of unassisted tuition revenue, the best available measure of personal financial resources spent on higher education by students and their parents.

Indirect Student Aid

Recent years have seen indirect student aid expenditures increase substantially at both public and private colleges and universities—from $587 million in 1966–67 to $1.4 billion in 1973–74 (table 2-A5). For the private sector as a whole, the increase has come in roughly equal amounts from general institutional funds ($162 million) and from public and private outside sources designated for student aid ($199 million, of which $75 million came from the federal government). As a percentage of educational and general income, the student aid deficit (what the institutions paid from general funds) increased from 2.9 to 4.0 percent within the private sector.

Because this increased use of unrestricted funds for student aid is often cited as evidence of the growing financial plight of private institutions,[5] it is important to stress that such increases taken in isolation—even increases relative to income—provide no information about financial weakness. It is essential to know what causes the growth in the deficit. If the increase results from enrolling additional students who require institutional financial help, or who can only pay a discounted price, what matters is whether the incremental operating costs incurred exceed the incremental revenues the new students bring in (their gross tuition and room and board expenses less any institutional student aid they receive). If the costs are less than additional net revenues, the institution is better off with the extra students than without them. The student aid deficit, or gap, is only one component of this marginal cost–marginal benefit calculation.[6]

On the other hand, constant enrollment but higher operating costs (such as energy bills or faculty salaries) may require tuition increases that not all students can pay, forcing additional institutional student aid in the form of tuition discounts. To the extent that the growth in the aid gap

5. See, for example, John F. Hughes and Patricia Smith, "Policy Options for Federal Consideration" (American Council on Education, Policy Analysis Service, April 1976; processed), p. 13.

6. For example, if a college charges $4,000 a year in tuition, and an additional student is enrolled with a $1,500 scholarship from the college, the latter will be worse off only if the marginal costs of that student's attendance exceed $2,500, even though the student aid gap has increased by $1,500. Note that average costs—expenditure divided by enrollment—are irrelevant here. Unlike the firm in standard price theory that in the long run must set price equal to average costs, a college faces no such constraint because it is able to engage in price discrimination; for example, it can charge different prices (stated tuition net of student aid discounts) in different markets based largely on family income or ability. Any time a college can enroll a student who can cover only marginal costs (and who is not taking the place of a student paying full tuition), it should do so. Such a student will not increase the costs that other students have to cover, either in the short or long run. If he did not attend, the fixed costs included in the long run would be unchanged, while the short-run costs that his attendance imposes would be offset by the net tuition paid.

is cost-induced, the financial status of the college is worse than it was the previous year, or than it would have been if all students had been able to pay the higher tuition. Thus only if the cause of growing student aid deficits is known is it clear whether they signal improving or worsening financial conditions.[7]

All types of private institutions devoted a larger share of educational and general revenue to student aid from 1966 to 1973 except for the research and the leading doctoral-granting universities (see table 2-A6). The expansion of federal and, to some extent, state aid programs enabled comprehensive colleges and universities II and liberal arts colleges II to increase their aid expenditures without dipping much further into their own general funds. The liberal arts colleges I were not so fortunate, however. Their student aid revenues grew slightly faster than educational and general revenue, but not as fast as their student aid expenditures.

In spite of some small increases in the student aid deficit, research universities suffered such large drops in student aid revenue that they were forced to reduce their aid expenditures (relative to income). The cutback in federal support of graduate students was a major factor. In the leading research universities, student aid from federal sources for every full-time-equivalent student actually fell from $268 to $200 between 1966 and 1973, and the fate of federal aid at other research universities was similar (table 2-A7).

DEPENDENCE ON STUDENT PAYMENTS

Taking gross tuition net of indirect student aid to represent the resources transferred from students to institutions,[8] over the 1966–73

7. The student aid deficit is discussed further in chapter 9 from the perspective of college presidents.

8. Net tuition is an imperfect indicator since some student aid can be used for room and board, as well as tuition. A more complete measure would be "net cash flow from and on behalf of students" (Hans H. Jenny, *Higher Education and the Economy* [American Association for Higher Education, 1976], p. 19), which adds room and board receipts to net tuition. Nevertheless, this chapter looks at net tuition relative to educational and general revenue, rather than at net cash flow relative to educational and general plus housing and food service revenues. College room and board receipts seem to keep pace with housing and food costs while college educational and general revenue follows the same course as general education costs; the price index for the former has been rising much more slowly than for the latter (D. Kent Halstead, *Higher Education Prices and Price Indexes* [Government Printing Office, 1975], pp. 31, 109), and it is therefore more useful to keep the two types of revenues separate. It should be noted, however, that because housing and food revenues have

period the share of educational revenue in the private sector contributed by students was generally inching down. This trend was far from universal, however, with research and doctoral-granting universities increasing—and the college categories reducing—their dependence on net tuition (table 2-A4).

Why did the reliance on student contributions increase at some types of institutions and fall at others? Liberal arts and comprehensive colleges could reduce their dependence on student revenues because the role of their gross tuition earnings had only slightly increased during a period when they were spending more of their operating funds on student aid. At the research-oriented universities, the federal government appears to be the culprit. Their gross tuition receipts assumed added importance, possibly because of slowing federal support for research, while falling federal support for graduate students reduced total student aid revenues (relative to income). This drop in federal indirect student aid has probably contributed to the financial dependence of research universities on students, but, in view of the stable student aid deficit, there is no evidence that the aid gap itself has had such an effect.

TUITION AND STUDENT AID EXPENDITURES

The relation of tuition revenue to student aid expenditures among institutions may be examined in a given year by comparing aid expenditures at different levels of tuition on a per student basis.[9] For instance, do more expensive colleges and universities also make more student aid available, and if so how much more relative to their tuition rates? One can see how the relation has been changing over the years by tracing the average fraction of tuition spent on student aid. Have higher tuition charges masked an increasing amount of "discounting" to maintain enrollments,

risen so much more slowly than other sources, comparing net cash flow to educational and general revenue plus housing and food receipts shows less increase in the dependence on student payments than comparing net tuition to educational and general revenue.

9. Since most students receive no student aid, total indirect aid expenditures should be compared to the number of recipients at an institution, rather than to full-time-equivalent enrollment. Unfortunately, data are not generally available so that an arbitrary assumption would have to be made about recipients as a fraction of enrollment. The evidence that is available indicates that such a fraction varies among institutions: higher aid per student probably reflects both larger grants per recipient and a larger fraction of the student body receiving aid. While aid per full-time-equivalent student does not equal the average grant awarded, it does reflect the potential for aid, allowing the number of recipients and the average grant to be determined by the institution.

Table 2-2. *Marginal Student Aid Expenditures per $100 Additional Tuition, Private Institutions of Higher Education, by Carnegie Classification, Academic Year 1973–74*

Classification[a]	Expenditure[b] (dollars)
Doctoral-granting institutions	
Research universities I	32
Research universities II	−16
Doctoral-granting universities I	17*
Doctoral-granting universities II	11*
Comprehensive institutions	
Comprehensive universities and colleges I	7*
Comprehensive universities and colleges II	13*
Liberal arts institutions	
Liberal arts colleges I[c]	14*
Independent (not church-affiliated)	12*
Catholic-sponsored	31*
Other church-sponsored	12
Liberal arts colleges II	3
Predominantly black	9
Predominantly white	
Independent (not church-affiliated)	−2*
Catholic-sponsored	15*
Other church-sponsored	20*
Two-year institutions	2

Source: American Council on Education, data tape of private institutions assembled from various Higher Education General Information Surveys for 1965–66 to 1973–74, conducted by the National Center for Education Statistics.

* Statistically significant at the 5 percent level of confidence.

a. See Glossary for a description of categories.

b. Per full-time-equivalent student. Marginal expenditures are calculated as 100 times the regression coefficient in:

$$\frac{\text{Student aid expenditures}}{\text{FTE enrollment}} = a + b \left(\frac{\text{tuition revenues}}{\text{FTE enrollment}} \right),$$

where a is the constant and b is the regression coefficient. The regression was estimated separately for each Carnegie category. The figures in this table should be interpreted as the additional aid per student associated with $100 higher tuition in 1973–74.

c. Predominantly white. There are no predominantly black colleges in the liberal arts colleges I category.

as a rising fraction would indicate, or have discounts not become a more substantial part of tuition, as a constant or declining fraction would suggest?

Not surprisingly, when student aid expenditures per full-time-equivalent student are examined by tuition level, it appears that, within and between Carnegie classifications, more expensive colleges and universities generally make more student aid available. (Research universities II are an exception where the reverse is true; see table 2-A8.) The additional aid that accompanied an additional $100 of tuition in 1973–74 is shown by Carnegie classification in table 2-2. In the five categories where the results are statistically significant (doctoral-granting universities and comprehensive institutions, and liberal arts colleges I), the table indicates that for every $100 by which tuition at one institution (say, college *A*) exceeded tuition at another institution (college *B*), college *A* would spend $7 to $17 more per student on aid than college *B*. For the other categories, it is not certain that there is any consistent relation between tuition and student aid, but the results suggest that in the leading research universities $100 of higher tuition elicited $32 in additional aid; that among the less prestigious research universities more expensive institutions actually gave out less in student aid than lower-priced universities; and that among the less selective liberal arts and two-year colleges, there is very little overall relation between student aid and tuition.

Breaking down the two liberal arts categories reveals substantial differences in the relationships between tuition and student aid. Selective Catholic colleges offset every $100 in higher tuition with $31 of additional student aid, compared to only $12 of aid from the other liberal arts colleges I. The diversity among the liberal arts colleges II explains the insignificance of the marginal aid expenditure calculated for the category as a whole. More expensive independent (that is, not church-affiliated), predominantly white colleges actually make smaller student aid grants than their lower-priced counterparts, while other church-related colleges make additional student aid available at the rate of $20 per student for every $100 higher tuition. Predominantly black colleges traditionally try to keep tuition low and student aid high, so the insignificant relation between marginal tuition and marginal student aid is not surprising.

These results indicate that indirect student aid can insulate only a limited number of students from much of the stated tuition differentials among private institutions in the various Carnegie categories. With the exception of the major research universities and selective Catholic colleges, at most 7 to 20 percent of the total student body could be completely sheltered from price differences, or at most 14 to 40 percent could have half of the additional tuition offset by student aid, depending on the Carnegie classification. Although these findings still do not describe the distribution of effective prices that low-income students face, they provide some information on how stated tuition differentials compare with the differentials actually encountered by students receiving aid.

They suggest, for instance, that posted tuition differentials among Catholic liberal arts colleges I overstate effective differentials more than those in any other category. At the other extreme, in the liberal arts II category, more expensive, predominantly white independent colleges actually offer less student aid than their less expensive counterparts. Apparently, the higher-priced colleges are much more dependent on student payments while those with lower tuition have other sources of support.

When the relation between tuition and student aid is examined over time (table 2-A9), it appears that discounts have increased in the comprehensive, liberal arts, and two-year colleges over this period, whereas in research and other doctoral-granting universities student aid has been shrinking as a fraction of tuition, at least since 1969–70, apparently because of declining federal support of graduate education. Black liberal arts colleges in particular registered spectacular growth, with student aid rising from 32 percent of tuition in 1966–67 to 60 percent in 1973–74. More outside support was the reason rather than greater use of general institutional funds.

Direct Student Aid

Direct student aid—defined as aid programs in which the government, not the institution, determines the amount and the recipient of the grant —is an important complement to indirect, institution-based aid because it increases students' general ability to purchase higher education. Direct student aid has become a popular form of student assistance for both federal and state governments, in part because most direct programs attempt to be neutral among schools (that is, they do not change tuition differentials).

Table 2-3 presents estimates of the amounts of direct aid given to students between 1972–73 and 1974–75 according to the type of institution. These estimates were derived on the following bases. First, since the funds for these programs flow directly to students, administering agencies often do not record expenditures according to institutional control. This is particularly true of the Social Security Administration and the Veterans Administration since neither agency considers its program primarily educational. Hence, the GI bill and social security benefit figures only approximate the actual distributions.[10] Second, the figures reflect the fact that basic educational opportunity grants were first funded in 1973–

10. The estimated distribution of GI bill benefits attempts to account for full- and part-time enrollment status, and number of dependents. Only trainees in two- and

74 with freshmen eligible that year and sophomores included the following year. Third, the interest subsidies involved in the guaranteed student loan program are assumed to be (a) the interest payments plus the special allowance paid by the federal government while the student is in school and for a nine-month grace period thereafter, together with (b) the special allowance that the government continues to pay during the repayment period. The figures in table 2-3 are therefore estimates of the present discounted value of these subsidies on the loans made that year.[11] These assumptions produce a subsidy equal to 37 percent of the loan. Finally, state direct student aid is taken as the difference between the amounts estimated from annual surveys of the National Association of State Scholarship Programs and the student aid revenues from state sources reported on HEGIS surveys.[12]

The most striking point shown by table 2-3 is how the GI bill dominates the other direct student aid programs, particularly in the public sector and especially in the two-year colleges. At four-year institutions, the distribution is more even, with private students receiving about 26 percent of the benefits while they represent about 30 percent of the enrollment. The impact of the 1976 revisions to the GI bill—in which the federal government will match contributions withheld from the veteran's pay while he or she was in the service—will not be felt for several years.

---

four-year public and private nonprofit institutions of higher learning are included. The data used for these estimates were given to the author by the Veterans Administration.

The distribution of social security benefits is even more approximate than that for the GI bill. The estimates are based on (a) monthly benefits received by students aged eighteen to twenty-one published in *Social Security Bulletin, Annual Statistical Supplement, 1974* (GPO, n.d.), (b) an estimate made by the Social Security Administration of the fraction of these benefits going to college students in 1972, and (c) the distribution of these benefits by level and control of institution attended, and by size of the family unit, as reported in the Spring 1973 Survey of Social Security Student Beneficiaries, 18–21 (taken from a printout provided by the Social Security Administration).

11. Additional assumptions of a 7 percent rate of interest on the loan, a 9 percent discount rate and market rate of interest, and an average of three more years of school including grace period with ten-year repayment period were adapted from Robert W. Hartman, *Credit for College: Public Policy for Student Loans*, A Report for the Carnegie Commission on Higher Education (McGraw-Hill, 1971), pp. 133–35. Data on guaranteed student loans made per year by level and control of institution were estimated from unpublished information provided by the Office of Education.

12. These data and the estimating procedures are described below.

Table 2-3. *Sources of Direct Student Aid, by Level and Control of Institutions of Higher Education, Academic Years 1972–73 to 1974–75*

Millions of dollars

Level of institution and source of aid	Public			Private		
	1972–73	1973–74	1974–75	1972–73	1973–74	1974–75
All levels						
GI bill	1,534.2	1,772.3	2,658.8	286.0	342.4	445.2
Social security benefits[a]	305.2	319.5	372.7	131.7	138.0	161.0
Basic educational opportunity grants	...	32.9	238.1	...	13.1	87.1
Guaranteed student loan subsidies	192.0	166.0	250.0	109.0	115.0	148.0
State aid	48.7	52.3	b	123.8	160.1	b
Total	2,080.1	2,343.0	b	650.5	768.6	b
Four-year institutions						
GI bill	860.9	852.1	1,051.4	260.9	302.1	381.8
Social security benefits[a]	210.9	217.8	254.1	121.9	130.7	152.5
Basic educational opportunity grants	...	20.5	142.9	...	11.0	75.6
Guaranteed student loan subsidies	159.0	137.0	207.0	98.0	104.0	134.0
Total (excluding state)[c]	1,230.8	1,227.4	1,655.4	480.8	547.8	743.9
Two-year institutions						
GI bill	673.3	920.2	1,607.4	25.1	40.3	63.4
Social security benefits[a]	94.3	101.7	118.6	9.5	7.3	8.5
Basic educational opportunity grants	...	12.0	93.6	...	1.7	11.2
Guaranteed student loan subsidies	33.0	29.0	43.0	12.0	12.0	16.0
Total (excluding state)[c]	800.6	1,062.9	1,862.6	46.6	61.3	99.1

Sources: See text and accompanying notes on pages 80–83. Unpublished data for basic educational opportunity grants and guaranteed student loans were obtained directly from the U.S. Office of Education.
a. Additions to total family benefits from eighteen- to twenty-one-year-old children attending college.
b. The HEGIS financial surveys for 1974–75 do not give a figure for state student aid funds channeled through the institution.
c. State data are not available by level of institution.

Social security benefits are concentrated slightly more heavily in the private sector (30 percent of the total) than full-time-equivalent enrollment (25 percent), but probably not more heavily than unmarried eighteen- to twenty-one-year-olds. (Public two-year colleges attract a greater number of older students.) Basic grants were also weighted in favor of the private sector—28 percent in 1973–74 and 27 percent in 1974–75 of total payments went to private students.[13] This distribution probably reflects higher private-sector tuition (which is not affected by the half-cost limitation) and higher private-sector participation, offsetting the greater concentration of low-income students in the public sector.

Unassisted Tuition

When direct and indirect student aid are combined and compared with total tuition and fee revenue as in table 2-4, an interesting fact emerges. The various levels of government pay out 24 percent more in student assistance to students of public colleges and universities than students of those institutions return in tuition. This is possible because some of the aid is used for living expenses and is largely due to the substantial GI bill benefits. In the private sector, student assistance from public sources amounts to only one-third of tuition, with aid from all sources raising the proportion to 46 percent. Although the fraction of tuition offset by student aid is much higher in the public than in the private sector (since private tuition greatly exceeds public rates), the average private student receives a larger amount of aid than his public counterpart: $940 as opposed to $617.

Because much of the student aid money reported in table 2-4 could be used to defer living costs as well as tuition and fees, not all of it accrued to the institutions as educational and general revenue. If it is assumed that the same fraction of student aid is used for tuition as tuition and fees constitute of total costs of education (tuition plus room and board) in each sector,[14] student aid paid $1,186 million toward tuition in the

13. This was the program's second year of operation and only freshmen and sophomores were eligible; the distribution of funds may be different when the program is fully operational.

14. In the public sector average tuition and fees charged was $553 in the 1973–74 academic year, with home-state and out-of-state rates weighted by 1972 enrollment, according to Arthur Podolsky, *Basic Student Charges, 1972–73 and 1973–74*, National Center for Education Statistics (GPO, 1975), table B1, and Ellen Cherin and

Table 2-4. *Total and Unassisted Tuition and Fee Revenue, and Tuition Gap, Public and Private Institutions of Higher Education, Academic Year 1973–74*

Description	Public		Private		Tuition gap per student (dollars)[a]
	Millions of dollars	Dollars per student[a]	Millions of dollars	Dollars per student[a]	
Total tuition and fee revenue	2,744.6	483	3,798.6	2,051	1,568
Student aid	3,499.0	617	1,741.4	940	...
Public sources[b]	3,404.2	600	1,252.2	676	...
Private sources	94.8	17	489.3	264	...
Student aid allocated to tuition[c]	1,186.2	209	1,088.4	588	...
Unassisted tuition revenue	1,558.4	275	2,710.2	1,463	1,186

Sources: Table 2-3; Paul F. Mertins and Norman J. Brandt, *Financial Statistics of Institutions of Higher Education: Current Funds Revenues and Expenditures—1973–74 Summary Data*, NCES 76-121 (GPO, 1976); and unpublished data from U.S. Office of Education, Division of Student Financial Aid.

a. Per full-time-equivalent student.

b. Includes public indirect aid, all direct aid, college work-study aid, and subsidies on national direct student loans in the following amounts (in millions): to public institutions, $240.7 for NDSL and $198.0 for CWS; to private institutions, $183.0 for NDSL and $93.0 for CWS.

c. Assuming the same fraction of student aid goes for tuition as tuition and fees constitute of total costs of education. (See text for further explanation.)

public sector, or 43 percent of total tuition and fee revenue, and $1,088 million, or 27 percent, in the private sector. This implies that the unassisted tuition revenue per full-time-equivalent student, that is, tuition revenue net of student aid from all sources allocated to room and board, was $275 at the average public institution and $1,463 at the average private school in 1973–74. In spite of the concentration of the GI bill at public institutions, student aid reduces the tuition gap from $1,568 to $1,186 (table 2-4).

Marilyn McCoy, *Supplementary Document: Data Values Used in the Development of Analysis Reports for the Study*, "State Financial Support of Higher Education: A Framework for Interstate Comparison—1973–74" (National Center for Higher Education Management Systems at Western Interstate Commission for Higher Education, 1976). Living costs were $1,077. At private institutions undergraduate tuition averaged $1,989 and room and board $1,174. Hence, tuition accounted for 62.5 percent of total costs of education in the private sector and 33.9 percent in the public sector. These proportions ignore miscellaneous costs like books and transportation and are too low for commuting students who continue to live at home. Nevertheless, they are useful approximations of the relation between tuition and other monetary costs of attending college in the two sectors.

Federal Support for Institutions

Federal institutional aid not designated for students has been an unstable source of revenue for private colleges and universities. When the private sector is examined by Carnegie classification, it is clear that the sharp drop in the proportion of federal support in institutional budgets has been concentrated in the research and doctoral-granting categories, while federal support for the other types of private colleges has been generally stable or rising over this period (see table 2-A10).[15]

It is interesting to note that the decline in the role of federal support at the research-oriented universities seems to have been offset by an increased reliance on tuition. A general coincidence between such falling federal support and the rising importance of tuition does not prove that the former trend was responsible for the latter. Nevertheless, the fact that in these university categories the federal share of income fell more than any other source and that no other source rose as much as tuition does bolster the possibility that one caused the other.

In view of the possible link between the two occurrences it is important to isolate the actual cause of the federal decline, as is done in table 2-5. Sponsored research is the only component of federal aid that has consistently fallen, due to very slow growth in basic research. Between 1967–68 and 1973–74, federal support for basic research, which accounts for 70 to 80 percent of all federal research and development money in universities, grew by 34 percent at public and by 19 percent at private universities. Whether deflating by the consumer price index or Kent Halstead's research and development price index,[16] these nominal increases represent decreases in real terms in federal support for basic research. Applied research, the other main object of federal funding, more than kept pace with educational and general revenue at both public and private universities. Federal support for development in the private sector actually fell

15. Federal support includes general appropriations, sponsored research, and other sponsored programs (including college work-study). In addition, beginning in 1968–69 when it was first reported as a separate item in the HEGIS surveys, "indirect costs recovered" are included. Although they are not identified by program sponsor, all indirect costs are allocated here to federal contracts since (a) the federal government provides most of the outside support for programs that involve indirect costs, and (b) federal contracts are more apt to have specific provisions for the recovery of indirect costs than those of state or nongovernmental sponsors. This approximation slightly overestimates the role of federal funding beginning in 1968–69.

16. Halstead, *Higher Education Prices and Price Indexes*, pp. 9, 76.

Table 2-5. *Federal Funding of Research and Development at Public and Private Universities and Colleges, Academic Years 1967–68 and 1973–74*

Amounts in millions of dollars

Type of funds	1967–68		1973–74		Percentage change, 1967–68 to 1973–74	
	Public institutions	Private institutions	Public institutions	Private institutions	Public institutions	Private institutions
Educational and general revenue	5,556.4	2,783.4	9,107.1	3,765.9	63.9	35.0
Federal government	803.5	768.5	1,174.0	913.5[a]	46.1	18.9
Basic research	607.5	643.3	812.7	764.5[a]	33.8	18.8
Applied research	161.5	92.0	312.6	126.6	93.5	37.6
Development	34.5	33.2	48.7	22.4	41.2	−32.5

Sources: 1967–68, educational and general revenue, O'Neill, *Sources of Funds*, pp. 34–35; other 1967–68 data were provided by the National Science Foundation; 1973–74 educational and general revenue are from National Center for Education Statistics, unpublished data; other 1973–74 data are from NSF, *Expenditures for Scientific Activities at Universities and Colleges, Fiscal Year 1975: Detailed Statistical Tables, Appendixes B and C,* NSF 76-316 (NSF, 1976), p. 8, and NSF, *Expenditures for Scientific and Engineering Activities at Universities and Colleges, Fiscal Year 1974,* NSF 76-303 (GPO, 1976), p. 11.

a. Includes $55 million in basic research for Draper Laboratories in Massachusetts, which, beginning in 1973–74, were reclassified; from being counted as a part of Massachusetts Institute of Technology they were transferred to the independent nonprofit sector.

between 1967–68 and 1973–74, but development is only a small part of total funding.

A curious point that emerges from table 2-5 is that between 1967–68 and 1973–74 federal research and development expenditures became more concentrated in the public sector of higher education relative to the private sector, even more concentrated than could be explained by differential growth rates. During this period, federal spending in the public sector grew at 72 percent of the rate of growth in university education and general revenue (46.1/63.9), while in the private sector federal funds grew only 54 percent as fast as general university income (18.9/35.0), indicating a shift in federal research and development funds away from the private sector toward the public. The less research-oriented public universities in particular seem to have gained at the expense of all levels of private research universities.[17] At the same time that federal support

17. In the private sector, the reduction in federal research and development funds was about evenly distributed between the top ten recipients and other private institutions: between 1967–68 and 1973–74 the proportion of federal research monies going to the top ten fell by 1.8 percentage points and the percentage to other insti-

was becoming more concentrated in public universities, the number of researchers was actually dropping in the public sector and rising in the private. Consequently, in terms of federal support per researcher, the shift toward public universities is even more pronounced:[18]

	1968–69		1972–73		Percent change, 1968–69 to 1972–73	
	Public	Private	Public	Private	Public	Private
Number of full-time-equivalent researchers	31,705	18,441	27,508	19,384	−13.2	+5.1
Federal dollars per researcher	26,377	41,944	41,466	46,304	+57.2	+10.4

There is no obvious explanation for this trend. Since peer review is the process by which most grants are awarded, the shift cannot be attributed to a conscious federal policy to favor public over private universities. Apparently proposals submitted by the public sector were "better" or disproportionately more numerous than those from researchers at private institutions. The rapid growth of applied research, disproportionately concentrated in public universities, may explain part of the shift. Differences in the indirect cost rates may be another factor,

---

tutions by 3.3 percentage points. In the public sector, the gains were concentrated below the top ten institutions, which increased their share of federal research money by 0.8 percentage point; the others enlarged their portion by 4.3 points. The percentage distribution of federal research and development funds for the two years was as follows:

	1967–68		1973–74	
Institutional category	Public	Private	Public	Private
Top ten recipients	18.4	24.4	19.2	22.6
Other recipients	32.7	24.5	37.0	21.2
Total	51.1	48.9	56.2	43.8

Data are from the National Science Foundation, *Expenditures for Scientific Activities at Universities and Colleges, Fiscal Year 1975: Detailed Statistical Tables, Appendixes B and C* (NSF, 1976), p. 16, for 1973–74; 1967–68 data obtained from the National Science Foundation.

18. The numbers of full-time-equivalent researchers are as of January 1969 and January 1973. The figures for federal funds per researcher are based on expenditures for 1968–69 and 1972–73. Expenditures for 1968–69 are estimated as the average of 1967–68 and 1969–70 expenditures. Figures were obtained from the following sources: number of researchers, NSF, "Survey of Scientific Activities of Institutions of Higher Education, 1967–68," NSF Form 411, provided by NSF, and unpublished tabulation for 1973, provided by NSF; federal funds per researcher, NSF, *Expenditures for Scientific Activities at Universities and Colleges, Fiscal Year 1975*, NSF 77-307 (GPO, 1977), p. 11.

since states often cover expenses such as pensions, insurance, or legal fees for institutions in the public system that private universities must include in their operating budgets. Given the importance of federally sponsored research to private universities and the increased reliance on tuition revenue to offset the shrinking role of federal support in their operating incomes, the competitiveness of research proposals from public and private universities is a question that warrants further investigation.

State Support for Private Higher Education

Three questions regarding state aid to the private sector of higher education are explored in this section. First, how much and what types of aid do various states provide? The spectrum ranges from New York, with its substantial and long-standing programs of both student and institutional aid, to Colorado, which prohibits the use of state scholarships at private institutions. Second, is there any explanation for the differences among states in the generosity of their aid? And, third, how does state aid to the private sector affect state support for public higher education? Specifically, does increased support for private higher education draw support away from the state's own institutions?

Level of Support

As in federal programs, those of the state can be separated into aid given directly to students and institutional aid. Student aid programs continue to be the dominant mechanism for channeling state funds into private colleges, whereas direct institutional subsidies are the main form of state support for the public sector.

STATE STUDENT AID

Student assistance can be defended as encouraging choice; it can be (and generally is) restricted to state residents, but it also helps private institutions compete more effectively for home-state students. A number of states have heeded the requests of their private sectors to provide student assistance usable only at private schools. Other states simply allow both public and private students to qualify for aid under the same program. Academic merit was the main qualification for student aid in the 1960s and earlier years, but most programs are now based on financial need. If need is effectively related to cost of education rather than to income only, private students will generally receive larger awards because of higher tuition. These two factors—private-only programs and cost-of-education provisions—help to explain why the average state grant awarded a student attending a private institution, $780 in 1975–76, exceeds the average given to his or her counterpart in the public sector, $457 (see table 2-A11).[19] An alternative explanation, that state aid recipients at private institutions are poorer than those at public colleges, does not seem valid, assuming the experience with federal student aid programs is comparable.[20]

STATE INSTITUTIONAL AID

Programs of institutional aid to private higher education are less common than student aid. In 1975–76, ten states appropriated $115 million in general-purpose aid to private colleges and universities.[21] In contrast

19. These figures are based primarily on data from Joseph D. Boyd's annual surveys of state scholarship programs with other sources added where Boyd's information seemed incomplete (see table 2-A11 for details). Since 1969 Boyd has collected data on the amount of state aid and the number of recipients, and in some years the fractions of dollars and of awards going to private students. Where possible, gaps in the data are filled by interpolation between other years.

20. In 1974–75, of the basic grant recipients still dependent on their parents attending private colleges and universities, 54 percent had family incomes below $7,500, compared to 65 percent of their counterparts at public institutions. In the supplementary grant program, 60 percent of the dependent private-school recipients and 70 percent of public-school recipients had low family incomes. (See Frank J. Atelsek and Irene L. Gomberg, *Student Assistance: Participants and Programs, 1974–75*, Higher Education Panel Reports 27 [American Council on Education, December 1975], pp. 19–20.)

21. The figures for institutional aid are from the yearly surveys by M. M. Chambers on state support for higher education reported by "key persons in each state." (See, for example, M. M. Chambers, *Appropriations of State Tax Funds for Operating Expenses of Higher Education, 1975–76* [National Association of State Universities and Land-Grant Colleges, n.d.].) Although the methods and sources used by Chambers are not as reliable as would be desired, his data are probably as good as— and are more readily available for more years than—the alternative series compiled by Lyman Glenny and Janet Ruyle, by Glenny and James Kidder for the Education Commission of the States, and by the National Center for Education Statistics. (Lyman A. Glenny and Janet Ruyle, *State Tax Support of Higher Education: Revenue Appropriations Trends and Patterns, 1963–1975* [Center for Research and Development in Higher Education, 1975]; Glenny and James R. Kidder, *State Tax Support of Higher Education: Revenue Appropriation Trends and Patterns, 1963–1973*, report 47 [Education Commission of the States, 1974]; and the annual publications of the National Center for Education Statistics, *Digest of Educational Statistics* and *Financial Statistics of Institutions of Higher Education*.) Chambers and others acknowl-

to federal institutional support, which is generally intended to purchase such services as research, the bulk of state direct aid is aimed at providing education of either a general or specific nature.

Although institutional aid has been increasing in recent years, in many states such programs are still blocked because the question of federal and state constitutionality of targeted aid has not been resolved and because of political reluctance to aid schools that the states do not control. With the June 1976 Supreme Court decision in *Roemer* v. *Board of Public Works of Maryland*[22] upholding a Maryland law giving private colleges a flat grant for each full-time student enrolled, the federal constitution should no longer hinder adoption of general institutional aid programs.[23] Aid to religiously affiliated colleges and universities continues to be impeded, however, by even stricter provisions in many state constitutions. In addition, there are direct and indirect prohibitions against aid to all private educational institutions in a number of states. By contrast, student aid programs can often invoke the "child benefit" theory, that the aid primarily helps the individual and only secondarily the institution, and be deemed constitutional when direct institutional aid is rejected.[24]

STATE AID TO THE PRIVATE SECTOR

When aid to institutions and to students are combined, state aid to private higher education appears as a growing but still small component of the budgets of both the states and the institutions. In 1972–73 state aid, on average, accounted for 3.3 percent of total educational and general revenue of the private institutions. State aid to the private sector accounted for 2.6 percent of total state spending on higher education in 1969–70, 2.8 percent in 1972–73, and 3.2 percent in 1975–76 (table 2-A12). More states are providing some type of aid—twenty states in

---

edge that his figures are most useful and consistent for analysis within a state over time rather than for interstate comparisons. (For more discussion of the relative merits of these sources, see Marilyn McCoy, *State Financial Support of Higher Education: A Framework for Interstate Comparisons* [National Center for Higher Education Management Systems at Western Interstate Commission for Higher Education, November 1975].)

22. *Roemer* v. *Board of Public Works of Maryland*, 426 U.S. 736 (1976).

23. Cheryl M. Fields, "Aid to Church Colleges Ruled Constitutional," *Chronicle of Higher Education*, vol. 12 (June 28, 1976), p. 3.

24. William H. McFarlane, A. E. Dick Howard, and Jay L. Chronister, *State Financial Measures Involving the Private Sector of Higher Education*, A Report to the National Council of Independent Colleges and Universities (Fall 1974; available from Association of American Colleges), p. 13.

1969, thirty in 1972, and thirty-seven in 1975—and in most states the dollar amounts are growing faster than the overall state higher education budgets.

Explanations for Differences in State Support

A common explanation offered for the diversity in state support for private higher education is, simply, that there is no consistent explanation apart from state idiosyncracies and unique histories. An alternative to this "nontheory" that random forces are responsible is the hypothesis that a state may have certain characteristics that determine how much aid it gives to its private sector. Using partial correlation analysis, this section attempts to determine whether there are consistent relationships between these characteristics and the amount of state aid. It first describes several factors that hypothetically could be associated with a state political climate favorable to private higher education. Next, these theoretical factors are approximated by quantifiable variables that, in turn, are tested empirically for their association with state support of the private sector.

THEORETICAL EXPLANATIONS

A number of motives could prompt a state to support its private sector. First, higher private-sector tuition may encourage legislators to ease the burden for residents who prefer a private to a public higher education by making more state aid available either to them or to their institutions. Second, higher education in general might be granted a high priority in the state. Third, perhaps the private colleges and universities are perceived as important institutions in the economy and society of the state, so that their welfare benefits the state as a whole. This might be particularly true in states where the private institutions enroll many home-state students. Fourth, the "costs" of the public system might affect state aid to the private schools, in particular the cost to the student (tuition), the cost to the state (subsidy), or the cost to society (total expenditures from all sources). A state that lacks a strong commitment to low-tuition public higher education, that is, where the "cost" to the public student is not low, might be more inclined to support high-priced private education than a state with very low public tuition. Alternatively, if there has been a trade-off between support for the public and private sectors, large amounts of aid to private higher education might be associated with a low state subsidy for the public system, that is, at a low "cost" to the state.

These explanations are not mutually exclusive nor do they exhaust the list of motives that could induce a state to provide aid for private higher education. Also, the direction of causality is not clear: a private sector enrolling many home-state students may attract more state support, but more state support, particularly in the form of nonportable student aid (that cannot be used in another state), could encourage students to attend private colleges inside the state. Hence, these motives must be tested simply for consistent relations with, rather than their effects on, state support of private higher education.

TESTING FOR CONSISTENT EXPLANATIONS

All of these motives suggest quantifiable state characteristics that can serve as proxies to test which motives, if any, are empirically related to state aid to private higher education. Precise definitions of the variables chosen as proxies for the four motives and the two alternative measures of state support for private higher education[25] are presented in appendix B, along with the results of partial correlation analysis relating the proxies for state characteristics with the measures of state aid (see tables 2-B1 and 2-B2). Partial correlations essentially give the correlation between two variables while controlling for the level of other variables.

From this analysis, the first explanation can be dismissed. There is no support for the assertion that higher private tuition encourages legislators to relieve the burden of those charges by granting offsetting state aid to the private sector. Tuition at private institutions in a state is not significantly related to either of the measures of state aid and, indeed, is negatively correlated with state aid relative to educational and general revenue. This relationship would be consistent with the notion that state aid helps private colleges and universities keep their tuition rates down in states where such aid represents a substantial portion of institutional budgets.

The second hypothetical motive—that a state has a general preference for higher education—seems largely unsupported with one exception. Two proxies for this motive were tested. The first—high school graduates as a percent of all men—is consistently unrelated to state aid. An

---

25. The measures of state support are state aid relative to (1) educational and general revenue of private institutions and (2) total state spending on higher education.

alternative was the share of state budgets going to higher education. It appears that state aid accounts for a larger share of the income of private institutions in states that spend a large fraction of their total budgets on higher education than in states with small fractions.

The third possible motive—that the private sector is considered important to the well-being of the state—is generally supported by the empirical analysis. In states where a large fraction of all students is enrolled in the private sector, or where many of the private students are state residents, there clearly tends to be more aid to private higher education.[26]

In testing the validity of the fourth possible motive—the nature of the "costs" of public higher education—the results depend on what "costs" are considered. In terms of the tuition cost to the student, the higher public tuition is (that is, the less committed the state is to low-priced public education), the more aid the private sector receives. Similarly, states are more generous to the private sector where the total cost, or cost to society, of public higher education is greater.[27] In this context, neither the cost to the student nor the cost to society is equivalent to the cost to the state, for the state and local subsidy per public student is consistently unrelated to state aid for the private sector. Apparently, if other factors are held constant, states with generous support for the private sector tend to have higher public tuition and higher total spending per public student than states with low private assistance, but their subsidies to the public systems are no different. Some states may support the private sector instead of increasing spending for the public sector, but even so, such trade-offs are not the dominant pattern.[28]

IMPLICATIONS

The main conclusion to be drawn from these correlations is that quantifiable and logical state characteristics are consistently associated with states' efforts on behalf of private higher education. The factors that seem most related to state aid are (1) an explicit desire to help a

26. The fraction of private students who are residents is strongly related to both measures of state aid while the size of the private compared to the public sector matters only for the share of state spending on higher education that goes to the private sector.

27. Cost to society is defined as the total educational and general expenditures per public student.

28. Using time series analysis, the next part of this paper investigates whether trade-offs exist in certain specific states.

private sector where it is an important force in the life of the state, (2) a high budget priority afforded higher education in general, and (3) a lack of commitment to low tuition at public institutions. It is particularly noteworthy that the level of state subsidy to public higher education is independent of aid to the private sector. In addition, there is no support for the notion that states with high educational attainment among the population are more favorably inclined to aid private higher education. Historical accident may be responsible for the structure of higher education in a state, but however it evolved, logical reasons, not just random factors, are clearly related to the state effort on behalf of private higher education and the importance of that aid to the institutions.

A Possible Trade-off between the Public and Private Sectors

Representatives of public and private higher education frequently view legislation affecting them as a zero-sum game: if one sector gains, the other must lose. As a consequence, they fail to speak with a united voice on behalf of higher education in general, particularly on state programs. Statements such as the following from the American Association of State Colleges and Universities are evidence that the notion of a trade-off between funding for public and private higher education is commonly held:

No federal or state aid program to the private or proprietary sector should be at the expense of public college students, either in terms of reduced appropriations for the public sector or increased tuition and student charges at public colleges. *"Choice" should never be at the expense of access to higher education.*[29]

The existence of a trade-off can be tested by estimating, using regression analysis, what state aid to public higher education would have been in the absence of aid to the private sector. A model of how state spending on the public system is determined should include effects of the economic position of the state, the priority attached to higher education relative to other demands on the state budget, the size of the public college and university system being financed, the availability of alternatives to financing the public system (that is, the private sector), as well as any effect resulting from the support of private higher education. The model could answer the question of the source of new funding for the private sector empirically. Does new funding come from monies that would

29. American Association of State Colleges and Universities, "Public Aid to Private and Proprietary Institutions" (policy statement adopted by the AASCU, November 1975; processed).

have gone to public higher education (the trade-off hypothesis), from reductions in other state programs, or from increases in state revenues?

Using such a model, individual equations relating state support for public higher education as the dependent variable to independent variables chosen to reflect the factors suggested above were estimated for eleven states that have sufficient longitudinal data.[30] Definitions and sources for the variables, along with the estimated equations, appear in appendix C.[31]

The regression analysis indicates that only in New York is the trade-off hypothesis clearly valid. In three states—California, South Carolina, and Ohio—there is strong evidence that the opposite is true—that state aid to public and private higher education move together. Alabama and Minnesota show neither a trade-off nor a positive relation, while the findings for the other five states are simply inconclusive.[32] Even though this

30. Because Joseph Boyd's state scholarship surveys began in 1969, only those states could be included that gave no aid to private students before 1969 but that did provide some aid in the next several years. New York and California are exceptions since data were supplied by state higher education officials.

31. The variable representing state aid to private higher education (PR) indicates how state support for the public sector (PUB) would respond to a change in the former, controlling for all other relevant factors and assuming the model is correctly specified. If the trade-off hypothesis were true, PR should have a negative effect on PUB. On the other hand, if additional state support for the private sector comes out of funds that would have gone to other programs or out of new revenue sources, then the relation between PR and PUB would be either positive or insignificant.

As in all regression analysis, the possibility exists of misspecifying the model, such as omitting some factor correlated with aid to both sectors. Nevertheless, the results should be more reliable in finding a trade-off than in proving the absence of one since most excluded variables would produce false positive or insignificant relationships between aid to the public and private sectors, rather than false negative ones.

The equations are estimated in both current and constant dollars. If legislators are subject to "money illusion" and primarily concerned with the nominal value of funds, the results of constant-dollar analysis should be given more weight since they indicate how additional real resources for the private sector would affect the real resources available to the public system. The analysis in nominal terms, however, probably better approximates the common perceptions of the relation between aid for public and private higher education. In the absence of money illusion, on the other hand, there should be little difference in the determination of spending in real or current terms.

32. More precisely, in New York, PR (state aid to private higher education) is significantly negative in both the current- and constant-dollar equations. In California, South Carolina, and Ohio, PR is significantly positive in current and constant dollars, although only at the 10 percent level of confidence in one of the Ohio equations. PR is insignificant in all equations for Alabama and Minnesota. In Tennessee, PR is significantly positive in the constant-dollar equation and significantly negative in current dollars. For each of the remaining four states, PR is significant in one equation but not in the other.

mixed picture is based on only eleven states, it at least indicates that the trade-off hypothesis is not valid as a general rule.

This variation in patterns of state funding for the two sectors defies simple explanation. It would be useful, however, to determine whether some state aid to private higher education is consistently associated with trade-offs, or with positive relationships, or even with insignificant relationships. Unfortunately, no clear pattern emerges.

Of the three states with a positive association between funding for the two sectors, California and Ohio have no programs targeted specifically at the private sector but only state scholarships usable at both types of institutions. Tennessee also has this type of funding but the empirical analysis was unable to determine whether a trade-off exists there.

The two states with no significant relation between aid to the public and private sectors, Minnesota and Alabama, both have programs of direct aid to private institutions. The other state with substantial direct aid is New York, where a strong trade-off is evident.

Of the five states that have student aid programs restricted to students attending private colleges, four of them—Iowa, Maine, North Carolina, and Texas—have a negative relationship between state support for the two sectors in either current or constant dollars (but not both). In the fifth state—South Carolina—both sectors seem to prosper together in real and nominal terms.

Perhaps the contrast between the results for New York and California is the most enlightening, for these two states exemplify opposite approaches to public support of private higher education. New York has a substantial private sector with a strong voice in state-level decisions that affect its welfare. It has the most extensive program of direct institutional aid for the private sector of any state (amounting to $57 million in 1975–76), a student aid program that is large in the aggregate ($55 million to students of private colleges), but relatively modest per recipient, (averaging $485 in 1975–76, see table 2-A11). California, on the other hand, has an extensive system of public two- and four-year colleges and universities, and a relatively small private sector that enrolls less than 10 percent of all students in higher education in that state. California emphasizes generous student aid (averaging $1,726 per private recipient in 1975–76) in place of any direct aid to private institutions. Although California and New York may differ in other important respects (such as fiscal capacity), when only the structure of higher education in these two states and the types of programs of aid for the private sector are considered, it is not surprising that state aid to the private sector in New York appears to come at the expense of the public sector, whereas in California gains for private higher education come as part of advances for the public system. Support for the private sector in New York seems to be determined in the context of the entire system of higher education in the state and subject to clear budgetary constraints. The student aid programs in California apparently have avoided such explicit budget trade-offs.

From this evidence it appears that without a special effort by the state to aid the private sector (such as programs of direct institutional aid or private-only student aid), there is no problem of a trade-off between state support for the two sectors. With programs targeted at private students or institutions, a zero-sum game is not inevitable, but may be possible. Although the analysis is not definitive, it suggests that aid to the private sector is only one of many factors that determine the level of state support for public higher education, and that its impact varies greatly among states.

Voluntary Support

Because private giving is primarily independent of government budget decisions and of fluctuations in enrollment, it provides an important element of diversity in an institution's "income portfolio." But giving, in turn, is dependent on a different set of factors—such as the stock market, general business prospects, alumni attitudes, and tax laws—which can affect private institutions as adversely as drops in enrollment or cuts in government spending. The first two forces, the stock market and the general economy, respond mainly to macroeconomic policies that are beyond the scope of this paper, as is analysis of changing alumni views. Tax policy toward the treatment of charitable giving, however, does have a direct impact on the financial position of private colleges and universities and is considered here.[33] This section describes the importance of voluntary support to different types of private institutions and their vulnerability to changes in these tax laws. It concludes with an estimate of the value to private higher education of the deduction from personal income taxes for charitable contributions.

33. Chapter 6 presents a more extensive examination of tax policies that affect higher education and analyses of alternative measures.

Reliance on Voluntary Support

Although the private sector as a whole depends on private gifts for 13.5 percent of its current educational income,[34] liberal arts II and two-year colleges received a much larger share of their educational and general revenue from private gifts—21.6 percent and 25.7 percent, respectively, in 1973–74 (table 2-A13). This greater reliance results largely from the heavy concentration of religiously affiliated schools that are particularly dependent on voluntary support. In liberal arts II, gifts accounted for 26.5 percent of income for Catholic colleges and 21.7 percent for other church-related institutions. For the forty-five predominantly black colleges, the share was 25.1 percent. Overall most types of institutions relied slightly less on private giving in 1973–74 than they did in 1966–67.

According to statistics compiled annually by the Council for Financial Aid to Education, of the total current- and capital-account gifts to the private four-year institutions responding to their survey, half comes from individuals (equally divided between alumni and others), nearly one-quarter is donated by foundations, while corporations, religious organizations, and miscellaneous sources contribute the remaining quarter (see table 2-A14). This pattern has remained stable over the past decade except for a general decline in the share of support coming from religious organizations.

The general pattern is repeated throughout the private sector with some small but important differences. Universities are more dependent on foundation support and less on religious organizations than the private sector as a whole. Universities also receive slightly more from alumni than from other individuals. The support for coeducational colleges is distributed much as for universities, except that religious organizations are more important and foundations less so, and alumni contribute

---

34. These figures include only current-account gifts for educational and general purposes. They exclude capital-account gifts (for construction or additions to endowment and the like) and gifts designated for student aid. These two excluded categories amounted to approximately 14 percent and 1 percent of educational and general revenue, respectively, for the private sector as a whole in 1973–74. (Data are from Paul F. Mertins and Norman J. Brandt, *Financial Statistics of Institutions of Higher Education: Current Funds Revenues and Expenditures—1973–74 Summary Data*, NCES 76-121 (GPO, 1976), and estimates derived from Julian H. Levi and Sheldon Elliot Steinbach, *Patterns of Giving to Higher Education III: An Analysis of Voluntary Support of American Colleges and Universities, 1973–74* (American Council on Education, n.d.).

less than other individuals. The single-sex colleges, on the other hand, rely much more heavily on contributions from individuals than on corporations, and women's colleges in particular rely on alumnae. Institutions that conduct a substantial amount of research and that have broader educational programs (universities and coeducational colleges) attract the most support from foundations and corporations.

Vulnerability to Tax Changes

Three tax provisions frequently cited as candidates for revision are the deduction of charitable contributions under the income tax, non-recognition of capital gains on appreciated property given to charitable organizations, and the deduction of bequests to charitable organizations under the estate tax. All three alter the effective price of giving. But their value depends on the volume of support that would be affected by a change in the laws, and the responsiveness of donors to such a change.

Individuals are the donors most apt to respond to changes in the tax treatment of charitable contributions. The income tax deduction lowers the price of giving by an amount equal to the marginal tax rate. People in the highest tax brackets are thus most affected, and they tend to make the largest gifts. The revisions in income tax deductibility could apply to corporations and foundations as well as individuals, but probably little voluntary support would be affected since much corporate giving could still be deductible as legitimate business expenses, and nonprofit foundations by definition have no taxable income against which to deduct even their current contributions.[35]

Large gifts, bequests, and gifts of property form the backbone of individual giving to higher education. A recent study[36] found that 30 to 40 percent of total voluntary support from all sources arrived in amounts of $5,000 or more from individuals. Less than 1 percent of the donations accounted for 72 percent of the amount received by private four-year institutions from individual contributors (table 2-6). These large gifts averaged $25,000 to $30,000 for the colleges and as much as $50,000 for universities; nearly half were property such as securities and real estate. Universities relied particularly on large property donations. Men's colleges depended the most on smaller gifts but, even for them, 0.2 percent

---

35. Changes in the tax treatment of individuals may affect their giving to private foundations and thus eventually affect contributions from these foundations.

36. Levi and Steinbach, *Patterns of Giving.*

Table 2-6. *Gifts from Individuals to Private Four-Year Universities and Colleges, Academic Year 1973–74*[a]

Gifts from individuals	All private four-year institutions	Uni-versities	Coeduca-tional colleges	Men's colleges	Women's colleges
Percentage of dollar value of individual gifts					
All individual gifts[b]	100.0	100.0	100.0	100.0	100.0
Gifts worth $5,000 or more	72.5	80.4	63.2	52.3	60.4
Gifts of property	36.2	42.3	35.1	38.1	33.3
Gifts of property worth $5,000 or more	34.3	40.5	32.9	34.6	29.0
Bequests, annuities, life contracts, insurance	40.7	46.4	35.3	21.6	36.8
Number of individual gifts (percent)					
All individual gifts	100.0	100.0	100.0	100.0	100.0
Gifts worth $5,000 or more	0.5	0.7	0.4	0.2	0.5
Gifts of property	0.8	1.2	0.8	0.5	0.9
Bequests, annuities, life contracts, insurance	0.9[c]	n.a.	n.a.	n.a.	n.a.
Average amount (dollars)					
Gifts worth $5,000 or more	39,264	50,464	29,190	28,137	25,395
Gifts of property	12,075	15,441	9,245	9,060	7,517
Bequests, annuities, life contracts, insurance	11,827[c]	n.a.	n.a.	n.a.	n.a.

Source: Julian H. Levi and Sheldon Elliot Steinbach, *Patterns of Giving to Higher Education III: An Analysis of Voluntary Support of American Colleges and Universities, 1973–74* (American Council on Education, n.d.).
n.a. Not available.
a. Includes both current- and capital-account gifts.
b. Gifts from individuals constitute 51.5 percent of total gifts to all private four-year institutions, 50.4 percent of those to universities, and 50.2 percent, 68.1 percent, and 65.0 percent of those to coeducational, men's, and women's colleges, respectively.
c. All institutions, not just private four-year institutions.

of the donors contributed more than half of the total amount of donations. Bequests accounted for 41 percent of all support from individuals. The average bequest amounted to approximately $12,000, but those that exceeded $5,000 accounted for 98 percent of the dollar value of all bequests and averaged nearly $100,000 each.

Put in the context of other sources of income for the private sector in 1973–74, total gifts (current and capital account) from individuals were equivalent to nearly 15 percent of educational and general revenue: bequests 5 percent and lifetime gifts almost 10 percent.[37]

37. These estimates are derived from the sources given for table 2-7.

Value of the Personal Income Tax Deduction

Estimates of the amount of giving to private institutions induced in 1973–74 by the charitable deduction are shown in table 2-7.[38] They indicate that lifetime giving by individuals would be reduced by 34 percent if the charitable deduction were eliminated and the average price of a dollar donated were raised from 68.6 cents to one dollar. In 1973–74 the entire private sector would have received an estimated $484 million from living individuals, instead of the $733 million it actually received with the deduction. This would represent a drop of 11.6 percent in total gifts, and 3.3 percent in educational and general revenue. For private four-year colleges, induced giving is a larger fraction of total gifts and of educational and general revenue—13.2 percent and 4.4 percent, respectively—than it is for the universities, because the former receive more of their income as gifts, and more of their gifts are influenced by the charitable deduction.

The increase in giving attributable to the charitable deduction exceeds the decrease in tax revenues because giving is estimated (in chapter 6) to be price-elastic: a 1.0 percent fall in price results in a 1.0 percent drop in tax revenue *and* a 1.1 percent increase in contributions received by colleges and universities. Of the $249 million in gifts to the private sector that the provision induced in 1973–74, $230 million (the tax subsidy) would have gone to the Treasury as income taxes if there had been no charitable deduction. It encouraged donors to give approximately $19 million more than they would otherwise have paid in taxes.[39]

The figures presented in this section show the charitable deduction

38. The calculations were made on the assumption that the average marginal tax rate of the donors is 31.4 percent and that the price elasticity of giving is −1.1, the same assumptions used by Emil Sunley in chapter 6, notes 50 and 51. If G = gifts, P = price of $1 in gifts, and $G = aP^{-1.1}$, when $P = 0.686$ and $G = 1,000$, then $a = 661$. Hence, when P rises to 1.0, G falls by 34 percent to $661. Since no good estimates exist of the responsiveness of bequests to changes in estate taxation, only the value of the income tax deduction is calculated here.

39. These figures underestimate by an indeterminate but probably small amount the benefits of the charitable deduction because they exclude induced giving to private foundations, which later is passed on to colleges and universities; corporate and foundation grants that match individual contributions; and a small amount of induced giving caused by the income effect. Though a substantial decline may be the eventual result, eliminating the charitable deduction would probably have little effect on foundation support in the short run. Corporate matching grants accounted for less than 4 percent of total corporate giving, and only 0.6 percent of total voluntary support in 1973–74.

Table 2-7. *Estimated Impact on Contributions to Universities and Colleges of the Charitable Deduction under the Individual Income Tax, Academic Year 1973–74*

Description	All institutions	All private institutions	Private four-year colleges
Gifts by living individuals (millions of dollars)			
With deduction[a]	920.4	733.0	490.2
Assuming no deduction under the tax law[b]	607.5	483.8	323.5
Induced giving[c]	312.9	249.2	166.7
Tax subsidy[d]	289.0	230.2	153.9
Gifts by living individuals as percentage of:			
Gifts from all donors (with deduction)	32.3	34.0	38.8
Educational and general revenue	3.7	9.6	12.9
Induced giving as percentage of:			
Gifts from all donors (with deduction)	10.9	11.6	13.2
Educational and general revenue	1.3	3.3	4.4

Sources: Derived from Levi and Steinbach, *Patterns of Giving;* Mertins and Brandt, *Financial Statistics of Institutions of Higher Education: Current Funds Revenues and Expenditures—1973–74.*

a. Estimated to include current- and capital-account gifts by combining NCES data from *Financial Statistics* on actual total current-account gifts with information from the ACE report on the ratios between current- and capital-account gifts, and between giving by living individuals and total gifts.

b. Line 1 × (1 − 0.340) (see text note 38).

c. Line 1 — line 2.

d. Line 1 × marginal tax rate of 0.314 (see text note 38).

from personal income taxes to be a fairly unimportant generator of income for private higher education, worth less even than the $272 million in direct aid the institutions received from state governments in 1973–74.[40] It is worth repeating, though, that this benefit is not distributed evenly among institutions in the private sector. Since the tax subsidy accounts for more than 90 percent of the induced giving, a system of tax credits ($1 credit for every $2 contributed) might be an acceptable alternative to the present deduction since it would approximately maintain the current level of giving, though not necessarily the current distribution of gifts. Any decision to eliminate or replace the charitable deduction must balance the loss to higher education and the distribution of the burden imposed with the equity and efficiency considerations discussed at length in chapter 6.

40. The $272 million includes general appropriations, sponsored research, other sponsored programs, and student aid revenues as reported in Mertins and Brandt, *Financial Statistics of Institutions of Higher Education: Current Funds Revenues and Expenditures—1973–74.*

Property Tax Expenditures

The tax expenditures involved with the general exemption from state and local property taxes for educational institutions are a true hidden subsidy: a subsidy because the owners of taxable property pay higher taxes than they would if the holdings of colleges and universities were included in the tax base, and hidden because the value of those holdings is unknown. In addition, many institutions recognize that they impose burdens on the local community that noneducational institutions cover with property taxes, and consequently make "payments in lieu of taxes," but there is little information on the amounts. Hence any estimates of the net subsidy due to property tax exemptions can only be approximate.

Such estimates were made using book values of institutional property holdings and the effective tax rates in each state to approximate potential tax liability, with a subsequent adjustment for payments in lieu of taxes by amounts that seemed consistent with findings of a 1969 study by the American Council on Education.[41] The major problems with these estimates stem from assuming that market value equals book value, which tends to underestimate the tax expenditures, while including properties (such as fraternities and faculty housing) that are not exempt in all states, and also ignoring probable reductions in the amount of property owned by educational institutions if they were subject to local taxation, which tends to overestimate the tax losses. In addition, even the direction of error in the estimate of payments in lieu of taxes is uncertain.

In spite of these problems, the potential property tax liability for the whole private sector was estimated at $185 million in 1971–72. Perhaps $9 million were paid in lieu of taxes, resulting in a net tax subsidy by state and local governments of about $176 million. If the ratio between tax subsidy and property book values had stayed the same, in 1973–74 the subsidy would have risen to $205 million.

Public and Private Support

One final question related to the financing of private higher education is: what fraction of the income for private institutions actually comes

41. See table 2-A15 for estimates, sources, and further description of estimating procedures.

Table 2-8. *Summary of Public and Private Support for Private Higher Education, Academic Year 1973–74*

Source of support and revenue	Amount (millions of dollars)	Percent of total support
Private sources, total	5,027.8	64.3
Unassisted tuition revenue	2,710.2	34.6
Gifts[a]	893.9	11.4
Endowment income	500.0	6.4
Miscellaneous educational and general revenue[b]	623.3	8.0
Student aid for tuition and fees[c]	300.4	3.8
Public sources, total	2,795.3	35.7
Direct institutional support[d]	1,695.3	21.7
Federal	1,408.0	18.0
State-local	287.3	3.7
Student aid for tuition and fees[e]	782.6	10.0
Federal	649.3	8.3
State-local	133.3	1.7
Tax expenditures	317.4	4.1
Charitable deduction[f]	112.3	1.4
Property tax exemption	205.1	2.6
Total support, public and private	7,823.1	100.0
Educational and general revenue	7,621.9	97.4

Sources: Tables 2-4, 2-7, and 2-A15; Mertins and Brandt, *Financial Statistics of Institutions of Higher Education: Current Funds Revenues and Expenditures, 1973–74*.

Note. This table allocates all components of educational and general revenue between public and private support. In addition, "total support, public and private" exceeds educational and general revenue by $201.2 million because (1) the tax expenditures associated with property tax exemptions ($205.1 million) were added to educational and general revenue, (2) the tax loss ($3.2 million) associated with student aid gifts that were allocated to living costs was subtracted from educational and general revenue, and (3) rounding reduced total support, public and private, by $0.7 million.

a. Net of tax loss and gifts designated for student aid. Calculated by reducing current-account gifts ($1,081.6 million: *Financial Statistics*, p. 9) by gifts for student aid ($80.9 million), then subtracting the tax loss estimated as 10.7 percent of gifts (current-account gifts from living individuals [34 percent] × the marginal tax rate [31.4 percent] — tax loss). See also table 2-7.

b. Includes sales and services of educational departments, organized activities of departments, and "other."

c. Student aid from private sources, from table 2-4, of $489.3 million × 0.625 (the fraction of student aid money used for tuition and fees) — $5.4 million tax loss on this fraction, as in note *a* above.

d. Includes general appropriations, sponsored research, other sponsored programs from government sources, and recovery of indirect costs.

e. Student aid from public sources, from table 2-4, of $1,252.2 million × 0.625 (see note *c* above).

f. Tax loss on current-account gifts from living individuals (1,081.6 million × 0.340 × 0.314 = $115.5 million) — $3.2 million ($80.9 million × 0.375 × 0.107) for exclusion of tax loss on student aid gifts allocated to living expenses. See note *a* above.

from private sources and what fraction from the public treasury, either through explicit appropriation or through implicit subsidies? When all forms of support for institutions of higher education, explicit and implicit, are separated according to their origin in either the public or private sectors of the economy, as in table 2-8, 36 percent of current support for private colleges and universities comes from public sources. The bulk of this support flows directly from various levels of government as general appropriations or support for specific programs.

This 36 percent represents only part of the monetary value that private institutions would place on current public programs. When student aid that was allocated to living costs ($469.5 million from public programs plus $3.2 million in tax subsidy on gifts allocated to living expenses) and the charitable giving for current- and capital-account purposes that was induced over and above the tax loss on current-account gifts ($133.7 million) are added onto the $2.8 billion of public support in table 2-8, and when it is recalled that the tax expenditure for the property tax exemption is based on an extremely low estimate of market value and that no attempt has been made to estimate the value of the favorable tax treatment of charitable bequests and gifts of appreciated property, public implicit and explicit support of private higher education is worth at least $3,401.7 million a year. This is equivalent to 45 percent of all the educational and general operating revenue for private colleges and universities in 1973–74.

The main conclusion to be drawn from this analysis is important. The private sector is not an "independent" sector, at least financially. Existing public policies play a crucial role in the financing of private higher education. Though many schools may still receive little benefit from government programs, the principle of public contributions, direct or indirect, to private colleges and universities is firmly established. One implication of this dependence is that policymakers must consider the inadvertent as well as the intended consequences of policy changes affecting higher education. Although the unconditional preservation of private institutions should not be a public goal, neither would the public interest be served by a total disregard for their fate. Along with the power to affect institutional well-being so substantially goes the responsibility to use this power wisely.

This financial dependence calls into question the operational independence—in terms of administration or educational offerings—of the private sector. The larger the amount of public support involved (or the share in total income), the more effective the threat of discontinuing government aid would be as a lever to enforce regulations. The method of support, however, is also important. The more indirect it is—tax expenditures at one extreme, grants directly to institutions at the other, with student aid in between—the less will be the call for public account-ability of the funds involved, and hence fewer regulations will be im-posed that intrude on institutional independence. Whether public support in 1973–74—$1,700 million in direct grants and contracts with institu-tions, $783 million in student aid, and $317 million in tax expenditures—is too large and too heavily concentrated in direct forms of aid to main-tain operational independence remains at issue.

APPENDIX A: STATISTICAL TABLES

Table 2-A1. *Distribution of Current-Fund Income of Private and Public Universities, by Source, Selected Academic Years, 1951–52 to 1973–74*[a]

Description	1951–52	1955–56	1959–60	1963–64	1967–68	1969–70	1971–72	1973–74[b]
Private institutions								
Source of income				*Percent of total income*				
Governments, total[c]	21.4	21.7	29.4	36.4	36.4	32.8	32.2	30.1
Federal[d]	15.5	18.5	27.0	33.6	34.3	30.5	29.1	26.8
State	5.8	3.0	2.4	2.3	1.5	1.9	2.2	2.5
Tuition and fees[e]	32.8	30.6	28.1	25.6	25.3	26.0	26.8	27.1
Gifts[f]	9.1	10.7	9.6	8.8	8.6	8.3	8.9	8.0
Endowment earnings	9.8	9.0	8.1	6.5	5.7	5.6	5.4	5.4
Sales, services, and related activities[g]	6.5	7.2	7.0	7.0	6.6	9.8	10.9	11.0
Other educational and general revenue[h]	3.2	4.2	2.6	2.0	2.9	4.8	2.6	1.1
Student aid grants	1.2	1.8	2.2	2.2	4.1	4.0	3.6	3.2
Auxiliary enterprises	16.0	14.7	12.7	11.4	10.4	10.1	9.6	9.3
				Millions of dollars				
Amount of income	580.5	747.9	1,210.0	1,933.4	3,255.5	3,869.9	4,495.7	5,191.8

Public institutions

Source of income	Percent of total income							
Governments, total[c]	58.1	59.3	61.5	62.8	59.9	59.3	58.0	57.6
Federal[d]	13.9	15.7	20.3	24.8	22.4	20.8	19.9	19.1
State	41.3	41.4	40.0	36.8	37.1	38.1	37.9	38.2
Tuition and fees[e]	11.7	9.9	9.5	10.0	10.7	11.8	13.1	12.3
Gifts[f]	2.8	3.1	3.5	2.8	2.8	2.6	2.7	2.2
Endowment earnings	1.1	1.0	0.8	0.7	0.5	0.6	0.5	0.6
Sales, services, and related activities[g]	7.1	7.0	6.5	5.8	6.9	7.6	8.5	9.2
Other educational and general revenue[h]	1.8	2.1	1.4	1.5	3.2	2.4	2.8	3.2
Student aid grants	0.5	0.8	1.1	1.2	2.6	2.6	2.2	1.9
Auxiliary enterprises	16.9	16.8	15.6	15.2	13.4	12.4	12.1	11.8
	Millions of dollars							
Amount of income	909.0	1,403.9	2,235.0	3,683.3	6,619.7	8,308.7	9,845.4	11,884.3

Sources and footnotes: Same as table 2-1.

109

Table 2-A2. *Distribution of Current-Fund Income of Private and Public Four-Year Institutions Other Than Universities, by Source, Selected Academic Years, 1951–52 to 1973–74*[a]

Description	1951–52	1955–56	1959–60	1963–64	1967–68	1969–70	1971–72	1973–74[b]
Private institutions								
Source of income				*Percent of total income*				
Governments, total[c]	9.5	10.3	13.9	22.1	13.3	12.7	12.7	12.9
Federal[d]	9.1	9.8	13.3	21.6	12.8	11.4	11.5	10.9
State	0.4	0.5	0.5	0.5	0.5	0.8	1.1	1.6
Tuition and fees[e]	37.4	35.3	36.3	35.0	41.1	42.9	43.9	43.5
Gifts[f]	11.6	13.8	13.6	11.6	10.9	10.6	10.3	10.6
Endowment earnings	7.7	7.6	7.0	5.1	4.6	4.7	4.1	4.1
Sales, services, and related activities[g]	3.4	3.4	2.9	1.3	3.1	3.0	4.9	5.2
Other educational and general revenue[h]	1.8	1.7	1.5	1.4	2.1	2.2	2.0	2.6
Student aid grants	1.3	1.9	2.0	1.9	3.4	4.1	4.1	4.1
Auxiliary enterprises	27.2	25.9	22.6	20.5	21.4	19.7	18.1	16.8
				Millions of dollars				
Amount of income	558.6	792.2	1,239.2	2,158.3	3,021.6	3,665.6	4,445.2	5,166.2

Public institutions

Source of income	Percent of total income							
Governments, total[c]	58.0	60.8	61.6	58.9	62.3	62.3	61.8	63.0
Federal[d]	9.5	8.2	10.8	10.3	11.8	9.9	11.1	10.7
State	46.3	48.8	48.1	46.4	48.0	49.3	47.2	48.4
Tuition and fees[e]	14.3	11.3	11.9	13.0	13.1	13.8	14.8	14.0
Gifts[f]	0.3	0.8	0.7	0.6	1.0	1.1	1.1	1.3
Endowment earnings	0.3	0.4	0.1	0.1	0.1	0.1	0.1	0.1
Sales, services, and related activities[g]	3.5	2.3	2.5	1.9	1.7	2.9	3.9	4.6
Other educational and general revenue[h]	1.2	0.6	0.6	0.8	1.1	0.8	1.0	1.2
Student aid grants	0.3	2.7	2.0	1.7	2.8	2.9	3.0	3.1
Auxiliary enterprises	22.0	21.2	20.6	23.0	17.9	15.7	14.3	12.2
					Millions of dollars			
Amount of income	379.0	498.6	816.6	1,281.8	2,641.6	3,701.1	4,749.8	5,879.4

Sources and footnotes: Same as table 2-1.

111

Table 2-A3. *Distribution of Current-Fund Income of Private and Public Two-Year Institutions, by Source, Selected Academic Years, 1951–52 to 1973–74*[a]

Description	1951–52	1955–56	1959–60	1963–64	1967–68	1969–70	1971–72	1973–74[b]
Private institutions								
Source of income			*Percent of total income*					
Governments, total[c]	1.2	2.3	1.0	1.6	3.2	4.6	5.9	6.4
Federal[d]	0.0	0.3	0.9	1.5	3.0	3.4	3.8	4.3
State	0.4	0.7	0.0	0.2	0.2	0.8	1.1	1.3
Tuition and fees[e]	41.0	42.5	48.3	50.0	52.9	50.3	50.0	51.2
Gifts[f]	12.1	13.2	14.0	13.4	11.0	12.2	11.9	12.7
Endowment earnings	2.1	2.4	2.5	2.2	1.5	1.6	1.6	1.7
Sales, services, and related activities[g]	0.6	0.3	0.7	0.6	0.4	0.4	0.7	0.7
Other educational and general revenue[h]	1.9	1.6	1.2	1.1	1.7	1.4	1.6	2.9
Student aid grants	0.4	0.9	0.6	0.6	2.1	3.0	4.4	5.2
Auxiliary enterprises	40.7	36.6	31.5	30.3	26.9	26.8	24.0	20.3
					Millions of dollars			
Amount of income	48.1	57.7	86.9	130.9	221.3	232.2	249.0	283.6

Public institutions

Source of income	Percent of total income							
Governments, total[c]	70.7	75.2	74.6	73.5	76.5	76.6	76.5	76.1
Federal[d]	0.8	0.5	1.4	1.7	5.0	4.7	6.3	6.0
State	28.8	31.1	29.4	31.5	37.3	40.2	41.2	43.6
Local	41.7	43.6	43.8	40.3	34.2	31.7	29.0	26.3
Tuition and fees[e]	15.5	10.0	10.7	11.8	13.2	13.2	13.5	12.8
Gifts[f]	*	0.1	0.4	0.3	0.3	0.2	0.3	0.3
Endowment earnings	1.4	0.3	0.2	0.1	0.1	0.1	0.1	0.1
Sales, services, and related activities[g]	1.0	0.9	0.6	0.4	0.3	0.4	0.3	0.4
Other educational and general revenue[h]	1.6	0.7	0.8	0.8	1.3	1.2	1.0	1.8
Student aid grants	0.5	0.2	0.5	0.3	1.3	1.7	2.6	2.9
Auxiliary enterprises	9.4	12.4	12.2	12.7	7.0	6.5	5.9	5.6
	Millions of dollars							
Amount of income	87.3	128.4	225.0	403.5	1,150.7	1,861.2	2,615.8	3,621.0

Sources and footnotes: Same as table 2-1.
* Less than 0.05 percent.

Table 2-A4. *Gross and Net Tuition and Fee Revenue and Student Aid Expenditure as Percent of Educational and General Revenue, Private Institutions of Higher Education, by Carnegie Classification, Academic Years 1966–67 to 1973–74*[a]

Institutional classification and revenue or expenditure item	1966–67	1967–68	1968–69	1969–70	1970–71	1971–72	1972–73	1973–74
All private institutions								
Gross tuition	46.5	46.3	47.8	48.4	49.4	49.6	49.9	49.7
Student aid expenditure	7.6	8.2	8.8	9.5	9.4	9.4	9.6	9.1
Net tuition	38.9	38.1	39.0	38.9	40.0	40.2	40.3	40.6
Research universities I								
Gross tuition	24.4	22.0	23.5	23.6	24.3	24.4	26.1	26.9
Student aid expenditure	8.2	8.3	8.6	8.9	8.6	8.0	8.1	7.6
Net tuition	15.9	14.6	14.6	14.4	15.3	16.0	17.6	19.0
Research universities II								
Gross tuition	39.7	36.8	41.6	42.2	42.4	43.4	44.1	44.3
Student aid expenditure	10.2	9.5	9.5	10.4	9.5	9.7	9.5	8.6
Net tuition	29.6	27.2	32.1	31.8	32.8	33.7	34.5	35.7
Doctoral-granting universities I								
Gross tuition	55.8	51.7	52.3	54.7	57.9	58.3	59.1	58.5
Student aid expenditure	8.1	8.3	8.8	10.0	9.9	10.0	9.6	8.4
Net tuition	47.6	43.3	43.5	44.7	47.9	48.3	49.5	50.1
Doctoral-granting universities II								
Gross tuition	67.8	69.2	68.6	69.5	69.4	69.2	69.9	69.3
Student aid expenditure	9.8	8.2	10.3	11.0	10.2	10.5	11.8	11.6
Net tuition	58.0	61.1	58.3	58.6	59.3	58.7	58.1	57.7

Comprehensive universities and colleges I								
Gross tuition	77.3	79.5	77.4	77.7	78.8	79.2	77.9	77.0
Student aid expenditure	7.3	8.7	9.5	10.3	10.0	10.5	10.9	10.6
Net tuition	70.3	71.4	68.1	67.5	69.0	68.8	67.2	66.6
Comprehensive universities and colleges II								
Gross tuition	71.3	71.7	72.9	73.0	74.5	74.6	72.8	71.4
Student aid expenditure	8.1	8.9	10.2	11.2	11.4	11.3	11.2	11.6
Net tuition	63.3	62.8	62.8	61.8	63.1	63.3	61.6	59.8
All liberal arts colleges I[b]								
Gross tuition	67.0	66.8	66.8	67.7	68.4	69.7	69.7	68.0
Student aid expenditure	10.4	10.9	11.3	12.2	12.2	12.6	13.0	12.0
Net tuition	57.2	56.4	56.2	56.1	56.8	57.9	57.9	56.7
Independent liberal arts colleges I (not church-affiliated)								
Gross tuition	66.4	66.4	66.1	67.1	67.9	69.5	69.4	66.8
Student aid expenditure	10.7	11.1	11.3	12.0	12.1	12.6	13.1	11.7
Net tuition	55.6	55.3	54.6	54.8	55.8	56.8	57.2	55.3
Catholic-sponsored liberal arts colleges I								
Gross tuition	65.8	65.6	64.7	64.9	64.6	63.9	64.5	67.2
Student aid expenditure	10.2	11.8	12.3	13.5	13.9	12.6	12.9	13.6
Net tuition	58.0	56.2	57.1	54.8	56.9	57.3	55.2	54.5
Other church-sponsored liberal arts colleges I								
Gross tuition	69.2	68.4	69.7	70.7	71.7	73.3	72.8	71.5
Student aid expenditure	9.5	9.9	10.9	11.8	11.8	12.5	12.8	12.0
Net tuition	59.7	58.4	58.8	58.8	59.9	60.8	60.0	59.5
All liberal arts colleges II								
Gross tuition	64.0	64.1	65.2	66.0	66.5	66.7	65.0	63.5
Student aid expenditure	9.0	9.9	11.0	13.9	11.9	12.6	13.2	13.6
Net tuition	55.5	54.9	54.9	54.8	55.2	54.9	52.9	51.6

(Continued)

Table 2-A4 (Continued)

Institutional classification and revenue or expenditure item	1966–67	1967–68	1968–69	1969–70	1970–71	1971–72	1972–73	1973–74
Predominantly black liberal arts colleges II								
Gross tuition	44.8	46.4	47.9	46.9	46.2	44.7	41.2	39.7
Student aid expenditure	11.6	15.4	20.0	20.7	21.4	24.5	22.6	22.5
Net tuition	33.1	30.5	27.5	26.1	24.8	20.2	18.6	17.3
Predominantly white liberal arts colleges II (not church-affiliated)								
Gross tuition	69.0	68.6	70.0	70.6	71.5	71.8	70.6	69.9
Student aid expenditure	7.6	7.7	8.8	9.3	9.7	10.0	10.9	11.4
Net tuition	61.7	61.5	61.4	61.8	62.0	61.6	60.9	60.4
Catholic-sponsored, predominantly white liberal arts colleges II								
Gross tuition	58.3	57.8	58.7	62.0	62.9	64.0	63.0	61.9
Student aid expenditure	9.6	10.3	10.4	21.1	11.1	10.8	12.8	12.4
Net tuition	52.8	53.4	52.4	53.5	54.6	56.1	53.7	51.8
Other church-sponsored, predominantly white liberal arts colleges II								
Gross tuition	68.4	68.8	69.5	69.1	69.3	69.4	67.4	65.1
Student aid expenditure	9.0	9.9	11.0	11.7	11.8	12.6	12.9	13.8
Net tuition	59.7	59.3	58.9	57.4	57.5	56.8	54.8	51.6
Two-year colleges								
Gross tuition	65.8	64.5	64.3	64.4	67.1	66.4	66.3	66.6
Student aid expenditure	5.6	7.0	6.7	7.8	7.6	8.6	10.5	10.5
Net tuition	61.3	60.3	59.3	58.4	61.2	60.7	58.5	59.3

Source: American Council on Education, data tape of private institutions assembled from various Higher Education General Information Surveys (HEGIS) for 1965–66 to 1973–74, conducted by the National Center for Education Statistics. For 1966–67 and 1967–68, funds for federally funded research and development centers were subtracted from educational and general revenue as reported by NCES.
a. Net tuition is gross tuition and fee revenue minus student aid expenditure. The figures for net tuition may not equal the difference between gross tuition and aid expenditure due to differences in the number of schools providing information in the three categories.
b. Predominantly white, as there are no predominantly black liberal arts colleges I.

Table 2-A5. *Indirect Student Aid at Public and Private Institutions of Higher Education, Academic Years 1966–67 to 1973–74*

Millions of dollars

Description	1966–67	1968–69	1970–71	1972–73	1973–74
Private institutions					
Public sources	88.1	145.0	164.1	194.6	207.5
Federal	79.0	127.1	137.2	148.8	154.4
State	8.8	17.5	26.5	45.1	51.3
Local	0.3	0.4	0.4	0.7	1.8
Private sources	247.8	303.8	406.0	479.0	489.3
Gifts and endowment	95.9	118.2	130.1	157.9	159.2
Institutional funds[a]	140.6	169.5	252.1	298.6	302.6
Other	11.3	16.2	23.8	22.5	27.5
Total	335.9	448.9	570.0	673.6	696.9
Public institutions					
Public sources	196.0	310.5	441.2	571.4	622.5
Federal	112.5	176.2	236.2	237.3	295.4
State	30.9	57.8	65.5	103.4	112.4
Local	3.9	1.6	2.5	5.8	5.0
Institutional funds[a]	48.7	74.9	137.0	224.9	209.7
Private sources	55.5	63.7	87.0	96.0	94.8
Gifts and endowment	44.7	56.8	77.1	86.8	84.2
Other	10.8	6.9	9.9	9.2	10.6
Total	251.5	374.3	528.2	667.4	717.3

Sources: 1968–69 and 1970–71, Kenneth A. Simon and W. Vance Grant, *Digest of Educational Statistics, 1971 Edition*, National Center for Educational Statistics, DHEW (OE) 72-45 (GPO, 1972), and corresponding edition for 1973; other years, Paul F. Mertins and Norman J. Brandt, *Financial Statistics of Institutions of Higher Education: Current Funds Revenues and Expenditures—1973–74 Summary Data*, NCES 76-121 (GPO, 1976), and corresponding issues for 1966–67 and 1972–73.

a. Institutional funds for student aid = student aid expenditures minus student aid revenues, that is, the student aid gap.

Table 2-A6. *Student Aid Revenue, Expenditure, and Gap as Percent of Educational and General Revenue, Private Institutions of Higher Education, by Carnegie Classification, Academic Years 1966–67 to 1973–74*[a]

Institutional classification and student aid item	1966–67	1967–68	1968–69	1969–70	1970–71	1971–72	1972–73	1973–74
All private institutions								
Revenue	4.0	4.6	5.5	5.6	5.3	5.4	5.3	5.2
Gap	2.9	2.8	3.3	3.9	4.2	4.1	4.2	4.0
Expenditure	6.9	7.4	8.8	9.5	9.4	9.5	9.6	9.1
Research universities I								
Revenue	5.7	5.9	6.1	5.8	5.4	4.9	4.8	4.8
Gap	2.5	2.4	2.5	3.1	3.4	3.2	3.3	2.9
Expenditure	8.2	8.3	8.6	8.9	8.6	8.1	8.1	7.6
Research universities II								
Revenue	6.1	7.1	6.9	6.7	5.5	5.4	5.2	4.3
Gap	4.0	2.9	2.7	3.7	4.0	4.2	4.3	4.4
Expenditure	10.2	9.5	9.5	10.4	9.5	9.7	9.5	8.6
Doctoral-granting universities I								
Revenue	5.2	5.1	5.2	6.0	5.5	4.9	4.9	4.0
Gap	3.4	3.8	3.6	4.0	4.4	5.0	4.9	4.4
Expenditure	8.1	8.3	8.8	10.0	9.9	10.0	9.6	8.4
Doctoral-granting universities II								
Revenue	4.1	3.4	6.1	6.5	6.2	6.1	5.8	4.8
Gap	5.7	4.7	4.2	4.4	4.0	4.5	6.2	6.9
Expenditure	9.8	8.2	10.3	11.0	10.2	10.5	11.8	11.6

118

Comprehensive universities and colleges I								
Revenue	4.0	4.8	5.6	5.8	5.1	5.5	6.1	5.6
Gap	3.4	4.0	4.1	4.7	5.0	5.1	5.0	5.2
Expenditure	7.3	8.7	9.5	10.3	10.0	10.5	10.9	10.6
Comprehensive universities and colleges II								
Revenue	3.8	4.9	5.5	6.9	6.1	6.2	5.8	6.8
Gap	4.3	4.3	5.0	4.8	5.8	5.6	5.5	5.1
Expenditure	8.1	8.9	10.2	11.2	11.4	11.3	11.2	11.6
All liberal arts colleges I[b]								
Revenue	6.1	6.8	6.9	6.5	6.8	6.9	6.9	6.6
Gap	4.2	4.2	4.7	5.8	5.6	6.0	6.2	5.5
Expenditure	10.4	10.9	11.3	12.2	12.2	12.6	13.0	12.0
Independent liberal arts colleges I (not church-affiliated)								
Revenue	6.8	7.3	7.3	6.9	7.4	7.2	7.4	6.7
Gap	3.9	4.0	4.2	5.2	4.7	5.4	5.9	5.2
Expenditure	10.7	11.1	11.3	12.0	12.1	12.6	13.1	11.7
Catholic-sponsored liberal arts colleges I								
Revenue	4.4	6.0	6.1	6.3	5.7	5.8	5.9	7.7
Gap	5.8	5.8	7.2	7.8	8.8	8.8	7.5	7.2
Expenditure	10.2	11.8	12.3	13.5	13.9	12.6	12.9	13.6
Other church-sponsored liberal arts colleges I								
Revenue	5.2	6.0	6.3	5.6	5.6	6.2	6.2	6.2
Gap	4.1	4.0	4.9	6.2	6.4	6.5	6.6	5.7
Expenditure	9.5	9.9	10.9	11.8	11.8	12.5	12.8	12.0
All liberal arts colleges II								
Revenue	4.6	5.9	6.9	11.7	7.7	8.3	8.8	8.6
Gap	4.6	4.3	4.7	4.4	4.7	4.6	4.9	5.3
Expenditure	9.0	9.9	11.0	13.9	11.9	12.6	13.2	13.6

(Continued)

Table 2-A6 (Continued)

Institutional classification and student aid item	1966-67	1967-68	1968-69	1969-70	1970-71	1971-72	1972-73	1973-74
Predominantly black liberal arts colleges II								
Revenue	6.4	13.2	14.6	15.4	17.1	21.0	19.0	17.0
Gap	5.7	2.2	5.5	5.3	4.3	3.5	3.7	5.4
Expenditure	11.6	15.4	20.0	20.7	21.4	24.5	22.6	22.5
Predominantly white liberal arts colleges II (not church-affiliated)								
Revenue	3.8	3.9	4.3	5.6	5.8	6.0	7.0	7.4
Gap	4.1	4.1	4.7	4.1	4.3	4.1	4.5	4.4
Expenditure	7.6	7.7	8.8	9.3	9.7	10.0	10.9	11.4
Catholic-sponsored, predominantly white liberal arts colleges II								
Revenue	4.7	5.8	8.3	8.1	7.4	7.1	9.1	8.5
Gap	5.0	4.7	3.2	3.5	4.3	4.0	3.9	3.8
Expenditure	9.6	10.3	10.4	10.6	11.1	10.8	12.8	12.4
Other church-sponsored, predominantly white liberal arts colleges II								
Revenue	4.7	5.6	6.2	7.2	7.1	7.5	7.4	7.6
Gap	4.6	4.8	5.4	5.0	5.3	5.6	6.0	6.7
Expenditure	9.0	9.9	11.0	11.7	11.8	12.6	12.9	13.8

Source: Same as table 2-A4.
a. Student aid gap = student aid expenditure minus student aid revenue. Revenue plus gap may not add to expenditure because of different numbers of institutions reporting.
b. Predominantly white, as there are no predominantly black liberal arts colleges I.

Table 2-A7. Sources of Revenue for Student Aid, Student Aid Expenditure, and Student Aid Gap, Private Institutions of Higher Education, by Carnegie Classification, Academic Year 1973–74 and Percent Increase over 1966–67

	Specific sources of revenue[a]						
Classification	Federal government (1)	State governments[b] (2)	Gifts (3)	Endowment (4)	Total[c] (5)	Expenditure (6)	Gap[d] (7)
	Dollars per full-time-equivalent student, 1973–74						
Doctoral-granting institutions							
Research universities I	209	57	136	389	772	1,094	322
Research universities II	150	16	88	69	305	584	279
Doctoral-granting universities I	95	33	30	31	156	321	165
Doctoral-granting universities II	63	[e]	38	60	163	423	260
Comprehensive institutions							
Comprehensive universities and colleges I	73	96	30	22	148	279	131
Comprehensive universities and colleges II	80	121	36	28	169	296	127
Liberal arts institutions							
Liberal arts colleges I	68	90	76	109	257	452	195
Liberal arts colleges II	138	158	61	32	248	385	137
Two-year institutions	135	128	80	29	224	245	21

(Continued)

Table 2-A7 (Continued)

Classification	Specific sources of revenue[a]					Expenditure (6)	Gap[d] (7)
	Federal government (1)	State governments[b] (2)	Gifts (3)	Endowment (4)	Total[c] (5)		
	Percent increase in current dollars per full-time-equivalent student, 1966–67 to 1973–74						
Doctoral-granting institutions							
Research universities I	−22	418	0	33	19	34	93
Research universities II	−17	e	4	57	7	29	66
Doctoral-granting universities I	25	−45	−46	24	6	50	146
Doctoral-granting universities II	−9	e	52	30	55	80	100
Comprehensive institutions							
Comprehensive universities and colleges I	143	153	100	38	151	163	179
Comprehensive universities and colleges II	248	195	50	33	186	143	102
Liberal arts institutions							
Liberal arts colleges I	106	−5	0	79	69	79	93
Liberal arts colleges II	237	210	39	88	226	167	102
Two-year institutions	286	300	129	14	250	202	24

Source: Same as table 2-A4.
a. Data cover only institutions reporting aid from each specific source.
b. Less than one-third of the institutions reported any state support for student aid.
c. The sum of columns 1, 2, 3, and 4 may exceed column 5 because the averages apply only to those institutions reporting any revenue from those sources.
d. Student aid gap = student aid expenditure − total student aid revenue.
e. Not calculated because of the small number reporting this source of aid.

Table 2-A8. *Student Aid Expenditure per Student by Tuition Level and Carnegie Classification, Private Institutions of Higher Education, Academic Year 1973–74*

Dollars per full-time-equivalent student

Classification	Gross tuition level (dollars)						All tuition levels
	0–749	750–1,249	1,250–1,749	1,750–2,249	2,250–2,999	3,000–5,000	
All private institutions	245	232	320	337	446	587	371
Doctoral-granting institutions							
Research universities I	a	a	a	836	949	975	1,094
Research universities II	a	a	a	635	579	564	584
Doctoral-granting universities I	70	a	295	261	372	657	321
Doctoral-granting universities II	a	a	361	284	415	560	423
Comprehensive institutions							
Comprehensive universities and colleges I	a	170	266	265	309	354	279
Comprehensive universities and colleges II	169	198	265	311	395	a	296
Liberal arts institutions							
Liberal arts colleges I	298	a	205	380	479	550	452
Liberal arts colleges II	483	286	360	384	420	373	385
Two-year colleges	160	191	222	182	241	368	245

Source: Same as table 2-A4.
a. No institutions in this bracket or too few to produce useful averages.

Table 2-A9. *Student Aid Expenditure as Percent of Tuition Revenue, Private Institutions of Higher Education, by Carnegie Classification, Academic Years 1966-67 to 1973-74*

Classification	1966–67	1967–68	1968–69	1969–70	1970–71	1971–72	1972–73	1973–74
All private institutions	17	18	18	20	19	20	22	23
Doctoral-granting institutions								
Research universities I	40	43	43	44	41	38	35	32
Research universities II	31	29	28	30	27	27	26	23
Doctoral-granting universities I	18	20	20	22	20	19	18	16
Doctoral-granting universities II	15	13	16	17	16	16	17	17
Comprehensive institutions								
Comprehensive universities and colleges I	10	12	13	14	13	14	14	14
Comprehensive universities and colleges II	12	13	15	17	16	16	17	18
Liberal arts institutions								
Liberal arts colleges I	17	18	18	20	20	20	20	20
Independent (not church-affiliated)	19	19	19	20	20	22	22	21
Catholic-sponsored	15	18	18	21	20	18	19	20
Other church-sponsored	14	15	16	18	17	17	18	17
Liberal arts colleges II	16	17	18	19	19	21	22	24
Predominantly black	32	36	43	46	47	56	56	60
Predominantly white								
Independent (not church-affiliated)	12	12	14	15	15	15	16	16
Catholic-sponsored	16	17	17	17	17	17	20	20
Other church-sponsored	14	15	16	18	18	19	20	22
Two-year institutions	14	16	14	17	16	19	19	23

Source: Same as table 2-A4.

Table 2-A10. *Federal Support[a] for Private Institutions of Higher Education as Percent of Educational and General Revenue, by Carnegie Classification, Academic Years 1966-67 to 1973-74*

Classification	1966-67	1967-68	1968-69	1969-70	1970-71	1971-72	1972-73	1973-74
Doctoral-granting institutions								
Research universities I	37.5	38.8	39.2	38.3	36.1	35.9	36.4	34.2
Research universities II	29.1	29.8	30.7	29.6	28.7	28.1	27.3	25.5
Doctoral-granting universities I	18.2	23.4	24.6	20.8	18.7	18.3	17.5	17.0
Doctoral-granting universities II	11.6	12.3	10.9	10.3	10.0	9.8	9.3	8.6
Comprehensive institutions								
Comprehensive universities and colleges I	5.3	5.4	6.4	5.2	5.1	5.0	5.4	5.3
Comprehensive universities and colleges II	5.5	5.9	6.2	6.1	5.6	5.0	5.0	5.7
Liberal arts institutions								
Liberal arts colleges I	4.3	4.6	4.3	4.1	3.9	3.9	3.9	3.4
Independent (not church-affiliated)	4.6	4.8	4.5	4.5	4.0	4.1	3.8	3.2
Catholic-sponsored	4.0	6.0	6.1	5.1	6.0	6.1	5.7	4.5
Other church-sponsored	3.6	3.3	2.9	2.5	2.5	2.6	3.1	3.4
Liberal arts colleges II	7.4	7.2	6.2	6.2	5.9	7.5	8.3	8.3
Predominantly black	22.5	23.3	19.8	19.4	22.1	24.3	25.4	27.5
Predominantly white								
Independent (not church-affiliated)	6.3	6.9	5.6	5.0	4.8	5.9	6.4	5.5
Catholic-sponsored	7.1	5.7	5.9	4.8	3.3	4.3	5.7	5.5
Other church-sponsored	4.8	4.9	4.2	4.4	4.2	5.4	5.7	6.0
Two-year institutions	7.6	8.3	8.9	8.5	8.8	10.7	13.8	14.0

Source: Same as table 2-A4.

a. Federal support includes general appropriations, funds for sponsored research and other sponsored programs (which includes college work-study), and "indirect costs recovered" starting in 1968-69 when they were first reported separately (see text, note 12). It does not include "student aid revenues—federal."

Table 2-A11. *State Government Assistance to Students at Public and Private Institutions of Higher Education, by State, Academic Years 1972–73 and 1975–76*

Average grant per recipient, in dollars

	1972–73		1975–76	
State	Public institutions	Private institutions	Public institutions	Private institutions
Alabama	o	o	o	o
Alaska	o	1,022	o	o
Arizona	o	o	o	o
Arkansas	o	o	238	476
California	407	1,270	486	1,726
Colorado	425	o	603	o
Connecticut[a]	431	739	488	794
Delaware	598	542	574	574
District of Columbia	o	o	o	o
Florida	675	1,103	1,122	1,216
Georgia[b]	o	398	298	446
Hawaii	o	o	451	o
Idaho	o	o	785	785
Illinois	500	1,058	428	1,190
Indiana	495	1,097	552	840
Iowa	502	876	398	1,204
Kansas	462	864	457	904
Kentucky	o	o	253	479
Louisiana	o	o	466	466
Maine	o	622	845	802
Maryland[c]	293	429	410	588
Massachusetts	274	914	297	903
Michigan	469	703	584	995
Minnesota	564	829	853	1,051
Mississippi	o	o	n.a.	n.a.
Missouri	o	o	257	657
Montana	o	o	288	o
Nebraska	o	o	350	o
Nevada	o	o	o	o
New Hampshire	o	o	o	o
New Jersey	610	743	602	829
New Mexico	o	o	o	o
New York	256	296	354	485
North Carolina[d]	o	n.a.	483	724
North Dakota	o	o	292	292

Table 2-A11 *(Continued)*

State	1972–73 Public institutions	1972–73 Private institutions	1975–76 Public institutions	1975–76 Private institutions
Ohio	314	745	310	725
Oklahoma	0	0	177	589
Oregon	357	438	398	448
Pennsylvania	485	804	451	710
Rhode Island	567	1,043	477	1,083
South Carolina	0	1,143	0	1,276
South Dakota	0	0	145	277
Tennessee	312	925	0	0
Texas	0	458	500	540
Utah	0	0	639	0
Vermont	672	792	426	1,285
Virginia	0	0	280	319
Washington[e]	484	843	336	336
West Virginia	272	681	329	1,182
Wisconsin	762	561	585	868
Wyoming	0	0	0	0
United States, total[f]	466	784	457	780

Sources: Derived from Joseph D. Boyd, "National Association of State Scholarship Programs: 7th Annual Survey, 1975–76 Academic Year" (Deerfield, Illinois: NASSP, 1975; processed), and first, fifth, sixth, and eighth surveys. Wherever possible, gaps in information on the distribution of funds between the public and private sectors were filled by interpolation between the years.

n.a. Sufficient data are not available to compute average award.

a. The 1972–73 average grant to private students does not include student aid from contracts with private institutions.

b. Data for the tuition grant program from the staff of the Georgia State Scholarship Commission.

c. Data for the senatorial scholarship program in 1975–76 from the staff of the Maryland state scholarship board.

d. The 1975–76 average grant to private students does not include aid to private institutions for needy undergraduate enrollees, nor tuition grants to each full-time North Carolina undergraduate attending a private school.

e. A tuition supplement program, begun in 1971, was ruled unconstitutional in 1973.

f. Unweighted average.

Table 2-A12. Total State Aid to Private Higher Education, by State, Selected Academic Years, 1969-70 to 1975-76[a]

| State | Total state aid | | | | | Percent of state higher education expenditure | | |
| | Amount (thousands of dollars) | | | Percent of private educational and general revenue[b] | | | | |
	1969-70	1972-73	1975-76	1969-70	1972-73	1969-70	1972-73	1975-76
Alabama	589	1,150	2,803	2.0	2.8	0.8	1.0	1.3
Alaska	0	754	0	0.0	28.4	0.0	3.2	0.0
Arizona	0	0	0	0.0	0.0	0.0	0.0	0.0
Arkansas	0	0	184	0.0	0.0	0.0	0.0	0.2
California	9,645	17,120	36,858	2.5	3.1	1.3	1.7	2.4
Colorado	0	0	0	0.0	0.0	0.0	0.0	0.0
Connecticut[c]	758	2,144	5,087	4.2	1.0	0.9	1.9	3.7
Delaware	0	15	106	0.0	0.3	0.0	0.1	0.3
District of Columbia	0	0	0	0.0	0.0	0.0	0.0	0.0
Florida	0	388	2,162	0.0	0.3	0.0	0.1	0.5
Georgia[d]	0	2,347	6,422	0.0	2.3	0.0	1.3	2.7
Hawaii	0	0	0	0.0	0.0	0.0	0.0	0.0
Idaho	0	0	20	0.0	0.0	0.0	0.0	*
Illinois	20,360	36,910	46,296	5.2	8.2	5.0	7.1	7.2
Indiana	1,602	4,240	8,664	1.6	3.5	1.0	2.0	2.9
Iowa	1,631	4,114	9,280	2.3	4.9	1.6	3.3	4.8
Kansas	47	1,046	3,000	0.2	4.1	0.1	1.1	2.0
Kentucky	0	0	908	0.0	0.0	0.0	0.0	0.5
Louisiana	0	0	1,664	0.0	0.0	0.0	0.0	0.8
Maine	31	148	509	0.2	0.6	0.1	0.4	1.1

Maryland[e]	1,160	1,039	1,086	1.2	0.8	1.3	0.7	2.8
Massachusetts	1,500	6,336	8,519	0.2	0.9	1.8	4.1	4.3
Michigan	7,755	7,749	15,762	8.8	6.9	2.5	1.9	2.8
Minnesota	475	4,050	8,955	0.8	4.9	0.4	2.3	3.4
Mississippi	0	0	n.a.	0.0	0.0	0.0	0.0	n.a.
Missouri	0	0	2,837	0.0	0.0	0.0	0.0	1.3
Montana	0	0	0	0.0	0.0	0.0	0.0	0.0
Nebraska	0	0	0	0.0	0.0	0.0	0.0	0.0
Nevada	0	0	0	0.0	0.0	0.0	0.0	0.0
New Hampshire	0	0	0	0.0	0.0	0.0	0.0	0.0
New Jersey	5,051	15,118	16,539	3.6	8.4	4.0	6.4	6.2
New Mexico	0	0	0	0.0	0.0	0.0	0.0	0.0
New York	58,073	63,937	112,135	3.7	4.5	9.3	7.8	8.9
North Carolina[f]	0	513	9,307	0.0	0.2	0.0	0.2	2.5
North Dakota	0	0	19	0.0	0.0	0.0	0.0	*
Ohio	0	7,111	8,629	0.0	2.6	0.0	2.3	1.9
Oklahoma	0	0	328	0.0	0.0	0.0	0.0	0.3
Oregon	704	204	446	2.5	0.6	0.8	0.2	0.3
Pennsylvania[g]	43,492	47,090	68,530	1.0	8.9	17.4	11.9	11.0
Rhode Island	825	1,178	1,508	1.6	1.8	2.9	3.3	3.2
South Carolina	0	148	7,423	0.0	0.3	0.0	0.1	3.5
South Dakota	0	0	120	0.0	0.0	0.0	0.0	0.3
Tennessee	0	833	0	0.0	0.6	0.0	0.6	0.0
Texas	0	3,000	8,100	0.0	1.4	0.0	0.6	1.0
Utah	0	0	0	0.0	0.0	0.0	0.0	0.0

(Continued)

Table 2-A12 (Continued)

| | Total state aid | | | | | | | |
| | Amount (thousands of dollars) | | | Percent of private educational and general revenue[b] | | Percent of state higher education expenditure | | |
State	1969-70	1972-73	1975-76	1969-70	1972-73	1969-70	1972-73	1975-76
Vermont	480	526	1,173	2.2	1.7	3.5	3.1	5.8
Virginia	0	0	267	0.0	0.0	0.0	0.0	0.1
Washington	0	1,114	578	0.0	2.5	0.0	0.6	0.2
West Virginia	39	90	890	1.5	0.5	0.1	0.1	0.9
Wisconsin	2,328	4,110	6,750	4.5	4.3	1.4	1.6	2.0
Wyoming	0	0	0	0.0	0.0	0.0	0.0	0.0
United States, total	156,545	234,522	403,864	2.8	3.3	2.6	2.8	3.2

Sources: The first three columns are estimates derived from Joseph D. Boyd, 1969-70, 1972-73, and 1975-76 surveys cited for table 2-A11, and from three publications by M. M. Chambers: *Higher Education in the Fifty States* (Interstate, 1970); *Higher Education and State Governments, 1970-1975* (Interstate, 1974); and *Appropriations of State Tax Funds for Operating Expenses of Higher Education, 1975-76* (National Association of State Universities and Land-Grant Colleges, n.d.). Revenue data in the fourth and fifth columns are from Paul F. Mertins and Norman J. Brandt, *Financial Statistics of Institutions of Higher Education: Current Funds Revenues and Expenditures, 1969-70*, DHEW (OE) 74-11419 (GPO, 1973), and corresponding volume, *1972-73*. Expenditure data in the last three columns are from the three Chambers publications cited above.

* Less than 0.05 percent.

n.a. Not available.

a. Total state aid for private higher education consists of state aid to students of private colleges and universities and state aid to private institutions.

b. 1975-76 revenue not available at time of publication; hence, third column for this group could not be calculated.

c. Contracted aid to students attending private institutions for 1972-73 is from *Higher Education in the States*, vol. 4, no. 1 (1973), p. 3.

d. Data for the tuition grant program from the staff of the Georgia State Scholarship Commission.

e. Data for the senatorial scholarship program in 1975-76 from the staff of the Maryland state scholarship board.

f. State aid to private higher education for 1972-73 is estimated from data in *Higher Education in the States*, vol. 4, no. 1 (1973), p. 13.

g. The 1969-70 state aid to private higher education data do not include Pennsylvania's education incentive program.

Table 2-A13. *Voluntary Support*[a] *as Percent of Educational and General Revenue, Private Institutions of Higher Education, by Carnegie Classification, Academic Years 1966–67 to 1973–74*

Classification	1966–67	1967–68	1968–69	1969–70	1970–71	1971–72	1972–73	1973–74
Doctoral-granting institutions								
Research universities I	11.0	10.1	10.6	11.3	10.6	11.6	11.6	10.9
Research universities II	9.1	11.2	11.5	10.5	10.2	9.3	8.7	9.5
Doctoral-granting universities I	13.2	12.8	13.3	14.4	12.4	12.7	11.7	11.1
Doctoral-granting universities II	8.7	7.1	7.8	7.2	7.8	7.5	7.2	7.0
Comprehensive institutions								
Comprehensive universities and colleges I	8.0	7.2	7.0	7.6	6.8	6.5	6.7	7.0
Comprehensive universities and colleges II	14.2	14.1	13.9	12.2	12.9	13.2	13.9	12.9
Liberal arts institutions								
Liberal arts colleges I	15.1	15.6	15.2	13.8	14.3	13.0	13.5	13.7
Independent (not church-affiliated)	12.9	13.8	13.6	12.2	12.8	11.3	12.2	13.1
Catholic-sponsored	26.2	23.6	23.1	23.0	22.8	23.2	23.8	21.6
Other church-sponsored	14.8	15.8	15.1	13.2	13.8	12.5	12.2	12.2
Liberal arts colleges II	23.8	23.1	22.6	22.5	21.5	21.2	21.9	21.6
Predominantly black	29.4	25.1	27.0	26.6	24.4	25.2	27.1	25.1
Predominantly white								
Independent (not church-affiliated)	19.1	19.8	18.2	20.1	18.2	17.2	17.8	16.6
Catholic	32.8	31.3	31.3	28.3	27.4	27.2	27.8	26.5
Other church-sponsored	20.2	20.0	19.6	19.8	19.8	19.6	20.4	21.7
Two-year colleges	31.8	30.1	32.4	31.0	28.5	28.2	25.4	25.7

Source: Same as table 2-A4.
a. Voluntary support includes current-account private gifts plus nongovernmental "sponsored research" and "other sponsored programs."

Table 2-A14. *Voluntary Support of Private Institutions of Higher Education, by Source and Type of Institution, Academic Year 1974–75*[a]

	Type of private institution				
Item	All four-year	Uni-versities	Coed-ucational colleges	Men's colleges	Women's colleges
Total voluntary support (millions of dollars)	1,226.8	648.5	426.6	17.9	64.5
Institutions reporting (number)	669	69	453	13	80
Source of support	*Percent of total support*				
Individuals	49.6	50.3	48.1	62.1	65.0
Alumni	24.8	26.6	21.4	31.2	41.1
Nonalumni	24.8	23.7	26.7	30.9	23.9
Living individuals[b]	28.4	28.0	31.1	48.7	44.1
Foundations	23.5	26.6	19.5	18.2	17.8
Corporations	14.4	14.9	14.0	7.0	9.0
Religious organizations	6.9	1.9	13.2	9.5	5.9
Other	5.7	6.3	5.2	3.2	2.3
Total	100.0	100.0	100.0	100.0	100.0

Source: Council for Financial Aid to Education, *Voluntary Support of Education, 1974–75* (CFAE, n.d.). Figures are rounded.

a. This table and statistics in the text exclude private two-year colleges because the CFAE data group them with public two-year colleges. Total voluntary support here includes both current- and capital-account gifts.

b. Gifts from individuals net of bequests. These individuals are also included in one of the two preceding groups.

Table 2-A15. *Estimates of the Tax Revenue Lost Due to the State and Local Property Tax Exemption for Private Institutions of Higher Education, Academic Years 1971–72 and 1973–74*

Millions of dollars

| | 1971–72 | | | | 1973–74 |
Level of institution	Book value of property	Tax loss[a]	Payments in lieu of tax[b]	Net tax subsidy	Net tax subsidy[c]
All institutions	14,189	185	9	176	205
Universities	5,273	69	4	65	73
Other four-year institutions	8,357	110	4	106	126
Two-year institutions	576	6	*	6	6

Sources: Paul F. Mertins and Norman J. Brandt, *Financial Statistics of Institutions of Higher Education: Property, 1970–71 and 1971–72*, NCES 75-114 (GPO, 1974); U.S. Bureau of the Census, *Census of Governments, 1972*, vol. 2, *Taxable Property Values and Assessment-Sales Price Ratios*, pt 1: *Taxable and Other Property Values* (GPO, 1973), p. 27, and pt 2: *Assessment-Sales Price Ratios and Tax Rates*, pp. 8, 33; John Caffrey, "Tax and Tax-Related Arrangements between Colleges and Universities and Local Governments," *ACE Special Report* (American Council on Education, August 12, 1969).

* Less than 0.5.

a. The estimates were derived by applying the ratio of the tax revenue to the sales value of property outside the standard metropolitan statistical areas in each state in 1971 to the book value of institutions' holdings of land and buildings in 1971–72.

b. In a 1969 survey of over 400 institutions of which 318 responded, Caffrey found that approximately 45 percent of private colleges and universities made some payment in lieu of taxes with a median amount for all institutions of $13,000 a year. The estimates here come from applying this percentage and this median to the total number of private institutions and allocating this estimated total payment among levels of private colleges according to their shares in the total income of the private sector.

c. These estimates assume that the net tax subsidy in 1973–74 is the same fraction of property book values as in 1971–72. The property values apply to September 1974 and were obtained directly from the National Center for Education Statistics.

APPENDIX B:
PARTIAL CORRELATION ANALYSIS OF STATE AID TO PRIVATE HIGHER EDUCATION

This appendix presents the partial correlation coefficients between state characteristics and state aid to private higher education relative to total state spending on higher education and relative to total revenues of private institutions (see tables 2-B1 and 2-B2). The variables used in the partial correlation analysis to test for a consistent relationship between state aid to private higher education and possible motives for such support are defined below, and are followed by the data sources. The letters in parentheses after the variables are keyed to the sources. All data are for the 1973–74 academic year unless otherwise noted.

Variables

Measures of State Aid

1. State aid to private higher education relative to total state spending on higher education. (A, C)
2. State aid to private higher education relative to educational and general revenue of private institutions. (A, C, E)

Proxies for Motives for State Support of Private Higher Education

Motive 1 (higher private-sector tuition)
> Private tuition = weighted average undergraduate tuition and required fees for students of private colleges and universities. (F)

Motive 2 (strong preference for higher education)
> Percent of high school graduates = men twenty-five years and older with at least a high school degree as a percent of all men twenty-five and over (data are for 1970). (G)

Share of state budgets going to higher education = total state appropriations for higher education as a percent of total state general expenditure. (C, H)

Motive 3 (private sector important to the state)

Total enrollment in private institutions of higher education as percent of total enrollment in higher education. (D)

Home-state students enrolled in private colleges and universities as a percent of total enrollment in private colleges and universities (data are for 1972–73). (This enrollment refers to resident, that is, nonextension, degree-credit students.) (D)

Motive 4 ("costs" of the public sector)

Public tuition = weighted average undergraduate tuition and required fees for home-state students of public colleges and universities. (F)

State subsidies per public student = expenditures from state and local sources per full-time-equivalent student in public institutions. (B)

Educational spending per public student = total institutional expenditures for educational and general purposes at public institutions per full-time-equivalent student. (B)

Sources

Key	Citation
A	Joseph D. Boyd, "National Association of State Scholarship Programs: 7th Annual Survey, 1975–76 Academic Year" (Deerfield, Illinois: NASSP, 1975; processed), and preceding surveys for 1973–74 and 1974–75.
B	Carnegie Foundation for the Advancement of Teaching, *The States and Higher Education: A Proud Past and a Vital Future* (Jossey-Bass, 1976).
C	M. M. Chambers, *Higher Education and State Governments, 1970–75* (Interstate, 1974).
D	Ellen Cherin and Marilyn McCoy, *Supplementary Document: Data Values Used in the Development of Analysis Reports for the Study, "State and Local Financial Support of Higher Education: A Framework for Interstate Comparison—1973–74"*

(National Center for Higher Education Management Systems at Western Interstate Commission for Higher Education, 1976).

E   Paul F. Mertins and Norman J. Brandt, *Financial Statistics of Institutions of Higher Education: Current Funds Revenues and Expenditures—1973–74 Summary Data*, NCES 76-121 (GPO, 1976).

F   Arthur Podolsky, *Basic Student Charges, 1972–73 and 1973–74*, National Center for Education Statistics (GPO, 1975).

G   U.S. Bureau of the Census, *Census of Population, 1970: General Social and Economic Characteristics*, Final Report PC(1)-C1, *United States Summary* (GPO, 1972).

H   U.S. Bureau of the Census, *State Government Finances in 1973*, Series GF73-no. 3 (GPO, 1974).

Table 2-B1. *Partial Correlation Coefficients between State Characteristics and State Aid to Private Higher Education Relative to Total State Spending on Higher Education*[a]

State characteristics[b]	Correlation							
	(1)	(2)	(3)	(4)	(5)	(6)	(7)	(8)
Proxy for motive 1								
Private tuition	.246	...	...	...	...	...	...	...
Proxies for motive 2								
Percent high school graduates	...	...	.017	...	...	...	...	...
State spending on higher education as percent of total state spending	...	...	...	.001	...	...	...	...
Proxies for motive 3								
Private enrollment as percent of total enrollment	.504*	.498*	.575*	.543*	.576*	.628*	.685*	.515*
Private home-state enrollment as percent of total private enrollment	.496*	.572*	.569*	.567*	.569*	.376*	.521*	.482*
Proxies for motive 4								
Public tuition	...	.534*	.565*	.562*	.569*	...	...	.611*
State subsidy per public student	...	...	...	...	...	.218	...	.341
Total educational and general expenditure per public student	...	...	...	...	...	...	.387*	...

Sources: See text of this appendix.
* Significant at 5 percent level of confidence.
a. For definitions of the variables, see text of this appendix.
b. Correlations are based on data for the thirty-one states that had some aid to private higher education in 1973–74.

137

Table 2-B2. *Partial Correlation Cofficients between State Characteristics and State Aid to Private Higher Education Relative to Total Educational and General Revenue of Private Institutions*[a]

State characteristics[b]	Correlation							
	(1)	(2)	(3)	(4)	(5)	(6)	(7)	(8)
Proxy for motive 1								
Private tuition	-.137	-.326	...	...	...	...	...	...
Proxies for motive 2								
Percent high school graduates	...	...	-.009	...	...	...	...	...
State spending on higher education as percent of total state spending	...	...	...	.420*	...	...	...	...
Proxies for motive 3								
Private enrollment as percent of total enrollment	.254*	.197	.030	.212	.031	.172	.217	-.034
Private home-state enrollment as percent of total private enrollment	.419*	.485*	.506*	.509*	.506*	.377*	.529*	-.433*
Proxies for motive 4								
Public tuition	...	.505*	.422*	.516*	.427*	...	...	.448*
State subsidy per public student	...	...	...	...	...	.136	...	.201
Total educational and general expenditure per public student	...	...	...	...	...	...	.476*	...

Sources: See text of this appendix.
* Significant at 5 percent level of confidence.
a. For definitions of the variables, see text of this appendix.
b. Correlations are based on data for the thirty-one states that had some aid to private higher education in 1973–74.

APPENDIX C: REGRESSION ANALYSIS OF STATE SUPPORT FOR PUBLIC AND PRIVATE HIGHER EDUCATION

In order to test for a trade-off between state aid to public and private higher education, equations in which state support for the public sector was a function of a number of independent variables, including state aid to private higher education, were estimated for eleven states using annual data between 1959–60 and 1973–74, in both current and constant dollars. Definitions of the variables, and a table that shows the regression results, are presented below.

Dependent Variables

PUB	State appropriations for public higher education (for both institutions and students), in millions of current dollars
RPUB	Same as *PUB*, except in millions of constant dollars

Independent Variables

PUBENR	Total enrollment in public institutions, in thousands
PR	The sum of state aid to private institutions of higher education and state assistance to private students, in millions of constant and current dollars
STREV	State general revenue, in millions of current and constant dollars
Y	Per capita personal income, in current and constant dollars
HE/STREV	Total state appropriations for higher education as a percent of state general revenue
PRENR	Total enrollment in private institutions, in thousands
TIME	Time trend: 1 in 1959–60, progressing to 15 in 1973–74
PRENR/ PUBENR	Ratio of total enrollment in private to total enrollment in public higher education
CPI	Consumer price index (fiscal years) (1967 = 100)
DUM	Dummy variable used in Iowa and North Carolina to indicate the second year of a two-year appropriation

Table 2-C1. Coefficients and Summary Statistics for Equations Estimating State Expenditures on Public Higher Education, Selected States

State and dependent variable[a]	Independent variables[b]											Summary statistics[c]	
	Constant	PUBENR	PR	STREV	Y	HE/STREV	PRENR	TIME	PRENR/PUBENR	CPI	DUM	Durbin-Watson	Standard error of estimate
Alabama													
RPUB	−27.15 (2.3)	0.67 (2.1)	5.82 (1.0)	0.05 (2.4)	...	768.00 (3.7)	−1.98 (4.3)	−2.83 (2.3)	...	...	...	2.23	1.84
PUB	−82.49 (8.8)	−0.26 (0.61)	1.16 (0.2)	...	0.05 (8.1)	1,082.30 (3.5)	...	−1.66 (0.9)	...	...	...	2.34	3.08
California													
RPUB	−230.25 (3.0)	0.09 (1.4)	7.08 (5.4)	0.05 (6.6)	...	5,061.10 (7.1)	−0.95 (2.6)	...	...	...	...	2.11	0.60
PUB	−438.44 (3.0)	0.30 (2.1)	8.99 (2.9)	0.04 (3.9)	...	5,641.20 (4.8)	−1.30 (2.2)	...	538.23 (2.1)	...	...	2.21	0.89
Iowa													
RPUB	−57.44 (9.6)	0.03 (0.3)	−0.66 (2.3)	0.09 (10.2)	* (1.6)	705.70 (11.3)	...	...	...	...	...	2.08	1.00
PUB	1.17 (0.02)	0.59 (2.1)	0.72 (0.5)	0.09 (3.5)	...	587.37 (3.3)	−0.56 (1.9)	...	...	−0.59 (0.9)	−1.06 (0.6)	2.00	1.39
Maine													
RPUB	−14.50 (2.2)	0.51 (2.3)	−2.03 (0.3)	63.70 (5.3)	* (0.1)	212.78 (6.0)	...	−0.80 (1.9)	...	...	...	1.65	0.49
PUB	−31.38 (5.9)	1.53 (5.1)	−18.18 (2.4)	0.05 (8.0)	* (0.7)	239.24 (10.7)	−3.33 (4.6)	...	40.72 (5.0)	−0.03 (0.2)	...	2.58	0.30

	C1	C2	C3	C4	C5	C6	C7	C8	C9	C10	C11	C12	C13
Minnesota													
RPUB	−19.04 (0.5)	0.85 (2.9)	−1.23 (0.3)	0.08 (2.6)	−0.03 (3.2)	...	...	...	108.68 (2.1)	...	...	2.09	3.09
PUB	−72.95 (4.3)	0.05 (0.3)	−1.27 (0.4)	0.09 (6.8)	−0.02 (2.1)	1,421.60 (7.8)	...	...	...	...	...	1.81	1.90
New York													
RPUB	−22.61 (0.2)	0.80 (2.7)	−3.07 (3.3)	0.04 (1.8)	−0.10 (1.5)	6,099.30 (3.8)	...	...	...	...	...	1.83	14.23
PUB	1,246.30 (9.1)	0.79 (2.5)	−2.49 (3.0)	...	−0.03 (0.6)	3,691.80 (3.9)	...	...	...	13.34 (6.4)	...	1.83	14.17
North Carolina													
RPUB	−23.35 (2.1)	0.39 (2.1)	0.17 (0.1)	0.07 (4.3)	−0.02 (2.7)	1,579.00 (14.5)	−9.54 (4.2)	...	...	...	...	1.75	2.01
PUB	−214.45 (4.1)	−1.19 (8.6)	−4.57 (4.7)	0.08 (6.5)	...	1,346.00 (10.6)	−840.99 (2.6)	...	...	3.00 (6.2)	−12.02 (4.6)	2.26	1.85
Ohio													
RPUB	−138.90 (3.1)	−0.36 (1.9)	1.78 (1.9)	0.07 (8.0)	0.02 (0.8)	2,583.50 (8.8)	−0.22 (1.2)	...	...	...	...	2.39	2.74
PUB	−128.13 (8.1)	−0.51 (4.2)	2.07 (3.2)	0.06 (6.1)	0.03 (2.2)	2,894.10 (10.5)	−0.18 (1.0)	...	...	...	...	2.19	2.94
South Carolina													
RPUB	−14.25 (6.6)	0.22 (1.4)	2.04 (4.2)	0.09 (5.2)	−0.02 (6.8)	691.40 (16.8)	...	...	...	...	...	1.49	0.79
PUB	−181.08 (5.9)	0.03 (0.1)	3.79 (4.3)	0.10 (2.7)	−0.05 (5.6)	...	...	...	...	2.46 (5.4)	...	1.96	2.28
Tennessee													
RPUB	−34.50 (2.2)	0.69 (5.2)	6.63 (3.1)	0.09 (5.0)	−0.02 (1.7)	815.30 (7.2)	...	−3.35 (3.7)	...	...	...	2.00	1.19
PUB	−120.30 (10.8)	−0.61 (3.4)	−7.59 (2.4)	0.03 (1.7)	0.02 (1.6)	584.00 (5.7)	...	...	...	0.95 (4.3)	...	2.06	1.07

141

(Continued)

Table 2-C1 (Continued)

State and dependent variable[a]	Constant	PUBENR	PR	STREV	Y	HE/ STREV	PRENR	TIME	PRENR/ PUBENR	CPI	DUM	Durbin- Watson	Standard error of estimate
												Summary statistics[e]	
Texas													
RPUB	−238.40	0.33	−0.58	0.11	...	2,386.50	...	−13.60	...	...	...	2.55	3.46
	(17.2)	(2.3)	(0.3)	(6.8)		(13.6)		(7.0)					
PUB	−162.86	−0.85	10.90	0.15	...	2,742.50	...	...	...	...	...	2.12	7.75
	(13.6)	(3.4)	(2.3)	(7.8)		(6.8)							

* Between 0.01 and −0.01.

Sources: PUB, M. M. Chambers, *Higher Education in the Fifty States* (Interstate, 1970) and Chambers, *Higher Education and State Governments, 1970–75* (Interstate, 1974). PUBENR and PRENR, National Center for Education Statistics, *Opening Fall Enrollment in Higher Education*, and NCES, *Digest of Educational Statistics*, relevant issues for both. (Before 1965–66, NCES did not break down state enrollments by public and private sector. Hence the distribution was estimated assuming that the ratio between the fraction of state enrollment in private institutions and the fraction nationally in private institutions in 1965–66 had remained constant back through 1959–60.) PR, the two Chambers volumes above and Joseph D. Boyd, "National Association of State Scholarship Programs: Fifth Annual Survey" (Deerfield, Illinois: NASSP, October 1973; processed), and preceding annual surveys (various titles), except for California and New York where actual values of student aid were provided by state higher education officials. STREV and Y, U.S. Bureau of the Census, *State Government Finances*, and U.S. Bureau of the Census, *Statistical Abstract of the United States*, relevant issues of both. HE/STREV, the two Chambers volumes cited above and the sources for STREV cited above. CPI, *Economic Report of the President*, February 1975.

a. PUB and RPUB, the dependent variables defined in text above, have fifteen observations per state.
b. The variables are defined in the appendix text. The numbers in parentheses are *t*-statistics.
c. R^2 is 0.99 for all equations.

142

Chapter Three

The Demand for Higher Education

Michael S. McPherson

EDITED BY DAVID W. BRENEMAN AND CHESTER E. FINN, JR.

MICHAEL S. McPHERSON is assistant professor of economics at Williams College. He thanks Joseph A. Kershaw, Stephen R. Lewis, and Roger Bolton for their helpful comments and Ben Schneider for research assistance.

Tables

Figures

COMPETITION between public and private colleges and universities is hardly a new phenomenon. But current events are markedly changing the context and the character of that rivalry. For the past two decades the burgeoning demand for higher education has meant that the contest for students between public and private institutions has affected the comparative rates at which enrollments in each sector could grow. In the next two decades, according to most observers, the likelihood is that total college enrollment will decline, or at best achieve a "steady state." If either occurs, competition between public and private colleges will become not a question of faster versus slower growth but, at least for some of them, a struggle for survival.

This chapter is concerned with one set of factors that will influence the outcome of this impending struggle for students: the determinants of student demand for higher education. The fast-growing literature on the various aspects of this subject is complex and often technical; the level of argument ranges from the most casual empiricism to highly abstruse econometrics. The principal aim here is to sort out the various economic, demographic, and social factors whose interplay will shape the future of enrollment demand, and, as far as possible, to assess their quantitative importance. No new forecasts are presented (though some existing forecasts are discussed). If the chapter achieves its aim, the reader will have a better conceptual grasp of the forces that are likely to determine future enrollment levels and a more realistic sense of what is known about those forces empirically. He will not come away with a neatly printed table showing enrollment by sector in 1990—a table that in any case would almost certainly be wrong.

It is worth emphasizing at the outset that no strong conclusion emerges from the following analysis whether enrollment declines are more likely to be felt at public or at private institutions, even in the absence of explicit policy changes. By themselves, demographic factors affect both sectors symmetrically (unless there is marked unevenness in the demographic trend for different population groups). Other social and economic factors affecting enrollment patterns appear to hold some pluses and some minuses for the private sector, so far as it is now possible to foresee their implications. The commonly voiced suspicion that the private sector will lose out in the years ahead relative to the public sector appears to rest partly on a "naive" projection of the trends in enrollment shares of the last two decades (when the public sector increased its share of students from about half to more than three-quarters) and partly on believing that public institutions will respond more effectively than private institutions to the changed environment—either through obtaining increased subsidies that widen the tuition gap or through more effective nonprice competition.

But caution is required on both counts. The validity of projecting on the basis of past trends is very much in doubt, since the rapid relative expansion of the public sector rested heavily on the community college movement, now abated, and the favorable effects of the general growth climate, now vanished. That climate was very good for public higher education, both in enabling it to maintain and to some degree increase its subsidies and—very importantly—in fostering the development of a stronger and more varied collection of public institutions. That such relative gains in the competitive position of public versus private colleges will continue in a time of general retrenchment and decline is far from a forgone conclusion. Dealing with such questions raises difficult political and economic issues concerning the response of the higher education system to conditions of adversity, which go well beyond the scope of the present chapter. But at least one can begin this discussion of the future with the pronouncement that the outcome of the impending struggle for students is in doubt.

The Changing Environment for Higher Education

Since the basic premise of this chapter (and, in some measure, the entire book) is that the demand for college enrollment will fall over the next decade and a half, it is necessary to discuss the reasons for that belief.

The dominant factor in the overall enrollment picture is the 15 percent decline in the college-age population (eighteen- to twenty-one-year-olds) that will occur between 1980 and 1990. Forecasters relying on this information have typically projected declining or at best stable enrollments until the 1990s. Thus Allan Cartter in 1976 forecast an overall enrollment decline of 6 percent between 1980 and 1990, despite his assumption that enrollment *rates* among the college-age population would rise.[1] The authors of *More than Survival* reached rather more optimistic conclusions by incorporating the assumption that enrollment among older and other "nontraditional" students will rise markedly. But

1. Allan M. Cartter, *Ph.D.'s and the Academic Labor Market* (McGraw-Hill, 1976).

they still project an enrollment decline among undergraduates during the 1980s, and only a 3 percent increase in total enrollment over that period.[2] Contrast these forecasts with the period from 1962 to 1972, when undergraduate numbers nearly doubled and total enrollment more than tripled.[3] The impact of demographic change is powerful indeed.

As noted, these forecasts depend on the assumption that enrollment *rates* will rise over the next decade as they have in the past. Unfortunately, the forecasts of future enrollment rates embodied in most projections are based more on guesswork and the extrapolation of trends than on any systematic theory.[4] Thus recent declines in enrollment rates, especially among white males, suggest that the coming drop in enrollment levels may be even more severe than purely demographic factors indicate.

The most plausible single explanation of this recent sag is the dramatic downturn in the labor market for college graduates that began in the late 1960s. This striking development and its implications for higher education and society have been extensively studied by Richard Freeman.[5]

Freeman's analysis indicates that this downturn, which has been reflected in reduced job availability and in starting salaries for college-level jobs that have been falling in constant dollars, is not the product of the recent recession, but instead has resulted from a fundamental shift in the supply and demand for college-educated labor. The number of college graduates increased enormously through the late 1960s as a result of large college-age cohorts and rising college and university enrollment rates. Meanwhile, growth in the sectors of the economy that draw most heavily on educated labor—including education, research and development, and government employment—has been slowing substantially. The consequence has been a depression in the college-graduate labor market that has sharply reduced the economic value of a college degree.

2. Carnegie Foundation for the Advancement of Teaching, *More than Survival: Prospects for Higher Education in a Period of Uncertainty* (Jossey-Bass, 1975), p. 45. This book also surveys other enrollment forecasts.

3. Full-time-equivalent enrollment. (See Cartter, *Ph.D.'s and the Academic Labor Market*, pp. 69, 89.)

4. This point is thoroughly discussed in Douglas L. Adkins, *The Great American Degree Machine: An Economic Analysis of the Human Resource Output of Higher Education* (Carnegie Foundation for the Advancement of Teaching, 1975), chap. 10.

5. See Richard B. Freeman, *The Overeducated American* (Academic Press, 1976), and other works cited therein.

Figure 3-1. *Alternative Projections of Freshman Male Enrollment as a Percentage of 1973 Enrollment, 1975–90*

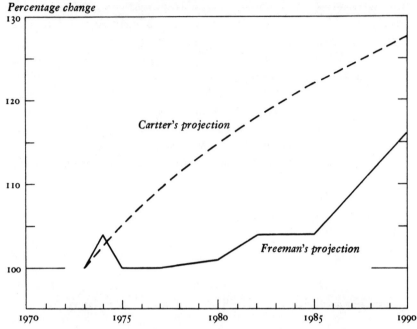

Percentage change

Sources: Allan M. Cartter, *Ph.D.'s and the Academic Labor Market* (McGraw-Hill, 1976), p. 69, and Richard B. Freeman, *The Overeducated American* (Academic Press, 1976), p. 75.

One hardly needs to be an economic determinist to believe that labor market changes of this magnitude may have played a major role in causing the decline in college enrollment rates in recent years. How long the depression and its retardant effects on enrollment rates will last depends on the ability of the economy to absorb additional college-trained workers and on the speed with which college enrollments decline and thereby reduce the excess supply. Barring a large shift in demand for educated workers, such as might result from a huge new energy program, the likelihood is that depressed conditions will continue until well into the next decade, if not longer.

One forecast of the potential implications is shown in figure 3-1 and table 3-1. Freeman forecasts rates of freshman male enrollment as part of a general model of supply and demand for educated labor.[6] As figure 3-1

6. The model is described in appendix B of Freeman, *The Overeducated American.*

Table 3-1. *Alternative Forecasts of Undergraduate Enrollment in Four-Year and Two-Year Institutions of Higher Education as a Percentage of 1973 Enrollment, Selected Years, 1975–90*[a]

		Forecast	
Year	Cartter	Freeman[b]
1973	100	100
1975	103	101
1980	118	111
1985	113	105
1990	111	106

Sources: Allan M. Cartter, *Ph.D.'s and the Academic Labor Market* (McGraw-Hill, 1976), p. 69, and Richard B. Freeman, *The Overeducated American* (Academic Press, 1976), p. 75.

a. Data have been converted to full-time equivalents.

b. Calculated by adjusting Cartter's estimates of male enrollment rates by Freeman's estimates of enrollment rates for freshman males. This is only an *approximate* calculation that (1) assumes in the Cartter data that male enrollment is half of total enrollment and (2) applies Freeman's estimates for freshman enrollment rates to total enrollment levels.

indicates, he predicts a declining freshman enrollment rate to the mid-1980s, in contrast to Cartter's forecast of a rising rate. Freeman's forecast enrollment rate does turn up sharply in the late 1980s because the small graduating classes of the 1980s eventually do move the labor market from surplus to shortage. Table 3-1 shows a rough estimate of the implications of Freeman's forecast for levels of undergraduate enrollment. Note that the downturn starts sooner, is somewhat more severe, but ends sooner than in a strictly demographic model like Cartter's.[7]

Forecasting is an imperfect art, and things may not turn out as anticipated. Certainly the potential exists, as Howard Bowen has emphasized, for continued enrollment expansion despite demographic decline: "The higher education industry might well double or treble in size during the balance of this century and a totally new kind of society might be created in which the level and the depth of education and the richness of culture would surpass that ever before achieved or even imagined."[8] This of course is a hope, not a forecast. But even if the political and social changes envisioned by Bowen are not forthcoming, it remains possible that other factors not considered here, including smaller family size and

7. For a conceptually similar but even more ominous forecast, see Stephen P. Dresch, "Demography, Technology, and Higher Education: Toward a Formal Model of Educational Adaptation," *Journal of Political Economy*, vol. 83 (June 1975), pp. 535–69.

8. Howard R. Bowen, "Higher Education: A Growth Industry?" *Educational Record*, vol. 55 (Summer 1974), p. 157.

increased enrollment among nontraditional groups (which is discussed below in relation to public-private competition) may work to ease the overall enrollment situation. But the two factors most likely to influence demand for at least the next decade are declining college-age population and a weak market for college-educated labor. Both point in the same direction: down.

Public-Private Competition for Students

In analyzing factors that will influence the competition for students between public and private institutions during the coming period of overall enrollment decline, it is useful to distinguish between (1) external environmental factors, largely beyond the control of the institutions and (2) factors that depend on the policies adopted by institutions in response to the changing environment.

It is, of course, hard to know what "external factors" will prove to be important—who in 1955 forecast the Sputnik era?—but it is possible to discuss the apparent implications for the public-private enrollment mix of several developments that have been very much on people's minds: the demographic decline, reduced economic returns to college, and the increase in enrollment demand among nontraditional (adult and non-degree-credit) students. (Among institutional policies, pricing policy has been getting the most attention lately, but the tuition gap and related issues are put aside for separate discussion in later sections of this chapter.) "Nonprice" competition between public and private institutions—through admission standards, geographical accessibility, and so on—is also quite important and has been somewhat neglected; it is the focus here.

External Factors

The essential theme in the following review of environmental factors is an important if unexciting one: while some factors favor the public and some the private sector, their impacts appear neither to be large enough nor uneven enough between sectors to have a decisive effect on the enrollment mix. In the absence of significant changes in the tuition gap or in the nonprice dimensions of competition discussed below, the public and private sectors are likely to share enrollment declines more or less in proportion to their present enrollment ratios. This is important because it says that the fate of the private sector in higher education is not going to be decided by factors outside its control.

THE DECLINING RATE OF RETURN

Apparently students have so far been responding to the weak market for college-educated labor by opting for more explicitly vocational and career-oriented programs at the expense of traditional and liberal arts programs. For example, Glenny reports in his large-scale survey of colleges and universities that 52 percent of the institutions surveyed reported increased enrollments in vocational and professional studies, while only 27 percent had such increases in traditional and liberal arts studies over the 1968–74 period.[9] This trend, if it continues, will probably benefit comprehensive colleges and universities and two-year colleges with their vocational orientation, and be harmful to liberal arts colleges. Since almost all liberal arts schools are private, and most enrollment at comprehensive and two-year institutions is in the public sector, this trend toward vocational education, if it continues, will favor the public sector.

But that the trend will continue is not so clear. There is a certain illogic in responding to a reduced economic payoff to college by making one's college pursuits more narrowly economic in aim. Students right now, caught up in a very uncertain and rapidly changing situation, are understandably responding to their felt need to gain a foothold in the labor market by becoming qualified for some job upon graduation. But as things settle down, this perspective may change. Conceivably, a bifurcation may occur, with vocationally oriented students becoming more intensely serious about career training, while other students, recognizing the reduced financial returns to a degree, approach college for its cultural and social, rather than its economic, rewards.[10] Or perhaps, as Earl Cheit has suggested, colleges will succeed in combining craft or vocational training with liberal arts offerings—aiming, with Marx, to make their students fishermen in the morning, carpenters in the afternoon, and critics in the evening.[11]

9. Lyman A. Glenny and others, *Presidents Confront Reality: From Edifice Complex to University without Walls* (Jossey-Bass, 1976), p. 26.

10. Both Richard Freeman and Stephen Dresch foresee something of this kind. (See Freeman, *The Overeducated American*, p. 192, and Stephen P. Dresch, "The College, the University and the State: A Critical Examination for Institutional Support in the Context of Historical Development," working paper W4-18 [Yale University, Institution for Social and Policy Studies, 1974; processed], chap. 5.)

11. Earl F. Cheit, *The Useful Arts and the Liberal Tradition* (McGraw-Hill, 1975).

Trends like these are not so negative for the private sector as the recent purely vocational bias. Many private institutions have much to offer in the way of "consumption" benefits—intimacy and small size, pleasant surroundings, fine programs to enhance cultural awareness and capacity—if such benefits come to be favored instead of labor market preparation, at least by some students. And it also needs emphasizing that a good general education may still be of value in the labor market over the long run[12]—though probably not so much as in the past. When the dust settles, it may well turn out that economic returns to more narrowly professional and vocational training have declined *more* than returns to general education and liberal arts education. It is too early to tell, and therefore premature to assume that private institutions will suffer disproportionately from these developments.

THE DEMOGRAPHIC DECLINE

A more detailed look at the emerging population profile raises some intriguing possibilities for differential effects on public and private institutions—though some at least, on closer examination, turn out not to be empirically important. If, for example, the drop-off in childbearing had been greater among higher-income than among lower-income families, the effects on elite private colleges might have been quite severe. But demographers who have explored this question have found the changes quite pervasive and surprisingly uniform among socioeconomic groups.[13]

Similarly, given the heavy geographic concentration of private higher education institutions (in 1972 the ten states with the highest private enrollment had 62 percent of the total whereas the ten states with the lowest had only 1.2 percent), one might expect that regional shifts in population would significantly affect the market for private enrollment. Regional forecasts do indeed suggest that population over the next several decades will continue its historic westward shift, with the most rapid

---

12. Theodore W. Schultz, among others, has stressed both the importance of general education and the long period over which its benefits accrue. (See his *Investment in Human Capital: The Role of Education and of Research* [Free Press, 1971].)

13. See James A. Sweet, "Differentials in the Rate of Fertility Decline: 1960–1970," *Family Planning Perspectives*, vol. 6 (Spring 1974), pp. 103–07; Ronald R. Rindfuss and James A. Sweet, "The Pervasiveness of Postwar Fertility Trends in the United States," CDE working paper 75-25 (University of Wisconsin–Madison, Center for Demography and Ecology, 1975; processed); and Ronald R. Rindfuss, "Recent Trends in Fertility Differentials Among Educational Groups," discussion paper 263-75 (University of Wisconsin–Madison, Institute for Research on Poverty, 1975; processed).

Table 3-2. *Regional Comparison of High School Graduation Rates,*
1970, and Share of Private in Total College Enrollment, 1969

Region	High school graduation rate (percent)[a]	Private enrollment as a percentage of total college enrollment
New England	81.8	55.2
Mideast	77.1	43.5
Great Lakes	78.8	24.3
Plains	84.5	24.3
Southeast	68.2	22.0
Rocky Mountain	80.2	20.0
Southwest	68.8	15.1
Far West	77.4	10.8
All states	77.9	26.2

Sources: Graduation rates, Kenneth A. Simon and W. Vance Grant, *Digest of Educational Statistics, 1971 Edition,* U.S. National Center for Educational Statistics, DHEW (OE) 72-45 (Government Printing Office, 1972), p. 50, and U.S. Bureau of the Census, *Census of Population, 1970, General Population Characteristics,* Final Report PC(1)-B2 through PC(1)-B52 (GPO, 1971); enrollment, George H. Wade, *Opening Fall Enrollment in Higher Education, 1969: Report on Preliminary Survey,* NCES, OE-54003-69-A (GPO, 1970).

a. Expressed as a percentage of the population aged seventeen years.

growth in the Sunbelt where private higher education has a small market share. But as it turns out the magnitude of the expected shifts does not appear great enough to affect materially the overall situation: this factor alone would increase the ratio of public to private enrollment between 1969 and 1990 by only about 1 percent.[14]

Potentially more significant are regional differences in high school graduation rates. As table 3-2 indicates, the Southeast and Southwest have by far the lowest rates today, and hence they have the greatest potential for growth in numbers of graduates. In fact, a rise in their graduation rates to the national average would be nearly enough to offset the expected decline in college-age population in those states in the 1980s. Since these are both regions with below-average private enrollments, this factor may do little for private higher education.

A final demographic consideration is the changing pattern of family size and so-called sibling overlap. Recently researchers have noted a marked increase in the number of families having several children of college age at the same time. This overlap phenomenon and the atten-

14. Calculated by assuming the ratio of public to private enrollment in each region stays constant. Based on projections of population distribution appearing in Regional Economic Analysis Division, "State Projections of Income, Employment, and Population to 1990," U.S. Bureau of Economic Analysis, *Survey of Current Business,* vol. 54 (April 1974), pp. 19–45.

dant financial squeeze on parents may be one cause of the recent decline in enrollment rates, although there is no hard evidence of this.[15] Presumably the effect on choice of a lower-cost public versus a higher-cost private institution, as well as on the "go, no go" decision itself, may be significant.

Declining fertility levels will cause the extent of sibling overlap as well as average family size to decline sharply during the 1980s. It is quite possible that this development will ease families' financial burdens enough to be a discernible plus for private colleges. If so, it will probably be the elite liberal arts colleges, which are perceived to provide a uniquely high-quality product, that will benefit the most.

NONTRADITIONAL CLIENTELES

The rapid rate of increase in enrollment of older, part-time, and non-degree-credit students has been a rare ray of hope for higher education and in the last few years educational planners and college administrators have seized on it eagerly. Although adult enrollment has indeed grown rapidly in recent years, several limiting factors make it very doubtful that a new golden age of higher education can be built around this clientele. First is the fact that the group aged twenty-five to thirty-four years, which has accounted for much of the growth in adult enrollment, is currently passing through the demographic boom that hit the colleges in the mid-1960s.[16] Its numbers will dwindle substantially by the

15. Data on sibling overlap and speculations on its effects are in David Goldberg and Albert Anderson, "Projections of Population and College Enrollment in Michigan, 1970–2000" (Lansing: Governor's Commission on Higher Education, 1974; processed; available from ERIC Document Reproduction Service); and Stephen J. Carroll and Peter A. Morrison, "Demographic and Economic Influences on the Growth and Decline of Higher Education," Rand Paper Series P-5569 (Rand Corporation, February 1976; processed). The few empirical studies of enrollment demand that have included measures of family size and sibling overlap have not found important effects. (See Gary T. Barnes, "Determinants of the College Going and College Choice Decision" [University of North Carolina at Greensboro, n.d.; processed]; Richard R. Spies, *The Future of Private Colleges: The Effect of Rising Costs on College Choice* [Princeton University, Industrial Relations Section, 1973]; and Moheb Ghali, Walter Miklius, and Richard Wados, "The Demand for Higher Education Facing an Individual Institution," scheduled for publication in *Higher Education*, vol. 6 [Amsterdam: Elsevier; November 1977].)

16. In fact the fraction of the population aged twenty-two to thirty-four enrolled as degree-credit undergraduates actually fell slightly between 1969 and 1973, even as the numbers enrolled grew substantially (Carnegie Foundation for the Advancement of Teaching, *More than Survival*, p. 32).

mid-1980s. Second, much of the recent adult enrollment increase apparently derived from Vietnam veterans under the GI bill, a force that is already waning.[17] Last, the declining economic returns to college discussed above are likely to have a depressing effect on enrollment of nontraditional students, a large proportion of whom are vocationally oriented.[18] Thus, although nontraditional enrollments will probably continue to increase, the effect on total enrollment is unlikely to be spectacular—perhaps enough to provide steady rather than declining numbers, as the enrollment forecasts in *More than Survival* indicate; probably not much more.

Unless demand among adults grows much faster than this, it will probably be met largely by public institutions, especially the two-year colleges, where most adults and nondegree students are currently enrolled.[19] Undoubtedly some private institutions, especially those in metropolitan areas, will succeed in attracting adult students in the future as they have in the past. But as long as adult education is largely vocational, and as long as many older students have families to support, few of them are likely to be willing to pay extra for the amenities private colleges have to offer.

There is, however, one important potential side benefit to private higher education in all this. That is the fact that increased enrollment of nontraditional students at public institutions will not be at the expense of private enrollment, and in fact may relieve some of the competitive pressure for traditional students.[20] In particular public two-year colleges (and some public four-year institutions) may continue to expand their nonacademic vocational offerings at the expense of academic programs,

17. Bishop and Van Dyk estimate that in their sample of adult students, the male attendance rate would have dropped by 40 percent if veterans attended at the same rate as other students. John Bishop and Jane Van Dyk, "Can Adults be Hooked on College? Some Determinants of Adult College Attendance," *Journal of Higher Education*, vol. 48 (January/February 1977), p. 51.

18. O'Keefe reports that half of the students involved in adult education are in occupationally oriented programs, and that more than half of all adult students cite a desire to advance in their jobs as a primary motive for enrolling. (See Michael O'Keefe, *The Adult, Education and Public Policy* [Cambridge, Mass.: Aspen Institute for Humanistic Studies, 1977], pp. 48, 50.)

19. Cartter reports that 92 percent of nondegree-credit students attend public two-year colleges (*Ph.D.'s and the Academic Labor Market*, p. 88), as do about half of the older degree-credit undergraduates (*Higher Education Daily*, vol. 4 [June 17, 1976], pp. 3, 4).

20. I am indebted to Stephen R. Lewis of Williams College for suggesting this point.

thus easing the competitive pressure with their principal private rivals, the two-year private colleges and the less selective liberal arts colleges.

Institutional Responses

The external factors just considered do not suggest a clear competitive edge for either the public or the private sector in their prospects for attracting students, at least among traditional groups. Differential prospects for regional growth marginally favor the public sector, but this may well be offset by declining family size, which will increase the ability of families to pay for private higher education. The differential effects on public and private enrollment of a declining rate of return to higher education seem impossible to predict at this stage. Among non-traditional students, the public sector probably has the advantage, though it is important to appreciate that expansion into this market will not cut into the private sector's present clientele.

With the effects of external factors being ambiguous, enrollment prospects for the two sectors are likely to depend heavily on the comparative ability of each to respond effectively to the coming period of stringency in enrollment and finances. Public and private colleges and universities alike will be strongly motivated to try to maintain enrollment in spite of the general decline. Doing so will require reaching out toward a larger share of a shrinking pool of eligible people—at least among traditional college-oriented age groups. While this canvassing will certainly extend to groups of students not presently going to college at all, it will also—as it has in the past—involve attempts by schools in one sector to attract students who would otherwise enroll in the other.

The prospect of intensified competition for a limited group of students has helped focus attention on the "tuition gap" between public and private institutions. But while price competition is important (and will be thoroughly discussed below) there are other conditions that may be equally so—quality, accessibility, selectivity, and variety of offerings—and that are less easily quantified than tuition differences; they may well be crucial in the years ahead. In fact, my own impression is that changes in these nonprice dimensions of public offerings were more important than changes in the tuition gap in explaining the great increase in the proportion of students enrolled in the public sector since 1960.

Geographic accessibility is the dimension of qualitative change that has been examined most intensively. Various studies have established that the cost savings involved in attending a local instead of a distant institution—perhaps $800 a year or more—do have a significant effect on the decision whether and where to attend college.[21] Historically, the competitive position of many urban private institutions has probably benefited from the more heavily rural concentration of state colleges and universities.[22] Thus the expanded enrollments at urban public universities in the last decade have undoubtedly increased the effective public-private cost gap for many private universities and colleges.[23] Similarly, the explosion in numbers and geographic dispersion of public community colleges must have absorbed many students who would otherwise have enrolled at the less selective private colleges in both metropolitan and smaller urban areas.

Changes in academic selection policies in the public sector have also helped to erode the competitive position of private institutions. The rapid growth of free-access community colleges has not only brought into higher education a whole new segment of students of "low ability" (as conventionally measured); it has probably also cut into the applicant pools of the many private colleges that are very unselective academically.[24]

21. The cost estimates are based on research by Howard P. Tuckman, "Local Colleges and the Demand for Higher Education: The Enrollment Inducing Effects of Location," *American Journal of Economics and Sociology*, vol. 32 (July 1973), pp. 257–68, and are expressed in 1975 dollars. Studies showing that geographic accessibility affects access include John Bishop, "Income, Ability, and the Demand for Higher Education," discussion paper 323–75 (University of Wisconsin–Madison, Institute for Research on Poverty, 1975; processed); Stephen A. Hoenack, "Private Demand for Higher Education in California" (Ph.D. dissertation, University of California, Berkeley, 1967); James W. Trent and Leland L. Medsker, *Beyond High School: A Psychosociological Study of 10,000 High School Graduates* (Jossey-Bass, 1968); and C. Arnold Anderson, Mary Jean Bowman, and Vincent Tinto, *Where Colleges Are and Who Attends?* (McGraw-Hill, 1972). Effects on choice are demonstrated by Meir G. Kohn, Charles F. Manski, and David S. Mundel, "An Empirical Investigation of Factors Which Influence College Going Behaviors" R1470-NSF (Santa Monica, Calif.: Rand Corporation, 1974), and Anderson and others, *Where Colleges Are.*

22. Even in 1970, following a decade of rapid expansion of urban public higher education, less than 60 percent of public enrollment was in metropolitan areas, compared with 70 percent of private enrollment. (See Carnegie Commission on Higher Education, *The Campus and the City: Maximizing Assets and Reducing Liabilities* [McGraw-Hill, 1972], p. 25.)

23. Probably the best known is the story of Boston University and the University of Massachusetts–Boston campus. (See John R. Silber, "Paying the Bill for College: The 'Private' Sector and the Public Interest," *Atlantic*, vol. 235 [May 1975], pp. 33–40.)

24. See Alexander W. Astin, Margo R. King, and Gerald T. Richardson, *The American Freshman: National Norms for Fall 1975* (Los Angeles: University of California and American Council on Education, Cooperative Institutional Research Program, Graduate School of Education, n.d.), p. 45. Leland L. Medsker and Dale

Meanwhile, as access barriers were falling for students of limited ability, the best of the public universities were becoming better and more selective, and comprehensive institutions were being developed for students of intermediate ability.[25] This emerging commitment to accommodate the needs of students at all ability levels, not only through differentiation of function among institutions (as in the three-tiered California system) but also through development of special remedial and honors programs at individual campuses, probably did much to enhance the appeal of public higher education.

All in all, there was a notable expansion in the variety of missions, academic programs, and life-style alternatives offered by public higher education in the 1960s. To a remarkable extent, public higher education managed to become all things to all people, and however valuable this policy was socially, it proved to be a highly effective marketing strategy.[26]

These developments were in good measure a natural consequence of rapid enrollment expansion. Geographic accessibility was enhanced by the construction of many new two-year colleges and by additional capacity in four-year institutions in areas (especially cities) where need was greatest. More varied educational offerings were feasible with the ready availability of funds and a burgeoning market among students. The question for the future is whether the competitive advantages of the public sector can—or should—continue to increase in a time of enrollment decline and financial strain. Certainly the pressure to attract students will be greater than ever. Yet many of the more obvious avenues

---

Tillery, in *Breaking the Access Barriers: A Profile of Two-Year Colleges* (McGraw-Hill, 1971), p. 126, note that ability distributions of students at public and nonsectarian private two-year colleges are essentially the same. And Astin and Lee, surveying the so-called invisible colleges, which are roughly equivalent to the Carnegie Commission's liberal arts II category, report that they have generally low levels of academic selectivity. (Alexander W. Astin and Calvin B. T. Lee, *The Invisible Colleges: A Profile of Small, Private Colleges with Limited Resources* [McGraw-Hill, 1972], chap. 4.)

25. The transformation of normal schools and teachers colleges into multipurpose state colleges and universities is described in E. Alden Dunham, *Colleges of the Forgotten Americans: A Profile of State Colleges and Universities* (McGraw-Hill, 1969).

26. R. E. Anderson's examination of the expressed college preferences of high-ability students suggests that the perceived quality of public institutions rose substantially relative to private colleges between 1964 and 1972. (Richard E. Anderson, "Private/Public Higher Education and the Competition for High Ability Students," *Journal of Human Resources*, vol. 10 [Fall 1975], pp. 500–511.)

of qualitative improvement appear to be foreclosed by the slackening market. It is hard to imagine that the geographic accessibility of public institutions can continue to increase as enrollments stabilize. Similarly, innovation and product differentiation through the simple addition of new programs and new institutions is probably at an end. New programs from now on will be at the expense of existing programs. The costs of risk-taking in such an environment will be very high, and the imperatives of bureaucratic self-protection at their most urgent. Much will depend on the quality of leadership, and experience is likely to be very different in different states. It is clearly important from a public policy standpoint that decisions about qualitative change in public higher education—developing new programs, opening or closing or relocating campuses, changing admissions or graduation requirements, and the like—be made with an eye to the overall educational needs of the community, and not with the aim of protecting the interests of any existing set of public institutions.

Private higher education is of course vulnerable to the same kinds of bureaucratic pressures and imperatives as the public sector; many of the difficulties of managing a university are a necessary (and worthwhile) price for its collegial nature. Accountability to a board of trustees is, however, not the same as accountability to a legislature, and one suspects that the additional layers of bureaucracy embodied in university-government relations and attendant rigidities of budgeting and allocation will weigh heavily on public institutions. Overall, it seems likely that the competitive position of public higher education in its nonprice dimensions will cease to advance relative to the private sector, and may well decline. If this is true, it suggests that the future of private higher education may not be so bleak as a simple projection of a declining enrollment proportion on a soon-to-be declining enrollment base would suggest. But it also suggests that the question of price competition—the tuition gap—may come to play an increasingly critical role.

Measuring the Tuition Gap

Discussion of the tuition gap issue has been clouded by conflicting claims about how wide the gap is, how fast it is getting wider, and how wide it is likely to become. These disputes derive partly from the use of different ways of measuring the gap and partly from different data

Table 3-3. *Public and Private Tuition Rates and Three Measures of the Tuition Gap, Selected Academic Years, 1929–30 to 1973–74*

Year	Tuition (current dollars)[a] Public institutions	Tuition (current dollars)[a] Private institutions	Ratio, private to public	Constant-dollar difference (1967 dollars)	Current-dollar difference as fraction of disposable income per capita
1929–30	63	226	3.6	318	23.9
1931–32	60	234	3.9	382	33.7
1933–34	65	227	3.5	418	44.8
1935–36	70	224	3.2	375	33.6
1937–38	70	228	3.3	367	28.6
1939–40	64	239	3.7	421	32.6
1941–42	78	251	3.2	392	24.9
1943–44	89	289	3.2	386	20.5
1945–46	91	273	3.0	338	16.9
1947–48	194	368	1.9	260	14.8
1949–50	177	416	2.4	335	18.9
1951–52	157	430	2.7	351	18.6
1953–54	139	464	3.3	406	20.5
1955–56	141	502	3.6	450	21.7
1957–58	162	584	3.6	501	23.4
1959–60	175	673	3.8	570	26.1
1961–62	194	796	4.1	672	30.3
1963–64	218	896	4.1	739	31.7
1965–66	241	1,045	4.3	851	33.0
1966–67	254	1,078	4.2	848	31.6
1967–68	279	1,152	4.1	873	31.7
1969–70	334	1,348	4.0	923	32.4
1971–72	385	1,591	4.1	994	33.5
1972–73	407	1,705	4.2	1,036	33.8
1973–74	428	1,815	4.2	1,042	32.3

Sources: Tuition, through 1967–68, June A. O'Neill, *Sources of Funds to Colleges and Universities* (Carnegie Foundation for the Advancement of Teaching, 1973), p. 44, and other years, NCES, *Financial Statistics of Institutions of Higher Education: Current Funds Revenues and Expenditures* (GPO), relevant issues, and NCES, *Fall Enrollment in Higher Education*, relevant issues; per capita disposable personal income and consumer price index, U.S. Bureau of the Census, *Historical Statistics of the United States, Colonial Times to 1970* (GPO, 1975), pt. 1, pp. 225, 210, respectively, and *Economic Report of the President, January 1975*, pp. 269, 301, respectively.

a. Gross tuition and fee revenue divided by full-time-equivalent enrollment, calculated as full-time enrollment plus one-third of part-time enrollment. Full-time-equivalent enrollment as reported by the institution is used for 1971–72 to 1973–74. Because of differences in definition of the enrollment rate the 1969–70 to 1973–74 series had to be linked to the 1929–30 to 1967–68 series by deflating the former by 1.13. (This brought the two methods of calculating the 1967–68 figure into agreement.)

sources. Thus, without becoming involved in a detailed discussion of alternative tuition price indexes,[27] it is useful here to determine what the price situation actually is, has been, and is likely to become.

The immediate problem is what measure of the tuition gap to use.[28] The two most popular are the ratio of private to public tuition and the dollar difference between them (adjusted for inflation), but each has its drawbacks. Presumably at any given time, it is the dollar gap rather than the ratio that influences the buyer when he or she is deciding whether the advantages of a private compared to a public institution are worth the added costs. But over time, the ability of the average buyer to pay the added cost of a private higher education rises with rising income, and the dollar difference measure (even adjusted for inflation) fails to allow for this. Therefore, a new measure of the tuition gap, in addition to the ratio and the real-dollar gap, is used below. This is the "income-deflated" gap, defined as the dollar gap deflated by a measure of average income. This last captures both the significance of dollar differences and the increase over time in ability to pay, and is probably the best simple index of the comparative cost situation of public and private higher education over time.[29]

A General View of the Tuition Gap

It is misleading to talk about "the" tuition gap, since prices at various categories of public and private institutions differ so greatly, and since different students even at the same institution pay various "net" prices owing to student aid. Nonetheless, some generalities are worth noting.

Table 3-3 shows several measures of the gap over the period from 1930 to 1974. The real-dollar difference between public and private tuition

27. For more detailed work, see D. Kent Halstead, *Higher Education Prices and Price Indexes*, U.S. Office of Education (GPO, 1975) and June A. O'Neill, *Sources of Funds to Colleges and Universities* (Carnegie Foundation for the Advancement of Teaching, 1973).

28. The tuition gap and the total cost gap between public and private colleges are not precisely the same. But, as noted in chapter 1, it is tuition rather than room and board charges that account for most public-private cost differences. While between 1961–62 and 1973–74 the tuition gap in 1967 dollars increased from $672 to $1,042, the difference in room and board actually declined in constant dollars from $122 to $72. Travel costs might affect the total cost gap considerably for some classes of institutions. But geographic accessibility is treated in the previous section as a nonprice competitive factor, and is not further considered here. Hence, it seems most useful to concentrate on tuition (or the tuition gap) as the key to the private sector's competitive financial condition.

29. I am indebted to Robert Hartman for suggesting this measure.

Table 3-4. *Ratios of Tuition at Private to Tuition at Public Institutions of Higher Education, by Level of Institution, Academic Years 1961–62 to 1975–76*[a]

Year	All institutions	Universities	Other four-year institutions	Two-year institutions
1961–62	4.2	4.0	4.6	6.1
1962–63	4.3	4.3	4.5	6.2
1963–64	4.3	4.3	4.3	6.6
1964–65	4.5	4.4	4.6	7.1
1965–66	4.5	4.2	4.5	7.0
1966–67	4.5	4.0	4.5	7.0
1967–68	4.6	4.2	4.6	6.2
1968–69	4.7	4.3	4.8	5.6
1969–70	4.7	4.2	4.8	5.8
1970–71	4.8	4.1	4.8	6.0
1971–72	4.8	4.1	4.9	6.1
1972–73	4.7	4.1	4.5	5.7
1973–74	4.5	4.2	4.2	5.3
1974–75	4.6	4.1	4.2	5.2
1975–76	4.6	4.1	4.3	5.2

Sources: 1961–62 to 1963–64, Kenneth A. Simon and Martin M. Frankel, *Projections of Educational Statistics to 1981–82*, NCES, DHEW (OE) 73-11105 (GPO, 1973); other years, ibid., . . . *to 1984–85*, NCES 76-210 (GPO, 1976).

a. Ratio of enrollment-weighted averages of tuition and fees paid by full-time, home-state undergraduate students.

has grown pretty steadily over that period, as increases in both public and private tuition have outpaced the rate of rise in the general price level. But neither the ratio nor the income-deflated gap has shown such consistency. Both those measures dipped quite low after World War II when public tuition rose very fast because of high fees charged to veterans on the GI bill.[30] But if recent years are compared to the prewar period, it is apparent that there has been no dramatic long-term change either in the tuition ratio or the income-deflated gap. Over time, the difference between public and private tuition has not risen faster than the ability of families to pay.

Even through the 1960s, when many observers were alarmed by the supposedly widening tuition gap, these data show little tendency for either the tuition ratio or the income-deflated gap to change. This is partly a function of the data series employed, since tuition ratios derived from U.S. Office of Education data on student charges did rise during

30. See O'Neill, *Sources of Funds*, p. 8.

the 1960s (see table 3-4).[31] Even this rise, however, was almost wholly the product of the rapid shift in public enrollment toward low-cost community colleges where the gap was greatest. Tuition ratios calculated separately for universities, four-year colleges, and two-year colleges from the Office of Education data were all fairly constant during the 1960s, as table 3-4 shows. This suggests two important points. First, another such massive enrollment shift toward two-year colleges is unlikely to occur, so a further rise in the tuition ratio from this source is not to be expected and, second, a properly calculated tuition price index, which, corrected for the shift in enrollment composition in the same manner that the consumer price index adjusts for changing consumption patterns, would not show a rising tuition ratio in these circumstances.[32] Reports of a widening tuition gap (at least in ratio or income-deflated terms) are greatly exaggerated.

A Closer Look at Recent Developments

This general picture omits important detail about what is happening at different types of private colleges and, given the existence of student aid, among students at various income levels. Tables 3-5, 3-6, and 3-7 attempt to sort out some of these developments by looking at how several different measures of the tuition gap changed at the various Carnegie classes of private institutions between 1966–67 and 1973–74.[33]

The three tables differ in the way they handle student aid grants. In principle one would like to know for each student the actual price he

31. The series used in table 3-4 measures tuition charged to full-time, home-state undergraduates; that used in table 3-3 measures tuition charged to all students. Presumably this accounts for the difference.

32. See Halstead, *Higher Education Prices.*

33. The gap measures are calculated by comparing prices at various Carnegie classes of private institutions (defined in the Glossary) to the average price at all public institutions. This is preferable to comparing particular Carnegie classes of public and private institutions, because the competition is not, in fact, that narrow. Highly selective liberal arts colleges, for example, compete with both public universities and four-year colleges. Less selective liberal arts colleges compete with public two-year colleges as well as other public institutions. Comparisons of public with private institutions by Carnegie class can also be found in Carnegie Commission on Higher Education, *Tuition: A Supplemental Statement to the Report of the Carnegie Commission on Higher Education on "Who Pays? Who Benefits? Who Should Pay?"* (Carnegie Foundation for the Advancement of Teaching, 1974), and National Commission on the Financing of Postsecondary Education, *Financing Postsecondary Education in the United States* (GPO, 1973).

Table 3-5. *The Public-Private Tuition Gap for High-Income Students, by Carnegie Classification, Academic Years 1966–67 and 1973–74*[a]

Classification[b]	Ratio: Tuition at private to tuition at public institutions			Difference in tuition at private and public institutions (1967 dollars)			Difference as percent of median family income			Difference as percent of disposable income per capita		
	1966–67	1973–74	Percentage change	1966–67	1973–74	Percentage change	1966–67	1973–74	Percentage change	1966–67	1973–74	Percentage change
Doctoral-granting universities	5.3	5.3	0	1,233	1,510	22.5	16.0	17.2	7.5	46.1	47.9	3.9
Comprehensive colleges and universities	3.6	4.0	11.1	745	1,040	39.6	9.7	11.8	21.6	27.8	33.0	18.7
Highly selective liberal arts colleges	5.2	5.1	−1.9	1,205	1,423	18.1	15.6	16.2	3.8	45.0	45.2	0.4
Less selective liberal arts colleges	3.2	3.4	6.3	635	841	32.4	8.2	9.6	17.1	23.7	26.7	12.7
Two-year institutions	3.0	2.7	−10.0	586	595	1.5	7.6	6.8	−10.5	21.9	18.9	−13.7

Sources: Tuition, public, Paul F. Mertins and Norman J. Brandt, *Financial Statistics of Institutions of Higher Education: Current Funds Revenues and Expenditures—1973–74*, *Summary Data*, NCES 76-121 (GPO, 1976) and corresponding publication for 1966–67, and NCES, *Opening Fall Enrollment in Higher Education*, 1966 and 1973 issues; tuition, private, U.S. Office of Education, unpublished data; median family income, D. Kent Halstead, *Higher Education Prices and Price Indexes*, U.S. Office of Education (GPO, 1975), p. 106; disposable income per capita, *Economic Report of the President*, February 1975, p. 269 (figures are averages of 1966 and 1967 and of 1973 and 1974 data).
a. Tuition is gross tuition revenue per full-time-equivalent student, assuming no student aid. See text for discussion of the method used to calculate the gap measures.
b. See Glossary for a description of the categories.

Table 3-6. *The Public-Private Tuition Gap for Average-Income Students, by Carnegie Classification, Academic Years 1966–67 and 1973–74*[a]

Classification[b]	Ratio: Tuition at private to tuition at public institutions			Difference in tuition at private and public institutions (1967 dollars)			Difference as percent of median family income			Difference as percent of disposable income per capita		
	1966–67	1973–74	Percentage change	1966–67	1973–74	Percentage change	1966–67	1973–74	Percentage change	1966–67	1973–74	Percentage change
Doctoral-granting universities	4.8	5.4	12.5	825	1,133	37.3	10.7	12.9	20.6	30.8	35.9	16.6
Comprehensive colleges and universities	4.2	4.6	9.5	697	929	33.3	9.0	10.6	17.8	26.0	29.5	13.5
Highly selective liberal arts colleges	5.7	5.7	0	1,025	1,195	16.6	13.3	13.6	2.3	38.3	37.9	−1.0
Less selective liberal arts colleges	3.6	3.6	0	564	660	17.0	7.3	7.5	2.7	21.1	20.9	−0.9
Two-year institutions	3.7	3.0	−18.9	579	513	−11.4	7.5	5.8	−22.7	21.6	16.3	−24.5

Sources: Same as table 3-5.
a. Tuition is tuition revenue net of student aid grants per full-time-equivalent student.
b. See Glossary for a description of the categories.

Table 3-7. *The Public-Private Tuition Gap for Low-Income Students, by Carnegie Classification, Academic Years 1966–67 and 1973–74*[a]

Classification[b]	Ratio Tuition at private to tuition at public institutions			Difference in tuition at private and public institutions (1967 dollars)			Difference as percent of median family income			Difference as percent of disposable income per capita		
	1966–67	1973–74	Per-centage change	1966–67	1973–74	Per-centage change	1966–67	1973–74	Per-centage change	1966–67	1973–74	Per-centage change
Doctoral-granting universities[c]	1.1	6.4	481.8	9	379	...	0.1	4.3	...	0.3	12.0	...
Comprehensive colleges and universities	9.5	11.0	15.8	601	707	17.6	7.8	8.0	2.6	22.5	22.4	−0.4
Highly selective liberal arts colleges	10.4	11.5	10.6	665	739	11.1	8.6	8.4	−2.3	24.8	23.5	−5.2
Less selective liberal arts colleges	6.9	5.2	−24.6	422	298	−29.4	5.5	3.4	−38.2	15.8	9.5	−39.9
Two-year institutions	9.0	6.0	−33.3	565	349	−38.2	7.3	4.0	−45.2	21.1	11.1	−47.4

Sources: Same as table 3-5.
a. Tuition revenue per aided full-time-equivalent student, assuming one-third of students receive aid.
b. See Glossary for a description of the categories.
c. See page 167, note 36.

has to pay, net of the value of whatever aid he receives.[34] The first table attempts to determine the prices facing high-income individuals who are not eligible for aid, by estimating prices without deducting any student aid. The purpose of the second table is to estimate the average net price faced by enrollees by deducting from gross tuition revenue per student the amount of money per student returned in the form of aid. That is, this calculation pretends that the grant aid is spread evenly among all students. The third table allows crudely for the fact that aid is dominantly for low-income individuals, by showing the net price the average aided individual would face if aid were received by one-third of all students.[35]

The tables show, first, that the gap differs greatly among types of institutions, with the widest gaps at doctoral-granting universities and more selective liberal arts colleges. Of course, these are generally the highest quality institutions, and that helps to offset the effects of the wider gap. Comparison of tables 3-5 and 3-7 also shows that in general student aid significantly reduces the gap facing low-income individuals, especially at the more selective liberal arts colleges.[36] (The relation of the effective tuition gap to students' family income level is pursued in more detail below.)

In examining changes in the gap from 1966–67 to 1973–74 shown in tables 3-5, 3-6, and 3-7, the general conclusion is that most types of private institutions have held their own fairly well, particularly with regard to the most relevant measure, the income-deflated gap. The main exceptions seem to be at the comprehensive universities and the less selective liberal arts colleges, where the prices faced by high-income students have been rising rapidly compared to the public competition.

34. This at least is true if students have good information about aid offers they might receive. Although such information is, in fact, often not readily available to students, the little evidence that exists suggests that students are about as responsive to changes in aid as to changes in tuition.

35. The one-third figure is consistent with Haven and Horch's finding that 37 percent of students in a 1969–70 sample received student aid. (See Elizabeth W. Haven and Dwight H. Horch, *How College Students Finance Their Education: A National Survey of the Educational Interests, Aspirations, and Finances of College Sophomores in 1969–70* [College Scholarship Service of the College Entrance Examination Board, 1972].) The general approach follows that used by the National Commission on the Financing of Postsecondary Education in *Financing Postsecondary Education*, p. 204.

36. The figures for doctoral-granting institutions in table 3-7 are not significant. Much of the very large amount of aid at these institutions consists of graduate fellowships, which often far exceed tuition and are not given on the basis of need.

This is worrisome, especially for the liberal arts colleges, which have plenty of other problems (see below). At this last group of colleges, the rapid rise in "posted prices" has been accompanied by a fairly dramatic narrowing of the price gap facing low-income students. Though part of this expanded aid has come from state and federal programs, much has been financed by the institutions themselves (see chapter 2). It is not clear how long these institutions can continue to raise the price for higher-income students in order to finance their operations, while holding it down for lower-income students, presumably in response to competitive pressure from public campuses.

But this danger signal, echoed less sharply at comprehensive colleges, stands in contrast to a general picture of a tuition gap that—at most institutions and for most students—has not been rising relative to their families' ability to pay.

A Further Note on Student Aid

When tables 3-5 and 3-7 are compared, the dollar gap is seen to be considerably narrower for low-income than for high-income students because private institutions provide more aid per student than public institutions do. But these tables cannot fully portray how the gap varies with income. Though the data do not exist to provide definitive estimates of this variation, a common pattern is shown in figure 3-2.

This figure demonstrates how the cost of a year's attendance at a public and a private institution might vary with a dependent student's family income. A student is assumed to pay $5,500 a year at a private college—$2,500 in tuition and $3,000 in other costs—and $3,500 a year at a public institution—$500 in tuition and $3,000 in other costs. Grant aid at the private institution is assumed to be provided to the extent of need as determined by the College Scholarship Service needs-analysis tables, less a $2,000 allowance for the student's own contribution through earnings and a loan.[37] This approximates a typical aid pattern at selective private institutions. The public school is assumed to offer no aid beyond the student's basic educational opportunity grant. The aid pat-

---

37. The need calculation is based on a table that shows the typical relation observed between need level and parental income level in a sample of students surveyed by the College Entrance Examination Board, found in Humphrey Doermann, "The Future Market for College Education," in *A Role for Marketing in College Admissions*, papers presented at the Colloquium on College Admissions, 1976 (CEEB, 1976), p. 52.

Figure 3-2. *Estimated Cost of Attending a Public or a Private Institution as a Function of Family Income*

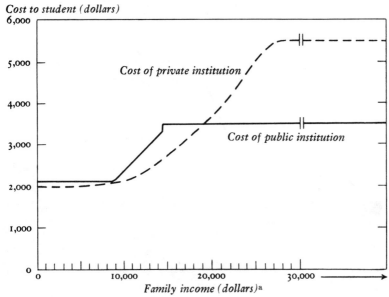

Cost to student (dollars)

*Family income (dollars)*a

Source: See text for the description of the calculations underlying the figure.
a. Assumes a family of four with $4,000 in exclusions and deductions from income for the purpose of cal-culating the basic educational opportunity grant.

tern depicted would apply to a student from a family of four that had $4,000 in allowable exclusions and deductions from its income.[38]

The resulting picture is probably a reasonable approximation of the cost situation facing a student of high ability (that is, one who is eligible to attend an elite private institution) in a state without an extensive state scholarship program or other aid to students at public institutions. If such a student comes from a very low-income family, he faces no tuition gap. And as income rises into the $6,000 to $12,000 range the cost gap actually becomes negative, because the basic grant drops off much faster with income than does aid based on the needs-analysis formula of the College Scholarship Service. The private college is as cheap or cheaper than the public college for students with family incomes up to something like $19,000 a year. Beyond that income level the comparative cost of the

38. Calculations of the relation between award level and income level for the basic grant are drawn from W. Lee Hansen and Robert J. Lampman, "Basic Opportunity Grants for Higher Education: Good Intentions and Mixed Results," *Challenge*, vol. 17 (November/December, 1974), pp. 46–51.

Figure 3-3. *Estimated Cost Gap between Public and Private Institutions as a Percentage of Family Income*

Cost gap as percent of family income

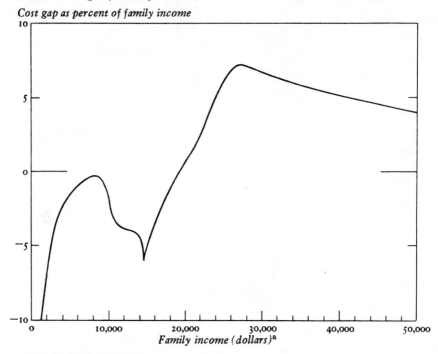

Family income (dollars)[a]

Source: Based on figure 3-2.

a. Assumes a family of four with $4,000 in exclusions and deductions from income for the purpose of calculating the basic educational opportunity grant.

private college rises rapidly. Figure 3-3 shows the dramatic rise in the cost gap relative to income as the family's income level rises.

The picture presented is somewhat exaggerated, inasmuch as most public colleges provide aid from their own (and other outside) funds, too, and because only the more affluent private colleges can provide aid to the full extent of need. But the point needs reinforcing that the tuition gap, especially among able students, hits hardest those families with income somewhat above the median. This, of course, is the source of concern over the "missing middle-income student" (really the missing upper-middle-income student) on some private campuses. Data on the income distribution of students suggest that this concern is not wholly misplaced: there has been a distinct drop-off in percentage terms in the representation of the upper-middle-income class in private higher education over the last decade.

Table 3-8 shows how the percentage distribution of full-time freshmen has been changing by income class. At private institutions other than universities, the percentage of students whose family income lay between the U.S. median and twice the U.S. median (roughly between $15,000 and $30,000 a year) fell substantially between 1966 and 1975.[39] It is interesting also that these types of private institutions are enrolling relatively more low-income students while some types of public institutions have tended to enroll more high-income students. This pattern of change can plausibly be related to the student aid pattern just described.

The Future of the Gap

Much of the concern about the future of private higher education has stemmed from the fear of a yawning tuition gap. But, as recent experience suggests, it is not really so clear that the gap will continue to widen.

The ratio of private to public tuition (gross of student aid) rose in the 1960s only for home-state undergraduates—apparently for other groups the gap narrowed. And even the rise that did occur was primarily due to the growth of community colleges—a phenomenon unlikely to recur. So a simple projection of recent trends would point to the continuation of something like the present ratio of private to public tuition.

An analysis of the underlying forces that determine the gap points in the same direction. Movements in the gap are governed by movements in costs and in the proportion of costs met by tuition. In an industry like higher education in which productivity increases are hard to achieve, there is good reason to expect unit costs to rise relative to the prices of other goods—unless quality falls.[40] But there seems little reason to expect

39. These data, from the survey of freshmen conducted by Alexander Astin and coworkers, are based on student-reported incomes. A similar pattern is shown in less detailed Census data, although in the latter the drop seems to come at somewhat lower income levels. (See U.S. Bureau of the Census, *Current Population Reports*, series P-20, no. 185 [GPO, 1969], and no. 286 [GPO, 1975].)

40. William J. Baumol, "The Macroeconomics of Unbalanced Growth: The Anatomy of Urban Crisis," *American Economic Review*, vol. 57 (June 1967), pp. 415–26.

Table 3-8. *Percentage Distribution of Freshman Enrollment in Public and Private Institutions of Higher Education, by Income Class, 1966, 1970, and 1975*

| Parental income | Universities | | | | | | Four-year colleges | | | | | | Two-year colleges | | | | | |
| | Public | | | Private | | | Public | | | Private | | | Public | | | Private | | |
	1966	1970	1975	1966	1970	1975	1966	1970	1975	1966	1970	1975	1966	1970	1975	1966	1970	1975
Less than half the median	12	7	9	8	7	7	21	14	16	12	10	15	17	21	20	16	14	27
Half the median to the median	27	26	27	19	23	19	33	35	33	22	27	30	30	37	38	30	31	34
The median to one and a half times the median	31	31	29	26	27	24	28	30	27	28	27	24	30	26	24	28	24	19
One and a half times to twice the median	14	16	16	15	16	15	11	12	13	15	14	12	13	9	10	13	12	9
More than twice the median	17	20	20	32	28	36	8	9	12	24	23	21	11	7	9	14	19	11

Sources: Calculated from data in Alexander W. Astin and others, *The American Freshman: National Norms for Fall 1975* (Los Angeles: University of California and American Council on Education, Cooperative Institutional Research Program, Graduate School of Education, n.d.); staff of the Office of Research, American Council on Education, *National Norms for Entering College Freshmen—Fall 1970*, ACE Research Reports, vol. 5, no. 6 (1970), and Astin and others, ibid., *Fall 1966*, vol. 2, no. 1 (1967); and official median income data from *Economic Report of the President*, January 1977, p. 216.

costs per student to rise more rapidly in the private than in the public sector in the years ahead—at least so long as financial pressures encourage tight management policies. Neither does it seem likely in the present and prospective political climate (as well as such things can be judged) that state government subsidies will expand to permit a drop in the share of costs covered by tuition in the public sector. A rise in the tuition ratio, then, if it comes, will probably be due to a rise in the share of costs borne by tuition in private institutions. But though this cannot be ruled out, there seems no obvious reason why it should occur.[41]

Even if the tuition ratio stays constant or falls moderately, there is of course little doubt that the real-dollar gap in tuition will widen, as it has for over twenty years, because costs will most probably continue to rise faster than the general price level. But the dollar gap should be judged in relation to ability to pay. And as figure 1-2 and table 3-3 indicate, since about 1960 there has been little tendency for either public or private prices or the gap between them to grow relative to income. Hence, there is good reason for optimism that private institutions will retain their competitive position in relation to public institutions in the years ahead, although experience will probably not be uniform either among the states or across types of institutions.

A final cautionary note: *ability* to pay cannot necessarily be equated with *willingness* to pay. While the cost of private higher education may not rise as a percentage of family income, the cost of private higher education will still be rising relative to the cost of other things that could be bought with that money. Currently, for an affluent family a private higher education costs about the same as a public higher education plus a new car or a trip to Europe. (The private sector must be glad that most parents do not give their children the choice among these options.) Quite plausibly in twenty years the difference will be two new cars or a modest summer cottage. Even though parents may be able to afford the private college choice, their willingness to pay for it remains imponderable.[42]

41. However, table 2-A4 indicates that the major research universities have shown increasing dependence on tuition in recent years.

42. Technically, this is a question of the income elasticity of demand for private higher education. This elasticity has typically been found to be rather high, but the studies available are hardly precise enough or powerful enough to settle the doubts raised above. (See Thomas D. Hopkins, "Higher Education Enrollment Demand," *Economic Inquiry*, vol. 12 [March 1974], pp. 53–65; Joseph E. Hight, "The Demand for Higher Education in the U.S., 1927–72; The Public and Private Institutions," *Journal of Human Resources*, vol. 10 [Fall 1975], pp. 512–20; and Barnes, "Determinants of the College Going and College Choice Decision.")

The Effects of Tuition on Enrollment

Measuring the tuition gap is only half the story—and in some ways the less important half—in examining the role played by tuition differences in determining public relative to private enrollments. The other half is the effects tuition prices have on student enrollment decisions. Much statistical work on this question has appeared in recent years and, although the areas of ignorance are vast, some systematic findings have begun to emerge.

Overview of Empirical Studies

The most important task in providing a nontechnical survey of statistical work in an area like the demand for higher education where results are not clear-cut is to endow the reader with a kind of "intelligent skepticism"—leaving him neither with a blind and unwarranted faith in the accuracy of the numbers nor with an equally uninformed disbelief in them. To achieve this, it is necessary not just to report and summarize findings, but also to convey some sense of the data and methods employed, and their strengths and limitations.

Most of the empirical studies that have examined the effects of price on enrollment decisions have followed the standard econometric practice of attempting to infer such effects from information about enrollment decisions students have actually made.

A few have instead employed the refreshingly straightforward technique of asking students what they would do if the price changed. Of course, it is hard to know whether students answer such questions honestly[43]—or whether, for that matter, they even know themselves how they would respond.

43. These studies have been based on surveys of students receiving financial aid who may have incentives to indicate to official questioners that the aid was decisive in their enrollment choice. (See Larry L. Leslie and Jonathan D. Fife, "The College Student Grant Study," *Journal of Higher Education*, vol. 45 [December 1974], pp. 651–71, and Daryl Carlson, "Student Price Response Coefficients for Grants, Loans, Work-Study Aid, and Tuition Changes: An Analysis of Student Surveys," Stanford Research Institute [paper presented to the Policy Development Group, Office of the Assistant Secretary of Education, U.S. Department of Health, Education, and Welfare, November 13, 1974; processed].) A critique and reinterpretation of Leslie and Fife's work is George B. Weatherby, " 'The College Student Grant Study': A Comment," *Journal of Higher Education*, vol. 46 (September/October 1975), pp. 601–06.

Much of the early work on enrollment demand was based on aggregate enrollment data collected by the U.S. government and involved either study of enrollment variation across the states for a single year or for the United States as a whole over time. The object of these studies was to try to determine how much of the observed enrollment variation could be accounted for statistically by variations in tuition rates and how much by other measurable factors such as income levels. The hope was that the statistical correlation between price and enrollment resulted from the effect of price on student enrollment decisions, and would therefore show how the average student would respond to a change in tuition. Most of these have been studies of "access" to higher education, aimed at explaining total enrollment, but two by Thomas Hopkins and Joseph Hight have examined public and private enrollment separately.[44]

More recently the focus of research has shifted from aggregate data to data on individual students. Studies in this vein include a nationwide study of access conducted by John Bishop and two studies by Stephen A. Hoenack (one jointly with William C. Weiler) focusing on demand for enrollment at a single public institution. While none of the above examined choice among alternative institutions, there have recently been several very intriguing studies of college choice based on individual student data. The best known of these are the Radner-Miller study for the Carnegie Commission (RM hereafter) and the Kohn-Manski-Mundel study for Rand (KMM hereafter).[45]

The methodology used in these studies of "choice" of institution is

44. State cross-section studies include Arthur J. Corazzini, Dennis J. Dugan, and Henry G. Grabowski, "Determinants and Distributional Aspects of Enrollment in U.S. Higher Education," *Journal of Human Resources*, vol. 7 (Winter 1972), pp. 39–59; Paul Feldman and Stephen Hoenack, "Private Demand for Higher Education in the United States," in *The Economics and Financing of Higher Education in the United States*, A Compendium of Papers Submitted to the Joint Economic Committee, 91:1 (GPO, 1969), pp. 375–95; and Thomas Hopkins, "Higher Education Enrollment Demand." Time series studies are Robert Campbell and Barry N. Siegel, "The Demand for Higher Education in the United States, 1919–1964," *American Economic Review*, vol. 57 (June 1967), pp. 482–94, and Hight, "The Demand for Higher Education."

45. Bishop, "Income, Ability, and the Demand for Higher Education"; Hoenack, *Private Demand for Higher Education;* Hoenack and Weiler, "Cost-Related Tuition Policies and University Enrollments," *Journal of Human Resources*, vol. 10 (Summer 1975), pp. 332–60; Roy Radner and Leonard S. Miller, *Demand and Supply in U.S. Higher Education* (McGraw-Hill, 1975); and Kohn and others, "Empirical Investigation of Factors Which Influence College Going Behaviors."

basically the following. The studies first try to impute to each student in a sample of students a set of available college-going alternatives, taking into account location, academic ability, and the like. They then gather information about the characteristics of the colleges available to the various students (their cost, selectivity, and so forth) and background characteristics of the students and their families. A statistical technique called conditional logit analysis is then used to infer how the characteristics of the colleges and the students interacted to produce the set of college choices the students actually made. In effect, the computer tries out alternative weighting schemes for the factors impinging on the decision process (cost, quality, family income), and selects the scheme that best accounts for the decisions the students made.

While models like these provide much the richest conceptual picture of the student choice process among existing studies and hold great promise for the future, their present formulations have some serious handicaps. First, the data demands are enormous, and do not come near to being met in practice. Most students are eligible to attend hundreds of colleges, and it is not practicable to determine which these institutions are, let alone the cost each student would face at each one (taking into account travel distance, financial aid, and so on)—nor would the computers be able to handle so much data. Even after simplifying by arbitrarily selecting out a subsample of schools for inclusion for each student (KMM) or grouping schools into a small number of types (RM), good measures of costs and other college attributes, which are essential for reliable estimation, are very hard to obtain.

The second problem is that in order to make the computations manageable, many constraining assumptions about the nature of the student choice process must be introduced a priori. RM, for example, boil down the student choice process so that the decisions of students at a wide range of income levels over ten types of institutions can be characterized by just two numbers—one showing the effect of college cost and family income and the other the effect of student ability and college selectivity. The authors then use the structural assumptions embodied in the model to translate these two estimated parameters back into a rich and detailed portrait of choices by students at various income levels over the various institution types. It is tempting but dangerous when confronted with the final product of such a study to interpret as empirical findings relationships that are in fact built into the model a priori—such as, for example, lower price responsiveness among higher income groups. Of course, to the extent that the underlying structural assumptions are accurate (and most seem at least plausible), a model of this kind can provide a remarkably comprehensive picture of student demand. Unfortunately, many of the assumptions are hard to verify empirically.[46]

Neither the KMM nor the RM model is particularly oriented toward the analysis of public-private college choice. Another choice model, that by Gary T. Barnes, is better adapted to this analysis. Barnes used a two-step formulation, the first step being the choice of whether to go to college, and the second, for those planning to attend college, the choice of whether to enroll at a public or a private institution.

All these types of studies, whether based on aggregate or individual data, have advantages and disadvantages in isolating the effects of price on enrollment decisions. The underlying purpose of such demand investigation is to identify a causal relationship: to infer what would happen to enrollment behavior (either the access or the choice decision) if prices changed. Successful estimation requires that three key prerequisites be met:

There must be adequate variation in the price variable. Conceptually, the goal is to measure the effect on enrollment of some set of institutions (or of all institutions) raising their price. To approximate this situation statistically, it is essential to observe similar students facing different prices at similar institutions. This is a real problem in the "choice" studies, because a good part of the difference in cost among different institutions that such studies can capture is related to differences in nonprice characteristics of the institutions—expenditures per student, selectivity, and

46. The RM results are a foundation stone for the comprehensive planning models currently in vogue. These models can be very useful as heuristic devices for illustrating the potential effects of policy changes, as well as for conveying something of the immense complexity of the higher education system and the enormous amount still to be learned about it. Good examples of models being used in this way are in the National Commission report, *Financing Postsecondary Education*, and its supporting volume by Daryl E. Carlson, James Farmer, and George B. Weathersby, *A Framework for Analyzing Postsecondary Education Financing Policies* (GPO, 1974). But the consumer should be aware that large gaps in present data and understanding are often filled by assumption, sometimes dubious assumption. (An egregious example is the use of the RM results for freshmen as estimates of the responsiveness of graduate enrollments to tuition changes! Ibid., pp. 46–55.) For further discussion, see Stephen P. Dresch, "A Critique of Planning Models for Postsecondary Education: Current Feasibility, Potential Relevance, and a Prospectus for Further Research," *Journal of Higher Education*, vol. 46 (May/June 1975), pp. 245–86.

others.[47] These sources of apparent price variation—really different prices for different products—are confounded with "real" price variation (where, for example, similar institutions in different states charge different prices) in ways that are very hard to sort out. The best way to counteract this problem would be through more extensive samples covering more states (none of the existing choice studies includes more than four states) and through more complete measures of the nonprice characteristics of the institutions. In the absence of such improved studies, it is not possible to be certain about either the direction or the severity of the bias introduced by this problem.[48]

Factors other than prices affecting enrollment behavior must be considered (the problem of ceteris paribus). In measuring the net relationship between prices and enrollment outcomes among a group or groups of potential students, it is necessary to allow for the presence of other factors, for example, parental income, education level, and student ability, that independently affect enrollment decisions. Several statistical techniques (the most common being multiple regression) have been used to control for these other social and demographic characteristics of students in the studies under review. Certainly the best measures of such variables are to be found in studies based on individual student data and this is one of their real strengths; the worst are in the time series studies. Further darkening the picture for time series studies is the fact that many background variables—incomes, educational attainment, and others—tend to change gradually over time along with the price variables. This problem (called multicollinearity) makes it hard to separate out the effects of different variables, and makes the results especially vulnerable to the omission of relevant variables.

In the case of higher education, it is necessary to control not only for the influence of "demand-side" variables such as income and ability but

47. For example, of three high-ability students from the Boston area, one may attend Harvard, another Boston College, and a third the University of Massachusetts–Boston. They will "pay" very different prices, but in fact (if admissible to all three colleges) face the same alternatives. Studying their choices in relation to their background characteristics may reveal something about the distribution of tastes for different types of colleges, but cannot, in the nature of the case, reveal *anything* about how their enrollment decisions would change if any or all of the college prices changed. In other words, the data would contain no information about the effect of price on enrollment.

48. Similar conclusions were reached in Dresch, "Critique of Planning Models," and in an unpublished review of the literature by Stephen A. Hoenack, "Description of Literature on Demand for Higher Education."

also for variation in characteristics of colleges and universities—such as quality, admissions selectivity, and geographical accessibility—that may affect demand.[49] The problem of determining the effects of nonprice institutional characteristics on enrollment demand is both important and difficult and has not been adequately addressed thus far.

The demand relationship must be identified. A paradox that delights newcomers to economics is that higher price lowers demand (or quantity demanded, to be precise), while higher demand raises price! How can one be sure in examining a body of data whether the causal arrow runs from price to enrollment or from enrollment to price? There is, unfortunately, no easy answer. The issue is problematic in all higher education demand studies (indeed, in all demand studies) but is perhaps most serious in cross-state regression analyses. The classic instance here is the observation of a high ratio of private to public enrollment in states where public price is high, notably in the Northeast. This may be evidence of a strong effect of prices at public institutions on the public-private enrollment mix; but it may instead show the effect of a strong private higher education sector on the political decisionmaking process whereby public tuition is set; or it may be due to a combination of both.[50] Typically, and perhaps inevitably, given inadequate empirical knowledge of the determinants of supply and price decisions made by political and nonprofit institutions, researchers in cross-state and other studies have simply assumed the problem away, building into their models the premise that causation goes from price to quantity.

All the studies discussed are vulnerable to all of these problems, although in differing degree; hence, there is reason for great caution in accepting their results. The difficulty encountered here is common to many areas of econometrics. While the "internal validity" of the studies is high—they are analytically rigorous, logically consistent, and technically up to date—their "external validity" or "believability" is rather

49. For example, states with high-priced private colleges tend to be those (like Massachusetts) with a concentration of prestigious schools. So cross-state differences in prices of private colleges largely reflect differences in "quality," and not differences in the cost of comparable colleges.

50. Statistical attempts to disentangle these effects (with indifferent success) are in Thomas D. Hopkins, "The Provision of Higher Education: A Market Interpretation" (Ph.D. dissertation, Yale University, 1971), chap. 4; Michael S. McPherson, "The Effects of Public on Private College Enrollment" (Ph.D. dissertation, University of Chicago, 1974); and Sam Peltzman, "The Effect of Government Subsidies-in-Kind on Private Expenditures: The Case of Higher Education," *Journal of Political Economy*, vol. 81 (January/February, 1973), pp. 1–27.

lower, since the empirical work rests on doubtful assumptions and weak data. The intelligent response to this state of affairs is clearly not to throw existing work overboard and await the perfection of data and methods. A more sensible response is to accept results only when they emerge consistently from studies employing a variety of methods and when they make good intuitive sense. There is probably not a single number in the whole enrollment demand literature that should be taken seriously by itself. But a careful review of the literature will show that there are some important qualitative findings and order-of-magnitude estimates on which there is consensus, and which do deserve to be taken seriously. (There are also some serious gaps.) The following review of findings attempts to convey such results.

Tuition and the Decision to Enroll

Some of the most conspicuous areas of agreement in this literature emerge in regard to the impact of prices on the access question—the decision whether to attend college. Tuition prices are, of course, only one of the factors that determine who goes to college, and by no means the most important one. The large sociological literature on the enrollment process suggests that motivational and other personal characteristics and family background factors generally predominate.[51]

Still, the one universal finding in the studies under review here is that price *does* affect access—every single one finds a significant negative relationship between the net price faced by students and their probability of attending college. There is apparently even some agreement on the magnitude of the price effect, as table 3-9 indicates. Translating the results of a number of demand studies into a common format suggests that a $100 cut in tuition (occurring in all colleges simultaneously) would lead to about a 1 percentage point increase in the enrollment rate (expressed as a percentage of eighteen- to twenty-four-year-olds).[52] Of

51. See the discussion and the survey reported in James W. Trent, "The Decision to Go to College: An Accumulative Multivariate Process," in *Trends in Postsecondary Education* (GPO, 1970), and Jonathan D. Fife, *Applying the Goals of Student Financial Aid*, Eric Higher Education Research Report 10 (American Association for Higher Education, 1975).

52. Details of the calculations underlying table 3-9 are available from the author. These calculations extend and in some cases correct those in Gregory A. Jackson and George B. Weathersby, "Individual Demand for Higher Education: A Review and Analysis of Recent Empirical Studies," *Journal of Higher Education*, vol. 46 (November/December 1975), pp. 623–52.

Table 3-9. *Alternative Estimates of the Effect of a Change in Tuition on the Enrollment Rate, Various Years, 1919–72*

Study	Type	Year	Price response coefficient[a]
Corazzini, Dugan, and Grabowski	National cross section[b]	1963	0.62
Hopkins	State cross section	1963	0.75
Barnes	Individual students	1970	1.53
Radner and Miller	Individual students	1966	0.05
Kohn, Manski, and Mundel	Individual students	1966	0.92
Hoenack	High school districts	1965	0.71
Hoenack and Weiler	Individual students	1972	1.46
Spies	Individual students	1971	0.05
Campbell and Siegel	Time series	1919–64	0.20
Bishop	Individual students	1963	0.90

Sources: Derived from the studies given in the first column, all of which are cited in the text (see index). Details of the calculations underlying the price response coefficients, shown in the last column, are available from the author. The calculations require correcting price response coefficients from various studies for price change since base year and for differences in enrollment base.

a. Increase in enrollment rate of eighteen- to twenty-four-year-olds (in percentage points) per $100 decrease in tuition, in 1974 dollars.

b. The data from the national sample were cross-sectionally stratified by the students' states of residence during high school, and average values were computed for each state's sample.

course, given the imprecision of each study taken individually, and the range of variation in results among the studies, nobody should be surprised if the true figure is half or twice as large as that.

It seems fair to call a price response of this order of magnitude "small." Cutting tuition in half, according to these estimates, would only raise enrollment by about 15 percent.[53] That the rate of price response should be fairly low (though not negligible) makes intuitive sense for a couple of reasons. First, tuition is only a fraction of the total cost facing a student—less than half when room and board is included, even less if forgone earnings are counted. Thus cutting tuition in half means perhaps a 20 percent drop in cost—or less—and seen in that light, the effect on enrollment seems quite reasonable.[54] The other point is the "one-to-a-customer" nature of the higher education commodity. When Coca-Cola's price drops, the company may attract some new customers, but the bulk of new purchases comes from present customers drinking more

53. The tuition-elasticity of enrollment demand, according to the estimate in the preceding paragraph, is about 0.3. (Remember that a 1 *percentage point* increase in the enrollment rate is equivalent to about a 3 *percent* increase in enrollment, since about one-third of the eighteen-to-twenty-four age group is enrolled.)

54. Thus demand is *inelastic* with respect to tuition, but somewhat *elastic* with respect to total cost.

Table 3-10. *Alternative Estimates of Comparative Price Responsiveness of Public and Private Enrollment, Various Years, 1927–72*

Study	Type	Year	Effect on enrollment of a $100 decrease in public price[a]		Rate of substitution of public for private enrollment	Effect on enrollment of a $100 decrease in private price[a]		Rate of substitution of private for public enrollment
			Public	Private		Public	Private	
(1)	(1)	(2)	(3)	(4)	(5)	(6)	(7)	(8)
Hopkins	State cross section	1963	0.95	−0.42	0.44	−0.20	0.42	0.48
Hight	Time series	1927–72	11.40	−0.44	0.04	−1.90	0.34	5.59
Barnes	Individual students	1970	1.80	−0.79	0.44	−0.46	0.98	0.47
Radner and Miller	Individual students	1966	0.11	−0.08	0.73	−0.08	0.10	0.80
McPherson	State cross section	1972	0.89	−0.64	0.72	...	...	...
Peltzman	State cross section	1966–67[b]	...	...	0.57	...	...	0.54
McPherson	State cross section	1968	...	...	0.58	...	...	...

Sources: See sources for table 3-9; column 5 = column 4 ÷ column 3, except last two figures, which are from the relevant studies; column 8 = column 6 ÷ column 7, except the Peltzman figure, which comes directly from his study.

a. Changes in enrollment rate of eighteen- to twenty-four-year-olds (in percentage points) per $100 decrease in tuition, in 1974 dollars.

b. Academic year 1966–67.

cokes. No matter what the price of higher education, nobody goes to college more than once.

A major implication of the low rate of price response is that attaining high enrollments through keeping tuition rates low across the board is a very expensive way to achieve access goals. Since most of the forgone tuition revenue resulting from a price cut would accrue to students who would attend college anyway, it apparently costs more than $4,000 in forgone tuition for each additional student attracted into college via a general price reduction.[55]

In principle a cheaper way to maintain high college enrollment or to raise it is to target low tuition (or student aid) on those groups that are most sensitive to price in their enrollment decisions. The most readily identifiable group consists of low-income students: a variety of studies indicate that they are significantly more sensitive to price than high-income students in deciding whether to attend college.[56] This finding supports the general presumption that subsidies should be targeted on low-income students and specifically suggests that the policy in most states of using government funds to keep tuition low at public institutions is hard to defend on access grounds.

Tuition and the Choice of Institution

To turn from access to choice is to address one of the central questions in the tuition gap controversy: how readily can students be moved from public colleges to private colleges (or the reverse) through changes in public relative to private tuition levels? The relevant evidence from a number of studies is summarized in table 3-10.[57] As columns 3 and 4 indicate, reduced tuition rates at public institutions will raise public enrollment, but the rise will come in large part at the expense of private enrollment. Similarly columns 6 and 7 suggest that lower private tuition will raise private enrollment partly by attracting students from public institutions.

In trying to form an opinion about how big or significant the price effects in table 3-10 are, there are two perspectives to keep in mind. On

55. See Jackson and Weathersby, "Individual Demand for Higher Education," p. 650.

56. Estimates of the magnitude of the effect differ rather widely across studies. See (among others) the studies by Hoenack, Barnes, Bishop, Kohn and others, Carlson, and Leslie and Fife, all cited above.

57. Details of the calculations underlying table 3-10 are available from the author.

the one hand, one can ask how many people get moved from one sector to the other by a price change of given magnitude. Here, as in discussing the access question, it seems right to say that the price effects are noticeable but not huge—though the disagreements among studies are even larger here than in the access literature. An order-of-magnitude guess is that a $100 price cut at public institutions would raise the public enrollment rate by 1 percentage point and reduce private enrollment by half that much. If this estimate is correct, it would suggest that the growth in the tuition gap that occurred during the 1960s accounted for something less than half of the shift in enrollment from private to public institutions that took place at that time.[58] The rest presumably resulted from the kinds of nonprice factors discussed above.[59]

The other perspective is to concentrate not on the absolute numbers of people affected by a price change, but rather on the question of where those people who *are* affected come from. There is considerable agreement among the studies surveyed that a substantial fraction of the people attracted to public institutions by a cut in public tuition would otherwise have enrolled in private colleges. Estimates of this fraction—the ratio of the number of people lost from private institutions to the number gained at public institutions when public tuition is reduced—appear in column 5 of table 3-10.[60] (The comparable figure for changes in private price appears in column 8.) Again discounting Hight's results, it appears that for every ten students attracted to public colleges by a wider tuition gap, between four and seven of them would otherwise have enrolled

58. The gap rose by about $350 (in 1967 dollars) from 1960 to 1970. By itself, this would have changed the public share of total enrollment from 55 to 64 percent. The actual share change was from 55 to 73 percent, about twice as large. Since the price effect was at least partially offset by rising incomes that tend to increase the private share, it is safe to say that the change in the tuition gap accounted for less than half the change that actually occurred.

59. Hight's findings of a very large price effect in his time series work probably resulted from his inability to allow for these nonprice factors. Improvements in geographic accessibility and the like at public institutions accompanied a gradual widening in the dollar gap between public and private tuition over the last twenty years. Hight's statistical procedures probably led him to attribute to his price variables effects that were in fact due to nonprice factors he could not include in his equations—the statistical counterpart to the impressionistic misjudgment many have formed that the widening tuition gap is the main cause of the declining share of private enrollment.

60. The table includes two studies that attempted to estimate this rate of substitution directly from cross-state enrollment data without estimating price effects: Peltzman, "Effect of Government Subsidies-in-Kind," and McPherson, "Effects of Public on Private College Enrollment."

Table 3-11. *Effect of Change in Public Tuition on Enrollment in Public and Private Institutions of Higher Education, by Family Income*

| Family income (dollars) | Price response coefficients[a] | | Rate of substitution of public for private enrollment[b] |
	Public enrollment	Private enrollment	
0–6,000	7.57	−1.92	0.254
6,000–10,000	4.89	−1.84	0.376
10,000–15,000	3.63	−2.01	0.554
15,000 and over	3.45	−2.81	0.814
All groups	4.53	−1.97	0.435

Source: Calculated from data in Gary T. Barnes, "Determinants of the College Going and College Choice Decision" (University of North Carolina at Greensboro, n.d.; processed).

a. Percentage point changes in enrollment rate per $100 cut in tuition at public four-year institutions.

b. Ratio of change in private enrollment to change in public enrollment resulting from a change in tuition at public four-year institutions.

in private colleges. Increases in the gap sufficient to significantly affect public enrollment would thus have quite serious effects on private colleges.

Furthermore, this tendency of public enrollment to substitute for private enrollment when the gap widens is even stronger among high-income students than others. As noted above, high-income students are less sensitive to price than low-income students in deciding whether to attend college. But there is evidence that high-income students remain somewhat sensitive to price in deciding *where* to go to college.[61] Thus a tuition cut at public institutions directed only at high-income students would raise total college enrollment very little, but might attract a fair number of students from private institutions. Calculations derived from Barnes's results support this reasoning (see table 3-11). They indicate that among upper-income students attracted to a public college by a tuition cut, more than 80 percent are drawn from private institutions, while among low-income students this would be true of only about 25 percent.[62]

Although the precise numbers should not be taken seriously, the tendency they suggest is probably real. Apparently the large subsidies

61. See particularly the studies by Barnes, "Determinants of the College Going and College Choice Decision," and Kohn and associates, "Empirical Investigation of Factors Which Influence College Going Behavior."

62. Similar results derived in a quite different manner can be found in McPherson, "Effects of Public on Private College Enrollment," chap. 3.

received by high-income students through low tuition at public institutions do little to augment total college enrollment. The striking implication for public policy is that if states were simultaneously to raise public tuition rates for high-income students and expand subsidies for low-income students, they could boost both private and total college enrollment at one stroke. By the same token, of course, policies to subsidize tuition rates at private institutions across the board would serve in good part to move relatively affluent students from public to private colleges (and to reduce the tuition bill for students who would attend private colleges anyway), and would do little to increase total college enrollment compared to alternative uses of the same funds.[63]

Tuition Effects by Type of Private Institution

Discussion to this point, like most of the work under review, treats "public" and "private" higher education as two homogeneous aggregates. Very little work has been done that provides any useful information about the tuition sensitivity of enrollment at different types of private institutions. This is unfortunate because for many purposes disaggregated information is essential. Certainly for planning at the institutional level highly aggregated data on private higher education as a whole are largely worthless. And planners of public policy at the state level will want to take into account the mix of types of private colleges in their state—the effects of state policy may depend heavily on the nature of any particular state's private higher education system. Moreover, as the discussion in chapter 1 makes clear, overall policy toward private higher education is (or should be) motivated in part by consideration of the unique roles and functions fulfilled by different kinds of private colleges and universities. Policymakers need to pay attention to the composition of private enrollment as well as its level.

Two steps are taken here to help answer the question of how different types of private institutions would be affected by reduced public tuition. First, the problem is discussed qualitatively by reviewing a set of factors that seem likely to affect the tuition sensitivity of enrollment at various types of private colleges. This is followed by a brief description of a cross-state regression analysis of the relation between public tuition and

63. I hasten to add that the desirability of pursuing such policies depends on a great many considerations other than the impact on enrollment levels, considerations extensively discussed elsewhere in this book.

public and private enrollment levels by Carnegie Commission classification. (See Glossary for an explanation of the categories.)

QUALITATIVE FACTORS

Distinctiveness of Offerings. The ability of private colleges to withstand competition from lower-priced public institutions depends perhaps most fundamentally on students (and parents) perceiving real and valuable differences in the experiences these institutions offer. These differences, which extend to matters of life-style and faculty-student relations as well as curriculum, are hard to judge summarily. But it does seem clear that the liberal arts colleges have a unique product to offer. The intimacy offered by their small size is matched almost nowhere in the public sector, and, as noted in chapter 1, their curricular distinctiveness also stands out. The less selective liberal arts colleges are probably less distinctive than the more selective, since they have had to accommodate a student clientele much like that at many state colleges. Worst off in terms of distinctiveness are the private comprehensive universities and colleges, which are quite like their public counterparts in size, curriculum, and life-style. Recently, some of these institutions have benefited from the surge of interest in vocational programs. But given the likelihood that these students are very price-sensitive, reliance on that clientele may actually intensify the threat of price competition from public institutions.

Reputation. This vital intangible quality can have a variety of sources —"from strong religious ties to a good record in employment placement, from a good climate to a good academic program."[64] While some institutions in all categories enjoy a fine reputation, the universities and the highly selective liberal arts colleges benefit especially. The ability to maintain a clear institutional identity is a key to establishing a reputation, and this has been a special problem for the less selective liberal arts colleges, which have often been forced to reorient themselves, relocate, even change their names in order to survive.[65]

Student Income Distribution. High-income students tend to be less sensitive to tuition than low-income students in deciding whether to enroll. Since students with wealthier parents also do not put a burden on the financial aid resources of a college, it is clear that colleges with a

64. Carnegie Foundation for the Advancement of Teaching, *More than Survival*, p. 72.
65. Astin and Lee, *The Invisible Colleges*, pp. 22–23.

Table 3-12. *Characteristics of Private Colleges and Universities, by Carnegie Classification, Academic Year 1972–73*

Percentage of institutions reporting each characteristic

Characteristic	Classification[a]				
	Doctoral-granting universities	Comprehensive colleges and universities[b]	Highly selective liberal arts colleges	Less selective liberal arts colleges	Two-year institutions
1. Parental income above $20,000 per year	55.0	41.4	49.1	30.8	26.8
2. Institution has 70 percent or more students from home state	31.8	61.0	21.9	44.8	56.3
3. Students have high school grade average of B+ or better	76.1	51.0	64.7	39.3	22.6
4. Institution has more than 70 percent of total educational and general revenue from tuition	18.1	71.6	52.5	42.0	45.5
5. Institution is located in standard metropolitan statistical area[c]	95.4	80.5	63.4	58.4	60.8

Source: Elaine H. El-Khawas, *Public and Private Higher Education: Differences in Role, Character, and Clientele*, Policy Analysis Service Reports, vol. 2, no. 3 (American Council on Education, December 1976), pp. 55, 57, 59.
a. See Glossary for a description of the categories.
b. Combines two subcategories of the Carnegie classification.
c. As defined by the U.S. Bureau of the Census.

wealthier clientele are likely to be less vulnerable to changes in public tuition levels. As line 1 of table 3-12 shows, this factor works in favor of universities and highly selective liberal arts campuses and against the other liberal arts institutions and private two-year colleges.

Market Area. A college that attracts students from farther away is not only going to be less sensitive to local competition, but also will have the opportunity as conditions change throughout its market area to draw more heavily from areas where the competition lags. The data on interstate student migration in table 3-12 suggest that private comprehensive and two-year institutions draw heavily on home-state students, and are therefore more sensitive to public tuition levels. Highly selective liberal arts colleges are again in a strong position.

Admissions Selectivity. This factor is important because it enables a college to survive a shrinking applicant pool. When a school is already at the point of admitting anyone who is not dangerous,[66] a dip in the applicant pool is disastrous. The key here is the ability to extend acceptances to a larger fraction of applicants without running into severe declines in student quality that will change the nature of the college, affect faculty morale, and so on. Evidence on the high school grades of entering freshmen (see table 3-12, line 3) substantiates that here again it is universities and highly selective liberal arts colleges that come out well, and private two-year colleges that do not.

Tuition Dependence. A heavy dependence on tuition revenue makes a college more vulnerable to competitive factors that reduce demand, and also less able to innovate, experiment, and weather bad times. Universities do distinctly well in this regard; the comprehensive institutions badly (see table 3-12, line 4).

Urban or Rural Location. Being located near a concentration of population not only reduces the effective cost gap for students located nearby, it also increases the opportunity for institutions to appeal to alternative clienteles in response to increased competition—especially to the older, employed students whose numbers have been growing recently. This factor weighs against liberal arts colleges and tends to favor the doctoral-granting and comprehensive universities (table 3-12, line 5).

Some very clear patterns emerge when the implications of these seven factors are summarized. The highly selective liberal arts colleges are apparently in a strong position on most of the dimensions considered (though it must be remembered that there is a wide gap between the most

66. See Joseph A. Kershaw, *The Very Small College* (Ford Foundation, 1976).

selective and the least selective among this group of colleges). The demand for enrollment at these institutions seems unlikely to be seriously threatened by price competition from the public sector. Not only are these institutions, at least the best of them, well situated in their own right, but owing to their relatively selective admissions they are in an ideal position to reach out into the applicant pool of other parts of the private sector, if need be—especially, one would guess, being able to attract the more affluent students from the less selective liberal arts institutions and the private comprehensive colleges and universities.

The doctoral-granting universities also appear to be relatively insensitive to public tuition levels. Their positions will of course depend heavily on developments in the graduate student market, which have not been considered here.

Most vulnerable to price competition from the public sector are the less selective liberal arts colleges, the comprehensive colleges and universities, and the private two-year colleges. The qualitative changes in public higher education in the last two decades, especially the expansion of state colleges and the community college movement, have tended to undermine the uniqueness of the offerings of these institutions. Lacking in admissions selectivity, typically anonymous in reputation (though with significant exceptions), these are the categories of institutions that, it appears, will prove most vulnerable if the tuition gap grows.

EMPIRICAL EVIDENCE

To what extent are these speculations supported by empirical evidence? A regression analysis based on 1972 data is broadly supportive, but it raises doubts on some points and certainly emphasizes the need for further research. Table 3-13 shows estimates of the net effect of changes in average public tuition levels on private enrollment rates by Carnegie classification.[67] The coefficients show the percentage increase in the private enrollment rate per $100 increase in public tuition. The results do indicate, as expected, a quite strong effect of public tuition levels on enrollments at less selective liberal arts colleges and a very weak (and

67. Enrollment rates were expressed as percentages of population eighteen to twenty-one years of age. Notice that these are measures of enrollment at institutions in the state. In principle, a better variable is enrollment of a state's residents, no matter where enrolled, but interstate student migration data by type of private institution are not available. All the regressions discussed include measures of income (personal income per capita) and educational attainment (fraction of adults who had attended college) among the independent variables.

Table 3-13. *Effect of Change in Public Tuition on Private Enrollment Rates, by Carnegie Classification, 1972*[a]

Classification[b]	Price response coefficient[c]	Percentage effect[d]
Doctoral-granting universities[e]	−0.014	−0.56
Comprehensive colleges and universities	0.059	2.19
Highly selective liberal arts colleges	0.593**	44.59
Less selective liberal arts colleges	0.781**	18.33
Two-year institutions	0.104	8.74
All categories of institution	−2.103	−4.36

Source: Derived from tuition and enrollment data from the Higher Education General Information Survey for 1972, conducted by the U.S. Office of Education.
** Statistically significant at 1 percent level.
a. Based on a cross-state regression analysis that controlled for per capita personal income and percent of adult population with some college education.
b. See Glossary for a description of the categories.
c. The effect on the enrollment rate (in percentage points) of a $100 increase in public tuition.
d. Percentage change in enrollment per $100 change in public tuition.
e. Utah, an extreme case, is excluded from this equation.

statistically nonsignificant) effect on private research and doctoral-granting universities. Unexpected is the relatively strong relation between public tuition levels and enrollments at more selective liberal arts colleges. The lesson here may be that even the highly selective liberal arts category is still quite broad. The so-called elite colleges, the thirty or so best-known private four-year colleges, have a disproportionate impact on many people's impressions of what private colleges are like, but in fact they make up only a small fraction even of the more selective liberal arts colleges. The evidence suggests that the less selective among the highly selective colleges may be rather more vulnerable to public competition than the earlier qualitative discussion was able to bring out. The insignificant effects on comprehensive universities and private two-year colleges are also a surprise. My inclination is to discount these last results, and believe instead the earlier qualitative discussion that suggests these institutions are sensitive to public tuition levels.

In addition to examining these correlations between public price and private enrollment, it is also revealing to look directly at the correlations between enrollment levels at various classes of public and private institutions. Estimates of these relationships (net of the effect of interstate differences in income and educational attainment) appear in table 3-14. The simplest interpretation of the figures in that table is that they measure the extent to which enrollment at a particular category of private institution will fall if a certain type of public enrollment is ex-

Table 3-14. Effect of Public Enrollment Rates on Private Enrollment Rates,
by Carnegie Classification, 1972[a]

Private enrollment classification[b]	Absolute effect[c]				Percentage effect[d]			
	All public	Public university	Other public four-year	Public two-year	All public	Public university	Other public four-year	Public two-year
Doctoral-granting universities[e]	−0.122*	−0.230*	−0.089	−0.139	−4.84	−8.39	−3.25	−5.07
Comprehensive colleges and universities	−0.047	−0.122*	−0.104	−0.024	−1.74	−4.40	−3.75	−0.87
Highly selective liberal arts colleges	−0.074	−0.085*	−0.155*	−0.108*	−5.56	−5.94	−10.84	−7.55
Less selective liberal arts colleges	−0.091	−0.053	−0.143	−0.128*	−2.14	−1.24	−3.33	−2.98
Two-year institutions	−0.064	−0.068*	−0.042	−0.098*	−5.38	−5.40	−3.33	−7.78
All categories of institution	−0.450**	−0.612**	−0.676**	−0.568**	−3.57	−4.65	−5.14	−4.32

Source: Same as table 3-13.
* Statistically significant at 5 percent level.
** Statistically significant at 1 percent level.
a. These figures result from a set of regressions across states in 1972 with enrollment rates in various categories of private institutions as dependent variables and enrollment rates in various categories of public institutions, personal income per capita, and percentage of adults with some college as independent variables.
b. See Glossary for a description of the categories.
c. Effect on private enrollment rate of a 1 percentage point change in public enrollment.
d. Effect on percent enrollment in private colleges of a 1 percentage point change in public enrollment.
e. Utah, an extreme case, is excluded from this equation.

panded—for example, that an increase in enrollment of 100 students at public universities will reduce enrollment at private universities by 23 students. This interpretation, though, requires the assumption that the causation flows from public to private enrollment, which is not clear. More broadly, the estimated coefficients do provide an index of the tendency for various categories of public and private enrollment to vary systematically against one another, and this presumably is a rough measure of the relatedness of their demands.[68]

What stands out in the table is the presence throughout of significant inverse relationships between public and private enrollment levels. While these are strongest between similar types of institutions (such as public and private universities),[69] it is also striking that, for example, changes in enrollment at public two-year colleges influence not just private two-year college enrollments, but also enrollments at private liberal arts colleges and maybe even private universities.

The results in table 3-14 corroborate the earlier findings that the less selective liberal arts colleges are quite sensitive to public competition, and again suggest that a substantial segment of the more selective liberal arts colleges may be so as well. Indeed, although the best of the liberal arts colleges and the doctoral-granting universities are undoubtedly in a relatively strong position, the results here and throughout seem to indicate that all segments of private higher education might be quite vulnerable either to a large increase in the tuition gap, or to other changes in public higher education that make it significantly more attractive to students.

Summary and Conclusions

The simplest way to summarize the findings of this chapter is to answer some basic questions about the future demand for higher education.

How real is the prospect of decline in overall enrollment demand in the next decade?

---

68. Extended discussion of the proper interpretation of relationships of this kind is in McPherson, "Effects of Public on Private College Enrollment."

69. The presence of a significant relationship between enrollments at public and private universities in the absence of a significant price effect may point to the importance of nonprice admissions policies that limit enrollment at public universities. (See ibid., chap. 4.)

Very. A weak employment market for college graduates is likely to reinforce the implications of the demographic decline, which by itself is enough to cause enrollments to drop. Growth in enrollment of non-traditional clienteles may offer some relief, especially for public institutions in urban areas, but prospects for further enrollment growth among adult and nondegree-credit students are more limited than many have supposed.

How close is the competition for students between public and private institutions?

Quite close. As noted in chapter 1 and several times in this chapter, many public and private institutions appeal to similar clienteles. This is especially true of state colleges and the less selective private institutions, where student profiles in terms of income, career ambitions, ability, and family background are quite similar.

Statistical evidence also suggests much substitutability between public and private institutions. It appears that when public campuses expand their enrollments, half or more of their new customers are students who would otherwise have enrolled in private colleges. As enrollments decline, the struggle between the sectors to enroll these students will intensify. The outcome is hard to predict, but one obvious conclusion is that the future of private higher education will depend heavily on decisions made in state legislatures and state colleges about pricing and other institutional responses to declining enrollments.

How important is the tuition gap as a competitive factor?

Evidence is clear that tuition prices have a significant impact on the public-private enrollment mix. In that sense, the tuition gap *is* important. Policies to affect it—whether by raising public tuition, providing tuition offset grants, or in other ways—can significantly affect enrollments in the two sectors.

It is not so clear that changes in the tuition gap have dominated past movements in enrollment rates, or that a widening tuition gap is inevitable for the future. The tuition gap has in fact not changed dramatically relative to ability to pay in the last decade; that it will do so in the coming decade is far from clear. The dramatic increases in public relative to private enrollment over the last two decades have probably had more to do with the proliferation of community colleges and with other qualitative changes in public higher education than with changes in the tuition gap.

It is difficult to predict the future course of qualitative developments in the two sectors, but there is reason for doubt that the relative position of the public sector in these nonprice competitive dimensions will continue to improve as the overall environment shifts from growth to decline. While this consideration suggests a less gloomy picture for the future of private higher education than some have foreseen, it also underlines once more the point that the private sector's prospects will indeed depend heavily on public-sector pricing decisions, as well as public-sector decisions concerning geographic and academic accessibility and other aspects of student recruitment policy.

Is the middle class being priced out of private higher education?

Assuming that financial aid offers follow the College Scholarship Service schedules, students with family incomes between $15,000 and $25,000 a year face a substantially wider tuition gap relative to their ability to pay than either richer or poorer students. In fact, for many low-income students, many private colleges are probably cheaper than public colleges. At the same time, the relative representation of the upper middle class in private higher education has been falling rather sharply. Although definitive evidence does not exist concerning the relative price sensitivity of enrollment by income level, it is reasonable to connect these two events, and conclude that the upper middle class is indeed responding to a price squeeze in private higher education.

To call this an hourglass effect, as some have done, seems extreme, since this group is still heavily represented in private colleges. Neither is it clear that the college destination of these students should in itself be an important concern for public policy. But as to the empirical question of the existence of this phenomenon, the answer appears to be yes.[70]

Where in the private sector is the competitive pressure likely to be most severe?

Not nearly enough is known about demand for different types of private institutions. Even if more were known, generalizations about the situation of various types of institutions would always have to be qualified by the special circumstances of each one. Still, the qualitative and quantitative evidence considered in this chapter suggests that the less selective private institutions are more vulnerable to public-sector

---

70. Discussion of the middle-income squeeze often involves the contention that costs of higher education have been rising over time relative to the ability of middle-income families to pay. This is a different issue from the question of the price *gap* faced by middle-income students compared to upper- and lower-income students discussed in the text. Although costs of higher education have risen over time there is no evidence that they have risen significantly relative to average incomes.

competition than others. This group includes the private two-year and comprehensive institutions, but the situation is perhaps worst for the less selective liberal arts colleges. Adding to the problems caused by the absence of national reputations and not very affluent student clientele is their predominantly rural location, which makes these institutions the least likely of any to enroll an appreciable number of nontraditional students.

There is evidence that these less selective liberal arts colleges, which enroll about one-quarter of the students in the private sector, are already in difficulty. They have been experiencing unusually rapid rises in their tuition rates compared both with public institutions and to other classes of private institutions. Scattered throughout the second survey of private higher education by Bowen and Minter are further signs of distress for these colleges—declining student quality, large shortfalls in enrollment compared to desired levels, and increases in student/faculty ratios. Bowen and Minter rated only one out of thirty of these places as being in a strong position in 1976.[71]

IT WOULD be pleasant to balance this portrait of distress with a description of that segment of higher education that is sure to enter the 1980s on a wave of strength and success. But probably there is no such segment, either in public or private higher education. It seems quite likely that the most elite private institutions will be among those best able to weather the storm, though even they will probably experience some adversity. It also seems worthwhile to repeat, in closing, that adversity and enrollment declines are likely to be experienced in both sectors, and it is really not clear in which one they will be the worse.

71. Howard R. Bowen and W. John Minter, *Private Higher Education: Second Annual Report on Financial and Educational Trends in the Private Sector of American Higher Education* (Association of American Colleges, 1976), pp. 11, 13, 26, 91.

Chapter Four

Federal Politics

Lawrence E. Gladieux and Thomas R. Wolanin

EDITED BY DAVID W. BRENEMAN AND CHESTER E. FINN, JR.

LAWRENCE E. GLADIEUX is director of the Washington office of the College Entrance Examination Board, and THOMAS R. WOLANIN is deputy staff director of the Select Subcommittee on Education of the House Committee on Education and Labor.

THERE IS wide popular support for the maintenance of a vital independent sector in higher education. Politicians and speechmakers have long extolled the virtues of diversity in American higher learning. It is a cause that readily commands the concern of federal policymakers.

Yet there exists no conscious, coherent national policy to sustain the dual system. Current federal programs that have an impact on private colleges and universities are a mixed bag, with many unintended and unanticipated effects. Despite the sympathetic rhetoric, Washington policy debates rarely focus systematically on the problems facing private higher education, nor are the concrete interests of the independent sector clearly discernible in the federal arena.

This chapter might be subtitled the "politics of ambiguity." Its purpose is to sketch some of the historical and political limits within which federal higher education policy is formulated and to analyze efforts to advance the cause of private colleges and universities in Washington.

Following a brief sketch of key legislation enacted in 1972, the chapter examines the politics of private higher education in Washington since that year, illustrating in the context of the most recent legislative debates the ambivalent relationships between independent higher learning and the national government, and the current impasse on the issues of "access" and "choice" in the federal student aid programs.

The chapter then poses and attempts to clarify the question: what is the community of interest among the private colleges and universities and how is it reflected in the federal policy arena? We conclude with our view of the prospects for a national solution to the dilemmas facing private higher education.

Major Changes in 1972

In the Education Amendments of 1972, Congress turned its back on institutional aid as a principal means of support for higher education and, instead, greatly expanded and elaborated the federal commitment to student aid.[1] Senate Education Subcommittee Chairman Claiborne Pell pushed through his notion of an individual student entitlement in the form of the basic educational opportunity grant (BEOG). The size of the award would be based on a standardized assessment of the student's (and his family's) financial strength, with a maximum grant of $1,400.

1. The Education Amendments of 1972, 86 Stat. 235.

The idea was to guarantee a resource floor for all students to finance postsecondary education. An alternative entitlement approach sponsored by Senator Walter F. Mondale, designed to ensure a greater degree of student choice among types of institutions, was set aside. Under the Mondale proposal, a needy student's eligibility would have been limited not by a flat ceiling, but by the actual costs of attending the institution in which he chose to enroll. A sliding scale of percentages would have determined how much of the student's expenses might be covered by the federal government.[2]

Congress did enact several key provisions in 1972 that were conceived at least in part as helping to protect the interests of private, higher-priced colleges and the students wishing to attend such institutions.

The BEOG half-cost rule. The BEOG formula calls for grants of $1,400 minus the student's family contribution, but not to exceed one-half the costs of attendance at the institution in which he enrolls. The half-cost restriction was added to ensure that no student would receive a "free ride" from the government (which a $1,400 grant would amount to at some low-tuition schools). It satisfied the traditional sentiment in Congress favoring at least some self-help on the part of the student (work and loans as opposed to grants). In addition, the half-cost limitation was intended to make the program "neutral" among different types of institutions. The legislators were persuaded that without it, inexpensive public institutions might become unduly attractive relative to higher-priced private colleges, since the basic grant would then pay all or nearly all of the student's costs at the public school.

The half-cost rule may not stand up under rational analysis (as argued in chapter 5 of this book), and on the face of it penalizing low-income students who choose to attend low-priced institutions may be a perverse way of safeguarding private colleges. But concern for the competitive position of the private sector was nonetheless part of the congressional intent, and the half-cost rule remains an article of faith among many private college spokesmen.

The campus-based funding trigger. In 1972 Congress anticipated that the Nixon administration would try to launch the basic grant program while largely abandoning the older, campus-based student aid programs. So it wrote into the law a requirement that the latter programs be funded

---

2. On this legislative history, see Lawrence E. Gladieux and Thomas R. Wolanin, *Congress and the Colleges: The National Politics of Higher Education* (Heath, 1976), pp. 91–114.

at specified minimum levels before the basic grants could become operational. Congress, particularly its authorizing committees, typically and instinctively builds the new on the old, rather than supplanting what already exists. The funding trigger headed off the administration's clear intention to follow the latter course in the case of the student aid programs. Congress was also mindful that private colleges and universities fared relatively better under the old programs than they would under the new basic grant program. Close to 40 percent of the supplemental educational opportunity grant (SEOG), work-study, and direct loan allocations went to private institutions, compared to a projected 20 to 25 percent share for the private campuses under the new basic grant program. Public schools stood to gain relatively more from basic grants because of their heavy concentration of low-income (hence, eligible) students and because of the fixed maximum grant that was unrelated (except for the half-cost rule) to differing tuition levels.

State student incentive grants. Congress also had the interests of private colleges partly in mind when it enacted the state student incentive grants (SSIG) program, a scheme for federal matching of state expenditures on need-based scholarships. The point of this program was to enlist the states in a new partnership to help advance equal opportunity objectives. States that already had student grant programs would be encouraged to increase their efforts and others would be tempted to follow their lead. The 1972 law imposed no requirement that the federally matched scholarships be geared to tuition costs, nor was it even required that the state programs be open to students in private institutions (though the latter has been mandated by the Education Amendments of 1976). But state scholarship programs generally favored students in the private sector, and the congressional sponsors of SSIG hoped to stimulate further growth in such aid. Over 50 percent of state student aid funds currently go to private college enrollees.[3]

These several gestures do not indicate a pronounced tilt toward the private sector, but were part of a rough, ad hoc balancing of public-private college interests in recent student aid legislation. In fact, there were tilts in both directions when it came to student aid.[4]

3. Joseph D. Boyd, *National Association of State Scholarship and Grant Programs, 8th Annual Survey, 1976–77 Academic Year* (Deerfield, Ill.: Illinois State Scholarship Commission, n.d.), p. 17.

4. These are discussed in greater detail by Robert Hartman in chapter 5.

Advancing the Cause in Washington in the Mid-1970s

During the legislative debates that culminated in the Education Amendments of 1972, spokesmen for private higher education were in the vanguard of those raising the alarm about the fiscal crisis of colleges and universities. Along with all of the other campus representatives, they proposed institutional aid based on enrollments as the primary federal remedy. But Congress, as noted above, was not persuaded and chose instead to put its priority and the bulk of the funding in student aid programs.

As chairman of the Special Subcommittee on Education, Representative Edith Green (Democrat from Oregon) had been the focus of bitter divisions over higher education policy within the House Committee on Education and Labor.[5] In addition, she led the fight for antibusing amendments in the committee, an issue that poisoned the atmosphere for all education policy discussions. Representative Green left the Education and Labor Committee in 1973 to become a junior member of the Subcommittee on Labor—Health, Education, and Welfare of the Committee on Appropriations and was replaced as chairman of the special subcommittee by James G. O'Hara (Democrat from Michigan). Widely admired for his intelligence, legislative skill, and effectiveness, O'Hara had previously devoted most of his efforts to labor issues close to the heart of his blue-collar constituency. He offered a fresh face and an open mind to those representing private higher education before the House. On the other side of Capitol Hill, the Senate Subcommittee on Education, overburdened as always with the whole gamut of education issues (divided in the House among three more specialized subcommittees), was initially more disinterested than hostile to the private sector's case.

Thus the Ninety-third Congress (1973–74) seemed to hold out a fresh opportunity to assist private colleges and universities, whose plight remained a live issue in Washington. In 1973, major reports by the Com-

5. It will be observed that the chairman of the Special Subcommittee on Education (changed in a 1975 reorganization to the Subcommittee on Postsecondary Education) plays a particularly prominent role in this discussion. He or she chairs the only congressional subcommittee devoted exclusively to postsecondary education. The Senate Subcommittee on Education is less specialized and has a wider jurisdiction. In addition, the generally low priority of higher education on the congressional agenda tends to magnify the role of the House chairman in the absence of much interest from anyone else.

mittee for Economic Development and the Carnegie Commission on Higher Education addressed the issue of the "tuition gap" and the financial health of the private sector.[6] In October 1973, Congressman O'Hara commenced a detailed series of hearings on federal student aid lasting into the summer of 1974. The chairman lived up to his reputation as a fast learner as he familiarized himself with the concepts, technicalities, and nuances of the jumble of federal programs providing assistance to postsecondary education.

As the Senate subcommittee was preoccupied with a variety of other issues, private-sector representatives pressed their case in the 1973–74 O'Hara hearings. In contrast to the 1972 sequence, this time the statement of the problem, the proposed solutions, and the reception from the subcommittee chairman were different.

The private institutions state their problem. The major plaint from the private sector remained constant—the dangers to its continued survival as a viable and healthy component of American higher education—but the emphasis shifted. The apocalyptic rhetoric of disaster gave way to a more subtle prognosis. For the previous three or four years the agents of the private sector had been drumming an unrelieved dirge at Congress: private colleges and universities were about to close their doors and soon just a few of the wealthiest would remain, the remnant of a once vigorous and extensive independent sector. Congress and the administration had not heeded these cries, and the dire predictions had not come true; large numbers of private schools did not shut down. The private sector's tale of woe began to lose credibility in Washington. Perhaps perceiving this new skepticism, spokesmen for the private institutions refined their case. Their campuses would continue to exist, they now argued, but the cost-cutting and belt-tightening required for survival were reducing them to hollow shells. The uniqueness and independence of the private sector were being steadily and perhaps irretrievably eroded. Private higher education, it was asserted, faced not the guillotine but a lingering death through malnutrition. In addition, the constant need to raise tuition rates in order to survive and the widening tuition gap threatened to make private colleges the exclusive preserve of the affluent. This would deny to many students of more modest means the kind of education that was only available at various types of

6. Committee for Economic Development, *The Management and Financing of Colleges* (CED, 1973); Carnegie Commission on Higher Education, *Higher Education: Who Pays? Who Benefits? Who Should Pay?* (McGraw-Hill, 1973).

private schools. It would also impair the stimulating intellectual climate that comes from an economically and culturally diverse student body.

Proposals to aid the private sector. While the primary concern of the independent colleges remained their institutional health and survival, they jumped on the only vehicle that seemed to be moving—student aid. Their spokesmen recognized that since 1972 aid for individual students was clearly the basic federal strategy. Funding for the cost-of-instruction grants authorized by the 1972 legislation remained part of their list of recommendations, as did some new institutional aid proposals, but these tended to be far down the list, more pro forma than the primary objective they had once been.

The focus was clearly on narrowing the tuition gap. Some of the early discussions in the Ninety-third Congress considered a federal tuition-offset program, which was in one sense a midway point between institutional aid and student aid, albeit one confined to the private sector. However, such a blunt federal intrusion into tuition policy and such clear favoritism for the private sector was obviously beyond the boundaries of political practicality, if not those of legitimate federal policy. The ranking minority member of the House subcommittee, Congressman John Dellenback of Oregon, observed, "This is not within our power or what we should be striving to do, to deal directly with tuition. That is an institutional and State decision and . . . ought to remain theirs and not ours."[7] Chairman O'Hara noted, "I don't see our role as coming in at this stage of the game and saying, all right, now, some States have chosen to favor public higher education and not to assist private higher education, therefore, we, Uncle Sam, are going to provide a compensating help to private education, we are going to, in effect, negate their decisions."[8]

The private institutions focused on strategies for modifying the collection of existing programs for student aid so that they would be more generous and above all more sensitive to tuition differences. Their leaders argued that they were willing to compete in the marketplace for students and asked only that the enormity of their competitive disadvantage, represented by the tuition gap, be reduced.

The refinement of the argument describing the plight of the private

7. *Student Financial Assistance* (Institutional Aid), *Hearings before the Special Subcommittee on Education of the House Committee on Education and Labor,* 93: 2 (Government Printing Office, 1974), pt. 7, p. 123.
8. Ibid., p. 120.

colleges and universities, the virtual abandonment of institutional aid, and the focus on the congressionally preferred policy of student aid demonstrated a significant advance in the political strategy pursued by private higher education. Following 1972, the higher education associations had been roundly criticized for their tunnel vision on institutional aid and for their political naiveté and ineffectiveness. During the Ninety-third Congress, by contrast, the private sector at least seemed to be playing in the right ball park.

The reception from the House subcommittee. As chairman of the House subcommittee, Representative Green had shown a special sympathy and concern for private higher education. The O'Hara hearings brought forth the usual expressions of goodwill for the private schools. As one private college president put it, "all of the rhetoric and most of the pieties are strongly and warmly supportive of diversity, pluralism, and a strong private sector."[9]

But the new chairman emerged from the hearings as a figure less friendly toward independent higher learning than his predecessor. O'Hara appreciated that some students' academic interests might be better served by private institutions. He also recognized that the private sector provided a measure of educational pluralism. But, overall, O'Hara seemed to view all postsecondary education as a largely undifferentiated product, no part of it being markedly more or less suited to the needs of different students. Private institutions did not seem to provide any unique experience for students, only a high price. As the hearings progressed, he also became frustrated by the lack of consensus among representatives of the private sector, who seemed to know what they did not want legislatively, but could not agree on what they did want. In addition, he was concerned about the total cost of the choice-related student aid proposals since he represented the Education and Labor Committee on the House Budget Committee and bore a large share of the responsibility for negotiating the budget ceilings for all of the Education and Labor Committee's many programs.

Most importantly, O'Hara doubted that using scarce dollars to subsidize student choice at higher-priced private institutions was the most appropriate federal priority. He was skeptical of tampering with tuition policies that had been traditionally left in state or private hands. The representatives of the public sector were also arguing that many students were still having trouble affording tuition at *any* school. Their case—that

9. Ibid., p. 93.

access was the issue and that low tuition was the best means to it—appealed to O'Hara. By the end of the hearings he had become a partisan of low-tuition public higher education, and he concluded one session of the hearings that had been largely devoted to the question of support for the private campuses by observing, "I think there are many roads to educational access . . . and one of those roads certainly is to provide a free, easily accessible system of Statewide community colleges. And I am not sure that is not one of the cheapest and easiest and best ways."[10]

All proposals to reduce the tuition gap became tainted, perhaps fatally, in O'Hara's view, by the 1973 reports of the Carnegie Commission and the Committee for Economic Development, which advocated *raising* public tuition to narrow the tuition gap. While witnesses for the private schools emphatically disavowed this approach and alternatively recommended means for lowering or holding down their own tuition rates, O'Hara associated the case for the private sector with an assault on low tuition.

In terms of federal policy, support for low tuition meant not advocating programs like price-sensitive student aid that could possibly encourage tuition increases. On the positive side, it meant that O'Hara, along with Senator Pell, favored those student aid programs, in particular, the basic educational opportunity grants, that promoted mass access to a postsecondary education.

During the 1973–74 hearings, the private educators' perception of O'Hara changed from that of an intelligent but uninformed neutral who could be persuaded to support their case to that of a man who was unsympathetic and unresponsive to their plight. Because O'Hara had been persuaded that the priorities in federal student aid policy lay elsewhere, the prospects that consensus on a choice-related student aid program would be worked out in the House subcommittee did not look good as the Ninety-third Congress adjourned.

A new legislative strategy. With new legislation addressed to the tuition gap seeming less and less likely, the associations representing the private sector, primarily the Association of Jesuit Colleges and Universities and the Association of American Colleges, shifted their legislative priorities.[11] Instead of pushing for new federal support for the private

10. Ibid., p. 128.

11. The Association of American Colleges has a mixed public-private membership of liberal arts colleges, but the overwhelming majority of its members are private liberal arts colleges. And it is primarily their point of view that the association represented before Congress.

institutions, the associations sought to preserve those aspects of the federal student aid programs that seemed particularly to serve—albeit inadequately—the interests of private schools and their students. This meant maintaining the campus-based student aid programs, which provided relatively flexible resources to meet student "need" above the level assured by the basic grant program. The private institutions also placed a high priority on retaining the so-called funding trigger, the requirement that these programs be financed to specified minimum levels before any basic grants could be awarded.

Most of the private-sector spokesmen were strongly committed to keeping the half-cost limit in the basic grant program as well. In their analysis, the half-cost limit meant that students applying to either a low-cost public school or a higher-priced private school would have at least *some* unmet financial need after receiving their basic grants. They reasoned that students in these circumstances would more seriously consider the private-college option, even though they would need to find substantially more assistance to attend the private school. Thus, the half-cost rule came to be identified as a key provision protecting the ability of the private schools to compete for students. While this concern had not been the primary intent behind its adoption in 1972, for many in the private sector it was becoming the touchstone of congressional concern for their well-being.

The shift in legislative priorities represented both a rational response to political prospects and the private sector's growing ambivalence toward the federal government. Those who thought Washington could be a constructive supporter of private higher education, if not its savior, had had their innings and apparently struck out. Those who approached the federal government defensively, inclined to "take the money and run," now dominated the private sector.

Early in the Ninety-fourth Congress (on February 20, 1975), Congressman O'Hara, without cosponsors, introduced two higher education bills, H.R. 3470 and H.R. 3471. The first was a simple extension of a potpourri of categorical and other programs, slated for only modest changes. H.R. 3471, on the other hand, was a detailed and complex student aid bill that represented some fundamental, indeed revolutionary, departures in national policy.

Since all of the federal higher education programs would be expiring in the Ninety-fourth Congress, these two bills, particularly H.R. 3471, had to be taken very seriously as the starting point for legislative action.

Of particular relevance to private higher education, H.R. 3471 removed the basic grant half-cost limit, O'Hara reasoning that it was unfair to deprive a needy student of federal grant money because of his or her choice of a school. The supplemental educational opportunity grant program would be administered directly by the Office of Education rather than by the campuses, and awards would be based on merit in addition to need. New federal capital contributions to the national direct student loan (NDSL) program would be terminated, and existing funds would be turned over to schools for their own loan programs. Student need was removed as a criterion for work-study. The state student incentive grant program was to be drastically changed, with funds allocated to states on the basis of their own support for higher education as measured by appropriations and by the degree to which they held down public tuition. In addition, states could use these funds not only for grants but also for work-study programs and to increase enrollment capacity at schools with no tuition charges. Finally, with respect to the guaranteed student loan (GSL) program, H.R. 3471 ended the eligibility of schools to serve as lenders.

The bill was not designed to discriminate against private higher education. Rather, it reflected O'Hara's policy preferences—support for low tuition, reward for student merit, cleaning up the abuses in the guaranteed student loan program, reducing student reliance on loans, and encouraging all students to be self-reliant by earning their education through work. But, regardless of the motivations of its author, H.R. 3471 was abhorrent to private higher education, a frontal attack on everything they cherished in federal student aid. It removed the one protection for their competitive position, half-cost; it took the sole campus-based grant program (SEOG) off the campus and diluted its need-relatedness; it terminated a second campus-based program (NDSL); it removed the need criterion from the third (college work-study); it ended institutional lending authority under the guaranteed student loan program; and it aggressively boosted the cause of their rivals, the low-cost public schools.[12] From the point of view of the private colleges, it would have been hard to design a more repugnant student aid bill.

H.R. 3471 confirmed the view among the private leaders that they

12. Campus-based student aid programs in which awards are determined on the basis of student need tend to benefit the private institutions since their students have more "need" (the difference between the costs of attendance and the students' own resources).

would receive no succor from Congressman O'Hara. Any lingering doubts were dispelled by O'Hara's (unsuccessful) attempt to repeal half-cost in a House-Senate conference dealing with a series of technical student aid amendments in June 1975. Within private college circles, H.R. 3471 guaranteed the ascendancy of the skeptics. One president reflected this view, explaining to the authors in mid-1976 that "attitudes toward the federal government have changed over the past few years. Private colleges are no longer looking to Washington for financial salvation; they just want to be left alone."

The private sector in a hostile environment. O'Hara's attitudes and H.R. 3471 combined with other developments to reinforce the skeptics' desire for greater distance from Washington and their low expectations for new federal help.

First, recent federal mandates in realms such as pension reform, occupational safety, education of the handicapped, and privacy of educational records, added to Title IX of the Education Amendments of 1972 prohibiting sex discrimination, imposed what seemed to be a crushing financial burden on schools struggling to survive on a thin margin and also threatened to subvert the independence of private institutions. They feared that any new legislation designed to aid them also carried a high risk of adding, perhaps in unforeseen ways, to their regulatory problem. "Our continued independence requires asking for less and getting less," explained one private university president.

Second, the Nixon and Ford administrations year after year had recommended termination of the campus-based supplemental grant and student loan programs, and they "zeroed" these programs in their budgets. Education appropriation bills were frequently vetoed, and money was often tied up by deferrals and rescissions. Retaining funds for existing programs with perhaps modest increases absorbed the energies and jaded the vision of private-sector leaders.

Third, private higher education now seemed to have no visible champions in either the executive branch or the Congress comparable to Daniel P. Moynihan in the first two years of the Nixon administration; Senator Wayne Morse, Pell's predecessor as subcommittee chairman; or Edith Green. Instead of vigorous allies and understanding friends, private higher education saw lukewarm enthusiasts—and James O'Hara.

Fourth, public sympathy for private higher education and public enthusiasm for education generally seemed to be on the wane. Combined with the economic recession and the deadlock between the President and

Congress, these attitudes hardly foreshadowed bold new federal initiatives in higher education.

It was not the best of times for federal support of private higher education, which quietly shelved the bright ideas advanced in the Ninety-third Congress and prepared to go to the barricades to hold on to what it had and to resist the O'Hara bill. This was also a rather easy and familiar course of action, absolving the private institutions from having to enter the hurly-burly of legislative innovation and compromise and allowing them simply to stand pat for the status quo.

COFHE enters the scene. Following the introduction of H.R. 3471, O'Hara held another round of student aid hearings in early 1975.[13] During these hearings a new actor emerged as an important spokesman for private higher education, the Consortium on Financing Higher Education (COFHE). Made up at the time of twenty-three "elite-prestigious" private schools, including those in the Ivy League and others like the University of Chicago, Stanford, and Duke, COFHE had been established in 1974 to provide research, planning, and consulting services to its members. In April 1975, it issued a report on federal student aid and adopted an aggressive legislative strategy, hiring its own Washington-based lobbyist. Using the rhetoric of the Ninety-third Congress, the COFHE report advocated modifying the basic and supplemental grants to achieve both "access" and "choice," and also proposed simplifying and conforming the two federal loan programs while ensuring a continued role for institutional lenders. The report generated considerable interest and comment since it was comprehensive and well written. While most of private higher education had pulled up the drawbridge and prepared to defend what it had, COFHE was the one highly visible group in the private sector still pushing for innovative federal action.

The student aid hearings generated almost no support for the O'Hara bill, either within the subcommittee or among the witnesses testifying for higher education. Indeed there was outspoken criticism of almost every facet of the chairman's bill, relieved only by polite references to its thought-provoking qualities and to the good intentions that surely lay behind it.

Apart from the chairman, the subcommittee seemed disposed to re-

13. *The Student Financial Aid Act of 1975*, Hearings before the Subcommittee on Postsecondary Education of the House Committee on Education and Labor, 94:1 (GPO, 1975).

orient the basic and supplemental grant programs along the lines recommended by COFHE. But this was not to be, for the COFHE proposals failed to win general support even within the private higher education community and the members of the subcommittee were not willing to go to the mat with their chairman and try to report out legislation to which he was hostile.

COFHE alone. COFHE billed its recommendations as broadly beneficial to all of private higher education while not antagonistic to the interests of the public sector. But despite diligent efforts, it aroused little enthusiasm among higher education representatives, except for limited endorsements from the Association of American Universities and the American Council on Education.

The political heart of the COFHE recommendations was a trade-off, repealing the half-cost rule to make basic grants more clearly an "access" program in return for supplementary grants more closely related to tuition costs to help ensure "choice." Although analyses by ACE and COFHE strongly challenged the view that the half-cost limit was a significant factor in student choice among types of institutions, it had by the spring of 1975 become a symbol, and there was an almost irrational attachment to it in many quarters of the private sector. The small private colleges were particularly adamant and, prodded by leaders of the Association of American Colleges and the Association of Jesuit Colleges and Universities, mounted a grass-roots letter-writing campaign to press for retention of the half-cost limit.

Perhaps most importantly, the trade-off proposed by COFHE entailed some risk; no one could guarantee that a more rationally structured and carefully targeted package of student aid programs would yield a net gain for the private schools. Risk-taking ran contrary to the defensive, protective mood that had overtaken the whole sector. COFHE found itself swimming against a strong tide.

Two other factors militated against private-sector support for these recommendations. Upon analysis, the COFHE formula for the supplemental grant program worked well for schools—such as those belonging to COFHE—that had exceptionally high tuition charges. But it was less well matched to the interests of the great mass of private colleges with more moderate tuition rates. In time, COFHE modified its proposal to focus on the "average" private college, but the damage had been done. The ecumenical glow of the COFHE report was dimmed, and its credibility on Capitol Hill was undermined. "At the tone the COFHE position will be . . ." was the mocking comment of one House staffer.

The issue of the supplemental grant formula reinforced a broader suspicion of COFHE within private higher education. It was perceived as an organization of rich schools that could afford to take risks. They were not so dependent on tuition or as close to the brink as most private institutions. If the gamble did not pay off, the COFHE campuses would still do well enough, but many of the others might go under. "Those COFHE guys come down from the mountain with this report and expect people to fall for it. The COFHE proposal would not have helped our institutions," remarked the spokesman for a group of private schools not affiliated with COFHE.

O'Hara and his colleagues. The members of the Subcommittee on Postsecondary Education who were sympathetic to the concept of the COFHE report, such as John Brademas (Democrat from Indiana), Frank Thompson, Jr. (Democrat from New Jersey), Edwin D. Eshleman (Republican from Pennsylvania), and Albert H. Quie (Republican from Minnesota), were unwilling to battle with O'Hara for several reasons.

They perceived, first, little public demand for and interest in legislative action on behalf of the private sector. The sprinkling of letters and witnesses advocating pro-private legislation amounted to a whisper rather than the outcry to which a representative legislature must give heed. Without any such effective political demand, involvement and action from sympathetic congressmen did not materialize, and there were just too many other lively items on the congressional agenda. Viewed from a distance, the higher education programs seemed to be working tolerably well, if not ideally.

O'Hara was also an old personal friend and a trusted and valued ally of the senior Democrats on the subcommittee, with whom he had stood shoulder to shoulder in many previous legislative battles. In 1972 there had been a zest for combat over higher education in part because Representative Green was a personal and political enemy of many of her opponents. In 1975–76, there was puzzled head shaking over O'Hara's bill and a search for some way to defeat H.R. 3471 without a confrontation. In addition, O'Hara was known to be campaigning for the Senate in Michigan even before he formally announced his candidacy in October 1975. His Democratic colleagues did not want to consume his energies or undermine his campaign by an acrimonious fight in the subcommittee.

More generally, they also had no stomach for repeating the bloodletting of 1972.

A third reason was that the COFHE recommendations were not supported by the majority of the independent institutions; they wanted to preserve the status quo. Besides being divisive, the report also provoked a reaction from the public sector. While willing to repeal the half-cost limit, the public institutions were unwilling to have their share of the supplemental grants reduced. As the umbrella association, the American Council on Education tried to mediate, but its efforts were only moderately successful. With open public-private warfare threatening, the subcommittee members backed away from a messy squabble in which it was unlikely that they could emerge as winners and about which they considered there was no real need to do anything anyway.

Finally, even if new legislation, as recommended by COFHE, were passed by the House, the prospects of a friendly reception in the Senate did not look good. Senator Pell let it be known early and clearly that he did not favor any further extensive modifications of the Higher Education Act of 1965. So a victory for the COFHE proposal in the House was likely to be short-lived and futile, since a divided House delegation to the conference committee would probably be beaten by senators united behind Pell.

House action. O'Hara expressed the hope that a higher education bill could be passed in the House during the summer of 1975. But apathy and lack of consensus produced a long delay. The first formal markup was not until November 10; a number of unproductive sessions followed, and there were frequent failures to achieve a quorum. Almost a full year passed, punctuated by brief flurries of public interest and flickers of enthusiasm as new ideas surfaced. COFHE came forward with its revised supplemental grant formula, Congressmen Thompson and John Erlenborn (Republican from Illinois) generated some interest with a discussion of variants on a basic grant-supplemental grant package, and ACE informally circulated a staff-developed "super BEOG," which combined the BEOG and SEOG into a single cost-related grant.

When the principals—O'Hara, Brademas, and Quie—finally got together informally to try to break the deadlock, the result was a firm if amiable stalemate. In time, it was agreed simply to reauthorize all of the existing higher education programs with minor changes and to make only "technical" amendments in student aid. O'Hara's proposals in H.R. 3471 and the BEOG-SEOG revisions suggested by COFHE and others were all abandoned. The reauthorization bill did contain one concession to each side. The compromise included a new "trigger" proposed by O'Hara to link funding of student aid to funding for several categorical programs of particular relevance to low-cost public institutions. In return, the reauthorization was limited to two years, which would force the next Congress again to face the student aid issues, perhaps in an environment more accommodating to innovations on behalf of the private sector.

The new bill that resulted from this agreement, H.R. 12851, was accepted by the subcommittee in late March 1976 without major changes. It did not include the guaranteed student loan program, which needed basic revision and further work. The two-year extension of the other programs was a limited victory for COFHE since the dominant sentiment elsewhere in the private sector was to try to hold on to the half-cost limit provision and the campus-based programs for as long as possible rather than exposing them to the whims of the next Congress.

Having achieved that modest success, COFHE stood with the rest of the private campuses as the House worked out a guaranteed student loan bill. The saga of H.R. 3471 and H.R. 12851 was repeated in miniature with respect to loans. O'Hara and Erlenborn floated a "Discussion Draft" that accomplished their policy objectives while conflicting sharply with the interests of private colleges seeking to continue as lenders. Another round of informal negotiations resulted in a loan bill, H.R. 14070 (introduced August 26, 1976), that essentially preserved the status quo for the private institutions, while accomplishing some important program reforms that were neutral among types of institutions.

Meanwhile in the Senate. While all of this was occurring in the House, the Senate was devoting much less attention to higher education, concentrating instead on revision of the Vocational Education Act of 1963.[14] Senator Pell did not introduce his omnibus education bill, S. 2657, until November 1975.[15] Senate markups concluded in April 1976 with most of the controversy still centered on issues unrelated to higher education. Pell achieved his objective of "refinements" in the higher education programs (with the exception of an overhaul of student loans) and a long reauthorization period of seven years. Senator William D. Hathaway (Democrat from Maine) raised the BEOG-SEOG, access-choice issue

14. 77 Stat. 403.
15. An important reason for the delay was the tragic death of Senator Pell's education counsel, Stephen J. Wexler.

and advocated a shorter extension, but he found little support among his colleagues and did not push hard, in part because private-sector representatives were spending most of their time on the House side where there was more active interest in their cause.

When the bulky House and Senate bills finally staggered into conference in September, there was very little at issue of importance to private higher education. The length of the extension was compromised at four years and the major House-Senate differences on student loans were worked out without upsetting the status quo for institutional lenders. While their ability to continue as lenders was not substantially curtailed, the private institutions did suffer at least a symbolic defeat. They were subjected to restrictions that did not apply to other lenders and that implied they were "suspect" in the eyes of federal policymakers.

The inactive executive branch. The administration played almost no role in the development of the higher education legislation. The bill it finally sent up to the Hill in early 1976 was essentially the same tired collection of proposals that Congress had rejected on several previous occasions, and it was treated with scarcely concealed disdain.

The minimal impact of the administration in recent higher education legislation has been in large part due to lasting policy differences during the Nixon-Ford years. Congress simply found unacceptable and did not take seriously the package of proposals that the administration doggedly advanced year after year. This pattern of congressional dominance and executive branch irrelevance contrasts with the more usual pattern in other policy arenas, where the administration sets the agenda and Congress responds.

Elsewhere on the Hill. This discussion has focused on the legislative authorization process and the interest of private higher education in the development of the Education Amendments of 1976.[16] The authorizing process leads to one set of decisions in which these interests are balanced with those of the public sector. Another pattern, however, might conceivably be established through the separate process of budgets and appropriations. Which authorized programs are actually funded, and at what levels, can make a substantial difference.

In recent years appropriations in the student aid area have roughly followed the choices of the authorizing committees: the basic grant program was phased in one year at a time, expanding to meet growing

16. 90 Stat. 2081.

student demand, while the campus-based programs have been sustained at stable or slightly increased appropriation levels. But new budget constraints and the mounting costs of basic grants could over time produce funding patterns adverse to private higher education's interests in student aid. Representatives of the independent sector will have to pay close attention to the budgetary process in the years ahead—a process now more protracted and complex as a result of new procedures and timetables established by the Congressional Budget Act of 1974.[17]

A Community of Interest?

The ambivalent attitudes of the private colleges and universities, their disparate needs and objectives, have in large measure contributed to the "politics of ambiguity" apparent in the legislative history of the 1970s. Private institutions no longer dominate American higher education as they did thirty, fifty, or one hundred years ago. Not only have enrollments dropped to less than 25 percent of the national total, but the private campuses no longer uniquely embody academic excellence, prestige, and quality, nor flexibility and innovativeness. Rapidly growing government-sponsored institutions have challenged the private sector of higher education along all of these dimensions.

Yet there remains a deep conviction that American higher education and society would be the losers if private institutions were allowed to decline and disappear. For this reason, as well as the natural survival instincts of human institutions, the health of private higher education has become a cause inspiring considerable passion and commitment. With finances and enrollments tightening in recent years, more and more independent institutions have felt increasingly vulnerable. A mood of growing unease has pervaded the private sector, along with a heightened sense of brotherhood and common cause in the face of adversity.

It is in this atmosphere that a new national organization was launched in mid-1976 designed to provide a "unified and persuasive national voice for independent higher education" in the United States. The private campuses have organized, for the first time, an exclusive lobby of their own, the National Association of Independent Colleges and Universities, to develop "public policies which promote, and public understanding

17. 88 Stat. 297.

which supports, the ability of independent higher education to continue to meet the education needs of America within our pluralistic system."[18]

But there is a considerable leap from such abstract solidarity to concrete issues of government policy, particularly federal. The fact is that the independent sector of higher education is quite fragmented in terms of attitudes and perspectives; there is a broad range in style, culture, and objective interest among the private colleges. Moreover, the federal government has never distinguished between public and private institutions in framing its policies; other divisions are usually more significant in the federal politics of higher education.

Attitudes toward Government Patronage

On a most fundamental question, private colleges and universities are traditionally ambivalent and divided: the propriety and risks of accepting public aid. Private higher education constantly finds itself on the horns of an inescapable dilemma: how much government patronage can independent institutions accept without ultimately sacrificing their independence? At what price salvation? Where to draw the line?

The private sector runs the gamut from campuses that have readily accepted federal money under almost any circumstances over the past two decades, to others that have succumbed more slowly as the enticements to do so became more attractive during the 1960s, to a fringe group that today still refuses virtually all federal support, usually with the exception of aid to students. For the rare institution in the latter category, independence is a matter of ideology, usually associated with a religious affiliation; funding is almost exclusively private, and the absence of tainted federal money on campus is sometimes used as a selling point in seeking aid from corporations and other private donors.

But in the mid-1970s all colleges and universities, public and private alike, seem to be growing increasingly restive under the mounting pressure of government mandates and rules. One observer recently suggested that the "agreeable patronage" of the federal government in support of higher education "has degenerated into an adversary relationship."[19] However, tensions have been embedded in the relationship all along.

18. *NAICU* (National Association of Independent Colleges and Universities, 1977), p. 1.

19. Earl F. Cheit, quoted in *Chronicle of Higher Education*, vol. 13 (September 27, 1976), p. 12.

Federal support emanates from various Washington agencies, each with its own purposes and needs, each concerned with the responsible stewardship of public funds. Educational institutions must be responsive if they are to seek government largesse; they must bend to the rules of accountability meant to ensure that money is spent for the purposes intended; and in recent years they have faced a growing list of nondiscrimination, affirmative action, and assorted directives designed to ameliorate social ills, along with increasingly complex and (as perceived by college administrators) cumbersome or arbitrary enforcement procedures.

Even those colleges that turn aside all but student aid funds must comply with a substantial volume of government regulations. Hillsdale College in Michigan, for instance, where 10 percent of the student body receives federal student assistance and no other federal money is involved, is vigorously protesting the applicability of Title IX sex discrimination regulations to its campus—so far without success. Federal patronage has a double edge.

A Diverse Constituency

The sheer diversity of the nation's 1,500 independent colleges and universities further confounds the relationship of private higher education to public policy. The problems of Harvard, Stanford, and the University of Chicago are obviously and vastly different from those of Kalamazoo, Our Lady of the Lake, and Piedmont Bible College.

When one scans the landscape of the private sector, chasms are readily apparent. Several variables stand out.

Scale. Most private institutions are small; about 90 percent have enrollments under 2,500. Several hundred must be termed tiny, with under 500 students. The major private universities, on the other hand, average over 10,000 students. Northeastern University enrolls nearly 40,000—in the same league with the major public universities.[20]

Scope. More than half the private schools are four-year, undergraduate, basically liberal arts institutions. There are about 250 two-year colleges and institutes, and over 350 theological seminaries, professional schools, and other specialized institutions. Graduate education and re-

20. Carnegie Commission on Higher Education, *A Classification of Institutions of Higher Education* (Carnegie Foundation for the Advancement of Teaching, 1973).

search are heavily concentrated in 35 universities in the private sector. These are highly complex, diversified institutions. Another 30 offer at least some doctoral training.[21]

Stature. Universities of international reputation, renowned liberal arts colleges, struggling local and regional institutions, little-known (sometimes dubbed "invisible") colleges all dot the map of private higher education.

Wealth. Some twenty institutions have endowments exceeding $100 million apiece. They account for over one-third of the endowed funds in the private sector, including Harvard with over $1 billion. The great majority of private colleges have endowments of less than $5 million, and several hundred have either none at all or barely a pittance.[22] Despite the fact that income from endowment has generally declined over recent decades as a share of institutional financing, endowed monies are a rough indicator of financial strength and educational "standard of living." The closeness of the fiscal margin and relative sense of security (or insecurity) thus vary widely among the private institutions.

Hence, while diversity remains a vaunted attribute of the independent sector, it means that the problems and perspectives of individual campuses diverge widely. Their frames of reference are simply not the same. The gaps are cultural. They are also pragmatic, for the management, marketing, and financial concerns vary considerably among private institutions. In this respect, the criss-crossing lines within the private sector may be as consequential as the public-private dichotomy itself.

Tuition rates. For purposes of public policy, one common denominator among the private schools appears to be the issue of the "tuition gap." Their dependence on relatively high student charges and their competitive disadvantage in the face of lower-priced, subsidized public institutions are a pervasive concern in the independent sector. Yet here again the line dividing the public and private sectors is not as clear-cut as one might expect. Average tuition in private institutions now runs in the neighborhood of $2,500, compared with something over $500 in the public institutions. But there is considerable overlap between the higher-priced public and the lower-priced private colleges and universities. Tuition rates in Ivy League schools and similar institutions are now near or over the $4,000 mark, but many small private campuses still charge

21. Ibid.
22. Council for Financial Aid to Education, *Voluntary Support of Education, 1974-75* (CFAE, n.d.).

less than $2,000. At the same time, some states have pushed tuition at public institutions well into the lower range of private-sector pricing.

A consequence of such overlap in pricing patterns is that it is very difficult to design programs of student assistance that will aid the entire private sector in equal measure. Particular types of private institutions, depending upon what they charge their students, will be affected in different ways.

The Tradition of Federal Neutrality

Even if higher education could resolve its ambivalence toward the national government and even if it could bridge internal gaps so as to present a united front in the federal policy arena, a fundamental fact would remain: federal policymakers are generally not disposed to "tilt" toward one sector of higher education or the other. This is not to say, of course, that public and private institutions benefit equally from all federal programs, but the intent has been to treat them evenhandedly— or at least to avoid arbitrary distinctions.

At the state level, the traditions are quite different. For the past century the states have moved with varying speed to establish and expand their own public systems of higher education. But during the past two decades, some twenty states have developed a variety of programs to support (or purchase educational services from) their private colleges and universities, and most states have developed programs of student aid, the majority of which are open to students attending either public or private institutions.[23]

This gradual evolution of state policy has meant that the public and private sectors of higher education are increasingly thrown into direct competition for funding. The independent institutions have organized effectively in some jurisdictions and the public campuses no longer have a lock hold on the state budget for higher education. Chapter 7 describes the conflict within some states as monies are set aside for private institutions and for scholarships, cutting into potential budgetary resources for the operation of public campuses. As one observer of these develop-

23. The handful of states that now restrict eligibility for state scholarships to students in either the public or private sector will have to change such policies if they are to continue to receive federal funds under the state student incentive grant (SSIG) program. Effective October 1, 1978, the Education Amendments of 1976 (90 Stat. 2081) require that state programs matched by incentive grants be open to students in both public and nonprofit private schools.

ments said to the authors, "the public institutions clearly view state money as *theirs* and there is always tension when the private campuses try to get in on the act."

In Washington, the public-private split is unlikely ever to be so clearly defined. The national government, after all, has always played a supplementary role while the states have had the basic responsibility for shaping and financing American higher education. Whether it be cancer research, space exploration, or educational opportunities for the disadvantaged, Washington supports higher education as a means to a variety of discrete federal purposes. And in doing so, it is essentially unconcerned about the public or private identity of the educational institutions that receive the funds.[24]

In the many federal programs that provide payments to the institutions themselves, public and private campuses generally have an equal shot at the benefits, and in practice the private sector claims a share of these funds that is roughly commensurate with its share of the higher education enterprise.

In the rapidly growing realm of student aid, however, neutrality is a murkier proposition. Federal student assistance has always been open to persons enrolled in both public and private institutions, but the important question is whether the specific terms of the programs should reflect the wide variations in pricing between and within the two sectors. With respect to student aid, neutrality and evenhandedness are in the eye of the beholder.

Federal Policy and the Price Structure of Higher Education

A corollary of the neutrality axiom is that federal policy does not seek to influence, much less dictate tuition levels. It implicitly accepts the price structure of higher education as given. Setting tuition rates is a state and institutional responsibility, an area where the national government has never presumed to play a role.

One school of thought holds that the states should restructure the way they support higher education, that is, they should raise public-sector tuition levels, thus narrowing the public-private tuition gap, and

24. On the historical assumptions and limits of federal policymaking for higher education, see Thomas Wolanin and Lawrence Gladieux, "The Political Culture of a Policy Arena: Higher Education," in Matthew Holden, Jr., and Dennis L. Dresang, eds., *What Government Does* (Sage, 1975), pp. 177–208.

redirect subsidies from operating support of public institutions to need-based student assistance. It is also argued (as in chapter 5) that Washington should design strategies to nudge the states in this direction. Federal incentives would be used to get them to "rationalize" the pricing of higher education.

It may be that the tuition differential is the nub of the private college dilemma, that the states are responsible for creating the problem, and that public policy alternatives that do not come to grips with it will be palliative at best. The fact is, however, that federal policymakers have been loath to tread on the sensitive tuition issue. Many things are possible politically, but a federal program to manipulate state subsidy and tuition policies seems beyond the pale. The federal government has never undertaken to "rationalize" prices in higher education. Student aid policies in effect help narrow the tuition gap for needy students, but they are not designed to reduce the gap for all students by revamping the price structure itself.

The Stakes for Private Higher Education

Where, then, do private colleges and universities find common ground in Washington? In many areas, their interests are essentially the same as those of public higher education, with differences only in emphasis and degree. In other policy domains, institutional interests diverge along public-private lines and even within the private sector itself.

Tax policies. Perhaps one of the most vital issues for the private sector is the federal income tax deduction for charitable contributions. Both sectors are affected by the charitable deduction (about one-fourth of voluntary support for higher education goes to public institutions), but private institutions have a far larger stake. Occasionally a voice is heard from the independent sector objecting to the public institutions "horning in" on private philanthropy, but spokesmen for public and private higher education are generally agreed on this issue.

Proposals to provide tax relief for families paying college expenses have often been introduced in Congress and consistently rejected for reasons spelled out elsewhere in this book. Twice in 1976, as on several previous occasions during the past decade, such proposals cleared the Senate, only to die in the face of House opposition. As yet, the idea's time has not come, though it keeps resurfacing in one form or another. Recent versions generally cover all expenses related to college attendance, not just tuition, and the credit or deduction usually has a fairly low ceiling (for example, $250 in the 1976 Senate measure), which means that the tax relief is likely to be the same regardless of the institution attended. Such a general credit would cost substantial amounts in forgone revenue, yet it would neither affect the tuition gap nor significantly reduce the cost of private higher education to the consumer.

Some private institutions nonetheless continue to favor the tax relief approach and lately there has even been some scattered support for the idea among spokesmen for public higher education.[25] However, a groundswell of support for college tax credits is still lacking in the higher education community.

Yet the concept has obvious political appeal. The 1976 version passed by the Senate was finally set aside largely because of strong pressures from the new congressional budget committees to avoid further revenue drain. The question is whether a tax credit scheme will ultimately find its way into law once the revenue picture eases, and whether it is really in the interest of private higher education to push for it.

Regulatory issues. In the main, public and private institutions are equally subject to the blossoming array of federal regulations impinging on higher education. Both public and private college leaders have spoken out on the question with increasing frequency and deepening concern. But many of the private schools feel especially threatened by the volume and scope of government mandates. Some are simply hard pressed to cope administratively with the problem. A small liberal arts campus with a president, a provost, a treasurer, and perhaps a business officer may have trouble just finding someone to read and interpret its obligations under new rules regarding sex discrimination, privacy of student records, occupational safety, and a host of other concerns. One private university spokesman argues that the combined impact of overlapping regulations "amounts to something like confiscatory behavior because of the amount of time and money required."

Moreover, private colleges tend to be more vulnerable to government demands because they operate on a closer margin financially. A federal decision to eliminate second-class postal privileges for college catalogs,

25. In earlier years a wing of the private sector strongly advocated tuition tax relief as a way to get federal support for higher education without the danger of federal control or the inconvenience of bureaucratic red tape. Representatives of public higher education, on the other hand, uniformly condemned the concept, particularly when it implied preferential treatment for parents of students in high-cost institutions.

for example, would deal a particularly heavy blow to many private institutions.

Representatives of private colleges in Washington are likely to devote increasing attention to regulatory issues. Test cases and other legal challenges on behalf of both public and private higher education may not be far down the road.

Research funding. Support for scientific research and development is the dominant source of federal funding that goes directly to institutions of higher education. The public-private issue has no bearing in this policy realm. The federal government purchases services from those educational institutions with the requisite capabilities, and the major beneficiaries tend to be a small number of research and graduate-oriented universities. Twenty institutions receive about 40 percent of total federal research and development funds to higher education; eleven of these are private. About one-third of the hundred universities receiving the largest overall federal support are private,[26] but institutions, public and private alike, have an overriding common interest in stemming the recent erosion of such support.

Changes in government research priorities may have subtle differential impacts on public and private higher education; a shift away from support of basic research, for example, may be somewhat more damaging to private universities. But federal research policy does not consciously treat public and private institutions differently.

Categorical programs. Similarly, there are no deep rifts along public-private lines when it comes to a variety of relatively small categorical aids for higher education, from "language and area studies" to library support and instructional equipment.

In all of the above areas—tax policy, regulations, research and development, and categorical support—representatives of private institutions will be found struggling alongside their public-sector counterparts to preserve current sources of federal funding and to avert unfavorable decisions and unwanted inroads. Lobbying here will typically be cooperative, reactive, and protective.

But what are the prospects that the federal government will take explicit action to undergird the private sector?[27]

---

26. National Science Foundation, *Federal Support to Universities, Colleges, and Selected Nonprofit Institutions, Fiscal Year 1974* (GPO, 1975), pp. 9–10.

27. It should be noted here that the bounds of permissible federal action on behalf of the private sector have in the past—and will continue to be—conditioned

Institutional aid. As one private college president has said about prospects for public funds to bail out private higher education, "don't count on it."[28] Since 1972 aid to students rather than institutions has been established as the principal mechanism of federal support. Symbolically, Congress opted to put purchasing power in the hands of needy students and to let them make their own choices in the postsecondary marketplace. The Education Amendments of 1972 did authorize "cost-of-education allowances" to institutions, but that program itself reflected the student aid priority by linking the institution's grant to its enrollment of federally aided students. Congress made clear that it was not assuming a responsibility for the well-being and survival of institutions, but rather was seeking to harness them to the realization of national objectives. Even this limited program of institutional support has yet to be funded and seems fated to remain on the books as nothing more than an expression of intent.

The cause of federal institutional aid remains alive in the higher education community, and it is still viewed in some quarters as an essential step to ease the plight of private higher education. But Congress still remains disinclined to legislate on behalf of institutions as such. Even less is it likely to legislate on behalf of *private* institutions alone, given the tradition of federal neutrality.

Student aid. If the government is going to do something to shore up the private sector of higher learning, it will most probably do so through strategies of student assistance and it will do so in the name of broadening and equalizing educational choice, not rescuing institutions. "Access" and "choice" have become code words in a controversy over who will get what, where, and how in the student aid programs.

The dollars at issue have multiplied during the past decade. Over $2.5 billion in federal appropriations were spent on need-based student assistance in the 1976–77 academic year. This more than triples the level of 1972–73 and the growth curve is likely to continue in the next two years as the basic grant program expands and as the authorized basic grant maximum award jumps from $1,400 to $1,800 in 1978–79, pushing pro-

---

at least in part by judicial decisions. This chapter focuses on federal legislative and executive policymaking for higher education, but the courts also play an episodic and uncharted role, particularly through their interpretations of the church-state strictures of the Constitution.

28. Edward Eddy, president, Chatham College, quoted in *Higher Education Daily*, vol. 4 (October 12, 1976), p. 6.

jected costs for this program alone to more than $2.3 billion (provided it is fully funded).

The federal government also invests substantial funds in education benefits under the GI bill and the Social Security Act. However, these are flat entitlements that are not adjusted according to individual financial circumstances or to costs of attendance at different schools. Representatives of private higher education in recent years have pressed the veterans' affairs committees of Congress to revive the post-World War II concept of subsidizing tuition as well as maintenance costs under the GI bill. To date, such efforts have failed. The social security and veterans' programs are shaped in policy arenas where higher education has relatively little influence.

A sizable federal investment is also associated with the guaranteed student loan program—for interest subsidies to students, special allowances to lenders, and payments on defaults. The issues here are complex and contentious, and neither policymakers nor higher education lobbyists are fully satisfied with the program, with its budgetary impact (over $500 million[29]), or with the continuing prospect of saddling millions of students with heavy loan obligations. Loans, however, will probably remain an inescapable component of student finance in both the public and private sectors of higher education. Washington will continue to play a role in stimulating the availability of loan capital, and Congress will periodically tinker with the guaranteed loan program (and perhaps alternative loan schemes) in an effort to serve students more effectively while tightening up on abuses.

Many private institutions, particularly the high-tuition campuses and those that operate as lenders under the program, have an especially important stake in guaranteed loans. For them, the guaranteed loan program commands a higher priority than it does for most of the public sector. They will continue to be particularly vigilant and sensitive to legislative remedies that might adversely affect their vital interests in student loan financing. But the program itself does not constitute a major issue dividing public and private higher education.

Therefore, the issues of access and choice—mirroring the interests of public and private, lower-priced and higher-priced institutions—will be thrashed out primarily in relation to the major federal grant programs, BEOG and SEOG. State student incentive grants and the other campus-

29. *The Budget of the United States Government, Fiscal Year 1978—Appendix,* p. 341.

based aid programs will also come into play as alternative strategies and potential trade-offs are debated. As the review of recent legislative history has shown, however, the resolution will not come easily.

Common Interests?

In summary, what can we say about the community of interest of independent colleges and universities in the federal arena? We conclude that:

• Private higher education has much at stake in Washington, but on most federal policy issues its interests are not far different from those of public higher education.

• Private higher education is as divided within itself—in terms of attitudes toward government, sectarian affiliations, size of institutions, orientation (undergraduate versus graduate and research), and wealth—as it is set against public higher education.

• Federal higher education policy generally skirts the public-private distinction by adopting a neutral approach and leaving the fundamental policy questions to the states.

• Public and private higher education are at odds in Washington to the extent that federal policy touches on the tuition gap, primarily through the student aid programs. But even in this realm the battle lines are blurred and consensus within the private sector is not easily achieved.

Prospects for a National Solution

This chapter started by contrasting the abundance of warm feeling toward private higher education among Washington policymakers with the absence of decisive federal action to meet private higher education's problems.

We have delineated and illustrated some of the implicit boundaries of federal policymaking that narrow the range of what the government is realistically apt to do in this area, and we have suggested that the tradition of federal neutrality might most easily be bent in the area of student aid so that more significant help could be made available to the private sector. It is difficult to avoid the conclusion, however, that the odds run counter to the development of a systematic national policy on behalf of independent higher education.

This assessment may prove false if the federal government is willing to intervene in the fundamental issue of pricing and the tuition gap. There are two basic approaches that Washington might take to close the gap: mandating or manipulating the states to raise tuition levels in the public sector (as advanced in chapter 5), or providing tuition off-sets to enable private institutions to reduce their charges to students. The former would constitute federal meddling in a traditional function of the states, and would do so in the name of higher rather than lower prices to students—politically a bitter pill, if not indigestible. The latter approach would require subsidizing higher-priced institutions according to a formula based on enrollments. The federal budgetary costs would probably be very high, even if the states participated; the payments would constitute a form of institutional aid, a concept Congress has rejected; and the policy would entail unabashed preferential treatment for one class of institutions, something Congress has long avoided.

To doubt the feasibility of such fundamental departures in the federal role is not to minimize the importance of the more circumscribed, ongoing debate on federal student assistance. The dollars involved are substantial and growing; the stakes for private higher education are very great and also growing. Particularly as the basic grant program looms larger in the scheme of federal aid, it becomes important for private higher education to seek a realignment of the access and choice objectives implicit in the student assistance programs. As the access program, basic grants, increasingly dwarfs all the other programs combined, private higher education's share of federal student aid funds, currently something less than one-third, will surely decline. Stemming that drift will require legislation to make either BEOG or some combination of the other programs more responsive to tuition levels and more supportive of student choice.

The most widely discussed and politically conceivable options include:

1. Making supplemental grants the principal policy vehicle for encouraging choice. This would require modifications in the current program to direct a greater proportion of awards to students attending higher-priced institutions.

2. Recasting the current basic and supplemental grant programs into a single tuition-sensitive grant that would serve as an entitlement for both access and choice—a "super BEOG."

3. Expanding the state student incentive grant program, which as

noted earlier would stimulate the growth of state scholarship programs that tend to favor students enrolled in independent institutions.

During the most recent legislative round, Congress held back from major revisions in federal student assistance policies (except perhaps for the changes in the guaranteed loan program). Some of the same factors may continue to work against significant change as the Ninety-fifth Congress reviews the student aid legislation. Three are particularly significant.

First, some key members are inclined to rethink the grant programs and to do something to enhance equality of choice. Yet Congress has in the past been ambivalent toward subsidizing students at expensive institutions. This sentiment worked against Senator Mondale's 1971 proposal of a variable entitlement geared to actual costs of attendance. Holding out for his own version of the BEOG, Senator Pell repeated many times, "Not everybody has to go to Princeton."[30] The question is how far Congress may be willing to go in underwriting a high-priced college education.

Second, every proposal that would revamp or tinker with the student aid programs is automatically analyzed by the higher education factions in terms of potential winners and losers among types of institutions. No segment of the academic community has yet shown any willingness to reduce its share of the pie to achieve the goal of a more balanced federal student aid strategy. The trade-offs built into various schemes are intricate and sometimes difficult to assess with precision, and the concerns cut across public-private lines. The fallout from the COFHE proposals suggests the underlying sensitivities and divergence of interests (at least perceived interests) within the independent sector.

Third, more generally, conditions of the mid-seventies seem to have produced a cautious, status quo orientation toward new federal legislation. One observer has noted "a kind of mutual exhaustion in higher education and government, not surprising after a decade of upheaval and rapid change."[31] Institutions of higher education are no longer looking to Washington for salvation as they may have been five years ago. Many of them are more concerned today about *protection* from potential harm at the hands of government.

Other factors may, however, improve the environment for federal action sensitive to the interests of independent colleges. President Carter

30. Gladieux and Wolanin, *Congress and the Colleges*, p. 105.
31. Harold L. Enarson, "The Endangered Partnership," Council for Advancement and Support of Education, *Case Currents*, vol. 2 (September 1976), p. 8.

arrived in the White House with a Democratic platform containing a pledge for student aid to achieve access and choice. Vice President Mondale can be counted on to remain a strong supporter of federal aid to higher education and may again advocate the kind of tuition-related student aid program that he sponsored in 1971. The House Postsecondary Education Subcommittee again has a new chairman, O'Hara having left the House because of his (unsuccessful) Senate candidacy. His successor, Representative William D. Ford (Democrat from Michigan), though he has yet to make his views fully known, may not be as unsympathetic to the private sector as O'Hara.

There is also the new voice of private higher education in Washington, the National Association of Independent Colleges and Universities. NAICU did not play a role in the 1976 legislation since it was not effectively organized until early fall, but its mandate includes vigorous advocacy of private higher education's cause in Washington. It must, of course, come to terms with the diversity of a membership that ranges between the high-tuition, highly endowed research universities and the lower-priced, traditionally black, and church-affiliated "invisible" colleges. Politically, it may opt for innovation and risk, or for the safety of the status quo and an arm's length relation with the federal government.

We suggest that there *is* room for creativity and change in federal policy and that independent higher education should shun the attitude of "take the money and run," which seems to have motivated some of its representatives in lobbying for a longer rather than a shorter extension of the student aid legislation in 1976. Congress compromised on the latter issue and gave itself four years to act again in this area. Private colleges and universities thus have another opportunity toward the end of the decade to tap a reservoir of goodwill among federal policymakers and to build into national higher education policy a genuine commitment to equal choice as well as equal access. The debate over the federal role remains open.

Chapter Five

Federal Options for Student Aid

Robert W. Hartman

EDITED BY DAVID W. BRENEMAN AND CHESTER E. FINN, JR.

ROBERT W. HARTMAN is a senior fellow in the Brookings Economic Studies program. He thanks Nancy J. Osher for research assistance. The chapter is based on research done under a grant from the Ford Foundation for a study of the relationships between federal aid and state support for higher education.

Tables

A PROMINENT ECONOMIST, upon returning from a mission to a Third World country, was asked for his general impression of its economy. His response—"Just about what you'd expect if the United Nations were managing an auto assembly plant"—seems as good a place as any to start a discussion of federal policy toward private higher education.

It is generally acknowledged that such a federal policy is needed, but the present panoply of programs represents, at best, a set of compromises designed to skirt the public-private institution issue. This accounts for one program providing air bags and another placing them in the trunk.

To limit the scope of the analysis, this discussion is confined to the federal role in financing undergraduate education. There are four principal themes. First, federal higher education programs have been modified (and multiplied) so as to minimize perceived harm to the private sector, resulting in an inefficient and inequitable set of programs. Second, any more direct federal approach to the public-private problem must take into account an even more central federal mission, that of providing access to higher education for students from lower-income families. Third, long-lasting solutions to the problems of the private sector depend on changes in the policies of state governments; federal solutions that take state behavior as given are both infeasible and unrealistically expensive. Finally, the federal government can help states reform their policies, but a realistic federal program involves the difficult task of revising, reforming, and phasing out existing aid programs in favor of a new policy providing the states with the incentives to change.

The first section examines briefly how the current set of federal programs have been distorted in an attempt to take the public-private problem into account. How the federal government could fully compensate for or attempt to influence the behavior of state governments that have created the public-private problem is discussed in the second section. The chapter concludes with a discussion of a recommended federal program and the budgetary constraints on such a plan.

The Current Federal Role

Before the Education Amendments of 1972 were enacted, federal aid to higher education was eclectic. For each problem that arose in the late 1950s and throughout the 1960s, a federal program responded. Sputnik's ascent was matched by the rise of national defense loans, graduate fellowships, and expanded research support. Facility shortages led to construction loans and grants. The discovery of poverty fathered educational opportunity grants and the college work-study program. Spiraling higher education costs threatened a middle-class raid on the Treasury via a tax credit; guaranteed loans were the cheaper compromise. Assorted other needs of higher education were addressed by small categorical programs.

Each of these programs gave rise to a full complement of guidelines, regulations, coordinating bodies, and regional panels that often seemed to be working at cross-purposes; but in fact there were so many different purposes underlying the laws that conflict was more or less inevitable. During this confused period, federal expenditures rose dramatically. Between 1962 and 1972, for example, expenditures for higher education in the U.S. Office of Education budget rose 343 percent, or 16 percent a year.[1]

While it is doubtful that any of these programs was undertaken with the private sector foremost in the minds of legislators, there is no doubt that it benefited greatly from the expansion of federal support during the sixties. As its share of enrollments dropped from 41 percent to 27 percent during that decade,[2] its share of federal payments to institutions (including research) fell only from 47 to 42 percent.[3] Moreover, in the rapidly growing student aid area, the private sector seems actually to have gained during the decade, its share rising from under 20 percent to 39 percent.[4]

By the time of the Education Amendments of 1972, several aspects of federal aid to higher education had begun to sort themselves out. First, and foremost, student aid was becoming the primary vehicle for federal purposes other than research.[5] Not only were veterans' GI bill benefits

1. Office of Management and Budget, Budget Review Division, "Federal Government Finances" (OMB, December 1974; processed), table 4, p. 11.
2. See table 1-5.
3. Derived from table 2-1.
4. Estimated from Felix H. I. Lindsay, *Financial Statistics of Institutions of Higher Education, 1959–60: Receipts, Expenditures, and Property* (Government Printing Office, 1964), p. 27, and Paul Mertins and Norman J. Brandt, *Financial Statistics of Institutions of Higher Education: Current Funds Revenues and Expenditures, 1969–70* (GPO, 1973), table 2, pp. 12-13.
5. Although research support from the federal government is of critical importance to a number of private universities, this chapter concentrates on federal education support, mainly for undergraduates. Research, graduate education, and medical school support are all so intertwined and complicated that they are beyond the scope of this chapter.

Table 5-1. *Federal Expenditures for Higher Education,*
by Type of Support, Fiscal Years 1965, 1970, 1972, and 1975

Type of support	1965	1970	1972	1975
	Millions of dollars			
Student aid	623	2,128	3,375	6,913
Veterans' readjustment benefits	43	665	1,437	3,479
Other	580	1,463	1,938	3,434
Institutional	331	1,459	1,389	1,661
Research	951	1,533	1,723	2,284
Total	1,905	5,120	6,487	10,858
	Percent			
Student aid	32.7	41.6	52.0	63.7
Veterans' readjustment benefits	2.3	13.0	22.1	32.0
Other	30.4	28.6	29.9	31.6
Institutional	17.4	28.5	21.4	15.3
Research	49.9	29.9	26.6	21.0
Total	100.0	100.0	100.0	100.0

Sources: Calculated from *Special Analyses, Budget of the United States Government, Fiscal Year 1977,* and issues for 1967, 1972, and 1974. Figures are rounded.

skyrocketing, but other forms of student aid were also expanding rapidly, while institutional payments declined in percentage terms after 1970 (table 5-1). Second, the ability of the private sector to hold its own in federal support, in spite of a declining share of enrollment, gave it a very substantial stake in the outcome of the 1972 legislation.

The 1972 education amendments did a great deal to clarify—but also to confuse—federal policy toward higher education. Three major new programs were authorized: basic educational opportunity grants (BEOG), formula institutional aid,[6] and state scholarship incentive grants (SSIG).[7] Each of these new authorizations was meant to address a federal policy goal, but each was fraught with political compromises, which limited the extent to which the programs really addressed the policy goals. In addition, the new programs did not replace old ones; rather, they were simply added onto existing programs, which were also renewed. These modifications and duplications, undertaken in part be-

6. Since no funds had been appropriated under this program by early 1978, analysis of its features has been omitted.

7. The SSIG program is examined at length elsewhere in this chapter; so are other aspects of the amendments not mentioned here.

cause of the perceived needs of private higher education, have served to confuse the thrust of federal support, as illustrated below.

Basic Educational Opportunity Grants

According to the conference report accompanying the Educational Amendments of 1972, basic grants were to be "the foundation upon which all other federal student assistance programs are based."[8] By using a national means test, the program was designed explicitly to channel federal student aid to students from low-income families. A maximum grant of $1,400, available to those whose families could contribute nothing to college expenses, was authorized, apparently as a compromise between higher and lower figures advocated by different legislators.[9] Much of the support for basic grants was prompted by the desire to increase access to higher education.

Although access for needy students is now generally agreed to be a primary purpose of federal higher education support, read in the terms of the basic grant program it is not entirely clear what access means. Specifically, access to what? Basic grants provide access to whatever $1,400 will buy. In 1972, when the enabling legislation was passed, $1,400 per academic year could be interpreted in several ways.

For example, since, in 1972–73, the average cost of room, board, books, and miscellaneous expenses for a commuter student at a typical public two-year college amounted to $1,435, basic grants could be interpreted as providing access to such a college with nominal tuition charges (about $200 in the 1972–73 academic year).[10] In this interpretation, virtually all of the federal funds are for noninstructional (nontuition) costs.

If, on the other hand, the framers of the law can be assumed to have known that most students were able to earn an average of $500 a year, then a $1,400 basic grant maximum might have meant access to institutions that cost the student $1,900, roughly a year's residence at a four-year public institution in 1972–73.[11]

8. *Education Amendments of 1972*, H. Rept. 92-1085, 92:2 (GPO, 1972), p. 167.
9. See Lawrence E. Gladieux and Thomas R. Wolanin, *Congress and the Colleges: The National Politics of Higher Education* (Heath, 1976), p. 106.
10. The half-cost rule, discussed below, somewhat modifies this statement.
11. Data on student budgets are from James B. Allan and Elizabeth W. Suchar, *Student Expenses at Postsecondary Institutions, 1973-74* (College Entrance Examination Board, 1973), p. vii.

It has recently been argued that, whatever the original purpose, the basic grants program *should* provide low-income students with enough money to pay all noninstructional costs.[12] Adopting such a rationale implies, first, that the basic grant law would need a perfecting amendment to scale up the maximum grant automatically in accordance with rises in the cost of living (or a specially designed index of room, board, and other expenses). A less desirable approach would be to legislate periodic adjustments, which was done in the Education Amendments of 1976. Second, it implies that if basic grants supply subsistence based on a needs test, the program would be as explicitly a redistribution of income and opportunity as any welfare program. That recognition solidifies the case for *federal* support inasmuch as there is broad concurrence that redistribution is properly a federal role.[13] Finally, and most important here, it implies that if basic grants are regarded solely as providing funds to cover the necessary noninstructional costs of attendance, then they have no particular role to play in solving the public-private problem in higher education. That is, by making basic grants independent of tuition charges incurred by students, the federal government would be saying, implicitly, that other federal or state programs are supposed to deal with this issue.

Several provisions included in the 1972 amendments were meant to be responsive to the needs of private higher education. Among these, the most significant was the half-cost limitation added to the basic grants program. Gladieux and Wolanin report that many private college spokesmen ". . . view the half-cost restriction as symbolic of federal concern for the protection of private higher education."[14] While it is probably unfair to subject symbolic concerns to empirical analysis, the half-cost

12. This approach is hinted at in Edward R. Fried and others, *Setting National Priorities: The 1974 Budget* (Brookings Institution, 1973), pp. 156 ff., and is spelled out in detail in Lois D. Rice, "Federal Student Assistance: Title IV Revisited," in John F. Hughes and Olive Mills, eds., *Formulating Policy in Postsecondary Education: The Search for Alternatives* (American Council on Education, 1975). By late 1975, the reformulation of the maximum grant into one based on noninstructional costs had been endorsed by the Carnegie Council on Policy Studies in Higher Education, the Consortium on Financing of Higher Education, the National Association of Student Financial Aid Administrators, and the National Student Lobby. (See College Entrance Examination Board, *Federal Student Aid Programs: A Comparison of Legislative Options* [CEEB, 1975].)

13. It also dramatizes the need to search out cases where other welfare programs might duplicate basic grant aid and where nonwelfare programs (for example, social security aid to students) might be integrated with basic grants.

14. *Congress and the Colleges*, p. 246.

provision so distorts the basic grants program that it merits dispensation from this stricture.

The half-cost limitation provides that basic grants shall be the lesser of (a) half the costs of attendance (tuition plus room, board, and other expenses), or (b) the basic grant entitlement ($1,400 minus the expected family contribution based on income and wealth). The half-cost provision has the effect, therefore, of reducing the grant entitlement only for low-income students attending relatively low-tuition institutions. For example, since nontuition expenses in the 1975–76 academic year had risen to an average of about $1,900,[15] the class of institutions affected by the half-cost provision was limited to those with tuitions under $900— almost exclusively public institutions, as can be seen from the average tuition and fees for 1975–76 in different types of institutions:[16]

Type of institution	Average tuition and fees (dollars)
Public: two-year	301
four-year	578
Private: two-year	1,652
four-year	2,240

In short, the half-cost provision "aids" the private sector primarily by reducing stipends to some basic grant recipients if they attend low-tuition institutions. The assistance to the private sector presumably stems from the fact that a grantee will view the incremental costs of attending a private institution as less than the difference in nominal charges. For example, assuming equal nontuition costs of $1,900 and using the average tuition figures noted above, a student whose family contribution is zero would observe that the costs of attending a four-year private institution are $1,939 higher than at a two-year public institution ($2,240 minus $301). Figuring that his basic grant will be only $1,100 if he attends a two-year public versus $1,400 if he attends the private institution, he will actually be subject to only a $1,639 net price differential. Thus the extra cost of attending a private institution is less with the half-cost provision than without it.

There are at least four difficulties with this approach to assisting the private sector. The first is that if the gap between public and private

15. Elizabeth W. Suchar, Stephen H. Ivens, and Edmund C. Jacobson, *Student Expenses at Postsecondary Institutions, 1975–76* (CEEB, 1975), p. ix. Average non-tuition charges ranged from $1,688 for commuters at public four-year institutions to $2,151 for residents at private four-year colleges.

16. Ibid., p. v.

prices is seen as the problem, then addressing it by narrowing the differential for only the most needy basic grant recipients, who constitute at most about 14 percent of all enrollees, seems futile.[17] Most enrollees who consider private higher education are not affected. Second, even if distorting the choice of institutions for a small share of all students were a plausible way to help private institutions, the disproportionate reduction for students from relatively low-income backgrounds needs further justification. For example, the reverse notion of imposing a federal tax on wealthy students who attend public institutions has the same price-narrowing effect and is superior on equity grounds. Third, as a result of the half-cost rule, two students of considerably different means might both receive the same basic grant. Finally, the half-cost limitation provides incentives for governing bodies of institutions with very low tuition *and* low-income student bodies to raise tuition rates, because the federal government picks up half the cost of the tuition increase for many aided students. While this kind of induced price change might help private institutions to the extent that it would narrow the tuition gap for everyone, it would work directly against the federal policy goal of providing access to higher education.

College-Based Aid

The Education Amendments of 1972 failed to simplify and clarify federal student aid by replacing, or at least integrating, previously existing college-based student aid programs (educational opportunity grants, college work-study, and national direct student loans) with the new basic grants program. Indeed, the law did the reverse by requiring that the existing programs receive appropriations of at least $653.5 million

17. According to the Office of Management and Budget, full funding of basic grants in 1977–78 will aid 1.3 million students (*The Budget of the United States Government, Fiscal Year 1977–Appendix*, p. 350). Enrollment of undergraduate degree-credit students in that year is projected at 5.7 million. (Martin M. Frankel and others, *Projections of Educational Statistics to 1982–83, 1973 Edition* [GPO, 1974], p. 38.) Only about 60 percent of basic grantees are from families with expected contributions of less than $300 (Office of Education, "Basic Educational Opportunity Grant Program, End of Year Report [1974–75 Academic Year]" [U.S. Office of Education, November 1975; processed]) and thus might be affected by the half-cost limit. Thus the 14 percent in the text is derived from $(1.3)(0.6)/5.7 = 0.137$. Even fewer students *actually* suffer a reduced award from the half-cost provision because some do attend higher-cost institutions.

before any basic grants payments at all can be made.[18] Congressional attachment to keeping an equitable balance between college-based aid and basic grants results partly from the relatively favorable treatment received by private institutions under the earlier programs. Over one-third of the funds in the college-based aid programs flows to the private institutions, even though the private sector accounts for less than one-fourth of total college enrollments. Unfortunately, programs that happen to produce favorable distributions among institutions may produce distortions and inefficiencies as well.

The college-based aid programs each have formulas to determine the allocation of 90 percent of the funds among the states. The remaining 10 percent is used to raise the "floor" percentage of need given all states to the highest possible level. The formula for supplemental educational opportunity grants is based on enrollment, which suggests a "general aid" focus, but the language of the act specifies that recipients must show exceptional financial need. College work-study funds are allocated on the basis of total enrollment, the number of high school graduates in the state, and the number of students from low-income homes, suggesting at least a partial emphasis on "access for low-income students"; but ironically, the 1972 amendments dropped the clause favoring "low-income" students in favor of one stating preference to be shown for those with "great financial need." The national direct student loan (NDSL) allotment formula is based on enrollment, and the law simply states that the purpose of the program is to make low-interest loans "to students in need thereof."

While the formulas establish limits on each state's share, how it is determined which colleges and universities get what is based on a complex system of institutional requests and panel approvals. Institutions send a "tripartite application" to the U.S. Office of Education for the three student aid programs. This form requires that they estimate the gross costs of attendance of needy students—those whose family contribution is less than the cost of attendance. From these gross costs, institutions must subtract both the total family contributions of the needy students and all "other" student aid received by such students including basic grants, institutionally funded work, loans and scholarships, state scholarships, veterans' benefits, and other types of loans and work. After

18. Public Law 92–318, Title IV, pt. A, sec. 411.

an adjustment for administrative expenses, these are transformed into institutional student aid "requests."[19] The requests, after further adjustment by the panels, plus review under a regional and national appeals process, are then reduced proportionately to fit the amounts appropriated and distributed under the state allocation formulas in the law.

An institution's request depends in part on the number of students it identifies as "needy." Because need is defined as the gap between the costs of attendance and the family's ability to pay, many students from quite prosperous backgrounds may be defined as "needy" because they are attending high-cost institutions, while less wealthy students are not considered "needy" because they are attending lower-cost institutions. This distinction is particularly important in looking at public-private differences. For example, a resident student at Harvard University, where the cost of attendance was $6,050 in the 1975–76 academic year, would have qualified as "needy" under an accepted needs-analysis system,[20] even if his family's income[21] were over $30,000. Yet a student from a family with an income of $20,000 at California State University at Hayward, which had a cost of attendance of $1,930, would not have qualified; nor would a commuter student at Mississippi Gulf Coast Junior College at Jackson (which cost $768) have qualified even if family income were about $14,000. To state the point only slightly differently, the measured "need" for a student from a family with an income of $10,000 would have been $668 at Mississippi Gulf, $1,830 at California State-Hayward, and $5,950 at Harvard. In short, the procedure for allocating college-

19. The requests are then examined by regional panels, which seem to reduce public and private institutions' requests by about the same percentage. In 1974–75, panels recommended the following percentage of requests:

Control	Supplemental educational opportunity grants	College work-study	National direct student loans
Public	84	89	81
Private	85	87	82

The data are from Lawrence E. Gladieux, *Distribution of Federal Student Assistance: The Enigma of the Two-Year Colleges* (CEEB, 1975), pp. 19–21.

20. College Scholarship Service of the College Entrance Examination Board, *CSS Need Analysis: Theory and Computation Procedures for the 1975–76 PCS and SFS Including Sample Cases and Tables* (CEEB, 1974), table F, pp. 96–99. Tuition rates are from Suchar, Ivens, and Jacobson, *Student Expenses.*

21. A couple with two children, filing jointly, one earner, no assets, no unusual expenses, one child in college.

based aid funds among colleges and universities is heavily weighted toward assisting students attending expensive private institutions.

Working in quite the opposite direction are the aspects of the need
assessment procedures having to do with offsets for other forms of student aid. Since an institution is supposed to subtract all other forms of
aid to needy students in determining its request for college-based funds,
institutionally funded student aid—important mainly in the private sector—reduces requests unless institutions shift such aid to students not
in need.

For state scholarships, the incentives in the college-based allocation
process are perverse. Suppose a state expands its state scholarship program and directs such aid to the private sector.[22] Private institutions in
the state would be required to report much larger "other aid" than
public institutions. Since the amount of college-based aid going to all
institutions in a state is fixed once the appropriations and state-allocation
formulas are applied, the private sector would receive a smaller share of
federal college-based student aid than before. Depending on the relative
magnitudes of the programs, the private sector's loss of federal aid could
nearly wipe out whatever it gained in state scholarships.

In sum, viewed as a process, the college-based aid programs fail to
articulate with the overall federal student aid program after the changes
introduced by the basic grants. Their state-allocation formulas do not
square with the law's intent concerning student selection. The student
financial need system rewards the private sector for enrolling some quite
well-to-do students and penalizes it for institutional or state aid granted
to lower-income students. Most of these problems arise because of the
failure to decide what role college-based aid is supposed to play.

How has college-based aid actually worked out?

Over the period following the 1972 amendments, college-based aid
requests grew at a rate of about 12 percent a year in the private sector
and 9 percent in the public (table 5-2). Federal allocations for such aid,
however, have grown more rapidly in the public sector. This is largely
because the share of public institutions in the college work-study program (69 percent) is larger than in the other programs (61 percent),
and the most rapid growth in funds over the 1974–76 period was in the
CWS program (56 percent growth as opposed to 10 percent).

More significantly, although the college-based aid programs were

22. This is typically the case. Over 50 percent of state scholarship expenditures
have gone to students at private institutions during the past few years.

Table 5-2. *Requests and Allocations for College-Based Aid,
by Private and Public Institutions, Fiscal Years 1974–76*

Millions of dollars

	Requests			Allocations		
Fiscal year	Private	Public	Private share (percent)	Private	Public	Private share (percent)
1974	582.4	1,027.4	36.2	260.6	454.1	36.5
1975	598.0	1,074.5	35.8	255.0	450.3	36.2
1976	718.0	1,202.1	37.4	320.9	582.0	35.5
1974–76	(11.6)	(8.5)	...	(11.6)	(14.1)	...

Source: U.S. Office of Education, Division of Student Assistance, application allocation tabulations for fiscal years 1974–76 for national direct student loans, supplemental educational opportunity grants, and college work-study (processed). Numbers in parentheses are the annual rate of growth (percent).

meeting a stable proportion (45 percent) of institutional requests in private institutions over this period, there was a $75 million increase in the gap between requests and allocations. (In the public sector allocations increased from 44 to 48 percent of requests, and the gap increased by $47 million). Such a growing volume of student need unmet by college-based aid would surely indicate—if the data are correct—that the ability to meet students' financial needs is eroding more rapidly in the private than the public sector.

Unfortunately there is reason to be wary when interpreting the rapid growth in institutional requests. First, the rapid growth of basic grants, veterans' benefits, and state scholarships—which should reduce institutional requests—has been difficult to estimate at the time request forms are filed. It appears that institutions have not fully accounted for the growth of these other programs.

Second, the College Scholarship Service liberalized the schedules of expected family contributions in 1975–76; that is, CSS lowered the family contributions across the entire income scale. A College Board study indicates that this change alone reduced aggregate family contributions (and increased need) for all higher education by about 10 percent (or $800 million). Since there was very little change in family contributions at lower income levels and massive reductions (over 30 percent) for students with family incomes above $12,000, the reduction of estimated family contributions was greater in the private sector than in the public, stimulating correspondingly larger increases in aid requests from the private sector.

Third, beginning in the 1975–76 academic year, the Office of Education allowed institutions to substitute a short-form application for the long form previously used in applying for college-based aid. The short form permits institutions to *omit* detailed reporting of basic grants, state scholarships, and the like, so long as their aid request grows no more than 10 percent a year. Apparently, many institutions have taken advantage of this.[23] It seems likely that public institutions, benefiting from the rapid growth in basic grants, chose to settle for a slow increase in funding for the college-based student aid programs rather than spell out their growing basic grant receipts and suffer probable cuts in their panel-approved, campus-based aid figures.[24]

Finally, in states where the formula allocation would yield slightly more than the floor percentage of need funded, there is considerable incentive for institutions to inflate their aid requests. By so doing, they may reduce the percentage of need met by the formula allocation sufficiently to make their states eligible for money from the 10 percent discretionary funds reserved to the commissioner of education.[25]

The conflicting tendencies within the system of distributing college-based aid make it very difficult to determine whether the private sector is actually benefiting or losing over time. The share of aid requests from that sector is distorted by a probable inability of aid officers to estimate outside aid, an incentive structure that discourages full disclosure, a needs-analysis system subject to abrupt changes, and fluctuating USOE procedures that may tend to favor public institutions. It is perhaps accidental, but still surprising, that with all the cross-currents of change occurring in student financial aid in recent years, the share of total funds for students attending private institutions has remained so stable (table 5-2). Whether this stability—which is no doubt regarded as a virtue by those who support college-based aid—will continue in the future is very much in question.

Although campus-based aid is generally given high marks for targeting assistance on relatively low-income students, the high participation

23. For fiscal 1977, an estimated 70 to 75 percent of institutional applicants used the short form. (Telephone interview, U.S. Office of Education, Division of Student Assistance.)

24. This practice may well have contributed significantly to the much slower growth in public requests (12 percent) compared with private requests (20 percent) in fiscal 1976 (table 5-2).

25. This point was brought to my attention by John Phillips, based on his experience as a USOE official during the 1971–76 period.

Table 5-3. *Number and Percentage Distribution of Dependent Undergraduates Receiving College-Based Aid, and Average Award, by Private and Public Institutions and Family Income, Academic Year 1974–75*[a]

Numbers in thousands

Type of aid	Family income below $7,500		Family income between $7,500 and $11,999		Family income above $11,999		Total number	Average award (dollars)
	Number	Percent	Number	Percent	Number	Percent		
Supplemental educational opportunity grants								
Total	190.0	66.2	78.4	27.3	18.6	6.5	287.0	540
Public	130.1	69.6	46.3	24.8	10.6	5.7	187.0	490
Private	60.0	60.3	31.7	31.9	7.8	7.8	99.5	660
College work-study								
Total	221.4	47.2	148.9	31.7	98.9	21.1	469.2	560
Public	149.1	53.6	89.8	32.3	39.5	14.2	278.4	600
Private	71.6	37.4	59.6	31.1	60.5	31.6	191.7	510
National direct student loans								
Total	230.7	40.1	185.0	32.1	160.3	27.8	576.0	690
Public	144.5	47.8	99.9	33.0	58.2	19.2	302.6	630
Private	85.5	31.1	85.2	31.0	104.0	37.9	274.7	770
All three programs[b]								
Total	642.1	48.2	412.3	30.9	277.8	20.9	1,332.2	...
Public	423.7	55.2	236.0	30.7	108.3	14.1	768.0	...
Private	217.1	38.4	176.5	31.2	172.3	30.5	565.9	...

Source: Frank J. Atelsek and Irene L. Gomberg, *Student Assistance: Participants and Programs, 1974–75*, Higher Education Panel Reports 27 (American Council on Education, 1975), tables 6, 7, 8, 11.

a. After this chapter was written, Atelsek and Gomberg published a 1976–77 version of the report: *Estimated Number of Student Aid Recipients, 1976–77*, Higher Education Panel Reports 36 (American Council on Education, 1977). The figures presented in this later version strengthen this chapter's appraisal of the impact of campus-based programs.

b. Derived by simple addition. The numbers do not represent unduplicated count.

of the private sector channels a significant proportion of the funds away from lower-income students. For example, in the total CWS program, nearly half of all dependent students who participate are from families with incomes below $7,500, and only about one-fifth are from families with incomes above $11,999. But in the private sector the share of lower-income students is under 40 percent, whereas nearly one-third come from the upper-income class (table 5-3). The differences between income distributions of aid recipients in the public and private sectors are least pronounced in the supplemental grants program, which has historically defined need most strictly, and significant in the CWS and NDSL programs (table 5-3). But care should be exercised in evaluating the income redistributive effects of the college-based aid programs, especially in the private sector, because of the fungibility of student aid funds. In 1974–75, for example, private institutions distributed an estimated $756 million in student aid from their own sources,[26] while distributing only $255 million in federal funds from the college-based aid programs (table 5-2). Inasmuch as the institutions are free to label aid from federal funds as being directed toward lower-income students, *even if such aid simply replaces outlays from institutional sources*, it would be misleading to regard the federal programs as being as redistributive as the data make them appear. Some significant part of that college-based aid reportedly spent on students with family incomes under $7,500 may well be simply a substitution of federal funds for institutional funds.

The enigma caused by the distributive outcome of the college-based aid program can be highlighted in the following way. According to table 5-3, in the 1974–75 academic year about 190,000 students from families with incomes below $7,500 received supplemental grants. About one-third attended private schools and received an average award of at least $660. In that same year there were a total of 874,000 dependent, full-time students from families with under $7,500 income enrolled in all collegiate institutions.[27] Therefore, 78 percent of lower-income students were not getting college-based grants, while 22 percent of them were being given substantial awards. At the same time, as indicated in table 5-3, about 260,000 students from families with incomes in excess of $11,999 were receiving college work-study aid or federal loans in amounts averaging somewhat less than $560 and $690, respectively. Over 60 percent of these students attended private institutions. Is there a sufficiently compelling public purpose being served in aiding the private sector through campus-based programs, which also results in: (1) treating some low-income students quite handsomely while the majority receives no aid at all (except for basic grants), and (2) awarding federal funds to a substantial number of students from relatively higher-income homes in the face of the failure to give aid to all students from lower-income backgrounds? To some observers, these consequences are de-

26. Frank J. Atelsek and Irene L. Gomberg, *Student Assistance: Participants and Programs, 1974–75*, Higher Education Panel Reports 27 (American Council on Education, 1975), p. 26.

27. Estimated from Washington Office of the College Entrance Examination Board, "Estimating the Unknown: Unmet Financial Needs of 1975–76 College Students" (CEEB, Washington Office, 1975; processed), app. A, table 2.

fensible because the programs enhance "choice." The next section discusses that concept and the various options for federal programs directed toward the private sector.

Alternative Federal Strategies toward Private Higher Education

Even if private higher education makes out pretty well under the present hodge-podge of special provisions and internal inconsistencies in federal laws, it might do even better if those laws were revised to clarify federal policy toward the private sector. Such clarification requires policymakers to make some hard choices, rather than to continue relying on the confused and sometimes unintended results of present policies.

First, let me spell out some assumptions about the federal role in "providing access" and "enhancing choice." With respect to the provision of access, I argue above that basic grants (without the half-cost provision) can be understood as providing all aided students with enough resources to meet noninstructional expenses. I am going to assume here that the program is understood that way and that appropriate amendments will be made in the basic grants law.[28] Unless these cracks are repaired in the foundation program, it will be difficult to make progress on other higher education goals.

By "enhancing choice" I mean a federal effort, which, at a minimum, enables all students to choose among the existing diverse educational offerings without debilitating financial burdens to themselves or their families. The justification for such a federal goal rests on the difficult-to-prove propositions that choice, per se, is of value to society and that present characteristics of the education marketplace imperfectly allow consumers' preferences to guide the allocation of resources to alternative educational offerings.

Some major part of the goal of enhancing choice, I assume, will be fulfilled by expanding the guaranteed loan program. Despite many problems, this program is designed well enough so that with some changes it

28. These are eliminating the half-cost limitation, raising the maximum grant to reasonable noninstructional cost levels (and maintaining such levels through indexing), and fully funding the amended program. The Education Amendments of 1976 merely raised the maximum grant to a higher fixed level, leaving future levels for later debate.

can provide all students with enough supplementary resources to attend a wide range of institutions.[29]

Some observers would have federal support for higher education stop right there—with a combination of basic grants for access and a (modified) loan program for choice. Such an approach—for which I have some sympathy—does imply a very restricted role for the federal government in the financing of higher education. And it means that the private sector will sink or swim depending on whether students are willing to borrow enough to cover the kind of tuition differentials that now exist. It also implies that access to higher education for lower-income students will only be realized in states that provide such students with low net instructional charges (that is, after student aid) and that the federal government is willing to take its chances on the states' doing just that.

But most observers do not accept such a limited role for federal support of higher education, and thus alternative goals and programs should be examined. One important distinction is helpful in discussing possible alternative strategies. This is the distinction between: (1) a federal strategy that takes the financing patterns of state governments more or less as a given, and determines federal goals and instruments by adjusting to these state policies; and (2) a federal strategy that attempts to influence state behavior, especially with respect to the treatment of private institutions.

Strategies with Fixed State Policies

If no conscious attempt is made to alter state policies, basic grants and guaranteed student loan programs may have to be supplemented to meet federal goals. Basic grants alone do not guarantee that a low-income student will be able to find an institution with low net charges for instruction, thus making access dependent on loans or other forms of support.

There are two main avenues by which the federal government can attempt to ensure access for low-income students without trying to change state policies—through institutional support or student aid.

A student aid approach would simply modify basic grants by defining the guarantee (maximum grant) level to include not only noninstructional costs but also $200 or $300 or $700 for tuition, picking whatever number matches current state pricing policies at those institutions to

29. For a discussion of some problems in the loan program, and some possible improvements that could be made, see Lois D. Rice, ed., *Student Loans: Problems and Policy Alternatives* (College Entrance Examination Board, 1977).

which it is decided students should have access. The analysis of this alternative is straightforward (such an approach costs money, it may induce tuition increases, and it hurts some private colleges), and it would run counter to the idea of focusing basic grants on noninstructional costs.

An institutional aid program that is cost-effective in providing access for low-income students is difficult to devise. In principle, any formula should reward institutions for enrolling low-income students (that is, basic grant recipients) at low net charges for education. One such formula would be:

$$\text{Payment per basic grant recipient} = x - \text{net charges},$$

where net charges is defined as tuition minus student aid from institution or state, and where x is simply the maximum bonus for keeping net charges at zero for basic recipients. As net charges rise, the bonus is reduced and becomes zero whenever net charges to needy students exceeds x. This program might be effective in rewarding institutions that keep their charges down,[30] but it would be disastrous for the weakest segment of the private sector. With the possible exception of the most heavily endowed institutions, private colleges would fare poorly under any formula that rewarded low net tuition. Indeed, if the maximum bonus were high enough, it is likely that low-tuition public institutions would proliferate,[31] worsening the private sector's position.

This approach to access would, in turn, make it nearly impossible to avoid some sort of additional federal program to preserve choice ("choice" in this case being interpreted as preventing a substantial part of the private sector from closing). Such an additional program would have to be one that consciously provided support to the private sector. Once again, there are many possibilities, but the 1975 proposal from the Consortium on Financing Higher Education (COFHE) can serve as an example.[32]

The COFHE proposal provided for a supplementary grant to be

---

30. A similar provision for institutional grants equal to $1,200 minus tuition was included in the original version of the Pell bill that culminated in the 1972 amendments. Senator Pell's intent was to keep tuition down. (See discussion in Laura Christian Ford, "Institutional Aid," *Journal of Law and Education*, vol. 1 [October 1972], p. 569.)

31. If x were $1,200, as in the Pell bill, low-tuition, two-year public institutions would collect about $1,000 for each basic grant recipient. This could make such institutions nearly cost-free to the operating government.

32. The following data are from Consortium on Financing Higher Education, "Federal Student Assistance: A Review of Title IV of the Higher Education Act" (Hanover, N.H.: COFHE, 1975; processed).

awarded to basic grant recipients *and others* who demonstrated considerable self-help (or received state or private assistance) and still had
considerable financial need. Specifically, the COFHE grant would have
been the lesser of $1,500 or one-half the amount remaining after deduct-
ing, from tuition and fees, the parental contribution less the maximum
basic grant, and $1,000. The first deduction from tuition and fees repre-
sents the family's ability to pay for instructional costs and the second
represents the student's contribution in the form of wages, borrowing,
state scholarships, or institutional grants. Assuming, as COFHE did,[33]
that the maximum basic grant would reach $1,600 in the 1975–76 aca-
demic year, the proposal rather ingeniously excluded most students at
public institutions by the requirement that each student pay the first
$1,000 in tuition and fees. Choice would have been enhanced primarily
for middle-income students by having the federal government share half
of their tuition costs up to a limit. For example, a student with a family
income of $17,500 (and a family contribution of $2,620) would have
paid all of the first $2,020 tuition, but only half the tuition between $2,020
and $5,020,[34] after which he or she would have paid all tuition charges.
Most of the beneficiaries of this plan would have come from middle- and
upper-income homes; few would have been basic grant recipients. Thus
this program should be understood as one enhancing choice for the
great majority of students, not just the poor and near poor. As such, it
offers real possibilities for helping the private sector by focusing aid on
those students who traditionally are attracted to that sector.

COFHE estimated that if 80 percent of the eligible students applied
for the grants, its proposal would have cost about $319 million in the
1974–75 academic year, or about one and one-third times the $240 million
spent on the supplemental grant program that year. The COFHE grants
would have benefited 671,000 students at an average grant of $475.
Sixty-five percent of these students (436,000) would have been in the
private sector, about four times as many as were aided by the SEOG
program in the private sector that same year. These students would
have constituted about one-quarter of all private full-time undergraduates. In all, the private sector would have received about 75 percent of
the funds.

33. Ibid., p. 28.
34. The supplementary grant would have reached its $1,500 maximum when
tuition is $5,020. The tuition at which the grant reached its maximum would have
risen with income. See appendix D in ibid.

While some of these benefits to the private sector would be attributable simply to the $80 million increase of expenditures over the $240 million spent on the supplemental grant program, the more important point is that the COFHE proposal would have been much more heavily skewed in favor of the private sector and its middle-income clientele than the current SEOG program. Given its purpose—to provide special help to students enrolled in the private sector—such skewing would be quite proper, and also a great deal more defensible than the existing program, which selects some students and excludes others for little apparent reason.

The combination package of an access-oriented institutional grant coupled with a choice-oriented student aid program represents a possible strategy for the federal government. Taken alone, neither of these programs would be very desirable. Institutional grants on their own would probably wipe out a sizable number of independent colleges, but they would help guarantee access for low-income students. The supplementary student grants, alone, would offer help to private institutions but there would be no guarantee that the $1,000 in self-help and other aid built into the formula would actually be forthcoming. As a consequence, many lower-income students attending medium-tuition public institutions might be unable to obtain grant funds to cover any part of tuition. This change, in turn, might induce some public institutions to raise tuition rates so that their students could become eligible for more federal funds. The upshot would be an indefensible situation in which the federal government shared part of the tuition of a lawyer's son at Harvard and shared no part of the fees paid by a dressmaker's daughter at the State University of New York.

Even though the two programs described here work at apparent cross-purposes, one driving public-sector prices down, the other ameliorating the damage, the package makes a good deal more sense than existing programs. It focuses the "access" money on the lower-income segment of the population (and the public sector) and the "choice" funds on middle-income students (and the private sector). By contrast, existing programs, to the extent that their purposes are similar to the ones described here, are defective. The half-cost provision of basic grants, the symbol of aid to the private sector, is targeted on low-income students and only worsens their access. The complex SEOG allocation singles out a few low-income students, mostly in public institutions, while discouraging state and institutional aid for the private sector.

However, the package, as described, has a major flaw. By not dealing with the source of the private sector's problem—the financing policy of the state—it is potentially a very expensive federal program. As long as states are expected and encouraged to hold down tuition to enable low-income students to attend college, they will hold down tuition for everyone. That will worsen the private sector's competitiveness and federal aid will have to be channeled into filling a widening tuition gap. This strategy could conceivably become an open-ended drain on the U.S. Treasury if pressures to save the private sector push up the supplementary grants to meet tuition increases and to liberalize grant eligibility.[35] Most disturbing of all is the fact that this potential drain on the Treasury is not really the result of federal policies, but rather of state actions.

Strategies Affecting State Policies

Starting with the assumption that a basic grant program furnishes all needy students with necessary noninstructional expenses, what would be the federal strategy for support of higher education *without* the constraint that current state financial practices remain unaltered? Once the possibility of federal action designed to change state behavior is introduced, many new policies become feasible.

GOALS

Before assessing federal alternatives it is important to specify what would be desirable characteristics of state financial policies from the federal government's point of view. There are three major characteristics that the federal government ought to—and, in fact, does—have an interest in fostering.

Access. An acceptable state financial plan would provide places at public or private institutions for low-income students at low net costs to such students.

Choice. A variety of institutions should be available to students, in-

---

35. An important issue, sure to arise if a COFHE-type plan were adopted, is the role of private needs-analysis systems (such as the College Scholarship Service and American College Testing Program) in determining federal aid. It is hard to imagine that federal officials would not attempt to take an active role in determining who can afford to pay how much, when such a determination becomes the basis for a quasi-entitlement. The issue, of course, exists under present programs, but it is obscured because of their complexity.

cluding especially institutions independent of state political control. An existing private sector should not be discriminated against by state policies; a nascent one should be encouraged.

Reduction of state barriers. Such practices as charging different prices for the same educational program to residents and nonresidents and prohibiting students from carrying state scholarship aid across state lines should be discouraged. These barriers lead to distortions in student choice and to costly and unnecessary duplication of curricula.

PERFORMANCE

It should be clear that state policies for the most part do not conform to all of these requirements. Strengths and shortfalls in existing state policies are briefly enumerated below.

Access. The record of the states in providing access to low-cost higher education is difficult to assess. A recent study by the Carnegie Council seems to indicate that about half of the states have failed to provide a sufficient number of "open-access spaces" in higher education.[36] Unfortunately, its definition of an open-access space includes a tuition level requirement, which may be a spurious indicator of real access because it ignores state student aid. A better measure of access would be net charges after state aid.

The net charge to the average *aided* public student is under $400 in all but a few small states (table 5-A1, column 3). Most of the major states, and most of the states with large private sectors, impose quite low net burdens on low-income students in public institutions. Moreover, the net charge measure of access seems to be only loosely correlated with public tuition levels: the lowest net charges are found almost randomly distributed among the states when the latter are arranged by tuition level.

Unfortunately, in many states, the *coverage* of the state scholarship program is slim: very few students receive such aid (table 5-A1, column 4). While it is comforting to know that Iowa has offset its rather high public tuition by a generous average state scholarship, it is not comforting to note that only 0.5 percent of public enrollees in Iowa received such scholarships in the 1973–74 academic year.

36. *The States and Higher Education: A Proud Past and a Vital Future*, A Commentary of the Carnegie Foundation for the Advancement of Teaching (Jossey-Bass, 1976), p. 46. The *Supplement* to the commentary (The Foundation, 1976; available from Carnegie Council on Policy Studies in Higher Education, Berkeley), figure A-3, lists seventeen metropolitan areas needing at least one more campus.

On the whole, it seems reasonable to conclude that most states have been performing fairly well in providing access to institutions with low net charges for their neediest students. Some accomplished this by charging low tuition in public schools. Others provided access even with relatively high tuition through substantial state scholarships serving a significant number of students (for example, Vermont, Pennsylvania, New Jersey, and New York; see table 5-A1). But in many states the fairly high public tuition charges were offset for only a few low-income students in 1973–74. Improvements could certainly be made in providing access for students in such states.

Choice. If the private sector is to survive, some balance is needed in the distribution of subsidies to public and private institutions. If state governments heavily support public institutions while holding back support for private ones, eventually the gap between public and private tuitions will widen and the differences in total expenditure per student will narrow. The amount of state (and local) expenditures per student in public and private institutions seems the most appropriate single indicator of how evenhanded state governments are in financing the two sectors.

On this measure, the states' performance in recent years is poor. Expenditures by state and local governments per full-time-equivalent student in public institutions typically run about $1,600 more than expenditures for students in private institutions. These differences seem to be no smaller in states with high proportions of private students, where the differential is important, than in states with relatively small private sectors.

I have estimated the percentage change in each state's higher education budget that would be occasioned if every state were to raise subsidies per student in the private sector to the public-sector level.

The results of this "leveling-up" show that, for the United States as a whole, state higher education budgets would have had to rise by 27 percent (about $2.9 billion) in the 1973–74 academic year (table 5-A2, column 4). More to the point, the cost for some states would be astronomical; Massachusetts, for example, would have to more than double its higher education expenditure and twenty-two other states increase theirs by over 25 percent.

While it would be desirable for states to treat the private sector more evenhandedly, the feasibility of such a policy, especially in states with relatively large private enrollments, is questionable not only on fiscal grounds but also on the grounds of rational self-interest. Everyone may agree that a Harvard student is as deserving of a subsidy as any University of Massachusetts student, but Massachusetts legislators will wonder why their taxpayers should be the ones to treat evenhandedly the Harvard student from Oregon.[37] At the same time, the Oregon legislature is under no pressure from Oregon higher education leaders to endow its emigrating residents with a state subsidy. Oregon colleges would prefer that the students stay home. So, in fact, an unfair and inefficient pattern of subsidies has prevailed between the sectors, largely because of the states' tendency to support all students at public institutions—a tendency that is unlikely to be changed radically by state action. To the extent that this stasis in state policies causes the private sector to contract, choice and diversity are impeded.

Reduction of state barriers. In recent years, major barriers have been erected to discourage students from crossing state lines for higher education. Public universities in 1973–74 typically charged about $1,000 more for the tuition of nonresidents than of residents, and in almost all cases nonresident tuition rates are rising faster than those of residents.[38] In addition, rapidly growing state scholarship programs typically restrict recipients to home-state colleges.[39]

Such barriers are reducing interstate mobility (table 5-A3). In 1968, over 81 percent of all enrollment was accounted for by students who attended college in their home state. By 1972, almost 84 percent of enrollees were stay-at-homes. In part, the increase of home-state attendance is caused by the relatively rapid growth in public institution enrollments, which are heavily local. But this differential growth accounts for less

37. I confess to a certain amount of cheating here. "Evenhandedness" is defined on a state-by-state basis, implicitly assuming that public-private competition is primarily intrastate. The Harvard example indicates that the relevant sphere of competition for some institutions crosses state borders. This means that table 5-A2 should be understood as only a rough approximation to the costs of evenhandedness. An alternative approach, focusing on state of origin of students, is discussed below.

38. See tables 6 and 7 in *Tuition: A Supplemental Statement to the Report of the Carnegie Commission on Higher Education on "Who Pays? Who Benefits? Who Should Pay?"* Prepared by the staff of the Carnegie Commission on Higher Education (Carnegie Foundation for the Advancement of Teaching, 1974). On the other hand, *changing one's residence* for purposes of reducing one's tuition seems to be getting easier.

39. See William H. McFarlane, A. E. Dick Howard, and Jay L. Chronister, *State Financial Measures Involving the Private Sector of Higher Education*, A Report to the National Council of Independent Colleges and Universities (1974), app. B.

than half of the increase in the proportion of students remaining in the state. The rest is due to declining out-of-state enrollment percentages in either the public or private sector, or both.[40]

The private sector has, by far, the most to lose from these mounting disincentives to interstate mobility. In 1972, one-third of all students attending private institutions were from out of state. In Vermont, New Hampshire, and the District of Columbia, over 70 percent of the private enrollees were from other jurisdictions. The destiny of the private sector in these states, in particular, is at the mercy of the students' mobility preferences and state scholarship rules in all the other states—not their own.

The private sector would be affected in varied ways by freer trade in students. As a class, private institutions gain from the adoption of portability of state scholarships if the number of students who now attend home-state public institutions but would shift to out-of-state private schools exceeds the number who now attend home-state private schools but would switch to out-of-state public colleges. Judging by the private sector's ability to draw out-of-state students even without portability, it seems likely that it would benefit from the change. However, individual private institutions could turn out to be big enrollment losers: namely, those for whom current nonportability requirements in effect provide captive students.

The private sector, on the other hand, would stand to lose from a reduction in nonresident tuitions at public institutions. Some of the students lured into out-of-state public schools would be students who would have attended private institutions had the nonresident public tuitions remained high.

Thus, although portability and reduction of nonresident barriers are desirable from a social point of view, it is open to question whether private institutions as a whole would benefit from such changes. Private colleges serving a local clientele and lucky enough to be in states with poor-quality public institutions would almost certainly lose out to public or private institutions in other states. High-quality private institutions with a national clientele, offering a product sharply differentiated from public institutions, probably would gain in enrollments.

40. On the basis of preliminary data for 1975, the decrease in interstate mobility seems to have slowed in public institutions. However, the fraction of out-of-state students attending private colleges continued to fall between 1972 and 1975, especially in the New England states. (See American Council on Education, *A Fact Book on Higher Education: Enrollment Data* [issue 2, 1976], pp. 76.90 and 76.91.)

Alternative Solutions

This review of federal policy goals and state performance highlights the major requirements of a program to supplement basic grants and loans. First, states should be encouraged to increase subsidies to the private sector; this must be done in a manner that allows subsidies to cross state lines or it will be ineffective in meeting the above goals. Second, those states with a good record in maintaining low net charges for low-income students should be encouraged to continue; other states should be encouraged to improve.

The states have three options open to them to meet these goals:

Option 1. Each state could maintain low public tuition rates and pay its own private colleges and universities an amount per student equal to the subsidy per student at public institutions for either (a) all students in private institutions or (b) all students in private institutions who are state residents.

Option 2. Each state could maintain low public tuition rates and give all students who attend out-of-state institutions or home-state private institutions grants equal to the public subsidy per student. This is sometimes referred to as a tuition offset program.

Option 3. Each state could raise public tuition rates and offset the increase in net charges for relatively low-income students by establishing (or more fully funding) a state scholarship program that is fully portable within and among states.

The first of these options is infeasible or undesirable, despite its apparent solution to the access and choice goals. If states were to grant private institutions an amount equal to the public student's subsidy for all privately enrolled students, many states would be expending substantial sums for residents of other states. (This can be seen by combining the data in the last columns of tables 5-A2 and 5-A3.) For example, Rhode Island would have had to raise its higher education budget in the 1973–74 academic year by 86 percent to provide all private college students with subsidies equal to that of its public sector (table 5-A2); but 52 percent of the private students were from out of state (table 5-A3). Thus this option implies that Rhode Island would have to increase its higher education budget by 45 percent (0.86 times 0.52) just to benefit out-of-state students. Rhode Island could argue that it is not its responsibility to provide for such students—and it would be right. Thus, even if the federal government could induce Rhode Island to undertake such subsidies for out-of-state students, the effort would be misplaced because no burden is imposed on the states that export those students.

On the other hand, each state could subsidize its private institutions just for resident students (for example, Rhode Island would pay Brown University a subsidy equivalent to that given to the University of Rhode Island per student for each Rhode Islander at Brown). The problem with this solution, if applied in each state, is that it would rigidify or worsen interstate immobility by providing an incentive for private institutions to favor home-state applicants. Thus neither possibility under Option 1 seems to be entirely consistent with the goals set out above.[41]

Option 2 represents state actions that would fully complement the basic federal programs and achieve federal goals. By keeping tuition low at public institutions, access to higher education is maintained for low-income students. At the same time, students who wish to attend private institutions are made to pay only the excess of the private schools' charges over the subsidy given in the public sector, because under this option a student carries with him a tuition offset grant equal to the subsidy given to students in public institutions in his home state.

This scheme can be illustrated as follows. In the 1973-74 academic year, Maine would have maintained its average tuition in public institutions at $534 (table 5-4). But instead of Maine residents facing average tuition rates of $2,356, $1,320, and $2,542 at Maine private colleges, Massachusetts public colleges (nonresident tuition), and Massachusetts private colleges, respectively, the students would be granted $1,772, the average subsidy paid to a Maine public institution student. This grant would reduce the net charges for a Maine resident to $584, −$452, and $770, respectively (table 5-4).[42]

This kind of change places the new financing burden on the state that sends its residents to home-state private colleges or to out-of-state schools. Since it is the home state that has failed to treat its residents equitably

41. A few states do employ small institutional aid programs for private institutions with some of the characteristics mentioned here. Pennsylvania and Illinois give grants to private institutions for state residents. Maryland, living up to its nickname (the Free State), pays private schools for all enrollees. New York's "Bundy aid" is based on degrees, regardless of the student's origin. (See *Higher Education in the States*, vol. 5, no. 1 [Education Commission of the States, 1975].)

42. Maine could limit its grant to actual tuition incurred, in which case the student bound for a Massachusetts public institution would receive only $1,320. However, Massachusetts would probably raise its nonresident tuition charges if an Option 2 scheme were widely adopted.

Table 5-4. *Nominal Tuition, Student Subsidy, and Net Tuition under Option 2, 1973–74*

Dollars per student

Item	Maine Public	Maine Private	Massachusetts Public	Massachusetts Private
Nominal tuition	534	2,356	1,320[a]	2,542
Subsidy per public student	...	1,772	1,772	1,772
Net tuition	534	584	−452	770

Sources: Tuition, Maine public, from Table 5-A1; tuition, private, from Marilyn McCoy, *State and Local Financial Support of Higher Education: A Framework for Interstate Comparisons, 1973–74*, Field Review Edition (Boulder, Colo.: National Center for Higher Education Management Systems at Western Interstate Commission for Higher Education, 1976); nonresidential tuition, University of Massachusetts, from *Tuition: A Supplemental Statement to the Report of the Carnegie Commission on Higher Education on "Who Pays? Who Benefits? Who Should Pay?"* Prepared by the staff of the Carnegie Commission on Higher Education (Carnegie Foundation for the Advancement of Teaching, 1974), table 7, p. 64; average subsidy per enrollee, from table 5-A2.

a. Nonresident tuition.

under current financing schemes—in the sense that it offers a substantial subsidy only if a home-state public institution is attended—the extra burden seems appropriately targeted. Moreover, the plan reduces the artificial barriers to attending private institutions or out-of-state public institutions and thus is consistent with national goals of fostering choice and diversity.

Tuition offset grants would cost the states an enormous amount of money, however. An estimate for 1973–74 can be derived as follows. Assuming that all students would have attended the institutions they actually attended that year, each of the 1.141 million students enrolled in out-of-state institutions would have received an average subsidy from their state of $1,950,[43] a total additional outlay of $2.2 billion. In addition, since two-thirds of all private students attended institutions in their home state (table 5-A3), another 1.189 million students (two-thirds of the 1973–74 private enrollment) would have received a state grant of $1,996,[44] a further cost of $2.4 billion.

Thus, as a ball-park estimate, achieving equality for private school attendees and those who went out of state would have raised state expendi-

43. The average subsidy per public student by state (table 5-A2) weighted by the number of students exported by each state (table 5-A4). This differs from the U.S. average reported in table 5-A2 because that table weights students by total public enrollment in each state.

44. This is the state subsidy weighted by students attending private institutions in their home state (table 5-A4).

tures for higher education in 1973–74 on the order of $4.6 billion, about 45 percent over their actual expenditures that year in the public sector.[45]

If this total is broken down on a state-by-state basis (as in table 5-A4) the big export states such as New Jersey would suffer a very large increase in their state outlays for higher education.[46] Compared to its support for the public sector alone in 1973–74, New Jersey's expenditures would have to more than double under Option 2. Some other states with large private sectors, like Vermont, would not fare so badly under this option because they have relatively few residents in private institutions or leaving the state. In any event, all states would suffer substantial budgetary increases for a full tuition offset program.

Probably because of its high cost, no one seriously supports an all-out Option 2 program. Since its major distinction lies in providing aid to private institutions, spokesmen for that sector have usually marched up to the brink of Option 2, whiffed the costs, and then compromised. An excellent case in point is *A National Policy for Private Higher Education*, a task force report by the National Council of Independent Colleges and Universities.[47] NCICU narrows Option 2 by limiting the grants to private-sector students only (even though from the student's point of view paying a near full-cost nonresident tuition at an out-of-state public institution is no different from paying private tuition) and also by limiting the proposed subsidy to 25, 50, or 75 percent of the average public subsidy.[48] The resulting tuition offset grant program costs only between $840 million and $2.5 billion. Federal matching grants were also advocated (with a 25 percent federal share used as an illustration) to ensure a partnership. However, no state allocation formula was proposed.[49] While this kind of compromise can perhaps be defended,

45. These estimates should not include state subsidies to the private sector (which would presumably be eliminated) and the probably lower public subsidy for non-residents that would almost certainly follow as nonresident fees were raised. On the other side, however, is the likelihood that enrollment would rise in the aggregate from such a new infusion of subsidies. I believe these considerations indicate that the estimate might be stretched to between $4 billion and $6 billion, foul line to foul line.

46. It is assumed that student export patterns of 1968 (the last year for which data are available) and home-state private school attendance patterns of 1972 prevailed in the 1973–74 academic year.

47. *A National Policy for Private Higher Education*, The Report of a Task Force of the National Council of Independent Colleges and Universities (Association of American Colleges, 1974).

48. Ibid., pp. 19–26.

49. Devising a state-aid formula for this purpose would not be easy. A straight matching grant would result in the lion's share of federal support going to those

it implicitly involves emphasizing choice more than access, because states would almost certainly be forced to divert funds out of public institutional support into the new grant program. Since the federal government has an interest in both goals, the compromise represented by Option 3 is the better alternative.

Option 3 is a state program that would supplement federal goals by vastly increasing state scholarship programs, financing them in large part by reducing state subsidies to the public sector. This decrease in subsidies would be achieved through a substantial increase in public tuition. Such a program would promote—or at least not worsen—access to higher education for lower-income students because the state scholarships they receive would offset (in some cases, more than offset) tuition increases.

At the same time, the position of the private sector would be enhanced in the following ways. State scholarship recipients would be able to carry their grants to all private institutions and to out-of-state public institutions, thus broadening their ability to choose among colleges.[50] Depending on the generosity of the average state scholarship and the number of students covered, this change might increase enrollment at private institutions, both home-state and out-of-state. The major help to private institutions, however, would probably derive from the rise in public tuition rates, which, for unaided students, would reduce the gap between public and private charges. To the extent that unaided (middle- and upper-income) students have been enticed into the public sector by its heavily subsidized tuition, such a change would provide significant aid to the private sector. Thus a shift from general support of public institutions to a state scholarship scheme with higher tuition is consistent with federal interests in both access and choice.

There are two major caveats. First, this option compromises "full evenhandedness" in that the financing scheme does not envision giving *all* students who attend private institutions a subsidy equal to the average public subsidy as was the case in Option 2. In the private sector, only

---

states whose past support for higher education had been poorest. New Jersey residents would get a disproportionate share of federal dollars mainly because New Jersey has provided the fewest public enrollment places, whereas Wisconsin, which ranks high on everyone's list of high-effort states, would get a disproportionately low share. Thus some other matching device would be required, which might raise federal costs even further.

50. If, however, out-of-state public institutions raise nonresident tuition by an amount equal to the state scholarship grant, the grantee would be no better off than before the change.

means-tested state scholarship recipients gain. However, as public tuitions are raised, the subsidy to public students is reduced and this lessens the discrimination against private school enrollees.

Second, as described here, the Option 3 program could be largely self-financing for each state in that the reduced public subsidies would offset the increased state scholarship costs. But, since some students would be better off than they are now (those who receive state scholarships and attend private or out-of-state public institutions), it follows that there must be some losers. These are the students whose family incomes are too high to qualify for state scholarships and who will face higher public tuition after the proposed change.

The solution proposed here, thus, while consistent with the basic federal goal of providing access to low-income students, suffers from the fact that it enhances choice partly by hurting unaided students and the public sector. I do not believe that defect is in conflict with federal goals, but it certainly creates political problems.

There is a direct response to these political difficulties that arise from offering nothing (but greater hardship) to relatively well-off students. If it is in the federal interest for such people to be assisted in obtaining higher education, two simple means of assistance could be made available to them: per capita federal grants to all institutions of higher education and federal tax credits for higher education expenses. Some combination of these two instruments would be the appropriate federal response to the need to provide a general subsidy for *everyone's* higher education (see the discussion of tax credits in chapter 6). For the more limited federal role of taking on major responsibilities jointly with the states, or of providing access and a reasonable amount of diversity, the Option 3 recommendation is more to the point and more efficient. Devotees of general federal aid to higher education should be made to fight the battle with the proper instruments (enrollment-based institutional grants and tax credits) and on the direct issue—not by blasting proposals for higher tuition and bigger scholarships as un-American activities.

Implementing a New Federal Strategy

I have argued thus far that the federal government should encourage states to redesign their financing schemes to feature greater reliance on portable state scholarships and less on institutional subsidies to public institutions. Such changes would complement the basic grant program to facilitate access and the federal loan program to facilitate choice.

How can Washington induce states to undertake such financing changes? There are several possibilities, all fraught with at least some political or practical drawbacks.

One method is to make the development of an adequate state plan a prerequisite for state residents' receiving basic grants or federally guaranteed loans. While this use of the federal stick would almost certainly be effective—basic grants and guaranteed loans combined aggregate to about $3 billion annually—it is impractical and inadvisable. Someone (presumably the commissioner of education) would have to approve "adequate state plans." But devising the criteria for acceptability is difficult, as is shown below, and it is asking too much of a federal official to cut off a state for failure to comply with arguable acceptability criteria. The threat of federal disentitlement to student aid for failure to comply is so awesome as to be both unbelievable and unenforceable (how would one say no to New York?). Finally, tying federal assistance in one set of programs to criteria for another creates paradoxes for federal policymakers. For example, a state with no private sector whose public institution charges zero tuition and serves all residents might not meet strictly drawn criteria for finance plans, but it is hard to see why basic grants should be withheld.

In contrast to the stick, a federal carrot could be employed to induce state reform. The object would be to design a system of federal payments to states that would reward desired changes in state financing. The obvious candidate for such a federal incentive program is state scholarship awards. There is a federal program with the right name—but unfortunately the wrong characteristics. These may clutter one's thinking about a well-designed federal incentive program, but I will use the program as a foil for my discussion.

The SSIG Program

State student incentive grants (SSIG) were made part of the federal higher education arsenal in the Education Amendments of 1972. In practice, the program works as follows. The annual appropriation, which has risen from $19 million in fiscal 1974 to $60 million in fiscal 1977, is allotted to fifty-six potentially eligible states and other jurisdictions ac-

Table 5-5. *Federal Funds for the State Student Incentive Grant Program as a Percentage of State Scholarship Funds, in Rank Order, by States, Award Year 1975–76*

State	SSIG funds as a percentage of total state scholarship funds
Pennsylvania	1.3
Illinois	1.6
New York	1.7
New Jersey	2.1
Vermont	2.2
Iowa	2.4
Minnesota	2.6
Indiana	2.7
South Carolina	2.8
Wisconsin	2.9
Colorado	3.6
Ohio	4.1
Michigan	4.3
Connecticut	5.1
Rhode Island	5.2
California	6.1
Massachusetts	6.2
Kansas	6.7
West Virginia	8.1
Oregon	9.7
Missouri	10.9
Texas	12.1
Florida	13.0
Washington	13.2
Maine	13.5
Kentucky	13.6
Arkansas*	24.1
North Dakota	25.9
Georgia	26.2
South Dakota	27.3
Maryland	27.5
Virginia	30.8
Delaware	40.5
Hawaii*	50.0
Idaho*	50.0
Louisiana*	50.0
Mississippi*	50.0
Montana*	50.0

Table 5-5 (Continued)

State	SSIG funds as a percentage of total state scholarship funds
Nebraska	50.0
North Carolina*	50.0
Oklahoma	50.0
Utah	50.0

Source: Joseph D. Boyd, "National Association of State Scholarship Programs: 7th Annual Survey, 1975–76 Academic Year" (Deerfield, Ill.: NASSP, 1975; processed), pp. 3, 18.
* State adopted a qualified state scholarship in 1975–76.

cording to their share of total enrollment. Any state that can demonstrate that it has a qualifying program and that it will increase state scholarship spending above a base year by at least as much as the federal allotment receives the amount allotted.[51] Before the program's inception, twenty-seven jurisdictions had qualified programs. By its first year of operation SSIG had thirty-nine participating jurisdictions; by 1976–77, over fifty jurisdictions qualified.

While this record of stimulating states to adopt scholarship programs looks impressive, the program design and funding level have combined to make it worthwhile for most states that did not have state scholarship programs to just barely qualify for support; once qualified there is no incentive to undertake a program reaching all (or most) eligible students. Thus, in the 1975–76 academic year most of the states with new state scholarship programs appropriated just enough money to meet the federal allotment (table 5-5).[52]

At the other extreme, states like Pennsylvania, Illinois, and New York already spend so much more on state scholarships than their federal allotment (table 5-5) that the matching provision of the SSIG program is irrelevant. These states get no more federal SSIG dollars if they expand their programs.

Thus, while the SSIG program may have been important in encouraging states to adopt scholarship programs, it currently provides an incentive for states to switch their financing toward scholarships only in cases where the state program is close to the amount made avail-

51. If a jurisdiction does not qualify, its share is reallotted to the others.
52. States with new state scholarship programs in 1975–76 are asterisked in table 5-5. A ratio of 50 percent signifies minimal qualification for SSIG; all but one newly qualified state are at the minimum.

able by the allotment formula. When appropriations are increased, the incremental amounts available to a state depend entirely on its share of total enrollment, which may or may not correspond to its need for, or willingness to expand, state scholarships.

In order for the SSIG program to really furnish a continuing incentive for states to transfer funds to state scholarships, receipt of federal funds must depend on marginal choices made by state legislatures. That is, the appropriate form of aid is an open-ended matching grant in which the federal government offers to pay x percent of each additional dollar spent on state scholarships. Under such a program state governments will be faced with a shift in relative costs of supporting higher education in different ways. A dollar spent on state scholarships will cost the state (100 minus x) percent of a dollar while an incremental dollar spent on traditional institutional support will cost the state a whole dollar. This kind of program would correspond precisely to the federal government's intent of inducing states to switch support to the scholarship mode.

The practical arguments against such an open-ended matching program are that aggregate costs can become uncontrollable or that a few states may garner a disproportionate share of the funds. These objections lead, as in the present SSIG program, to closed-end (fixed appropriation) grants with state allotment formulas.[53] But these undesirable features of open-ended matching programs can better be solved by defining carefully the characteristics of state scholarship program funds eligible for matching and perhaps by placing speed limits on growth of an individual state's receipts.

The SSIG legislation and regulations define the characteristics of a state scholarship program that must be met before the state becomes eligible for federal grants. For the purpose here, the key criteria in the current SSIG system are:

Who is eligible? The law provides that state scholarships must be available only to students with "substantial financial need," which regulations of the Office of Education leave defined in various ways: limiting eligibility to those students whose family contribution is less than $2,800 (which corresponds to a gross income of about $24,000 in the 1976–77 College Scholarship Service system); to those whose parents' "net in-

---

53. Higher education is by no means unique as a federal program area where open-ended matching funds have been eschewed. Indeed, the only pure open-ended matching programs I can think of are aid to families with dependent children and Medicaid. For the demise of another matching program see Martha Derthick, *Uncontrollable Spending for Social Services Grants* (Brookings Institution, 1975).

come" (not defined in the regulations) is less than $20,000; or to those selected under a state system approved by the commissioner of education.

How much can they get? The law limits the state scholarship program to a $1,500 maximum per full-time student per academic year.

How will the grant be determined? Under SSIG rules, states may determine a student's scholarship award in any way they please provided that they assess a student's expected family contribution by using either the American College Testing Program, the College Scholarship Service, the basic grant or income tax needs-analysis system (or any other one approved by the commissioner, "which produces an expected family contribution reasonably comparable" to these systems). There are no criteria as to the treatment of costs of education in determining the award.[54]

Which institutions may the recipient attend? The Education Amendments of 1976 specify that "effective with respect to any academic year beginning on or after July 1, 1977, all nonprofit institutions of higher education in the State are eligible to participate in the State program."[55]

A New State Scholarship Matching Program

Most of these rules and regulations are not consistent with a reasonably designed federal-state scholarship matching program. Assuming that the purpose of spelling out the characteristics of a qualifying plan is to ensure that critical federal purposes are implemented, that some leeway is left for state variation on less urgent issues, and that safeguards are built in to prevent uncontrolled expenditure growth, federal criteria under a reformed program would be very different from the current law governing state scholarship incentive grants:

1. The single most important mandatory criterion ought to be the full and free portability of the state scholarships. The unwillingness of all but a very few states to adopt this on their own largely justifies federal intervention.

2. While it is essential to insist that family income be a determinant of scholarship eligibility, setting a national income level cut-off is unduly constraining. If an income level limit is set in the legislation, it should be a level related to each *state's* average income. For example, eligibility could be limited to dependent students whose family income falls below the state median family income.

54. All of the above from P. L. 92-318 and from the SSIG regulations published in the *Federal Register*, vol. 39 (May 31, 1974).

55. Sec. 123(b)(4).

3. If the income level for eligibility is specified as suggested, the needs-analysis systems used by the various states should be left entirely up to them. But if eligibility is tied to a maximum "expected family contribution," as in the current SSIG program, the federal government should annually review and reserve the right to disapprove the needs-analysis system used. Allowing private organizations to set eligibility criteria for a federal matching program delegates power to the wrong authority.

4. The federal-state scholarship matching program should be fully integrated with basic grants by requiring that college-going expenses counted for grant eligibility be limited to those in excess of expenses covered by basic grants. In addition, states should be required to insist that their scholarship applicants apply for basic grants, or at least that they base their grant computations on such an assumption.

5. To accommodate states that choose to make a gradual transition to rational pricing, federal regulations should permit state scholarship programs to make grant awards that vary with tuition. It would be desirable to segregate the costs attributable to this part of the state scholarship program, with a view toward phasing out such matching: this would convey the message that in the long run it is rationalization of prices that the federal program is intended to stimulate.

6. To safeguard federal outlays and to ensure that states do not move too precipitously, each state's award could be made subject to a "speed limit." For example, after an initial-year determination of a state's federal grant (based on a percentage of the volume of its state scholarship program), subsequent grants could be limited to no more than a 20 percent increase over the previous year. This would allow latitude for substantial expansion of state scholarships, while imposing some constraints on overall federal outlay growth.

Paying for the New Program

No specific matching rate for federal aid to state scholarship programs can be advocated with confidence at this time for several reasons. First, the adoption or expansion of a state scholarship program by a particular state does not necessarily impose a net burden on that state's taxpayers if subsidies are transferred from existing support of public institutions. Since some such substitution is an intended result of the policy and supporting program characteristics set out above, it is difficult to find a "burden" for the federal government to "share." Second, the main source of resistance to the proposed program of shifting state subsidies is likely to be the politically powerful losers: those in the upper half of the income distribution who now attend heavily subsidized public institutions in the home state, and the public institutions they attend. The proper subsidy rate is, therefore, the minimum level that persuades state legislators that offending these groups is worth the fight. It may be possible to examine the political advantages of providing benefits to private-sector and out-migrating students for state scholarship packages of varying sizes to see whether a federal rationale can be devised. (For example, the federal matching rate could be set so that, in most states, the federal grant provides the funds for the newly entitled private and out-migrating students. The selling point of this approach would be that Washington is paying for all the burdens that such students impose on the state.) Unfortunately, such an exercise would require very good data from a representative group of states, and such data are not currently available.

The matching rate for state scholarships would, in any event, be limited by the availability of federal funds. With states expected to allocate over $600 million of their own funds for state scholarship programs in the 1977–78 academic year,[56] a fifty-fifty federal matching program would cost at least $300 million if there were no stimulus to total state scholarship spending and would cost a great deal more if states responded to the incentive offered. Thus one way to arrive at a matching rate is to ask how much leeway there might be in the federal higher education budget and then assess what matching rate such a budgetary margin could support.

I start with an estimate of the "no policy change" federal student assistance budget for the 1977–78 academic year. This is shown in the first column of the table below (all figures in the table are in billions of dollars):[57]

Kind of assistance	"No policy change" budget	Cost of higher ceiling authorized in 1976	Elimination of half-cost provision
Basic grants	1.692	0.700	0.400
College-based aid	0.950	...	...
State student incentive grants	0.060	...	...
Guaranteed loan subsidies	0.537	...	...
Total	3.239	0.700	0.400

56. See the estimate by the Congressional Budget Office, reported in *Higher Education Amendments of 1976*, House Rept. 94-1086, 94:2 (GPO, 1976), p. 30.

57. The first three items in the first column are from *Making Supplemental Appropriations for the Fiscal Year Ending September 30, 1977*, H. Rept. 95-166, 95:1

The "no policy change" budget represents what the student assistance budget would be if basic grants were fully funded at the $1,400 maximum award level, the fiscal 1977 appropriations levels for college-based aid and SSIG programs, and the estimated cost of guaranteed loan interest subsidies. The total outlay of $3.2 billion reflects more than a tripling of the budget for these programs over a five-year period. Moreover, the Education Amendments of 1976 authorized an $1,800 maximum award level for basic grants, which would raise higher education student spending by about $700 million in the 1978–79 academic year (second column) provided that Congress actually appropriates the funds. Finally, if the suggestion raised earlier in this chapter were followed— that the half-cost provision of basic grants be eliminated—an estimated additional $400 million in federal student assistance costs would be incurred.

All told, then, the federal student assistance budget would be increased by over $1 billion over current policy if changes that have to be ranked as more fundamental to federal purposes than state scholarship matching are implemented. For all practical purposes, congressional action and good sense have already preempted any rise in federal student aid spending. The possibilities, therefore, for a big push in the direction of added funding for state scholarship matching depend entirely on how much Congress is willing to cut into the existing student assistance base. The place for such cutting, in my view, is clearly in the college-based aid programs, for reasons that are spelled out at length above.

I CONCLUDE with an observation on what seems to be poetic justice and an eerie symmetry. A federal reform that induces states to treat the private sector more evenhandedly and, at the same time, to maintain the complementary state provision of access for low-income students involves trading off college-based aid dollars for state scholarship matching dollars. There are obviously limits to the rate at which this conversion of federal funds can take place—limits defined by the ability of institutions to adjust to changes in federal funding sources. But since it is the private sector that has the largest stake in the college-based aid programs and, in the long run, would benefit the most from expanded state scholar-

---

(GPO, 1977). The last item, which is current-year funded, is the fiscal 1978 estimate of the U.S. Office of Education. The figures in the last two columns are author's estimates.

ship matching, it is reasonable to assign to that sector a large role in determining how quickly college-based aid should be scaled back to fund the new matching program. The inspirational theme for the private sector is, therefore, to "ask not what new federal dollars are your due, but ask at what rate you are willing to give up college-based aid for the new program." This amounts to asking the private sector to accept at the federal level a policy remarkably similar to what it is asking of public institutions at the state level: to accept reform of existing programs with little or no added financing.

From the point of view of someone looking at the private sector's problems from a social perspective, there is little question that the more fundamental shift in federal policy—away from college-based student aid toward state scholarship matching—and the state shift away from institutional subsidy toward student aid—would be desirable. Continuing past trends in federal-state aid could lead to continuing crises, especially in the coming decade. But the private sector cannot reasonably expect federal policy to downgrade its more direct responsibilities—particularly the support of basic grants—in order that its own institutions be preserved. Instead, private institutions should surely be willing to support a reasoned program of replacing college-based dollars with a revised state scholarship program.

APPENDIX: STATISTICAL TABLES

Table 5-A1. *Tuition, State Aid, and Recipients of Aid as a Percentage of Enrollment in Public Institutions of Higher Education, by State, Academic Year 1973–74*

Amounts in dollars

State	Nominal tuition[a]	State student aid per recipient	Net tuition to average aided student	Recipients of state aid as a percentage of enrollment
Vermont*	1,000	625	375	22.6
Pennsylvania*	832	491	341	33.3
New Hampshire*	829	0	829	0
Ohio	738	298	440	13.0
Indiana*	657	513	144	7.4
Rhode Island*	598	559	39	6.4
Minnesota	574	534	40	5.3
South Dakota	564	0	564	0
Iowa*	547	500	47	0.5
Maine	534	0	534	0
Michigan	529	544	−15	4.2
Virginia	528	275	253	0.2
Maryland	526	287[b]	239	7.9[b]
New Jersey*	525	523	2	20.9
South Carolina	520	0	520	0
Kentucky	500	0	500	0
Nebraska	500	0	500	0
Connecticut*	487	454	33	2.5
Delaware	481	632	−151	0.5
Montana	459	0	459	0
New York*	459	251	208	40.9
Alaska	445	0	445	0
Wisconsin	445	461	−16	9.0
Illinois*	443	442	1	17.6
Nevada	443	0	443	0

Table 5-A1 *(Continued)*

Amounts in dollars

State	Nominal tuition[a]	State student aid per recipient	Net tuition to average aided student	Recipients of state aid as a percentage of enrollment
New Mexico	437	0	437	0
Kansas	433	482	−49	0.3
Utah*	430	0	430	0
Oregon	428	416	12	4.4
Colorado	424	450	−26	14.0
North Dakota	420	232	188	2.3
Alabama	409	0	409	0
Georgia	405	0	405	0
Florida	404	1,073	−669	1.0
Missouri*	399	171	228	3.1
Washington	398	298	100	2.8
Massachusetts*	395	287	108	6.9
Arkansas	389	0	389	0
Oklahoma	373	0	373	0
Wyoming	362	0	362	0
Mississippi	358	0	358	0
Tennessee	346	293	53	2.4
Idaho	339	0	339	0
North Carolina	339	n.a.	n.a.	n.a.
Louisiana	303	0	303	0
West Virginia	290	261	29	3.2
Arizona	242	0	242	0
Texas	239	0	239	0
Hawaii	160	0	160	0
California	133	383	−250	2.9
Washington, D.C.	115	0	115	0

Sources: Average tuition, Carnegie Foundation for the Advancement of Teaching, *The States and Higher Education; a Proud Past and a Vital Future: Supplement to a Commentary of the Carnegie Foundation for the Advancement of Teaching* (The Foundation, 1976; available from Carnegie Council on Policy Studies in Higher Education, Berkeley), figure A-18; aid, derived from Joseph D. Boyd, "National Association of State Scholarship Programs: Fifth Annual Survey, October 1973" (Deerfield, Ill.: NASSP, 1973; processed); enrollment, Marilyn McCoy, *State and Local Financial Support of Higher Education: A Framework for Interstate Comparisons, 1973-74,* Field Review Edition (Boulder, Colo.: National Center for Higher Education Management Systems at Western Interstate Commission for Higher Education, 1976), p. 83.

* One of the thirteen states with the highest ratio of private to total enrollment.

n.a. Not available.

a. Computed by weighting average tuition by full-time-equivalent enrollment. The states are ranked from highest to lowest.

b. Figures for aid and public recipients are from the Maryland State Scholarship Board.

Table 5-A2. *State and Local Support for Higher Education and Cost of Equalization of Support, by State, Academic Year 1973–74*

Amounts in dollars

	Average state and local support per full-time-equivalent student			Percentage increase in support required to equalize private-public subsidies[b]
State[a]	Public	Private	Difference	
Massachusetts	1,633	65	1,568	128
Rhode Island	2,088	100	1,988	86
New Hampshire	1,255	2	1,253	77
Vermont	1,332	100	1,232	74
Pennsylvania	1,935	465	1,470	47
New York	2,581	746	1,835	40
Connecticut	1,854	129	1,725	58
Utah	1,607	13	1,594	61
Iowa	2,123	195	1,928	42
Missouri	1,780	81	1,699	37
Indiana	2,007	102	1,905	38
Illinois	2,317	436	1,881	31
New Jersey	2,013	346	1,667	29
Ohio	1,393	148	1,245	31
Maine	1,772	24	1,748	38
Tennessee	1,680	25	1,655	38
South Dakota	1,340	10	1,330	30
North Carolina	2,151	54	2,097	37
South Carolina	2,097	186	1,911	31
Idaho	1,837	0	1,837	29
Minnesota	1,771	140	1,631	27
Nebraska	1,765	1	1,764	29
Georgia	2,023	56	1,967	26
Maryland	1,656	104	1,552	21
Arkansas	2,014	0	2,014	22
Kentucky	2,144	0	2,144	22
Florida	2,005	205	1,800	20
Oklahoma	1,073	0	1,073	19
Louisiana	1,071	66	1,005	16
Texas	1,698	229	1,469	17

Table 5-A2 (Continued)

Amounts in dollars

State[a]	Average state and local support per full-time-equivalent student			Percentage increase in support required to equalize private-public subsidies[b]
	Public	Private	Difference	
West Virginia	1,641	30	1,611	19
Delaware	1,635	16	1,619	17
Virginia	1,519	20	1,499	21
Wisconsin	2,389	432	1,957	14
Michigan	1,933	92	1,841	16
Alabama	1,628	119	1,509	16
Washington	1,740	14	1,726	15
Kansas	1,635	210	1,425	13
Mississippi	1,735	0	1,735	13
Oregon	1,456	109	1,347	14
California	1,938	213	1,725	12
Montana	1,581	6	1,575	10
Colorado	1,504	16	1,488	13
New Mexico	1,571	6	1,565	9
Hawaii	1,331	0	1,331	6
Alaska	3,748	212	3,536	15
North Dakota	1,171	12	1,159	5
Arizona	1,806	0	1,806	5
Nevada	1,570	0	1,570	1
Wyoming	2,102	c	2,102	c
District of Columbia[a]	3,045	5	3,040	447
United States	1,881	262	1,619	27

Sources: McCoy, State and Local Financial Support of Higher Education, 1973–74, pp. 35, 83, 91, and Carnegie Foundation for the Advancement of Teaching, The States and Higher Education: A Proud Past and a Vital Future (Jossey-Bass, 1976), p. 65.

a. States are ranked by share of enrollment in private sector except for the District of Columbia.

b. Difference in third column times number of private full-time-equivalent enrollees divided by total state subsidies for higher education.

c. Wyoming has no private institutions.

Table 5-A3. *Residence Status and Migration of Students in Public and Private Institutions of Higher Education, Fall 1968 and Fall 1972*

State	Home-state enrollment as percent of total enrollment		Percentage point difference,	Out-of-state enrollment as percent of sector enrollment, 1972	
	1968 (1)	1972 (2)	1968–72 (3)	Public (4)	Private (5)
Alabama	84.8	86.9	2.1	9.0	30.4
Alaska	79.4	90.1	10.7	8.9	4.9
Arizona	81.3	82.7	1.4	14.9	49.5
Arkansas	84.7	85.9	1.2	9.3	32.9
California	92.8	94.1	1.3	1.7	17.7
Colorado	68.9	69.9	1.0	25.6	4.5
Connecticut*	77.3	82.9	5.6	6.6	32.4
Delaware	58.8	55.5	−3.3	40.9	53.9
District of Columbia	23.1	31.0	7.9	5.2	72.8
Florida	84.3	85.5	1.2	6.5	39.2
Georgia	78.3	80.9	2.6	12.3	40.3
Hawaii	78.9	86.5	7.6	6.8	·27.8
Idaho	78.2	74.7	−3.5	13.9	54.2
Illinois	86.2	89.2	3.0	2.3	22.1
Indiana	72.2	76.3	4.1	13.3	45.9
Iowa*	71.1	74.6	3.5	14.6	39.5
Kansas	79.0	82.2	3.2	12.2	43.2
Kentucky	76.1	80.2	4.1	13.9	39.2
Louisiana	87.5	88.1	0.6	5.7	34.1
Maine	64.8	71.3	6.5	11.4	69.2
Maryland	81.1	81.5	0.4	15.6	32.1
Massachusetts*	66.6	67.7	1.1	5.8	42.7
Michigan	86.8	90.2	3.4	5.7	21.8
Minnesota	82.3	83.8	1.5	7.9	36.9
Mississippi	87.2	89.8	2.6	8.1	18.1
Missouri*	74.9	79.6	4.7	9.1	40.8
Montana	84.5	82.9	−1.6	14.6	31.1
Nebraska	75.1	80.6	5.5	9.	46.2
Nevada	82.1	81.0	−1.1	13.2	69.3
New Hampshire*	46.7	46.2	−0.5	32.9	73.0

Table 5-A3 *(Continued)*

State	Home-state enrollment as percent of total enrollment 1968 (1)	Home-state enrollment as percent of total enrollment 1972 (2)	Percentage point difference, 1968–72 (3)	Out-of-state enrollment as percent of sector enrollment, 1972 Public (4)	Out-of-state enrollment as percent of sector enrollment, 1972 Private (5)
New Jersey	87.6	90.3	2.7	3.3	19.6
New Mexico	81.1	85.3	4.2	12.4	27.7
New York*	88.1	88.7	0.6	2.3	20.5
North Carolina	71.1	76.0	4.9	12.1	45.3
North Dakota	83.4	83.5	0.1	13.8	29.2
Ohio	80.9	84.3	3.4	7.8	33.8
Oklahoma	83.9	86.7	2.8	7.2	31.7
Oregon	82.5	80.5	−2.0	10.7	51.4
Pennsylvania*	80.3	82.3	2.0	5.6	28.3
Rhode Island*	63.8	64.0	0.2	15.8	52.3
South Carolina	75.6	82.3	6.7	10.9	32.1
South Dakota	77.0	77.4	0.4	14.2	45.0
Tennessee	71.7	76.1	4.4	10.7	56.1
Texas	90.1	89.5	−0.6	5.2	22.3
Utah*	67.6	64.0	−3.6	15.7	59.3
Vermont*	39.9	45.6	5.7	31.1	78.8
Virginia	75.5	78.8	3.3	15.4	41.2
Washington	85.0	87.6	2.6	6.6	31.4
West Virginia	69.6	72.7	3.1	20.5	52.5
Wisconsin	78.2	83.9	5.7	8.9	38.8
Wyoming	78.4	79.5	1.1	18.3	0
United States	81.5	83.8	2.3	7.6	33.1

Sources: Column 1, W. Vance Grant and C. George Lind, *Digest of Educational Statistics, 1973 Edition,* U.S. Office of Education (GPO, 1974), p. 79; column 2, ibid., *1974 Edition* (1975), p. 73; column 3, column 2 minus column 1; columns 4 and 5, McCoy, *State and Local Financial Support of Higher Education, 1973–74,* p. 135.

* One of the ten states with the highest share of enrollment in private institutions.

Table 5-A4. *Cost of Tuition Offset Grant Program (Option 2), and Cost as a Percentage of Expenditures in Public Sector, by State, Academic Year 1973–74*

	Number of students		Cost of subsidizing out-migrating and home-state private students	
State	Out-migrating[a] (1)	Attending private institutions in home state[b] (2)	Amount (thousands of dollars) (3)	As a percentage of state subsidy to public sector (4)
Alabama	11,599	10,254	35,577	25.3
Alaska	2,359	786	11,787	60.1
Arizona	7,536	2,063	17,336	11.2
Arkansas	7,766	5,542	26,802	35.5
California	48,165	94,634	276,744	17.0
Colorado	11,412	11,687	34,741	24.7
Connecticut	44,082	27,049	131,877	116.3
Delaware	6,266	1,454	12,622	41.4
District of Columbia	9,920	12,443	68,095	220.5
Florida	32,434	24,136	113,423	33.0
Georgia	16,885	14,986	64,475	33.8
Hawaii	8,045	1,460	12,651	29.4
Idaho	7,645	2,948	19,459	48.0
Illinois	82,538	83,101	383,786	65.0
Indiana	21,814	25,105	94,166	41.4
Iowa	22,893	19,126	89,206	64.5
Kansas	12,881	6,461	31,624	25.7
Kentucky	12,939	9,882	48,928	31.6
Louisiana	9,128	10,769	21,310	20.6
Maine	6,890	2,639	16,885	43.4
Maryland	35,977	15,756	85,670	50.6
Massachusetts	43,725	89,237	217,127	120.6
Michigan	21,971	33,356	106,947	21.5
Minnesota	18,770	19,480	67,741	37.7
Mississippi	6,988	6,491	23,386	21.7
Missouri	22,418	24,717	83,900	44.8
Montana	5,153	1,439	10,422	30.1
Nebraska	8,106	6,570	25,903	34.9
Nevada	3,435	28	5,437	22.3
New Hampshire	7,758	3,464	14,084	67.2

Table 5-A4 *(Continued)*

	Number of students		Cost of subsidizing out-migrating and home-state private students	
State	Out-migrating[a] (*1*)	Attending private institutions in home state[b] (*2*)	Amount (thousands of dollars) (*3*)	As a percentage of state subsidy to public sector (*4*)
New Jersey	119,425	40,370	321,667	120.0
New Mexico	6,717	2,346	14,238	25.7
New York	140,196	213,755	913,548	88.7
North Carolina	12,824	25,976	83,459	31.1
North Dakota	4,817	871	6,661	23.2
Ohio	51,961	55,002	148,999	46.2
Oklahoma	9,203	10,861	21,529	24.4
Oregon	10,181	6,140	23,763	20.0
Pennsylvania	78,874	103,898	353,664	91.0
Rhode Island	8,810	9,455	38,137	87.3
South Carolina	11,727	14,230	54,432	44.1
South Dakota	4,559	3,038	10,180	42.2
Tennessee	13,402	15,608	48,737	32.0
Texas	22,297	51,883	125,958	22.6
Utah	3,183	10,627	22,193	32.5
Vermont	4,024	2,332	8,466	49.1
Virginia	40,040	14,981	83,577	46.0
Washington	13,448	13,581	47,030	20.4
West Virginia	6,666	4,214	17,854	24.2
Wisconsin	17,708	15,854	80,180	23.0
Wyoming	3,516	0	7,391	27.4
United States	1,141,076	1,188,994	4,382,862	42.9

Sources: Column 1: a percentage distribution of out-migrating students, calculated from fall 1968 data in Grant and Lind, *Digest of Educational Statistics, 1973 Edition*, p. 79, was applied to the total number of out-of-state students in the United States in the fall of 1972, from *Digest of Educational Statistics, 1974 Edition*, p. 73; column 2: home-state enrollment as a percentage of private-sector enrollment (from table 5-A3) was multiplied by private full-time-equivalent enrollment from McCoy, *State and Local Financial Support of Higher Education, 1973–74*, p. 91; column 3: columns 1 and 2 were summed, then multiplied by state and local support per public full-time-equivalent student (from table 5-A2) for each state; column 4: derived from *State and Local Financial Support of Higher Education, 1973–74*, pp. 83, 85.

a. Fall 1972 data.
b. Fall 1973 data.

Chapter Six

Federal and State Tax Policies

Emil M. Sunley, Jr.

EDITED BY DAVID W. BRENEMAN AND CHESTER E. FINN, JR.

EMIL M. SUNLEY, JR., deputy assistant secretary of the Treasury for tax policy, was a senior fellow in the Brookings Economic Studies program from 1975 to 1977. He thanks Bruce Davie for helpful comments.

Tables

MUCH of the current public support of private colleges and universities takes the form of direct and indirect tax subsidies. The principal subsidies are the income tax deduction for charitable giving, an individual's tax exemption for scholarships and fellowships and for social security and veterans' benefits, the additional personal exemption granted for students, and a nonprofit institution's exemption from property taxes. Any changes in these provisions can have an important impact on private higher education.

In recent years there has been increased interest in providing tax relief for middle-income families faced with high college expenses. This led to a number of proposals for a tax deduction or a tax credit for tuition expenses. In addition to the usual equity and efficiency considerations, these proposals, if enacted, would affect the allocation of educational resources between public and private schools.

Federal, State, and Local Tax Subsidies

The Congressional Budget and Impoundment Control Act of 1974 requires the annual federal budget to include a listing of the various tax provisions, generally called tax expenditures, which are subsidies or incentives for particular activities or groups. The act defines tax expenditures as the "revenue losses attributable to provisions of the federal tax laws which allow a special exclusion, exemption, or deduction from gross income or which provide a special credit, a preferential rate of tax, or a deferral of tax liability."[1]

Higher education benefits from nine tax expenditures shown here in table 6-1. Seven of these provide direct benefits either to students or institutions of higher education and two provide only indirect benefits. Excluded from this list of preferences are a number of small items.[2] Also excluded is the income tax exemption of educational institutions which, like the separate taxation of individuals and corporations, is considered part of the normal structure of the income tax. Tax exemption, however, by itself is not important for colleges and universities because even if

1. 88 Stat. 299.
2. Tuition remission granted faculty children is exempt from taxation although the Internal Revenue Service in 1976 indicated an interest in changing this rule, only to back down in response to the political outcry. Many college presidents live in college-provided houses, but this in-kind benefit is not considered taxable compensation. Finally, forgiven indebtedness under federal student loan programs, for example, for those who enter teaching careers, is not considered income.

Table 6-1. *Estimate of Federal Tax Expenditures That Benefit Higher Education, Fiscal Year 1977*

Millions of dollars

Type of benefit and expenditure	Revenue cost		
	Private institutions	Public institutions	Total
Direct benefit			
Deductibility of contributions other than bequests to educational institutions[a]	580	200	780
Deductibility of bequests to educational institutions	225	50	275
Unrealized capital gains on gifts and bequests to higher education	60	20	80
Parental personal exemptions and tax credits for students aged nineteen and over	240	475	715
Exclusion of scholarships and fellowships	110	110	220
Exclusion of GI bill benefits for higher education	40	150	190
Exclusion of student survivor benefits under social security	25	75	100
Total, direct	1,280	1,080	2,360
Indirect benefit			
Deductibility of state and local taxes[b]	30	1,020	1,050
Exemption of interest on general purpose state and local debt[b]	15	415	430
Total, indirect	45	1,435	1,480
Total, direct and indirect	1,325	2,515	3,840

Sources: Author's estimates, partially based on data in *Special Analyses, Budget of the United States Government, Fiscal Year 1977*, pp. 125–27.

a. Includes some gifts to primary and secondary schools.

b. Assumes that 9.5 percent of state and local general expenditures and debts are for higher education (U.S. Bureau of the Census, *Governmental Finances in 1973–74* [Government Printing Office, 1975], p. 18).

these institutions were taxed as corporations they generally would have no net income and thus would be nontaxable.[3] The importance of tax exemption is that it qualifies them to receive deductible contributions.

3. A recent study by Carol Van Alstyne and Sharon L. Coldren concluded that the rapid increases in social security taxes have vitiated the tax exemption of non-profit institutions. (Van Alstyne and Coldren, "The Costs of Implementing Federally Mandated Social Programs at Colleges and Universities" [American Council on Education, 1976; processed], pp. 24–25, 53.) The study advocates shifting a portion of the social security tax burden to general revenue sources. Their argument is not convincing. To the extent that social security taxes are borne by labor, they impose no burden on colleges and universities. Tax exemption for education does not re-

Charitable Deduction for Gifts and Bequests

Individuals and corporations may deduct contributions to nonprofit educational institutions. For individuals the total deduction for contributions for all charitable purposes generally may not exceed 50 percent of income. (For corporations the corresponding figure is 5 percent of net income.) For most gifts of appreciated property, however, a 30 percent limitation applies. In addition, individuals may deduct contributions only if they itemize their personal deductions instead of claiming the standard deduction.

Under present law individuals may claim a current tax deduction for a charitable gift of a remainder interest. The usual arrangement is to transfer property to a trust, with the provision that the income is to be paid to certain individuals (say, a wife or children) over a specified period of time or during their entire lives; at the end of that period or at their deaths, what remains of the trust goes to charity. The allowable tax deduction is equal to the present value of the expected remainder interest.[4] Many colleges and universities have established charitable remainder trusts to receive property from donors who want to retain a lifetime interest.

Charitable bequests to educational institutions are deductible without limit under the federal estate tax.[5] This preference will reduce federal tax receipts by $275 million in fiscal 1977.[6]

The deductibility of gifts and bequests to educational institutions and unrealized gains on gifts and bequests are the only tax expenditures that benefit private colleges and universities more than public institutions, simply because the former rely far more on voluntary support. Although the private institutions enrolled only one-fourth of all students in 1974–

quire exemption of employees of colleges and universities from social security or income taxes any more than separation of powers requires state and local employees to be exempt from federal income taxes.

4. Before the Tax Reform Act of 1969, it was possible to favor the income beneficiary over the remainder beneficiary. The 1969 act tightened the rules governing current deductions for future charitable interests.

5. This preference is included in table 6-1 even though the Congressional Budget Act limits tax expenditures to income tax preferences. The impact of this provision on charitable bequests is discussed in the next section.

6. "Hearings on Estate and Gift Tax Reform" (Testimony of Senator Edward M. Kennedy before the Senate Committee on Finance, May 17, 1976; processed), tax expenditure table.

75, they received three-fourths of all gifts and bequests to educational institutions.[7]

The charitable deduction has long been criticized by tax reformers as basically inconsistent with a comprehensive definition of income. Moreover, the deduction is inequitable: it is worth more to high-income taxpayers than to low-income taxpayers, and nothing at all to those who do not itemize or who are nontaxable because their incomes are too low.[8] This basic inequity has led to a number of proposals to replace the charitable deduction with a tax credit that would provide the same benefit per dollar of charitable giving regardless of the taxpayer's income tax bracket.[9] Even if the rate of the tax credit were set high enough to provide a sufficient incentive to maintain total charitable giving, the amount of charitable giving going to higher education would be sharply reduced. (The impact of the charitable deduction on giving and the impact of proposed changes in the law are discussed in the following section.)

Unrealized Appreciation

The increase in the value of a capital asset, such as corporate stock, land, or a painting, is generally taxed at capital gains rates when the asset is sold. However, if such property is transferred by gift or at death, the increase in value is not subject to tax.[10] In addition, the taxpayer generally is able to claim a charitable deduction for the current market

7. Table 1-5, and Council for Financial Aid to Education, *Voluntary Support of Education, 1974–75* (CFAE, n.d.).

8. Not all tax experts accept this view. Boris Bittker of Yale Law School has argued that the charitable deduction is necessary if one wants to tax net income. (See Boris I. Bittker, "The Propriety and Vitality of a Federal Income Tax Deduction for Private Philanthropy" in *Tax Impacts on Philanthropy Symposium* [Tax Institute of America, 1972], pp. 145–70.)

9. This is strictly true only if the government would make payments to individuals with too little tax liability against which to use the full amount of the credit. Such a credit is generally said to be refundable.

10. In the case of gifts, the donor's basis (or the fair market value if lower) becomes the donee's basis. This carryover of basis, however, is unimportant in the case of tax-exempt organizations, which are not taxable on gains realized on the sale of the property. The Tax Reform Act of 1976 extends the carryover basis treatment to bequests, but only with respect to appreciation after 1976. This change will provide a tax incentive to leave low-basis property (that is, property on which there has been substantial appreciation in value) to charity and high-basis property to heirs, other things being equal.

value of the property even though the gain has never been recognized for tax purposes. It is thus more advantageous to give property to charity than to sell it and give the after-tax proceeds to charity. In certain cases, the tax savings from the gift of appreciated property can exceed what the taxpayer would realize after tax if he or she sold the property.[11] In these cases one may well ask whether the taxpayer has really given anything away.[12]

In 1973, contributions of property reported on individual income tax returns amounted to $1.3 billion, or 9 percent of all contributions. Gifts of appreciated property are most important in the higher income classes. Taxpayers reporting an income of more than $200,000 in 1973 gave away $400 million in property and $360 million in cash.[13]

There is no sound theoretical reason for treating gifts of appreciated property more favorably than gifts of cash. The preference for appreciated property magnifies the inherent inequity of the charitable deduction itself. The basic justification for retaining the present tax rules is that colleges, universities, and charitable organizations rely heavily on appreciated gifts for support, and any change would significantly reduce this particular source. Moreover, it might be argued that appreciation on gifts to charities should only be taxed if the appreciation on noncharitable gifts is also taxed.

11. For example, assume a 70 percent taxpayer possessing an asset with a zero basis (that is, acquired at no cost) that is now worth $1,000. If he sold the asset he would pay capital gains taxes of $350 (capital gains generally being taxed at half the rate of ordinary income), leaving $650 after tax. By giving the property away, he realizes a tax savings of $700. Thus he is $50 better off by giving the property away. If the taxpayer is subject to the minimum tax (see below) the tax savings from giving the property away is even greater. If the property is sold, the taxpayer could pay $399 in capital gains and minimum tax. He then would be almost $100 better off by giving the property away. The Tax Reform Act of 1976 included itemized deductions (other than medical and casualty) in excess of 60 percent of adjusted gross income as a new preference under the minimum tax. For taxpayers affected by this change, the tax incentive for charitable gifts is reduced. (Note that the minimum tax for individuals is a tax of 15 percent on the sum of various tax preference items not included in the regular tax base, reduced by either $10,000 or half the regular tax liability, whichever is greater.)

12. If the alternative is not to sell the property but instead to hold it until death when it could pass to the heirs with the gain never being recognized for income tax purposes, then one might conclude that the gift of appreciated property reduces the net estate and in this sense the taxpayer has given something away.

13. U.S. Internal Revenue Service, *Statistics of Income—1973, Individual Income Tax Returns* (Government Printing Office, 1976), table 2-5.

Extra Personal Exemptions and Tax Credits

In general, a person with gross income of $750 or more cannot be claimed for the $750 dependency exemption. An exception to this gross income test is made for a taxpayer's child who is either a full-time student or is less than nineteen years of age. The full-time student exception was provided in 1954 to aid parents with children in college. To claim the dependency exemption, however, the parent must provide more than half the student's support.[14]

This provision in effect provides a double personal exemption for students. The parent may claim the student as an exemption and, in addition, the student may claim himself on his own tax return. Since the tax saving from each extra personal exemption increases with the parent's marginal tax rate, it is worth more to high-income families. There is no tax relief for parents of students who provide more than half of their own support. The provision thus indirectly discriminates against students who are generally self-supporting.

Simple repeal of the extra exemption, however, would cause a serious tax disincentive for students who work part time during the school year or who work during the summer. If a student over age eighteen earned $750, the parent then would lose the dependency exemption even though the parent provides more than half of the total support.[15]

There have been many proposals to replace personal exemptions with a per capita tax credit that would be worth the same regardless of the taxpayer's marginal tax rate. Under such a system, Congress would be able to differentiate between two families at the same income level with and without children in college; and it would not provide a larger tax break for a high-income family with children in college than for a low-income family in the same situation.

In 1975, Congress provided a credit of $30 for each taxpayer and dependent. Under 1976 law, this credit was increased to the greater of $35 per capita or 2 percent of the first $9,000 of taxable income. As a result of these changes, parents eligible to claim extra student exemptions may

14. An exception to the support rule is provided for cases where support is provided by several taxpayers. Since 1954 scholarships have been ignored in determining whether the parent meets the support test for the dependency exemption.

15. As the student's income rises from $749 to $751, the parent would lose a $750 deduction which could be worth as much as $525 in tax savings. The exceptions to the gross income test for students and children less than nineteen years are necessary if this notch problem is to be avoided.

now be able to claim extra per capita credits as well. Most high-income parents will not benefit from the extra $35 credit since 2 percent of the first $9,000 of taxable income will provide a larger total credit.[16]

Scholarships and Fellowships

Individuals may generally exclude scholarships and fellowships from taxable income under the federal income tax. Individuals who are candidates for a degree, however, cannot exclude payments for teaching, research, or other services, such as part-time employment that is a prerequisite for a scholarship or fellowship, unless those services are required of all degree candidates. Individuals who are not candidates for a degree may exclude no more than $300 a month for thirty-six months.

The usual rationale for the present exclusion of scholarships and fellowships is that they are similar to gifts and inheritances that are not taxed under the income tax. The exclusion, like the extra personal exemption, discriminates against students who have to work. Their earnings are fully taxable. This provision often permits a college or university professor to convert $300 per month of sabbatical pay, which might be viewed as a payment for past or future services, into a tax-free fellowship.

Like all exclusions from gross income, the exclusion for scholarships and fellowships provides a tax benefit that increases with the individual's marginal tax rate. For many students this exclusion provides no tax benefit because the student would have no tax liability even if the scholarship or fellowship were included in income.[17] The largest benefit goes to students with other sources of income, married students where the spouse has taxable income, and nonstudents who receive fellowship income.

In recent years there has been considerable litigation over whether certain payments, such as payments by hospitals to interns and resident doctors, payments to teaching fellows and research assistants at colleges and universities, and sabbatical payments, are fellowships or compensation. Given these administrative difficulties and the basic inequity of exempting scholarships and fellowships, it would seem reasonable at the very least to limit the exclusion to students who are candidates for undergraduate degrees. An alternative would be to limit the exclusion to tuition and fees and require any payments for living expenses to be in-

16. A family with $9,000 of taxable income would have a $180 credit unless eligible for six or more per capita credits.

17. In 1976, a single individual may have $2,450 of income a year before paying tax and a married couple with no children $3,600.

cluded in gross income. This would favor private colleges and universities where tuition is higher. It would also reduce uncertainty as to what is or is not excludable. For example, sabbatical payments would clearly be taxable.

GI Bill Benefits

Education payments under the GI bill are designed to compensate veterans for opportunities lost while in the service. These payments, which vary with the number of dependents and the type of training, are exempt from income tax. Like the exclusion from income of scholarships and fellowships, this is worth more the higher the veteran's tax rate bracket. The equity of the tax system would be improved if veterans' benefits and all other transfer payments including social security benefits were made taxable. The personal exemption and the low-income allowance can ensure that poor families are not subject to the income tax.

Servicemen who enter the armed forces after 1976 are no longer eligible for the same GI bill benefits. Instead they can contribute between $50 and $75 of their monthly military pay to an education trust fund. The Veterans Administration will match every dollar with two dollars when the funds are withdrawn to meet education expenses.[18] The tax treatment of this new system is unclear. Presumably the payment by the Veterans Administration is tax exempt, but servicemen must pay tax on their contributions.

Student Benefits under Social Security

Under social security a child is entitled to benefits if his or her parent is disabled, retired, or deceased. The child must be under the age of eighteen or a student between the ages of eighteen and twenty-one. All social security benefits including student benefits are nontaxable. The student benefit thus includes a tax subsidy for education. Since most students would be nontaxable even if the social security benefits were included in income, the tax savings from the exclusion is only $100 million a year.

Deductibility of State and Local Taxes

The federal government aids state and local governments by means of two important tax subsidies. Both of these subsidies provide sizable

18. Veterans' Education and Employment Assistance Act of 1976 (90 Stat. 2383).

indirect benefits for public higher education. First, individuals who item-ize their personal deductions can deduct state and local taxes. That low-ered federal revenue by $11.1 billion in 1977. Since about 9.5 percent of state and local expenditures are for higher education, deductibility should be viewed as a $1 billion subsidy to public higher education.[19] Because only those who itemize get any direct benefit from deductibility, this provision is a kind of indirect revenue sharing for high-income states (and wealthy suburbs). Another indirect benefit is the incentive pro-vided for state and local governments to adopt progressive taxes so as to maximize the value of deductibility.

The second indirect subsidy to higher education through state and local governments is the exemption from federal taxation of the interest on state and local debt. The major impact of this provision is to permit state and local governments to float bonds at a lower interest cost than would be possible if the interest were subject to the federal income tax. The major criticisms of tax-exempt financing are that it is inefficient and inequitable.[20] It is inefficient because it costs the federal government more in forgone revenue than it saves state and local governments in interest costs. It is inequitable because it is worth more to high-income investors and thus it erodes the progressiveness of the individual income tax.

Taken together, the two federal tax subsidies for state and local gov-ernments imply that government expenditures for public higher educa-tion are subsidized indirectly whether they are tax or debt financed. These tax subsidies provide few benefits for private higher education.[21]

Deduction of Education Expenses

The deductibility of certain educational expenses was not included in the list of tax subsidies given in table 6-1. The present tax code does not specifically permit a deduction for educational expenses. Instead, certain educational expenses are deductible under the general section in the

19. About 3 percent of state and local expenditures for higher education go to private institutions. Thus in table 6-1 a small portion of the tax expenditure for deductibility of taxes is allocated to the private institutions.

20. See, for example, Richard Goode, *The Individual Income Tax* (rev. ed.; Brookings Institution, 1976), pp. 133–38.

21. In some states private colleges and universities can, in effect, borrow in the tax-exempt market to finance new buildings. For example, New York's State Dormi-tory Authority has issued tax-exempt bonds on behalf of private colleges and uni-versities.

code that permits a deduction for ordinary and necessary business expenses. Thus education expenses incurred to maintain or improve skills necessary for the taxpayer's present job are deductible, but expenses to prepare for a new job or to qualify for a new trade or business are not.[22] Admittedly, the line between deductible and nondeductible educational expenses appears rather arbitrary, but a tax on the net income must permit a deduction for ordinary and necessary business expenses, and such a deduction can hardly be viewed as a subsidy.

The deduction permitted under present law, however, is not neutral between education while on the job and education prior to obtaining employment. To remove this bias, however, would alter the basic justification for permitting a deduction for education expenses.[23]

Property Tax Exemption

The principal state and local tax subsidy for higher education is the exemption of educational institutions from property taxes. This exemption is generally mandated by state law, although the property tax is mainly a local tax. The scope of the property tax exemption varies from state to state with some of them taxing fraternities, housing facilities, and certain income-producing property owned by colleges.

There is almost no data on the amount of real property that is exempt from the property tax. It is generally assumed that about one-third of all property is tax-exempt, although the percentage is obviously much higher in college towns.[24] In aggregate, the property tax exemption may save colleges and universities $205 million a year in taxes.[25]

The property tax exemption is usually justified as an encouragement to institutions providing public services that would otherwise have to be provided—adequately or inadequately—by the governments themselves. The value of the exemption, however, bears little relationship to what governments would have to appropriate directly to supply the services. Property tax exemptions can impose severe fiscal problems on college towns that must supply municipal services to exempt as well as

22. The line between deductible and nondeductible educational expenses is drawn not in the code but in the regulations.

23. In the last section of this chapter I refer to the various justifications for giving some tax relief for education expenditures.

24. L. Richard Gabler and John F. Shannon, "The Exemption of Religious, Educational and Charitable Institutions from Property Taxation," in Commission on Private Philanthropy and Public Needs, *Research Papers*, vol. 4, *Taxes* (U.S. Department of the Treasury, 1977), p. 2535.

25. Table 2-8.

taxed property. Although many colleges and universities make voluntary payments to local governments, these payments are clearly less than the value of the exemption itself.

Property tax exemptions have somewhat different implications for public and private educational institutions. In the case of public institutions, the fiscal impact of the exemption could be offset by an intergovernmental transfer from the state to the local government. A state reimbursement of local governments for the revenue loss due to tax exemption of private institutions would, however, represent an indirect transfer from the government to the private sector.

Sales Tax Exemption

Forty-five states, the District of Columbia, and many local governments impose sales taxes. Educational institutions and other tax-exempt organizations generally do not pay sales taxes on the goods and services they buy, even when they are the final purchaser. Also, college tuition and fees for room and board are exempt from state and local sales taxes. If tuition were subject to the sales tax, this would work to the relative disadvantage of private colleges and universities. Alternatively, a sales tax could be imposed on the value of educational services received whether or not tuition is charged. This approach would be neutral between public and private schools, but it would be quite complex and would impose a heavy administrative burden on state and local governments.

Other State and Local Tax Subsidies

Forty-two states and the District of Columbia impose individual income taxes, and some municipalities or counties in eleven states also impose local income taxes. Charitable contributions generally are deductible under these taxes, and thus the issues relating to deductibility under the federal income tax discussed in the following section apply equally to most state and local income taxes. The District of Columbia, however, limits the charitable deduction for contributions to organizations that do substantial work in the District.

Two states, Indiana and Michigan, provide tax credits for contributions to institutions of higher education within the state.[26] In the case

26. *Higher Education in the States*, vol. 5, no. 3 (Education Commission of the States, 1976), pp. 128, 132–33.

of Indiana, there is no charitable deduction but a dollar-for-dollar credit is allowed for contributions up to 20 percent of income or $50 per return ($100 for a joint return), whichever is less. This provision, in effect, permits Indiana taxpayers to earmark a part of their taxes for higher education and, given the value of the federal tax deduction, it reduces to less than zero the cost of charitable contributions eligible for the credit. For public institutions, the state government could offset the impact of this provision simply by reducing general fund appropriations so that the institutions have no net increase in revenues.

In the case of Michigan, the credit is in addition to the state income tax deduction for the contribution. The credit is equal to one-half of the contributions but not more than 20 percent of state tax liability or $100 ($200 for joint returns). Since only half of the eligible contribution can be credited, this provision does not make the price of giving negative.[27]

The special provisions in the District of Columbia, Indiana, and Michigan discriminate against colleges and universities located outside their jurisdictions. Since most private colleges and universities have alumni spread more widely geographically than public institutions, these provisions thus tend to discriminate against private institutions.

The Tax Treatment of Philanthropy

Policy questions relating to higher education and the tax treatment of philanthropy can be grouped as follows. First, are tax incentives for giving justified? Second, are the present incentives equitable? Third, what schools benefit from the charitable dollars? Fourth, are the tax incentives efficient in encouraging additional giving? Fifth, what impact would proposed changes in the tax treatment of philanthropy have on giving to higher education?

Justification

The principal justification for tax incentives for philanthropic giving is that they foster decentralized decisionmaking and encourage activities

27. Even for a federal taxpayer at the 70 percent level the price is not negative because the tax savings from the credit reduces the federal deduction for state income taxes.

with important social benefits that governments would otherwise have to provide. For example, private colleges and universities clearly are close substitutes for public institutions, with the important exception that almost all liberal arts colleges are in the private sector. If private colleges and universities were to close, state governments, and probably the federal government, would have to assume a greater burden of financing higher education through direct expenditure programs. The traditional argument for philanthropy, however, is not just survival. The philanthropic dollar can provide the margin for excellence, and many (but by no means all) of the most distinguished colleges and universities are private. It is also contended that an independent private sector has a vital role to play in initiating new ideas and approaches to higher education.

A viable private sector in higher education may require unconditional government subsidies, but it does not require that the subsidies take the form of tax incentives for philanthropic giving. One possibility would be to provide unconditional grants or possibly tax credits to students who attend private colleges and universities. This would ensure pluralism based on student choice rather than pluralism based on the preferences of large donors.[28]

Equity

The fundamental criticism of the income tax deduction for charitable giving is that it is inequitable. The inherent inequity is clearly seen when the tax incentive is compared with an equivalent direct government expenditure program.[29] Instead of the tax deduction for charitable giving, the government could provide matching grants to charitable organizations that are supported by private philanthropy.

No bureaucrat or politician, however, would ever propose the following federal expenditure program with matching provisions equivalent to the present system of tax deductions. The matching rate would be zero for taxpayers who have no tax liability or who do not itemize their per-

28. For a discussion of alternatives to ensure pluralism, see Gerard M. Brannon and James Strinad, "Alternative Approaches to Encouraging Philanthropic Activities," in Commission on Private Philanthropy and Public Needs, *Research Papers*, vol. 4, pp. 2361–88.

29. Stanley S. Surrey has most effectively compared tax incentives with direct government programs. (See, for example, Surrey, *Pathways to Tax Reform: The Concept of Tax Expenditures* [Harvard University Press, 1973], pp. 223–32.)

sonal deductions.[30] For taxpayers who itemize and who are in the 14 percent tax rate bracket, the matching rate would be 14 cents for every 86 cents given to charity. The matching rate would then increase with income. It would be dollar-for-dollar for taxpayers in the 50 percent tax rate bracket, and for taxpayers in the highest tax rate bracket, for every 30 cents given to charity the government would contribute 70 cents to the same charity. In addition, the matching rate would be increased for any taxpayer giving appreciated property to charity, and the amount of the increase would depend on the amount of appreciation. In the extreme, a taxpayer in the 70 percent tax bracket who sold $100 of fully appreciated property (with $65 left after paying taxes) would inform the government that he wanted $100 contributed to charity. The government would pay the $100 to charity and, in addition, it would mail the taxpayer a check for $5. The taxpayer would then have $70 in cash instead of the $100 of appreciated property.

Not all tax experts accept the view that the charitable deduction is inequitable. Bittker contends that it is fundamentally different from other personal deductions. He argues that there are many different definitions of income, but that the concept of consumption is central and is the only definition that has the benefit of consensus. He concludes then that what one gives to charity can properly be viewed differently from spending in other respects.[31]

Most tax experts view individuals as voluntarily making gifts to philanthropic organizations. Presumably spending money in this way gives them more satisfaction than spending in other ways or adding to savings. Even though there are significant public benefits from philanthropic organizations justifying government subsidy, one cannot justify a subsidy scheme that provides, in effect, for the government to match private contributions at a rate that depends on whether the taxpayer itemizes his deductions, that increases with income, and that is higher when appreciated property is given.

Bittker has also pointed out that the charitable deduction ensures neutrality between giving time and money.[32] Under present law, if a tax-

---

30. Taxpayers have a choice of itemizing their personal deductions or claiming the standard deduction. Most low-income taxpayers claim the standard deduction.

31. Boris I. Bittker's views are summarized in *Giving in America: Toward a Stronger Voluntary Sector*, Report of the Commission on Private Philanthropy and Public Needs (the Commission, 1975), p. 110.

32. "The Propriety and Vitality of a Federal Income Tax Deduction," p. 166.

payer gives $100 to a charity he deducts that from income. If he gives time worth $100, he does not get a tax deduction, but at the same time he does not include the value of his time in income. Thus the person who gives $100 of time is left in the same tax position he would be in if he had earned $100 and had given it to charity (assuming he itemizes his deductions). If the tax incentive for giving were made more equitable by providing a credit instead of a deduction, there would no longer, be this neutrality between giving time and money.

The equity issue relating to the deduction for charitable bequests is very similar to that in the case of the income tax deduction. By making charitable bequests, wealthy individuals can, in effect, direct what otherwise would have been government revenues to organizations they select. Given the progressive estate tax rate schedule, the deduction for charitable bequests reduces estate taxes more for large estates than for small ones. Thus the estate tax deduction behaves like a government matching grant with the matching rate increasing with the size of the estate.

The Distribution of Voluntary Support

The better-off colleges and universities receive a disproportionate share of charitable giving whereas schools in danger of closing receive relatively little. Table 6-2 gives the distribution for private institutions in 1974–75, ranked by voluntary support per student. Those in the top 10 percent received 37 percent of all donations for the private sector (an average of $2,713 per student), while the top 20 percent received well over half. Voluntary support averages only $188 per student for the bottom 50 percent of the 616 colleges and universities—only 13 percent of the total.

Table 6-3 distributes the top thirty and the lowest thirty recipient institutions by Carnegie Commission categories. The top thirty schools are mainly research universities I and liberal arts colleges I. The bottom thirty are comprehensive colleges and universities I and liberal arts colleges II. These distributions confirm that the less selective institutions, those that may have difficulty surviving if higher education enrollments shrink, receive very little voluntary support.

The distribution of voluntary support reflects decentralized decision-making, and many would contend that that is a primary virtue of tax subsidies. It must be recognized, however, that it is the donors and not the government who determine how the funds are distributed. One can

Table 6-2. *Distribution by Decile of Voluntary Support Received by Private Colleges and Universities,[a] Ranked by Support per Student, Academic Year 1974–75*

| | | Voluntary support | |
| | Number of schools | Amount (millions of dollars) | Percent of total |
Decile[b]			
1 (highest)	59	429	36.6
2	73	233	19.9
3	89	158	13.5
4	82	114	9.7
5	68	86	7.3
6	80	66	5.6
7	53	38	3.2
8	48	27	2.3
9	36	13	1.1
10 (lowest)	28	7	0.6
Total	616	1,171	100.0

Source: Council for Financial Aid to Education, *Voluntary Support of Education, 1974–75* (CFAE, n.d.). Figures are rounded.

a. Excludes professional and specialized schools. Includes 70 major universities, 13 private men's colleges, 80 private women's colleges, and 453 private coeducational colleges.

b. Deciles are defined by enrollment, that is, each decile includes 10 percent of total enrollment for the 616 schools.

argue that the distribution of gifts should more closely reflect the public's preferences as expressed through government.

Efficiency

How one evaluates the desirability of present tax incentives for charitable giving depends in part on what impact these incentives have on the amount of giving. If the incentives induce little additional giving and do so at a high cost to the government in forgone revenue, one would conclude that the incentives are inefficient. Repealing them would have little effect on charitable giving, and it would improve tax equity. If, at the other extreme, tax incentives strongly influence the amount of donations, those who propose to improve tax equity by changing the tax treatment of charitable giving must also consider what the effects will be on the philanthropic sector of the economy, and on its various parts, including higher education.

Table 6-3. *Distribution of Sixty Private Institutions*[a] *Receiving Voluntary Support, by Carnegie Classification, Academic Year 1974–75*

	Rank by voluntary support per student	
Classification[b]	Top thirty schools	Bottom thirty schools
Doctoral-granting institutions		
Research universities I	7	0
Research universities II	1	0
Doctoral-granting universities I	1	2
Doctoral-granting universities II	0	0
Comprehensive institutions		
Comprehensive universities and colleges I	0	12
Comprehensive universities and colleges II	0	2
Liberal arts institutions		
Liberal arts colleges I	15	1
Liberal arts colleges II	5	8
Other		
Two-year institutions	0	0
Professional and other specialized institutions[c]	1	2
Unclassified	0	3

Sources: Council for Financial Aid to Education, *Voluntary Support of Education, 1974–75*, and *A Classification of Institutions of Higher Education*, A Technical Report Sponsored by the Carnegie Commission on Higher Education (Carnegie Foundation for the Advancement of Teaching, 1973).

a. The thirty institutions receiving the most voluntary support and the thirty institutions receiving the least.

b. For explanation of the classification system, see Glossary.

c. The schools classified as "professional and specialized schools" by the Council for Financial Aid to Education are excluded. However, three of the schools in the top or bottom thirty were classified as "professional and other specialized institutions" by the Carnegie Commission and thus appear here.

INCOME TAX DEDUCTIONS

In 1973, the latest year for which complete data are available, individuals reported $13.9 billion of charitable giving on their income tax returns (table 6-4). Except for the lowest income classes, the amount of giving as a percent of income increased as income rose. Families with between $10,000 and $50,000 of income gave less than 3 percent of income to charity, and families with income above $200,000 gave 8.8 percent.[33] In the lowest income classes, only a minority of taxpayers itemize

33. Adjusted gross income, as used in table 6-4, is an imperfect measure of income. One problem is that half of net long-term capital gains are excluded. Since capital gains are an important source of income for high-income families, giving as a percentage of income is overstated for the highest income classes.

Table 6–4. *Charitable Contributions Reported on Individual Income Tax Returns, by Adjusted Gross Income Class, 1973*

Adjusted gross income class (thousands of dollars)	Number of returns with contribution deduction (thousands)	Total adjusted gross income (millions of dollars)	Total contributions			Contributions other than cash[a]		
			Amount (millions of dollars)	Percent of total	Percent of AGI	Amount (millions of dollars)	Percent of total	Percent of AGI
0–5	1,062	3,983	296	2.1	7.4	11	0.9	0.3
5–10	5,287	41,230	1,669	12.0	4.0	69	5.4	0.2
10–15	7,237	90,412	2,591	18.6	2.9	110	8.6	0.1
15–20	6,024	104,337	2,561	18.4	2.5	115	9.0	0.1
20–30	4,642	110,374	2,674	19.2	2.4	149	11.7	0.1
30–50	1,552	57,377	1,496	10.8	2.6	101	7.9	0.2
50–100	552	36,499	1,176	8.5	3.2	171	13.4	0.5
100–200	105	13,675	606	4.4	4.4	158	12.4	1.2
200 and over	24	9,411	828	6.0	8.8	393	30.8	4.2
Total	26,486	467,296	13,896	100.0	...	1,276	100.0	...

Source: U.S. Internal Revenue Service, *Statistics of Income—1973, Individual Income Tax Returns* (GPO, 1976), table 2.5. Figures are rounded.

a. Excludes additional deduction due to carryover from prior years.

Table 6-5. *Charitable Contributions Reported on Taxable Individual Income Tax Returns, by Adjusted Gross Income Class and Type of Recipient, 1962*

Adjusted gross income class (thousands of dollars)	Total contributions		Contributions to educational institutions	
	Amount (millions of dollars)	Percent of total	Amount (millions of dollars)	Percent of total
0–5	922	13.0	6	2.3
5–10	2,849	40.2	28	10.7
10–15	1,261	17.8	21	8.0
15–20	458	6.5	16	6.1
20–25	250	3.5	13	5.0
25–50	· 556	7.8	43	16.5
50–100	331	4.7	44	16.6
100–200	178	2.5	32	12.4
200 and over	291	4.1	58	22.2
Total	7,095	100.0	262	100.0

Source: U.S. Internal Revenue Service, *Statistics of Income—1962, Individual Income Tax Returns* (GPO, 1965), table E. Figures are rounded.

their deductions. Many are aged sixty-five or older, and these taxpayers have relatively high giving rates.[34]

Very little is known about the distribution of charitable contributions by type of recipient. Only once has the Internal Revenue Service published these data and that was for 1962.[35] About 4 percent of the contributions went to educational institutions, presumably mostly colleges and universities. As shown in table 6-5, educational institutions depend primarily on high-income families for their gifts; over half of the gifts in 1962 came from families with incomes over $50,000. These same families accounted for only 11 percent of all charitable giving. This suggests that any tax changes affecting the incentives of high-income families to make charitable gifts will have a substantial impact on educational institutions.

The basic empirical question is to determine whether high-income families give more than low-income families because their after-tax incomes are higher or because their price of giving a dollar to charity is

34. For taxpayers over the age of sixty-five, adjusted gross income may not be a good measure of income because social security payments are excluded.

35. The tax forms do not require the taxpayer to classify contributions by type of recipient. Thus the IRS for 1962 classified each contribution on the basis of the name of the organization. Not all contributions could be classified.

lower. For cash gifts, the price is equal to one minus the marginal tax rate. For gifts of appreciated property, the price or net cost of making a gift is even lower because appreciation is not taxed. As is shown in table 6-4, gifts of property become very important only in the highest income classes.

The data given in table 6-4 are consistent with either the income effect or the price effect as an explanation for charitable giving. That is, in the absence of any tax incentives, it may be the case that charitable giving would increase more rapidly than income—the income elasticity may be greater than 1.[36] On the other hand, it may be the case that charitable giving is not very responsive to income, but is responsive to its price. As income increases, the value of the tax deduction increases and thus the price of charitable giving decreases. If charitable giving is explained by this price effect, then giving is responsive to tax incentives. If the price elasticity of giving is less than -1,[37] then the additional giving induced by the tax incentives is greater than the government's forgone revenue, and this is what is meant when one says that the tax incentives are efficient.

The first empirical studies of philanthropic giving concluded that the incentive effect of the tax deduction was quite weak. Using data from the 1962 income tax records, Taussig concluded that tax incentives account for no more than 2 or 3 percent of total giving.[38] Thus the revenue cost of the incentive, about 30 percent of total giving, far exceeded the additional giving induced by the incentive. Schwartz subsequently estimated giving to be more responsive to tax incentives than Taussig, but the induced giving was still less than the forgone taxes.[39] If the conclusions of these two studies are accepted, one would conclude that tax in-

36. The income elasticity is defined as the percentage increase in giving divided by the percentage increase in income. If the elasticity is greater than 1, giving increases more rapidly than income, all else remaining constant. If it is equal to 1, giving increases proportionately to income. If it is less than 1, giving does not increase as rapidly as income. If the income elasticity is zero, giving is unrelated to income.

37. The price elasticity is defined as the percentage increase in giving divided by the percentage decrease in price. Giving is elastic with respect to price if, for example, a 10 percent net decrease in price induces a greater than 10 percent increase in giving.

38. Michael K. Taussig, "Economic Aspects of the Personal Income Tax Treatment of Charitable Contributions," *National Tax Journal*, vol. 20 (March 1967), pp. 1–19.

39. Robert A. Schwartz, "Personal Philanthropic Contributions," *Journal of Political Economy*, vol. 78 (November-December 1970), pp. 1264–91.

centives are inefficient in inducing additional giving. Feldstein has shown, however, that these studies have serious methodological problems and that the results, particularly Taussig's, should not be relied upon.

In a series of papers, Feldstein has marshaled considerable evidence that tax incentives are efficient. He and various colleagues have used a time series of cross sections based on the value of itemized charitable contributions in each adjusted gross income class for even years 1948 through 1968,[40] cross sections of individual tax records for both 1962 and 1970,[41] a cross section of household survey data that included information on those who did not itemize deductions and on wealth,[42] and data from another survey that included many low- and middle-income families that did not itemize their personal deductions.[43] The estimates of the price elasticity obtained in these studies cluster around -1.2, with some indication that low- and middle-income families are at least as responsive to the tax incentives as high-income families.

Using a random subsample of 5,402 returns from the Brookings 1973 Tax File, I have reestimated the basic equation used by Feldstein in analyzing 1970 tax return data. He assumed a constant elasticity relationship between charitable giving and both income and price.[44] The income and price variables are defined so that they do not depend on the taxpayer's

40. Martin Feldstein, "The Income Tax and Charitable Contributions: Part 1—Aggregate and Distributional Effects," *National Tax Journal*, vol. 28 (March 1975), pp. 81–100.

41. Martin Feldstein and Amy Taylor, "The Income Tax and Charitable Contributions: Estimates and Simulations with the Treasury Tax Files," in Commission on Private Philanthropy and Public Needs, *Research Papers*, vol. 3, pp. 1419–39.

42. Martin Feldstein and Charles Clotfelter, "Tax Incentives and Charitable Contributions in the United States: A Microeconometric Analysis," *Journal of Public Economics*, vol. 5 (January–February, 1976), pp. 1–26. This study uses data from the Survey of Financial Characteristics of Consumers, conducted in 1963 and 1964 by the Board of Governors of the Federal Reserve System.

43. Michael J. Boskin and Martin S. Feldstein, "Effects of the Charitable Deduction on Contributions by Low Income and Middle Income Households: Evidence from the National Survey of Philanthropy," in *Research Papers*, vol. 3, pp. 1441–51.

44. That is, he assumed that a given percentage change in price (or income) will induce the same percentage change in giving regardless of income (or price). The basic specification is:

$$\log G_i = \beta_0 + \beta_1 \log P_i + \beta_2 \log Y_i$$
$$+ \beta_3 MAR_i + \beta_4 AGE_i + e_i,$$

where G is charitable giving, P is price, Y is income, MAR is a dummy variable indicating whether the taxpayer is married, AGE is a dummy variable indicating whether the taxpayer is over sixty-five, e is the error term, and the subscript i refers to a single return.

charitable giving. Income is defined as adjusted gross income minus the tax that would have been paid if no gifts to charity had been made. The price variable is based on the taxable income that the individual would have had if no gifts had been made.[45]

When the Feldstein equation is reestimated using the 1973 data it explains somewhat less of the variance in charitable giving than the Feldstein-Taylor equation for 1970. The estimated price elasticity is also closer to unity.[46] One can only speculate why these two estimates differ. When returns eligible for the 50 percent maximum tax on earned income are omitted, my estimated price elasticity is -1.19, very close to that estimated by Feldstein and Taylor. The maximum tax did not exist in 1970 and its introduction in 1971 increases the price of charitable giving. Under the maximum tax, personal deductions are, in effect, allocated between earned income and other income. Thus the marginal tax rate for computing the tax savings from giving depends on the split between earned and other income. It is possible that taxpayers eligible for the maximum tax have been slow in adjusting their level of giving to its higher price. Such an effect would tend to reduce the estimated price elasticity. Both the 1970 Feldstein-Taylor equation and mine for 1973, however, imply that giving is quite responsive to its price.

The regression results are very sensitive to the model estimated. For example, in the Feldstein equation, income is defined as adjusted gross income minus the tax that would have been paid if no gifts to charity had

45. For taxpayers who had property income—dividends or capital gains—it was assumed in computing the price variable that a portion of their gifts, depending on the taxpayer's income class, were property other than cash. Thus the price variable takes into account the possibility of appreciated gifts but it is independent of the actual amount of gifts of property made by the taxpayer. It was further assumed that the ratio of discounted gain to value was 50 percent. Feldstein and Taylor, in "Income Tax and Charitable Contributions," more fully discuss the technical problems of specifying the estimating equation. Feldstein and Taylor were able to allow for state income taxes in addition to federal taxes. This was not possible here because state data are not in the 1973 Brookings file. Since state income taxes are much lower than federal, this does not appear to be a serious problem.

46. The estimated equation is as follows:

$$\ln G = -2.715 - 1.005 \ln P + 0.774 \ln Y$$
$$(0.444) \quad (0.129) \qquad (0.049)$$
$$+ 0.403 \, MAR + 0.578 \, AGE.$$
$$(0.095) \qquad (0.074)$$
$$r^2 = 0.295.$$

The numbers in parentheses in this and the following equations are standard deviations.

been made. But adjusted gross income is a poor proxy for before-tax income. If income is defined as adjusted gross income plus excluded capital gains minus the tax that would have been paid if no gifts to charity had been made, the estimated price and income elasticities are changed substantially, with giving being much more responsive to price in this model than in the first estimate.[47]

These first two estimates assume constant price elasticity across all income classes. By introducing an interaction variable to the regression model, it is possible to permit the price elasticity to vary with income.[48] Although the price, income, and interactive terms are all statistically significant, one must be cautious in relying on the results since the price and interaction variables are highly correlated. To the extent that one can rely on this equation, it implies that the price elasticity is about zero for a family with $10,000 of income, about -1.0 for a family with $100,000 of income, and -1.3 for a family with $200,000 of income.[49] This in turn implies that high-income families are highly sensitive to the price of giving but that low-income families may be very insensitive. This result runs counter to Feldstein, who concluded that low- and middle-income families are at least as responsive to tax incentives as high-income families.

If it is accepted that the price elasticity of charitable giving is about -1.1, about halfway between the estimates obtained by Feldstein and the first estimate (-1.005) obtained above, this means that the tax incentive for charitable giving induces more giving than it costs the government in forgone revenue. To illustrate, suppose that in the absence of any tax incentives, taxpayers would each give $1,000 to charity. If introducing

47. The estimated equation is as follows:

$$\ln G = -0.944 - 1.356 \ln P + 0.573 \ln Y^1$$
$$\quad (0.383) \quad (0.122) \qquad (0.041)$$
$$+ 0.489 \, MAR + 0.533 \, AGE.$$
$$\quad (0.095) \qquad (0.075)$$
$$r^2 = 0.287.$$

where $Y^1 = AGI +$ excluded capital gains $-$ tax that would have been paid if no charitable gifts had been made.

48. When this is done the following result is obtained:

$$\ln G = -0.933 + 3.872 \ln P - 0.420 \ln P \ln Y$$
$$\quad (0.523) \quad (0.773) \qquad (0.066)$$
$$+ 0.618 \ln Y + 0.405 \, MAR + 0.552 \, AGE.$$
$$\quad (0.054) \qquad (0.094) \qquad (0.074)$$
$$r^2 = 0.300.$$

49. In this model the price elasticity is equal to $3.872 - 0.420 \ln Y$.

the charitable deduction reduces the price of giving by 30 percent, this would induce taxpayers to increase their philanthropic giving to $1,480.[50] The tax savings would be $444 (0.3 × 1,480). Thus giving is increased by $480 at a cost to the government of $444. Put another way, repeal of the charitable deduction would reduce giving in this example by almost one-third.[51] The reduction for educational institutions would be even greater than one-third, since their donors tend to be in high tax rate brackets. This fact clearly has important policy implications that are discussed below after looking at the impact of estate tax rules on charitable bequests.

ESTATE TAX DEDUCTIONS

Under the federal estate tax law a deduction for charitable bequests is allowed in determining the taxable estate. Unlike the income tax law, the estate tax contains no limit on the amount that can be deducted for property transferred to charitable organizations. Charitable bequests account for nearly one-third of the voluntary support by individuals for colleges and universities, and most of this support (88 percent) goes to private institutions.[52]

In 1973 estate tax returns were filed for about 9 percent of all decedents. Charitable deductions were claimed on 21,000 returns, about 12 percent of all those filed that year. For all estates, one-third of the charitable deduction was in excess of 50 percent of the estate. Put another way, if Congress limited the charitable deduction to 50 percent of the estate, one-third of such charitable bequests would no longer be deductible.[53]

The Tax Reform Act of 1976 liberalized the marital deduction and replaced the estate tax exemption with a tax credit. The act, however, will

50. Holding everything else constant, $G = aP^{-1.1}$. Thus if $G = 1,000$ when $P = 1.0$, a must equal 1,000. When P is reduced to 0.7, G increases to $1,480. This ignores the small income effect.

51. The average marginal tax rate appears to be 0.314, which implies that giving would drop by roughly 34 percent if the charitable deduction were eliminated. (The average marginal rate is estimated from the Brookings tax file.)

52. Julian H. Levi and Sheldon Elliot Steinbach, *Patterns of Giving to Higher Education III: An Analysis of Voluntary Support of American Colleges and Universities, 1973–74* (American Council on Education, n.d.), p. 4.

53. For details on charitable bequests reported on estate tax returns, see Emil M. Sunley, Jr., "Dimensions of Charitable Giving Reported on Federal Estate, Gift, and Fiduciary Tax Returns," in Commission on Private Philanthropy and Public Needs, *Research Papers*, vol. 4, pp. 2319–36.

have little impact on the very large estates, which account for most of the charitable bequests. Unless the tax treatment of charitable bequests affects the lifetime accumulation of wealth, its major impact is to alter the division of the estate between taxes, charity, and heirs. An important question then is how much additional charitable bequests are induced by deductibility. If the additional bequests are less than the revenue cost of the incentive, deductibility increases the amount of the estate available for distribution to heirs. On the other hand, if deductibility induces more charitable bequests than its revenue cost, it reduces bequests to heirs, thus decreasing the transfer of wealth to the next generation.

The tax treatment of estates, including that of charitable bequests, may affect the lifetime accumulation of wealth, the amount of lifetime gifts, and even contributions to heirs. If one treats the size of the estate as independently determined and abstracts from the impact that the estate tax may have on heirs, the deductibility of charitable bequests poses an empirical question very similar to that posed by the income tax deduction for charitable gifts. It is necessary to separate the wealth and the price effects of the charitable deduction: that is, do wealthy decedents tend to leave more to charity because they are wealthy or because the tax deduction reduces the net cost of making a charitable bequest? Boskin has investigated this question using a random sample of estate tax records filed in 1970.[54] He found that the deduction for charitable bequests is efficient, that is, it increases charitable giving at least as much as it decreases tax revenue. Only for the very largest estates, those greater than $1 million, did he conclude that the deduction is not fully efficient. These estates, however, account for a disproportionate share of charitable bequests. His findings suggest that proposals for change in the tax treatment of charitable bequests must take into account their likely impact on recipient organizations.

Impact of Proposed Changes

In recent years there have been a number of proposals to alter the tax treatment of philanthropy both under the income tax and the estate tax. An evaluation of these proposals must take into account their impact on charitable organizations. Given the apparent efficiency of the present tax incentives, changes that improve equity could greatly reduce charitable

54. Michael J. Boskin, "Estate Taxation and Charitable Bequests," *Journal of Public Economics*, vol. 5 (January–February 1976), pp. 27–56.

giving to those organizations, including private colleges and universities, that depend on gifts from high-income individuals and wealthy decedents. Even proposals not directly affecting charity, such as reductions in marginal tax rates and increases in the standard deduction, can have an indirect impact on charity.[55]

Unfortunately, data linking donors to recipients are scant. Low-income families tend to give mostly to religious organizations and high-income families to education and the arts. There is some evidence that people with large estates also make more bequests to educational institutions than the less wealthy.[56] Despite the severe data problems, Feldstein and Boskin have attempted to estimate the impact of proposed changes by type of recipient.[57] Their results indicate the direction of changes; the actual numbers should not be taken at face value. Some of the results are reported here because they highlight the trade-off between increased equity and the impact of any changes on colleges and universities.

Repeal of the income tax deduction for charitable giving would treat giving the same as most other personal expenditures. Feldstein estimates that this would reduce total giving by about 20 percent. Educational institutions would lose between 48 and 65 percent because repeal of the deduction would increase the price of giving more for high-income individuals.

The most frequently discussed change in the income tax deduction is to replace it with a tax credit. This would improve equity by making the price of giving the same for all taxpayers. (Charity would still be favored over most personal expenditures.) If the rate of the credit is set sufficiently high, total support of charitable organizations can be maintained. A tax credit, however, would reduce the incentive for high-income individuals to make gifts and increase it for low-income individuals. Thus charitable organizations that look to high-income individuals

55. Higher education would be doubly served by increased direct expenditures financed by higher marginal tax rates at the upper end of the income distribution, since the higher rates would, in turn, induce additional giving to educational institutions.

56. See Sunley, "Dimensions of Charitable Giving Reported on Federal Estate, Gift, and Fiduciary Returns." Data on recipients of charitable bequests from estate tax records are particularly unrevealing because bequests often go to a private foundation and no one knows what types of organizations the foundation will support.

57. Martin Feldstein, "The Income Tax and Charitable Contributions: Part II—The Impact on Religious, Educational and Other Organizations," *National Tax Journal*, vol. 28 (June 1975), pp. 209–26; and Boskin, "Estate Taxation and Charitable Bequests."

for their support would be worse off, the converse being true for those largely supported by the low-income groups. Feldstein has estimated that a 30 percent tax credit is more than sufficient to maintain total giving. The credit, however, would reduce lifetime gifts received by educational institutions by about 20 percent. Religious organizations and health and welfare organizations would receive increased contributions.

Eliminating the preference for appreciated property by taxing the unrealized appreciation at the time of the gift would improve equity by treating gifts of cash and property other than cash in the same fashion. Feldstein estimated that this change would reduce charitable giving by 3 percent. Educational institutions would expect an 8 percent decrease in the funds they receive from living individuals.[58]

Boskin estimated that repeal of the deduction for charitable bequests accompanied by an across-the-board rate reduction would decrease charitable bequests by one-half or more. Charitable bequests to education would be sharply curtailed. Treating all assets as if sold at death would also have a significant impact on giving to educational institutions unless charitable gifts were excluded from the proposal.[59]

I conclude that any change in the tax treatment of philanthropy would have an important impact on educational institutions, particularly on those private colleges and universities that rely heavily on voluntary support. It may be that the decrease in private support is too high a price to pay for improved tax equity. It would be possible, however, to expand direct government support for colleges and universities and to offset the overall reduction in private support, although it would be virtually impossible to ensure that the same campuses benefited.

New Tax Incentives for Higher Education

Concern over the increasing costs of higher education has spawned a number of proposals for new tax incentives, which, if enacted, could affect the relative competitive positions of private and public institutions. The proposal that has received widest support would permit a tax deduction or credit for college tuition and other related expenses. The Senate approved tax credits for higher education in 1967, 1969, 1971, and

58. Feldstein's results are reported in *Giving in America*, Report of the Commission on Private Philanthropy and Public Needs, p. 145.

59. Michael J. Boskin, "Estate Taxation and Charitable Bequests."

twice in 1976. But none of the tax credits has survived the legislative process and been enacted into law. A possible alternative to tax deductions or credits for college expenses would be a tax incentive for families to save now for future college expenses. This is similar to incentives presently available for retirement savings.

Tax Deduction or Credit

Each year a number of bills are introduced into Congress to provide some form of tax recognition for the personal costs of higher education. These bills typically provide a tax deduction or credit for the expenses of higher education that may be claimed by either the student, the spouse, or the parent.

Just what form of tax recognition for education expenses might be appropriate depends on the purpose of the proposal. John K. McNulty has identified five possible purposes—perfecting the definition of taxable income; improving tax equity; subsidizing education; redistributing income, wealth, or educational opportunity; or correcting the allocation of educational resources.[60]

DEFINING TAXABLE INCOME

Some tax experts believe that the costs of higher education are incurred to create human capital and that in order to properly measure taxable income these costs should be amortized over the expected working life of the student.[61] An immediate deduction of expenses for higher education would not be in order, nor would a deduction by parents for expenses incurred for their children. Thus, this rationale is not in keeping with the kinds of tax credits that the Senate has passed five times. Expenses for higher education may have a large consumption component that, under this reasoning, should not be deductible, and there is no practical way to separate this component from the investment component.

It is not clear, either, that the current federal tax system is biased against investment in human capital. As outlined in the first section above, the law directly or indirectly provides significant tax relief for higher

60. John K. McNulty, "Tax Policy and Tuition Credit Legislation: Federal Income Tax Allowances for Personal Costs of Higher Education," *California Law Review*, vol. 61 (January 1973), pp. 1–80.

61. See, for example, Richard Goode, *The Individual Income Tax*, pp. 80–92.

education. The fact that tuition and fees cover only a part of the costs of education indicates that investments in human capital are subsidized, not only by tax breaks but also by direct federal, state, and local expenditure programs. Human capital may already be treated as generously as physical capital.

TAX EQUITY

The second justification for a tax allowance is that it is necessary in order to improve tax equity. Families with expenses for higher education have less taxpaying ability than other similarly situated families with no educational expenses. That is, a family with an income of $20,000 and education expenses of $2,000 has the same taxpaying ability as another family with $18,000 of income and no education expenses. The tax equity justification is carried one step further when it is argued that families with children in private colleges and universities have less taxpaying ability than other similarly situated families with children in public colleges and universities and that a tax deduction for tuition would tend to equalize their taxpaying ability. Here, however, it must be recognized that the additional costs of private colleges and universities are incurred voluntarily.

There seems to be no general rule under the income tax governing which personal expenses are deductible and which are not. The major items that are deductible, such as extraordinary medical expenses, casualty and theft losses, and other taxes, are largely involuntary. They are deductible primarily to equalize the ability to pay income taxes. Involuntary expenses such as food are not deductible. Consumer interest and charitable contributions, however, are deductible even though they, like education expenses, are largely voluntary. The charitable deduction, however, as pointed out above, is generally justified as an incentive for giving and not as being necessary to improve tax equity or to perfect the definition of taxable income. All one can rationalize is that education expenses should be deductible because they are at least as deserving as the various types of consumption expenditures already allowed, and this is a very weak line of reasoning on which to introduce a new tax incentive.

Proposals for deductions generally have been considered less fair than proposals for tax credits. It is argued that deductions, unlike credits, are worth more the higher the family's marginal tax rate. This objection can in theory be answered by recognizing that the desired degree of progressivity in the income tax can be maintained—even with deductions—by changing the marginal tax rate schedules so that each income class would still pay the same average amount of tax. Then, within each class, families with education expenses would pay less and families without education expenses would pay more.

EDUCATION SUBSIDY

Providing a subsidy for education is a third purpose for a tax deduction or credit. A subsidy may be justified if it is shown that because of market imperfections or side effects (externalities) there is too little investment in education. Market imperfections may arise because students and their families may not be able to finance profitable investments in human capital if banks and other private lenders are reluctant to make loans where the only security pledged is anticipated earnings. Federal loan guarantees are a more direct solution to this problem than a tax subsidy.

There are side effects when the social benefits of additional investments in education, such as an increase in total knowledge, exceed the private benefits considered by the students and their families in deciding on further education. The various direct and indirect subsidies for education, however, reduce private costs paid by students and their families below social costs, and may fully compensate for the social benefit externalities. (The externality argument for further subsidizing education is only valid if it can be shown that the social benefits of additional investment in education exceed the private benefits anticipated by students and their families by a greater amount than the social costs exceed the private costs.) Furthermore, some argue that recent evidence of surpluses in certain professions is an indication that there may not be a need to subsidize additional investment in education, but this places great weight on the "manpower training" function of higher education, only one of its purposes.

If one wants to provide additional subsidy to education, a tax credit is preferable to a tax deduction. A credit of, say, 30 percent of tuition, reduces the cost of tuition for all students and families by 30 percent. The value of the credit, unlike a deduction, does not vary with income level, or, more specifically, with the marginal tax rate.[62]

62. This is true only if the amount of the credit is not limited by the amount of tax liability before the credit.

Because any tax credit for tuition expenses reduces the price of education relative to other goods and services, such a subsidy would encourage at least some additional investment in education. Since most of the credits that have been proposed, however, constitute such a small part of a student's total costs of education, it is unlikely that a credit would induce much new enrollment. In that case the credit will essentially be a tax relief measure, with the justification for it resting primarily on tax equity rather than on its capacity to induce increased investment in education.

DISTRIBUTION OF INCOME, WEALTH, AND EDUCATIONAL OPPORTUNITY

Subsidizing education is surely an inefficient way of redistributing income or wealth given that these objectives could more easily be achieved through changes in the income, estate, and gift taxes, or by introducing an annual net wealth tax. The goal of redistributing educational opportunity would justify a refundable tax credit. Such a credit could be available for students and their families with no tax liability before the credit. It could also be phased out for high-income families, and a larger credit per dollar of expenditures could be provided low-income families than for high-income families. Phaseouts or a higher credit at certain income levels become very complex if the credit may be claimed by either the student or his family. One possible rule would be to provide that the credit must be claimed by the parents if the parents provide more than half of the student's support. The rate of the credit and its phaseout would then be based on the parents' income. This solution, while simpler than basing the credit on the combined income of the student and his parents, may involve a notch problem: as the amount of support provided by the parents exceeds 50 percent, the credit is shifted from the student to the parents, and its value may be reduced. For example, if the credit is 50 percent when claimed by the student with low income and 25 percent when claimed by the parents, the value of the credit is sharply reduced when the parents shift from providing 49 percent of the support to 51 percent.

ALLOCATION OF RESOURCES

One type of misallocation of resources occurs when public colleges and universities are subsidized more than private institutions. A tax credit could be designed that would tend to make the choice between public and private schools more neutral. In the extreme, only expenses at private colleges and universities would be eligible for the credit. Another possibility would be to limit the credit to expenses in excess of the average tuition and fees at public schools.

A credit of this sort may very well be unacceptable politically. It would be argued that the credit would subsidize Cadillac educations at elite schools and provide no encouragement for students seeking lower-priced education at public schools, particularly community colleges. This objection does not take into account that the social costs of education may be nearly the same at public and private schools and that the price of private schools appears higher mainly because public schools receive more direct and indirect government subsidies. It might also be argued that a credit available only after a minimum level of expenditures has been incurred would tend to conflict with the goal of equalizing educational opportunities.[63]

The tax credit approved in 1976 by the Senate (but later dropped) eventually would have provided an annual credit equal to the first $250 paid per student for tuition, fees, books, supplies, and equipment required for courses.[64] Room and board was not to be included, presumably so as not to discriminate against students who live at home. The expenses were to be paid by an individual for himself, his spouse, or his dependents, and the credit was refundable, thereby benefiting citizens who had no tax liability before the credit. To qualify, the student would have to enroll full time at an institution of higher education or at a vocational school. Those in graduate study and taking recreational or noncredit courses would not have been eligible. Expenses already covered by tax-exempt scholarships, fellowships, or GI bill benefits would not have been reimbursed under the scheme, nor could educational expenses used for the credit be deducted as ordinary and necessary business expenses. The revenue cost of the credit would have been $500 million in 1978, and it would have increased to $1.1 billion by 1981. The parents of students in private institutions would have received only about 25 percent of these amounts.

63. Robert Hartman argues in chapter 5 that the proper federal response to this inefficiency is to induce states to reform rather than providing subsidies to private institutions.

64. To reduce the revenue cost of this provision, the Senate limited the maximum credit to $100 per student in 1977 and provided that this maximum would have been increased by $50 a year until it reached $250 in 1980. As mentioned above, similar tax credit schemes are continually being proposed either in the House or Senate; it is a very live issue.

Given its specific features, the $250 tax credit would primarily have been a tax relief measure for middle- and upper-income families. Since the credit could have been claimed by parents, it was not aimed at perfecting the definition of taxable income. Even though the credit would have reduced the net cost of attending college, it would have had little effect at the margin since total expenses for full-time students substantially exceed $250 a year. The credit might have influenced some potential students who were deciding whether to go to college. Such students are most likely to be from low-income families and there are more efficient ways to reach them.

The additional income represented by the transfer would have been allocated among education expenditures, other consumption, and savings based on the relevant income elasticities. It seems likely, therefore, that only a small portion of the $250 credit would have been spent on more education. The credit, if enacted, might have increased total expenditures on education if it had enabled colleges and universities to raise tuition rates. Under this scheme, the credit would have become an indirect subsidy for colleges and universities.

It is unlikely that such a credit would have much impact on the choice between public and private institutions because it would not change the absolute cost difference; but it would increase the relative cost advantage of public institutions,[65] and might therefore tip the choice of some students in favor of public schools. If tuition increases fully absorbed the credit, then it would have no impact on the absolute or relative cost differences, and thus it would not affect the choice between public and private institutions.

Senator William V. Roth, Jr., sponsor of the 1976 tax credit, has stressed the increasing costs of higher education as the primary reason for providing tax relief for middle-income families. In a "Dear Colleague" letter he indicated that the average total cost of a public university increased 40 percent in the previous five years.[66] For a private university, the increase was 35 percent. What he did not point out is that during the same period, median family income of families with a head of household aged forty-five to sixty-four, an age group likely to have children in

65. Assume, for example, that before the credit is introduced public institutions cost $2,500 a year and private institutions $5,000. A $250 credit would reduce the costs to $2,250 and $4,750 respectively. The absolute price difference is still $2,500. The cost of a public institution, however, has decreased from 50 to 47 percent of the cost of a private institution.

66. Letter from Senator William V. Roth, Jr., dated June 16, 1976.

college, grew even more rapidly. Contrary to common belief, over the last fifteen-year period (1960–75) the cost of college did not increase more rapidly than income.[67]

THE CRUCIAL ISSUES

The question of a tax credit for higher education finally boils down to two issues. First, should the next $1.1 billion of federal funds for higher education be spent on middle-income tax relief or on expansion of other federal education programs? Here, it must be recognized that a tax credit for higher education is very likely to lead to a similar credit for primary and secondary education. Extending the credit would raise constitutional issues and would be expensive in terms of forgone tax revenue. Second, if one wants to provide relief for middle-income families, is it necessary to do so through the tax system? Direct federal grants to colleges and universities based on the number of full-time students would permit colleges and universities to reduce tuition and fees by a corresponding amount, and at the same time a direct program would be subject to the usual annual review of expenditure programs. It would also be simpler to administer, requiring checks to be mailed to only 3,000 institutions of higher learning rather than requiring seven million families to claim the credit on their income tax returns.

An Incentive for Savings

An alternative to a tax deduction or credit for higher education would be to provide an incentive for families to save now for future college expenses. One possibility would be to permit individuals and their parents to establish special accounts similar to the individual retirement accounts permitted under the Employee Retirement Income Security Act of 1974.[68] Annual additions to the accounts would be tax deductible up to a maximum amount of $1,500, or 15 percent of earnings. The earnings on the special savings accounts would not be taxed currently. Qualified withdrawals could be made for higher education and possibly for retirement, the downpayment on a house, or extraordinary medical expenses, and these withdrawals would be taxed at that time.[69] Unqualified with-

67. See figure 1-2 and chapter 1, appendix.
68. 88 Stat. 829.
69. If the taxpayer is subject to a higher marginal tax rate at the time of withdrawal than when the funds were put in the special account, the benefit from tax deferral will be reduced and possibly eliminated.

drawals would be subject to an additional penalty tax to recoup the advantage of tax deferral.

The plan described above would permit tax deferral on savings for higher education. Assuming that the individual or the parents remain subject to the same marginal tax rate, this tax deferral is equivalent to exempting from taxation the earnings on the amount of income the taxpayer has "at risk," that is, the amount that would ordinarily be available after income tax.[70] The accounts would be more attractive than investing in tax-exempt securities because the accounts could hold investments that would earn the normal interest rates and not the lower tax-exempt rates. Since the value of deferral depends on the marginal tax rate, the savings incentive is markedly inequitable, being worth more to families in high tax rate brackets than in low ones.

The proposal for special savings accounts raises two fundamental questions. First, should an incentive be provided for individuals and parents to save for college and possibly for other purposes similar to that which is now available for retirement savings? It can be argued that an income tax is inherently biased against savings and that a consumption or an expenditure tax would not distort the choice between consumption now and consumption in the future.[71] Providing special tax recognition for savings would reduce this bias and would increase the incentive for individuals and parents to save now for future college expenses.

Second, what impact would the special savings accounts have on total savings? It may be that total savings are not very responsive to their rate of return and that a generalized incentive for savings would not increase the total amount of savings.[72] Even if savings are responsive, the special savings accounts may not increase savings but instead merely shift the form of savings. That is, up to the limitation, individuals and parents who would have saved anyway or who already have substantial deposits would transfer part of them to the special accounts without increasing

70. If $1,000 is put into the account that would otherwise be taxed at m percent, then the amount at risk is $(1 - m)$1,000. After n years the account has increased to $(1,000)(1 + r)^n$, assuming the account grows at r percent a year. This amount is then withdrawn and taxed at rate m, leaving $(1 - m)(1,000)(1 + r)^n$ after taxes. This is clearly the same as the amount that would be available if the amount at risk, $(1 - m)$1,000, was invested in a tax-exempt account earning r percent a year.

71. See, for example, William D. Andrews, "A Consumption-type or Cash Flow Personal Income Tax," *Harvard Law Review*, vol. 87 (April 1974), pp. 1113–88.

72. Recent empirical work by Michael Boskin suggests that savings may be more responsive than generally believed. (See "Taxation, Savings and the Rate of Interest," *Journal of Political Economy*, vol. 86 [April 1978], forthcoming.)

their annual savings. The special savings accounts then become little more than tax relief for those individuals and parents who face the costs of higher education and have assets to transfer to the special accounts. This is precisely the group least in need of tax relief.

To make the incentive more effective, it would be possible to permit a tax deduction only for savings in excess of, say, 7 percent of income. The tax treatment of the savings accounts then becomes more complex. It would be necessary to keep track of tax-paid and tax-deferred contributions to the account. Tax-paid contributions, that is, contributions equal to less than 7 percent of income, would not be taxed again when withdrawn from the account. The deferrred earnings on these contributions would be taxed.

If the primary objective of the special savings accounts is to increase total savings and not just to provide tax relief for individuals and families facing the costs of higher education, there are probably superior policies to tax incentives. It may very well be that the way to increase total savings and investment is to run a government surplus while maintaining full employment with low interest rates through an easy monetary policy.[73]

Summary and Conclusion

Higher education benefits from a number of tax subsidies at the federal, state, and local levels. These subsidies operate in myriad ways. Philanthropic contributions to higher education are favored under the income and estate taxes. Families of students benefit from additional personal tax exemptions. Student aid is exempt from taxation. State and local taxes are deductible under the federal income tax, which reduces the tax cost of additional state and local expenditures for higher education. State and local borrowing is subsidized in the tax-exempt market. The property owned by educational institutions is generally exempt from state and local property taxes.

These tax subsidies taken together hardly constitute a rational program of support for higher education. In designing a comprehensive income tax, none of these tax incentives would be retained. They generally benefit the well-established schools that receive most of the charitable contributions, high-income families for whom the extra personal exemption

73. The government surplus in this scheme provides the savings (that is, withdrawal of demand for current resources) to finance the investment.

is worth more, and public colleges and universities that also benefit from direct state and local expenditures. The only tax subsidies that benefit private more than public institutions are the special preferences for charitable giving.

In recent years the special treatment of philanthropic giving has come under increasing attack as an inequitable subsidy that is worth more to high-income donors than to those with low incomes. Recent empirical evidence, however, suggests that these tax incentives are efficient in that they induce more additional giving than they cost in terms of forgone tax revenue. There have been a number of suggestions to convert the tax deduction to a tax credit in order to make the subsidy more equitable. Even if the amount of charitable giving were maintained, the tax credit would induce a shift in giving away from educational institutions that depend on high-income donors. A flat-rate tax credit cannot maintain total giving and at the same time maintain the amount of giving to higher education. In short, policymakers are faced with a trade-off between the inequity of the present tax incentives and their efficiency in encouraging donations to higher education. If the tax incentives for philanthropic giving are going to be made more equitable, these changes should be a part of a program that includes additional direct government support for higher education.

Although the present tax incentives are under attack, there have been a number of proposals for new tax incentives. The most common of these are proposals for a tax deduction or a credit for tuition expenses. Credits have passed the Senate five times only to be dropped by the final conference committee. On examination these credits are found to be mainly tax relief for middle-income families. Generally they are not an incentive for additional expenditures for education. Nor under most versions do they increase the competitive position of private institutions vis-à-vis public ones. The next $1 billion for education should not be spent on a tuition credit program. An alternative to tax credits for tuition would be a tax incentive to encourage families to save now for future college expenses. These proposals would provide little benefit for low-income families. Their major impact is likely to be tax relief for middle- and upper-income families who already have substantial savings. I conclude that additional tax incentives for higher education either in the form of tax credits for tuition or tax incentives for savings are undesirable.

Chapter Seven

The Politics of State Aid

Robert O. Berdahl

EDITED BY DAVID W. BRENEMAN AND CHESTER E. FINN, JR.

ROBERT O. BERDAHL is professor of higher education at the State University of New York–Buffalo.

DURING the 1960s, expansion and affluence allowed both public and private colleges and universities to pursue their own separate interests. Neither felt it necessary to mobilize against the other or to try to use state power to the other's disadvantage. Private enrollment grew almost every year between 1950 and 1976, although it was a steadily declining percentage of the total (see table 1-5). Some individual private institutions had begun to suffer from the widening tuition gap between the private and public sectors early in this period, but this was not a general policy issue until the late 1960s, and then only in a few states. As late as 1969, Lewis Mayhew could observe: "Lip service is usually given to the need for both public and private higher education. . . . But the fundamental problems of private education, with few exceptions, are left untouched."[1] The squeaking private college wheel was not yet making enough noise in most regions to get state oil. However, several developments already under way were soon to alter that situation drastically.

First, some federal higher education programs enacted in the 1960s required public- and private-sector coordination. As statewide boards of higher education were established in more jurisdictions, increasing from twenty-six in 1959 to forty-six ten years later, some of their planning also included private-sector concerns.

Second, associations of private colleges and universities were formed in more states, increasing from fewer than ten in 1960 to thirty-nine in 1977, and many of these became active in state politics. Their cause was aided by the plethora of commission reports and other studies appearing between 1968 and 1975 that drew public attention to the financial distress of their member institutions.

Third, a provision of the Education Amendments of 1972 authorized states to establish comprehensive postsecondary planning commissions. Forty-eight such units (called 1202 Commissions) have been created (or designated) since 1974, and they are required by law to be "broadly and equitably representative" of all postsecondary education in a state.

The private sector has come in for special scrutiny in some jurisdictions. By 1969, Illinois, Missouri, New York, Oregon, and Texas had all issued reports on its condition. Those in New York and Illinois led to new programs of direct state grants to private institutions.[2] Between 1970

1. Lewis B. Mayhew, *Long Range Planning for Higher Education* (Washington, D.C.: Academy for Educational Development, 1969), pp. 154–55.
2. *New York State and Private Higher Education,* Report of the Select Committee on the Future of Private and Independent Higher Education in New York State

and 1975, twenty-one other states included private-sector problems in their planning in one way or another and a steady increase in state aid to private higher education followed. By 1976–77 forty-seven states conducted student aid programs, and thirteen to nineteen states (depending upon the definitions used) offered some sort of direct aid to private institutions.[3] While the dollar amounts channeled to the private sector have grown faster in most states than total state higher education outlays, the aggregate expenditure of state funds for this purpose still remains modest, accounting for about 3 percent of private-sector educational revenue and less than 3 percent of total state spending on higher education.[4]

With very few—and sometimes dramatic—exceptions, public-private relations in higher education today are still fairly cordial at the state level, and most state programs of aid to the private sector have not generated serious controversy. But as the private sector attempts to influence future state policies for public colleges and universities, this situation is likely to change. In jurisdictions where there will probably not be enough students or public funds to sustain all the institutions in both sectors at their accustomed levels of size and activity, it is fair to predict that the normal political process will lead to greater acrimony as resources are divided. Some tension is already visible, and the chief task of this chapter is to begin accounting for it in some systematic way.

Dealing first with the present situation and issues that, so far, have provoked debate but little heated controversy, I next discuss the probable effects of retrenchment and how states are likely to divide their restricted budgets between the public and private sectors. I have emphasized developments in California, New York, and Ohio because they present interestingly varied conditions. In California, the private institutions enroll a low percentage of college students (about 10 percent)

(Albany: State Education Department, 1968); commonly referred to as the Bundy Report after its chairman, McGeorge Bundy. Commission to Study Non-Public Higher Education in Illinois, *Strengthening Private Higher Education in Illinois: A Report on the State's Role* (Springfield: Illinois Board of Higher Education, 1969); commonly referred to as the McConnell Report after its chairman, T. R. McConnell.

3. For a listing of these various programs, see *Higher Education in the States*, vol. 5, no. 3 (Education Commission of the States, 1976), and Joseph D. Boyd, "National Association of State Scholarship and Grant Programs: 8th Annual Survey, 1976–77 Academic Year" (Deerfield, Illinois: NASSP, n.d.; processed). It may be noted that four states confine their student aid to those attending public institutions, and in several more jurisdictions certain aid programs are similarly restricted.

4. See chapter 2.

and, apart from student aid, there are few state programs that provide aid to the private institutions; in Ohio, the percentage of college students in private higher education falls in the middle range (about 23 percent) and state programs aiding the private sector are a bit more diversified; New York has both a heavier proportion (about 40 percent) of its students in private institutions and a richer blend of direct and indirect state aid programs than either of the other states.

In each of the three states I interviewed leaders of public and private higher education, persons in the executive and legislative branches of state government, and in other relevant organizations (for example, state-wide coordinating boards and state associations of independent colleges). I tried to discover what kinds of issues aroused greatest disagreement regarding aid to private higher education. Not surprisingly, I found conflict increasing roughly apace with state involvement.

Current Features of State Support

State handling of taxes, student aid, contracts with private colleges, and institutional aid has a significant effect on private higher education but has not yet led to much intersector rivalry. However, "invasion of turf" —establishing new public institutions where private campuses are already in existence—and altering public tuition rates are much more contentious issues in this respect, though even these need not necessarily involve confrontation.

Tax Issues

Most states grant tax exemptions to private college property. Some exempt private institutions from state sales taxes. Some grant their colleges powers of eminent domain. Eleven jurisdictions allow independent institutions to use the tax-free state bonding process to finance their capital construction. I found no instances where policies of this type have inflamed public-private relations. In fact, California state university leaders helped to remove the 100-acre limitation on private college property tax exemptions in the early 1960s, while private leaders supported state referenda authorizing large sums for construction bonds for state institutions.

Two states—Indiana and Michigan—also allow voluntary contributions to private colleges to be credited against state income taxes. A sim-

ilar bill nearly passed in 1969 in California, but no effort has been made
since then to make such legislation a priority in that state. Most private
college associations evidently see their time better spent pursuing other
forms of state aid.

Attitudes toward Student Aid

The politics of student aid at the state level appear less complex than
at the national level where the growing rivalry between public and private college spokesmen over issues such as access and choice is highly
vocal (see chapter 4). Some of the state student aid programs are themselves quite intricate; before 1974, for example, New York had seven
scholarship, seven grant, and two loan programs. But except for a few
states (such as Colorado, Missouri, and Tennessee) where political campaigns and lawsuits were mounted against providing subsidies to students
attending church-sponsored colleges, most disagreements in this policy
domain have been straightforward, predictable, and voiced in reasoned
terms.

The Americans United for Separation of Church and State, the American Civil Liberties Union, and similar organizations have generally opposed state programs of aid to students attending sectarian colleges.
But since the recent Supreme Court decision upholding direct state aid
to such colleges in Maryland, a lower court's finding of unconstitution-
ality of the Missouri state student aid program has already been reversed,
and this particular line of opposition will probably diminish.[5] To my
knowledge, leaders of the public sector have played no overt role in these
campaigns. Rather, the impetus has come from the ranks of civil liber-
tarians and religious fundamentalists who believe so ardently in total
separation of church and state that they oppose all state funds for church-
related colleges, even those flowing indirectly via student grants.

Public leaders may not have openly fought the creation of state student aid schemes, but it is hardly surprising that they assign lower priority
to programs that funnel state resources into private as well as public
campuses (and sometimes even out of state) than they do to their own
fiscal well-being. This inherent preference is merely magnified in a period
of inflation, tight state budgets, and impending enrollment shrinkage.
In Ohio, for example, the state's perennial ranking in the bottom fifth in

---

5. *Roemer* v. *Board of Public Works of Maryland*, in *United States Law Week*,
vol. 44 (June 22, 1976), p. 4939.

support (per student) for public postsecondary institutions discourages state campus leaders from giving more than rhetorical support to further increases in the state student aid program.

In California, by contrast, I found widespread and active support for continued expansion of the state student aid programs among almost all the groups I spoke with, including leaders of public higher education. Why the difference? Continued population growth and enrollment increases certainly help to mute public-private rivalries, and the state's history of generous support for higher education helps, too. It is also my impression that public leaders do not feel especially threatened by a private sector that enrolls a mere 10 percent of the student population, or by state aid channeled to students via programs that their own students also benefit from. The state colleges and universities of California receive about half the awards and roughly one-fifth of the funds supplied by the student assistance programs.

Priorities in Student Aid Programs

There may be no general discord about the funding of student aid programs as such, except for the obvious preferences mentioned above, but there quite often is disagreement over objectives and priorities. This was apparent in the three states I studied in depth.

CALIFORNIA

Disagreement between the public and private sectors on the form student aid should take is apparent in California. For example, the Association of Independent California Colleges and Universities (AICCU) is currently pushing to amend the college opportunity grant (COG) program to make it easier for recipients to attend private institutions. This program was begun in 1969 to supplement the state scholarship program by aiding minority and low-income students who were not necessarily able to obtain scholarships via conventional selection methods. The original COG legislation tied the program explicitly but not exclusively to the community college system. A change in 1971 loosened this restriction to one requiring that at least 51 percent of first-year recipients be enrolled in community colleges, but also continued the differential support pattern whereby smaller grants were given for the first year than for the next three. (In 1975–76, $900 for subsistence was the maximum allowed a freshman in contrast to up to $2,500 for tuition and fees plus

$900 for subsistence for an upperclassman). More COG students entered private institutions after the 1971 change, but their customary share (approximately 16 percent of all COG recipients) was difficult to maintain with the first-year ceiling. In the meantime, newly elected Governor Jerry Brown had joined forces with Assemblyman John Vasconcellos and others in the legislature to increase COG program funds to $9 million in 1975–76, marking, as one observer told me, "a real shift in priorities from helping middle-income students and private institutions through the scholarship program to first helping low-income students via the COG."

Mindful of these facts, the AICCU persuaded a leading member of the legislature's Black Caucus to introduce a bill allowing first-year COG recipients to use up to one-quarter of the total amount previously available for the entire four years. AICCU cited a 1975 study of 1,600 graduates from twenty Los Angeles high schools indicating that private campuses enrolled a higher percentage of low-income students than the public senior institutions they were eligible to attend. Advocates of the COG amendment also encouraged the impression in some minority circles that "streaming" disadvantaged blacks into community colleges was treating them as second-class citizens.

The AICCU–Black Caucus alliance was powerful enough to get this bill passed over the combined opposition of Assemblyman Vasconcellos, the California Community College System, and the California State University and College System (CSUC). Vasconcellos, a seasoned and powerful figure in state higher education policy, argued against the COG revision as "favoring choice at the probable expense of access." The opposition from the community colleges and CSUC stemmed from self-interest, the former because they might lose students, the latter because CSUC anticipated receiving more community college transfer students than the private institutions.

Since Governor Brown vetoed the bill, the issue may be reopened. It is noteworthy, however, that the 1975–76 debate was civil and open, and that the disagreements have not materially affected the generally cordial relations between the public and private sectors in California.

OHIO

In Ohio, recent disputes about state student aid emerged somewhat differently: the access versus choice issue was joined not over the merits of two separate programs but rather in relation to the inner workings of the single Ohio instructional grant (OIG) program. Furthermore, the low-income and minority spokesmen this time took the more traditional position in favor of access via student aid for the neediest.

The OIG program began in 1969 to aid students from low- and middle-income families by providing state grants prorated according to both absolute need and differential college prices. Initially, the maximum stipend available to students was $300 at state institutions and $900 at independent campuses, with eligibility ceasing when family income reached $10,000. The "dual ceiling" in the program is significant, for by giving a student a markedly larger grant at a private college than he would receive at a state institution, OIG obviously narrows his net tuition gap. It follows that the private sector's interest lies in enlarging the eligible student population (chiefly by raising the income ceiling), in expanding the maximum grant level, and in seeing that the program is fully funded. The first concern of the public institutions, of course, is to boost their own state subsidies rather than to expand the OIG program.

In 1974 and 1975, OIG alterations were considered both by a Citizens' Task Force on Higher Education, authorized by the legislature and appointed by the Board of Regents, and by the regents' own Advisory Committee on Student Aid. The first group split between a majority that favored sizable increases in the OIG population, grant limits, and income ceilings, and a minority that feared full funding for the neediest students would suffer if resources were stretched and if many more students were made eligible. In particular, the minority report noted that the expense and nuisance of recruiting and educating disadvantaged students might tempt college admissions officers to favor those with higher incomes and "return to the pre-Ohio Instructional Grant days when private colleges were the exclusive preserves of middle- and upper-income white youth." They cited a sudden drop in the number of low-income OIG recipients in 1973 as evidence that their concern was not baseless.[6]

The regents' advisory committee explained that low-income recipients had declined in number, at least partly because fewer students had applied for grants, and that enlarging the OIG program was therefore desirable. The committee, however, considered full funding of larger grants more urgent than expanding eligibility.

By the time the Board of Regents took up its 1976 master plan, OIG stipends had risen to maximums of $600 and $1,500 and the gross family

6. *Citizens' Task Force on Higher Education, State of Ohio, Final Report* (Columbus, Ohio: Ohio Board of Regents, 1974).

income ceiling had been boosted to $17,000. In its draft plan, the board called first for full funding at those levels, second for still larger grants, and third for extension of eligibility and a higher income ceiling. That is where the situation stood in 1977, with private leaders applauding this portion of the regents' draft plan (though not other parts) and lobbying in Columbus for larger OIG appropriations, and with public-sector spokesmen continuing to pursue their separate quest for increased institutional support.

NEW YORK

In New York I encountered little public-private tension within the student aid area, although there is a great deal on other issues. Controversy had flared briefly in 1971 when the "Big Six" major private universities called for full-cost tuition charges in the state institutions and for greatly expanded state student aid to facilitate access for low-income students. The immediate critical reactions by the State University of New York (SUNY) and the then tuition-free City University of New York (CUNY) put those proposals onto the back burner, although the general idea of linking increased student aid to higher public-sector tuition continues to rouse interest in New York, as elsewhere. In Albany, as in Columbus, the spokesmen for public institutions can be counted on to work harder for operating subsidies than for state student aid appropriations.

Portability

Some states have moved toward limited portability of student aid awards through reciprocity agreements with neighboring jurisdictions, and others may follow suit, but the reluctance of elected officials to send their taxpayers' money out of state makes broader portability unlikely, at least without strong federal incentives. Nor are the interests of the private institutions monolithic on this issue: although private campuses generally have a higher proportion of out-of-state students than those in the public sector, many private colleges draw primarily from a local or regional recruiting area, and these are threatened by schemes that allow students the option of taking their subsidies across state lines.

More sharply than any other issue in the realm of student aid policy, portability thus points up the disparate self-interests of individual private colleges and universities and the need to work out carefully balanced compromises so that the private sector can speak with one voice at the state capital.

In New York, for example, the private campuses with many out-of-state students derive more benefit from increases in the direct institutional grants (the so-called Bundy aid), which they receive for each degree awarded, regardless of the recipient's state of residence.[7] By contrast, those independent campuses patronized chiefly by New Yorkers favor the tuition assistance program (TAP), which is restricted to state residents. The legislative agenda of the Commission on Independent Colleges and Universities (CICU) must balance such rival goals before it can speak for the entire private sector, and even then CICU must expect more help from some schools on certain issues than on others.

Similarly, in California the present priorities of the Association of Independent California Colleges and Universities (AICCU) reflect the heterogeneous nature of its membership. Institutions with the highest tuition charges would welcome state appropriations for the tuition grant program, passed in 1974, which authorizes each eligible student to receive a $900 grant once enrolled in an independent institution. The bill was supported and signed by Governor Ronald Reagan before he left office; but his successor agreed with critics of the bill (including Assemblyman Vasconcellos) that the money would be better invested in expanding the college opportunity grant program. Hence, the tuition assistance scheme has never been funded. The AICCU decided, in those circumstances, not to press the matter but rather to seek further increases in the state scholarship program where traditionally it can expect public-sector support. As noted above, AICCU is also pushing for alterations in the COG program to make it more helpful to private institutions.

Contracts with Private Colleges

Sixteen states used contracts to aid independent institutions in 1976.[8] In most cases their purpose was to educate state residents at private medical and dental schools so that new public facilities would not have to be built. It is hard to classify these arrangements, since some state programs assisting private medical and dental schools are not called contracts (for example, Ohio's aid to Case Western Reserve University), whereas other

7. Based on the recommendations of the Bundy Report, see p. 323, note. 2.
8. *Higher Education in the States*, vol. 5, no. 3 (1976), p. 148.

contracts in fact turn out to be direct capitation grants (for example, Oregon's contracts for the secular education of state residents).

Nevertheless, contracts and similar devices constitute a straightforward way of channeling state funds directly to private institutions. I encountered little opposition to this procedure in the three states I visited, probably because of the modest scope of these programs and their built-in accountability. Contracts usually have a specificity that calms anxiety about the private use of public funds and assures adequate postaudits.

But such protections do not satisfy everyone. California has a lawsuit pending and Ohio has imposed legislative limitations on contracts. Experience in these two states suggests that the mere absence of rancor between public and private leaders does not alone make a special arrangement like intersector contracts succeed. Something more is needed, perhaps a sound initial law and flexible implementation combined with a positive commitment by the leadership of all affected institutions.

CALIFORNIA

A current lawsuit seeks to test the constitutionality of state contracts with private medical schools, a program now costing about $1.5 million a year. The plaintiffs' initial concern was the state's contract with a religiously controlled medical school, but a state legislative counsel opinion, when solicited by the Student Aid Commission, reasoned that even contracts with medical schools at Stanford and the University of Southern California were prohibited by article IX, section 8, of the state constitution, which says: "No public money shall ever be appropriated for the support of any sectarian or denominational school, or any school not under the exclusive control of the officers of the public schools. . . ." The private institutions' position is that contracts for services are not "support" in the forbidden sense of that word.

OHIO

The Ohio state legislature in 1973 authorized $1 million for the 1973–75 biennium for contracts between state institutions and approved private campuses "to provide courses of study, including graduate programs, not otherwise available to students at state-assisted institutions."[9] This restriction limited the uses of the program (a comprehensive uni-

9. *State of Ohio, Appropriation Acts Passed at the One Hundred and Tenth General Assembly of Ohio at the Regular Session Begun and Held in the City of Columbus, Ohio, January 1, 1973 to December 10, 1974, Inclusive* (State of Ohio, 1975), p. 74.

versity like Ohio State could not easily find any qualifying programs in nearby institutions), but an interpretation allowing contracts with regional consortia did result in some public-private cooperation, particularly in the Cincinnati area. Several public university presidents I interviewed judged the programs to have been of marginal help to their institutions, but a private leader was cautiously supportive:

The initial experience with contracts for services was really inconclusive. Applications were solicited on relatively short notice, and the pattern was only just beginning to come in vogue when the funds ran out. Some of the projects funded were relatively mickey-mouse, but another time around they could surely be more significant.

Both contracts for services and grants by the Board of Regents for special innovative projects won endorsement by the 1974 Citizens' Task Force on Higher Education. The contract funds were not repeated, however, and in 1977 the legislature was instead considering the board's request for $5 million to fund selected innovation and system improvement plans.

Direct State Aid

Some states have given direct aid to their private colleges since colonial times, but only recently have two related issues become politically sensitive: the constitutionality of such aid and institutional accountability for the money. Relating particularly to the experience in the three states, I asked the question: since these issues expose so many raw nerves, why is direct aid still considered desirable?

Both the New York Bundy Report and the Illinois McConnell Report had concluded that aid *via* the student turns out essentially to be aid *to* the student, and both had accordingly recommended programs of direct grants to private colleges and universities. A progress report of the California Joint Committee on Higher Education put it even more bluntly:

The obvious and logical way to aid California's private colleges and universities is not by indirect measures such as [instituting] public tuition or increases in state scholarships but by direct subventions to those institutions under applicable planning and budgetary procedures.[10]

CALIFORNIA

Sometimes, however, the most "obvious and logical way" is blocked by practical considerations. The California constitution clearly barred

10. Joint Committee on Higher Education, *The Academic State* (Sacramento: California Legislature, 1968), p. 39.

direct state aid, and the report accordingly urged that it be amended. Two routes were followed. A Constitution Revision Commission had been created by the legislature in 1963, and in 1969 its committee dealing with education provisions took up the issue of state relations with private higher education. In 1970 the full commission adopted a recommendation for the addition of this language to a revised constitution: "The Legislature may provide for aid to nonprofit institutions of higher education but only for a nonsectarian, educational, public purpose."

The earliest that the proposed amendment could reach the public ballot was 1972. In late 1969, AICCU judged that public opinion in the state was already favorable to such a constitutional change, and therefore turned to the legislature to try to get the revision approved that same year. In the Sacramento give-and-take, the opposition grew more vocal. The amendment sailed through the assembly, but an informal alliance between the Americans United for Separation of Church and State and the California Teachers Association (CTA) was able to block the necessary two-thirds majority in the Senate. The Americans United were concerned about the church-state issue, and the CTA presumably did not wish to see the precedent established of allowing state funds to go to private institutions, even at the postsecondary level.[11] There were no overt moves by the state colleges and universities themselves to oppose the constitutional amendment.

This defeat caused AICCU to rework its strategy; it thereafter pushed for increases in indirect assistance via students, a channel raising no constitutional issues in California. By 1976 several private college leaders indicated to me that the 1970 defeat had been a disguised blessing. While acknowledging that the public leaders had not openly joined the issue, they nevertheless felt that public-private relations were more relaxed in the absence of direct aid and, further, that their own institutions were better off without the accountability measures linked to such aid elsewhere in the country.

NEW YORK

In New York, the so-called Blaine amendment blocks state assistance to sectarian institutions, but unlike the California provision it does not prohibit support for private, nonsectarian institutions. Thus, even though

11. For an account of these efforts to amend the California constitution, see Fred A. Nelson, *Independent Higher Education in California* (Sacramento: Joint Committee on the Master Plan for Higher Education, 1973), pp. 126–32.

the voters refused to repeal the Blaine amendment in 1968, the following year the legislature followed the Bundy Report recommendation and authorized direct grants to private colleges and universities judged by the State Education Department to be "nonsectarian." Over half of the 100 nonseminary independent colleges and universities were initially deemed eligible. The funds, amounting to about $20 million at first, were allocated on the basis of degrees awarded, with the sums increasing from the associate through the doctoral level. Research by O'Keefe indicates that, although other forces were already at work on Catholic colleges and universities, the lure of the "Bundy money" sped further moves to "desectarianize" them.[12] By 1976 the number of eligible campuses had risen to ninety-one (out of the then 115 institutions), and the appropriations had reached $66 million.[13] I found no evidence of public-sector opposition to the development and extension of this program, and many signs of support from both the state and city universities.

Private college accountability for direct state assistance runs the gamut from simple postaudits, through intermediate levels of interaction such as private-sector participation in statewide master planning, all the way to empowering the state to terminate academic programs in independent universities. New York is the only state with all three forms of accountability, but the Board of Regents had those powers long before the advent of Bundy grants. Before 1969, the regents had concentrated on chartering institutions and registering degree programs, but since the beginning of state assistance and 1971 legislation including the private sector more fully in state master planning, the regents' oversight of independent colleges and universities has become more rigorous. To guard against excessive state intervention and to discourage end-runs around the regents, the Bundy Report had recommended the formula system described above. This meant that state officials needed only to certify the campus statistics regarding degrees awarded. It also meant that little could be gained by starting a public-private imbroglio over respective

12. Edward M. O'Keefe, "The Influence of New York State Aid to Private Colleges (1968) and Universities on the Process of Change Taking Place in Catholic Institutions of Higher Learning" (Ph.D. dissertation, State University of New York at Buffalo, 1974).

13. State Education Department, University of the State of New York, Office of Postsecondary Research, Information Systems and Institutional Aid, "Bundy Aid Program, 1969–1977: A Historical Report on New York State Colleges and Universities Receiving State Aid under Section 6401 of the Education Law" (OPRISIA, July 1977; processed).

shares of the state budget, since the formulas were supposed to determine the outlays. In fact, inflation and widening tuition gaps have led the private institutions to call repeatedly for more generous Bundy formulas, and these were increased in 1973 and again in 1976. So while a formula approach may simplify the relationship, it certainly does not eliminate the normal pressures of the political process.

Ad Hoc Decisions

Outside the main categories of state aid to private higher education lies a special world of individualized arrangements involving political decisions. When Athens College, the oldest private liberal arts college in Alabama, asked the state to take it over, the Commission on Higher Education recommended against such a move because facilities at nearby public campuses were underutilized. But the state superintendent of public instruction, whose jurisdiction includes the two-year colleges, offered to absorb Athens College and run it as an upper-division unit. The legislature agreed and the state system thus grew, "rescuing" a private college by ending its private status.

Similar scenarios could be constructed for state takeovers or rescues of private institutions in other jurisdictions. Florida, for example, took over private New College despite the political backlash.[14] And in New York it appears that noneducational considerations played a major role in state decisions to subsidize Cazenovia College and the Polytechnic Institute of New York. (In one case, the institution was so deeply in debt with state dormitory bonds that officials felt obligated to save the college and avert bond defaults.)

When state systems of public colleges and universities were growing rapidly in the mid-1960s, it was not uncommon for them to absorb private and municipal institutions. The difference in the mid-1970s is that excess capacity in many jurisdictions means that the state systems have no obvious need for the additional student places.

OHIO

Sometimes educational and political considerations are complementary. In Ohio, for example, it made sense on both counts for the Board of Regents to promote a quasi-merger between Rio Grande College (a declining private campus in the rural southeast) and Rio Grande Com-

14. David Riesman, "New College," *Change*, vol. 7 (May 1975), pp. 34–43.

munity College (a public institution authorized in 1974). So the community college board contracted with private college trustees to develop
and operate the community college on the existing campus. The two
boards found a common president and the state underwrites the arrangement with a million-dollar contract. Later, a similar contract was nego-
tiated to provide curricular cooperation between Wilmington College,
another private liberal arts school, and Southern State General and Technical College. But before other struggling private colleges in Ohio could
line up for kindred arrangements, the Board of Regents issued a general
statement on public policy toward independent colleges in Ohio, which
cautioned that the "Wilmington College and Rio Grande College prece-
dents will be narrowly interpreted. In those cases, location and unavail-
ability of other services in the area were important considerations."[15]

CALIFORNIA

A somewhat different example comes from California where friends
of California Western Law School, a private institution in some distress,
recently sought a state takeover. In this case, however, the Association of
Independent California Colleges and Universities not only refrained from
pushing for such a development, but many of its leading members opposed the proposal. They sensed that their credibility with state officials
and their colleagues in the public sector would be damaged were they
to pretend that the state needed another law school in the public sector.

NEW YORK

To my knowledge, New York is the only state where serious efforts
have been made to establish general policy guidelines for failing institutions and to try to reduce ad hoc decisions in this area. In 1974 the Board
of Regents appointed an Advisory Commission on the Financial Problems of Postsecondary Institutions. Chaired by former Harvard President Nathan M. Pusey, the commission consisted of sixteen men and
women, mostly heads of public and private campuses in New York state.
Its charge, in effect, was to advise the state on how best to conduct institutional triage, sorting out threatened colleges into those whose troubles
were mild and temporary, those whose problems were so deep as not to
merit use of limited resources, and those whose situations were serious
but soluble with state assistance. Its 1975 report offered general guide-

15. Ohio Board of Regents, *Public Policy toward Independent Colleges in Ohio*
(Columbus: Ohio Board of Regents, 1975), p. 15.

lines for the board and suggested a number of useful procedures for obtaining and weighing fiscal data from the institutions and criteria for deciding when and how to intervene; but it left to the staff the task of speaking bluntly about the possibility that some institutions might best be left to die.[16]

The Pusey Report carried a dissent from Robert L. Ketter, president of the State University of New York at Buffalo, charging that the commission had virtually ignored both the mounting financial distress of the public sector and the overriding problem of maintaining and improving quality during years of retrenchment. These omissions, Ketter said, pointed to the need for a long-range fiscal plan for higher education in the state, rather than merely suggesting ways to tinker with the system to keep the maximum number of institutions afloat.

Because the Pusey Report appeared just as the massive city and state fiscal crises were drawing headlines, and because it was followed in 1976 by a controversial new regents' statewide plan for postsecondary education, the recommendations were temporarily shelved. But, in January 1977, the regents again considered them and approved them essentially unchanged. The future will show how far these new procedures can swing the balance in New York from political to educational considerations. One assumes that concerned citizens, students, parents, and faculty will always try to appeal an adverse finding to the governor and legislature. If so, the board may have trouble making its decisions stick.

Private-Sector Interests in Public-Sector Issues

This review of state aid to private higher education has shown occasional disagreements but little heated confrontation. It is important, however, to look also at the obverse, at state policies toward public higher education and the private sector's reactions to them.

Establishing New Institutions and New Programs

Perhaps the most traumatic event in this category is the creation of a new public institution in a region in which some long-established private college has recruited most of its students. Sometimes this development has broadened access for students, but sometimes the market overlap has

16. *Report of the Regents Advisory Commission on the Financial Problems of Postsecondary Institutions* (Board of Regents of the University of the State of New York, 1975); commonly referred to as the Pusey Report after its chairman, Nathan M. Pusey.

been great and the lower price of the public institution has tended to drain prospective students away from the independent college. Two notable examples are Boston University whose president, John Silber, waged an articulate and aggressive campaign against the expansion of the Boston campus of the University of Massachusetts, and the similar, if less noisy, friction between the (old and private) University of Dayton and the (new and public) Wright State University.

Even in California, where public-private cooperation has been the norm, controversy arose in the 1960s over proposed expansion of one University of California campus. Under President Clark Kerr's leadership, the university was considering broadening its San Francisco medical school into a general-purpose campus, and the University of San Francisco, a Catholic institution, did not hide its displeasure. But the issue evaporated when Kerr was fired by the Board of Regents—not for this reason—and the San Francisco campus remained a medical school.

Change of mission also roiled the waters around Long Island. The State University of New York College at Old Westbury had been set up as a center for educational innovation that would recruit students from a very wide base. When, over the years, this did not work out, Old Westbury proposed more traditional programs such as business administration. Nearby private institutions, not threatened by the original mission, protested to the Board of Regents that such programs would be unnecessarily duplicative and that SUNY's low tuition would attract their own students. The staff of the State Education Department investigated and got the institutions to reach an agreement whereby most of their interests were protected.

Even new programs within existing missions at public institutions may draw criticism from affected independent colleges. Thus complaints were heard from both Saint Louis University and Washington University when the Missouri Board of Higher Education approved a new doctoral program in education at the St. Louis campus of the University of Missouri. The two private institutions already had such programs and argued that a third within the region was not needed.

An issue in Ohio concerned a private college establishing a new law school before its public neighbor could obtain the necessary approval. A leader of the independent institution tartly explained this to me:

Concerning "invasion of turf," it would be fairer to put more onus on public institutions. The branches of the state universities have been particularly prone thoughtlessly . . . or selfishly through empire building to offer upper-division and even graduate work, for example, contrary to regulation. . . .

There have been a dozen accusations of intrusion against public institutions for every one against the private.

Tuition Rates

Another policy area where private interests are obviously involved is that of tuition levels for state institutions. But it does not always breed acrimony. I encountered two instances where private-sector representatives knowingly refrained from joining a campaign to raise tuition in the public sector. The first was in California where Governor Reagan came to office on a platform critical of the University of California's leadership and of its free tuition policy. The tuition gap was even then large enough to tempt some leaders of independent colleges to support higher public tuition, but, with the exception of some University of Southern California trustees who were strong Reagan supporters, most private spokesmen refrained from comment. Certainly, the AICCU took no formal part. Why? No one gave me a wholly satisfactory explanation, but I sensed both a strong commitment to access on the part of private leaders and a desire to maintain cordial relations with their public counterparts. Siding with a conservative governor on behalf of a policy that assaulted one of the firmest tenets of public higher education was no way to retain allies who, over the years, had been generally sympathetic to the interests of private colleges and universities.

A somewhat similar development occurred in Ohio in 1971 when Governor John J. Gilligan succeeded James A. Rhodes. Gilligan was attracted to a variation of the "Yale plan" whereby students could borrow sizable sums to pay for their higher education in state institutions and then pay back the loans out of later earnings. The governor allegedly invited the presidents of the Ohio private colleges to support this idea, but the Association of Independent Colleges and Universities of Ohio and most of its individual members declined to do so.

These two examples illustrate the maxim that sometimes things that do not happen are as important as those that do. These are isolated instances from both California and Ohio, but it is perhaps no coincidence that public-private relations are generally good in both states. New York (described in the following section) is another story.

The Politics of Retrenchment

It is not altogether surprising that present-day programs of state aid to private higher education in most jurisdictions came into being in an atmosphere of relative calm, and that they have given rise to minor state-house disputes rather than pitched battles among competing interests. The programs have been modest in size and their presence did not pose acute threats to the welfare of other institutions, particularly in an era when enrollment and state higher education appropriations were both mounting.

But that is probably not going to be the case in the future. The politics of retrenchment are apt to be far bloodier than the dynamics of growth. Two issues are paramount: the fear that the allocation of state support for higher education is becoming a zero-sum game in which more money for one institution or program means less for another; and the related possibility of uneven retrenchment in which some colleges and universities absorb more than their share of falling enrollment and of appropriations that barely keep pace with inflation.

Like most fears and apprehensions, these need not be verified in order to have practical consequences. The zero-sum perception is notoriously hard to prove or disprove, but institutional leaders who believe in it will conduct themselves differently in the annual budget and appropriations cycle than they would if they assumed total expenditures on higher education to be growing. And even if states' fiscal conditions improve and total postsecondary outlays do increase, declining enrollment may yet create strained relationships over the issue of which institutions will absorb what share of retrenchment. That problem, while easier to document, is less likely to be resolved in the public forum: the college a student selects is only in part related to variables that government can influence, at least in the short run.[17]

The Zero-Sum Game

Although her findings are admittedly tentative and inevitably based on years past rather than future, Susan Nelson's conclusions in chapter 2 should soften concerns over zero-sum state funding of higher education. Only where there are substantial "special efforts" (for example, programs of direct institutional or student aid confined to the private sector) is there much chance of a public-private trade-off within the state budget. Those are, however, the very conditions that many private leaders push for: large and distinctive programs of assistance for their own institutions and students.

17. See chapter 3 for a discussion of price and nonprice factors in student decisionmaking.

New York offers a particularly interesting case in point, both because it already has such substantial "special efforts" and because Nelson cites it as a possible instance of present-day budget trade-offs between the public and private sectors.

The Board of Regents projects that state expenditures for postsecondary education will rise over the next four years by about $100 million a year but will always remain below 12 percent of estimated state revenues.[18] (The 1975–76 proportion was 12.3 percent.) Its statewide plan for postsecondary education does not offer detailed dollar breakdowns, but it does point to a real budgetary squeeze. For example, the proposal to boost the state's share of senior college operating budgets (net of tuition revenue) of the City University of New York from the traditional 50 percent to 80 percent by 1979–80 implies a jump of over $100 million in state support at 1976 enrollment and price levels. At the same time, the plan recommends regularizing state aid to independent institutions, multiplying enrollment at New York private colleges and universities by a figure adjusted through time to reflect 25 percent of the standard cost per student at state institutions. Although the regents provide no timetable for attainment of these ratios, it appears that the $160 million-odd going directly and indirectly to independent institutions from the state would have to rise to at least $250 million, again at 1976 enrollment and price levels.

To this must be added other sizable increases such as those proposed for the tuition assistance program ($15 million more in 1977–78) and medical and dental education ($5 million more in 1977–78).[19] It is no wonder therefore that the State University of New York leadership would begin to worry about SUNY's future funding. Where was all this state money to come from, if not from SUNY's budget increments?

The regents' recommendations for SUNY itself did not provide much reassurance. Their high enrollment projections for 1980 and 1984 were 17,000 and 37,000 students below SUNY's own *low* estimates for those years. The plan was sharply critical of SUNY's failure to plan its graduate programs more efficiently and spoke of the coming need to cut back all doctoral programs by one-third, with the public sector clearly foremost in mind. The regents also proposed that tuition levels at both SUNY

18. Since most of the pertinent issues are conveniently touched upon in *The Regents Statewide Plan for the Development of Postsecondary Education, 1976* (Albany, State Education Department, 1976), I focus on reactions to this document.

19. Ibid., p. 85.

and CUNY be set at, and periodically be revised to reflect, one-third of the cost of undergraduate study and 40 percent of the cost of graduate study.

SUNY's concern about the regents' intentions in a tight budget situation was heightened by another section of the plan proposing that the board play a larger role in SUNY and CUNY budget review than it had in the past. The argument was that the budget process needed to be linked more closely with statewide planning and program goals, and that only they, the regents, were in a position to do this. They were already charged with reviewing private college requests, and proposed increases in state funding for CUNY pointed to a greater need to link Albany's budgetary oversight with the regents' broader educational planning function.

In the best of times, powerful institutions with years of precedent on their side could be expected to oppose changes in basic procedures relating to their income. In this particular context, SUNY had to contend not only with zero-sum worries and with fears of a regents' bias favoring the private sector, but also with a well-organized and powerful group of private colleges.

An additional aggravation was the tuition assistance program, which had seemed immune from serious dispute because of the distant possibility that if the state did accept the regents' recommendation and fund private institutions on a formula basis pegged to public-sector appropriations, there might emerge a common interest in expanding the total higher education budget. In the short run, however, fears of zero-sum state funding precluded much beyond surface cordialities between the two sectors.

The Wessell Commission findings will probably not appreciably affect the situation.[20] This five-member panel was appointed by Governor Hugh L. Carey in August 1976 in accordance with legislation passed months earlier that provided emergency state aid to the City University. It was charged, inter alia, with recommending broad state policies for the financing and governance of the state and city universities and the community colleges; appropriate relationships with private higher education; and the future role of the Board of Regents in postsecondary education. It had also to assess the effects on public policy of emerging

20. Temporary State Commission on the Future of Postsecondary Education; commonly referred to as the Wessell Commission after its chairman, Nils Y. Wessell.

trends in college attendance, manpower requirements, and other social developments. The commission issued its report in March 1977.[21]

Its recommendations include additional moneys for the CUNY senior colleges to maintain "funding parity between the City and State systems." The two public systems, in fact, should be restructured "to preserve and enhance the quality, specific missions, and tradition of access characteristic of higher education in New York." Among its other suggestions is the revision of the tuition assistance program. The commission also stressed the importance to the private sector of maintaining quality and advised increasing Bundy aid for Ph.D. degrees. It saw the Board of Regents, once reorganized, as taking a more forceful role in policy-making and planning.

The Wessell Report does not provide authoritative new answers to the highly contentious issues discussed above; its objectives are broadly similar to those of the regents' plan but it seeks slightly less costly solutions. In any case, its recommendations have been widely ignored so far.

Nevertheless, the rest of the country may still be looking to New York as the possible harbinger of things to come in states where trade-off situations are likely to occur as public and private sectors vie for limited state resources.

Of course today's social and budgetary priorities need not last forever. Walter Adams suggests that they could be recast to exploit more fully higher education's potential contributions to society:

In the 1960's, the government decided, as a matter of national priority, to win the international competition for the conquest of outer space. . . . If and when it decides that a similar program of investment in human capital and the mobilization of our research talent is required to cope with today's formidable challenges—energy, environment, health, the cities, coexistence, and, indeed, the problem of human survival—we would quickly find that the surplus of trained manpower is in reality a deficit, and that our universities suffer not from over- but under-capacity. A new "Manhattan Project" to revitalize the nation's intellectual, scientific, technological, and economic capability would quickly convert a demonstrable need into effective demand for the services of higher education.[22]

While the present climate of opinion does not seem likely to produce such a radical reordering of priorities, it is well to recall from time to

21. *The Report of the Temporary State Commission on the Future of Postsecondary Education in New York State* (State of New York, March 31, 1977).

22. "Financing Public Higher Education," *American Economic Review*, vol. 67 (February 1977, *Papers and Proceedings, 1976*), pp. 86–89.

time that so-called inexorable forces are in fact mostly created by human beings who can and occasionally do change their minds.

Fears of Uneven Retrenchment

Even if zero-sum situations are avoided, enrollment declines may still exacerbate public-private relations in higher education. Painful retrenchments will be required in certain states, and some institutions may have to close. Most closings to date have occurred in the private sector, generally involving little-known campuses (see table 1-1). This is partly because the small private college is usually the most vulnerable to drops in enrollment, being so dependent on tuition, and partly because it is so ticklish politically to suggest closing a public institution.

Oregon and Georgia shut down several public campuses during the depression of the 1930s. But although recent statewide planning studies in South Dakota and Montana have discussed the need to shut or merge some state campuses, public outcry blocked such moves. (In Montana the planners had the bad fortune to pick on Senator Mike Mansfield's alma mater.) In some other states the planning process came up with more palatable alternatives. In Minnesota, for example, the Higher Education Coordinating Commission recently completed an intensive study of the future of Southwest State University, an institution faced with sharply declining enrollment. A revised mission and reduced size are the chosen remedies for that campus, although both closure and merger were also considered.

In 1975, Wisconsin Governor Patrick J. Lucey requested the state's consolidated university system to produce a plan for cutting back or closing down institutions. The university's reply stressed that a more orderly route to savings without damage to quality or access would be through the continuation and acceleration of its own system of program audit, review, and elimination. That is the approach now being followed, and no institutional closings have occurred.

Frank M. Bowen and Lyman A. Glenny have recently studied retrenchment styles in five states and found system administrators learning how to make selective rather than across-the-board responses to major cutbacks.[23] With additional experience perhaps public-sector retrench-

23. *State Budgeting for Higher Education: State Fiscal Stringency and Higher Education* (University of California at Berkeley, Center for Research and Development in Higher Education, 1976).

ments will be better handled and, although never pleasant, somewhat less traumatic than in the past. It is important to bear in mind that some large state campuses could shrink by thousands of students without having to close. One Ohio public university leader noted that if his institution were cut back by 5,000 students, a painful but not mortal wound, that would equal the closing of five to ten small private colleges.

State Options

The real questions relate to whether a state wishes consciously to plan for retrenchment in its public sector; how its policies will affect the private sector; and what sort of balance, if any, the state wishes to maintain between the two. There are four main policy options:

1. To continue the status quo, letting the chips fall where they may.

2. To consciously maintain some desired ratio between the two sectors by balancing the major variables.

3. To move to a free market model, with tuition charges approaching true costs, increased student aid, and heavy emphasis on individual choice.

4. To act decisively to protect public institutions as the first state priority, regardless of the consequences for the private sector.

Politically, Option 1 is attractive because it already exists. But it leads to ad hoc responses to passing crises and to inconsistent policies. Advocates of this option usually choose not to notice that the status quo is rarely neutral, and that existing patterns of state institutional subsidies, student aid programs, tuition charges, and private college assistance packages usually add up to preferential treatment for some campuses or institutional types. Laissez-faire may be impartial, but it is seldom even-handed.

Option 2 may be supported by two groups. A few state associations of independent colleges prefer this kind of definite state goal (so long as the private-sector share is large enough) in contrast to the uncertain results of the free market model of Option 3. And critics of laissez-faire may feel that Adam Smith's "invisible hand" operates no better in education than they think it does in economics. They believe that with accurate statistics, well-run computers, and planning skills, persons of goodwill can produce results that will be superior to those of the market. But this option is politically difficult. As Wildavsky has pointed out,[24] de-

24. Aaron Wildavsky, *The Politics of the Budgetary Process* (Little, Brown, 1964).

cisionmakers are uncomfortable when asked by planners to decide between major policy alternatives, especially when institutional survival may be at stake. For example, the former New York state budget director expressed himself this way:

If there's not new money, then the state's greatest interest is pursued by supporting that institution which can survive, which can offer access and quality education at a low cost. It's not clear [via prior planning] which can do that.[25]

There are, of course, other grounds for criticism of the second option. Scholars such as Kenneth E. Boulding, Howard R. Bowen, Burton R. Clark, Harold L. Enarson, and Martin A. Trow have warned of the snares of prescriptive planning by those who may be unfamiliar with local situations and perhaps unaware of the limits of rational intervention. Others doubt the adequacy of much of the data being used. Former SUNY Chancellor Ernest L. Boyer, for example, attacked overreliance on state education department enrollment projections:

It behooves us not to complicate our problems by caricature. It's absolutely careless to talk with specificity and glassy-eyed grandeur about enrollments in 1990. This represents either ignorance or arrogance.[26]

Several limited versions of Option 3, the free market model, have already been described. The Big Six (major private universities) in New York had proposed in 1971 that SUNY tuition rates should be doubled and state student aid funds increased to permit students to "vote with their feet" as to which institutions would survive. John Silber presented a "voucher plan" to the Massachusetts state legislature in 1975.[27] It called for a sum of money for each qualified high school graduate that the student could use at the college of his choice within the state. And, in New Jersey, a Commission on Financing Postsecondary Education recently recommended a set of policies whereby institutional subsidies would be reduced and direct student assistance dramatically increased.[28]

This option always produces mixed and strong reactions. Many private leaders like it because they are confident that their institutions would

25. Peter C. Goldmark, Jr., quoted in Amy Plumer, "Overseeing Higher Education's Collapse," *Empire State Report*, vol. 1 (November 1975), p. 417.

26. Quoted in Amy Plumer "Higher Education's Empty Pocket Blues," *Empire State Report*, vol. 1 (October 1975), p. 397.

27. See John R. Silber, "Paying the Bill for College: The 'Private' Sector and the Public Interest," *Atlantic*, vol. 235 (May 1975), p. 40; and Silber, "The 'Private' Contribution to Public Higher Education" (Testimony delivered before the Education Committee, General Court of Massachusetts, February 24, 1975 [reprinted by Boston University, 1975]).

28. Commission on Financing Postsecondary Education, State of New Jersey, "Financing in an Era of Uncertainty" (March 1977; processed).

prosper in a "fair fight"; some educational reformers see it as the best way to make sluggish colleges and stodgy universities more responsive to student and social needs; and some politicians think it would relieve them of the need to make unpopular decisions. On the other side, public higher education groups such as the American Association of State Colleges and Universities fight the free market option bitterly believing that it favors student choice at the expense of access; other policy analysts (such as Howard Bowen) warn that it could move American higher education too far toward consumer tyranny and point out that colleges exist to change people as well as to serve them; and many politicians want no part of such a controversial issue.

Option 4—that of providing maximum protection to the public sector during severe retrenchment—has, to my knowledge, nowhere been proposed as formal policy, but a gloomy scenario was outlined by Robert M. Rosenzweig, vice president for public affairs at Stanford University. Noting that the spectacular growth of college enrollments in the 1950s and 1960s had for the most part been effected by expanding the capacity of the public sector, Rosenzweig wondered whether the declines of the 1980s and 1990s would mostly be met by shrinking that capacity, or would "the instinct to survive in the public sector have the effect of shifting the burden to the private [sector]?" He went on to speculate that in the normal course of events:

A variety of subsidies, both open and hidden, will be devised to prop up faltering public colleges and universities. . . . We will see . . . more active recruiting of students by public institutions. . . . At the same time the inclination to lessen the price disadvantage of private institutions by such devices as generous state scholarship programs is likely to change. Statewide planning bodies may be expected to give heavier weight to the need to protect earlier investments than to the desirability of maintaining a more balanced educational system. Increased pressure on the main subsidy to private education, the charitable deduction, may be expected because the need for the institutions it supports will seem less compelling. In a variety of ways, some of which cannot now be predicted because necessity has not yet required their invention, the weight of public policy will shift toward the narrow negative goal of not contracting public systems.[29]

Politically, this model presents something of a mirror image of the free market option, and it is just as unlikely to be fully implemented. No state may go so far as to repeal the tax exemptions currently allowed pri-

29. "The Future of Private Higher Education: The Case of California" (speech prepared by Robert M. Rosenzweig, Stanford University, February 27, 1976; processed), pp. 9–10.

vate college property, yet it is altogether possible that public-sector distress signals will bring efforts to reduce the amount of direct state assistance to private institutions, or even to reduce state student aid programs.

Guideposts for the Future

The few general observations made in this paper and summarized below are offered more as plausible hypotheses in need of testing than as
firm conclusions:

1. State aid to private higher education in one form or another is now
given in most states. But in only a few of them does such aid constitute
more than 5 percent of private college revenue or of state higher education expenditures, and rarely has it been the source of significant political
controversy. The programs are growing rapidly, however, and further
struggles for limited state funds and enhanced competition for students
may spark controversy where little now exists.

2. It is therefore prudent to ask whether certain kinds of conditions
and certain kinds of policies generate more conflict than others—the idea
being *not* to seek false comity, but rather to find ways of confining the
inevitable tensions to tolerable levels.

3. There are few quarrels over state aid to private institutions via tax
exemptions or the use of state credit for bond issues. Indirect state aid via
the students is generally less contentious than direct payments to institutions. Within the latter category, contracts seem to raise fewer sensitive
issues than grants.

4. More conflict tends to arise in states with large and longstanding
private sectors that enroll a high percentage of home-state students, and
in those with relatively new public institutions that have grown rapidly
during the 1960s. (Often these are the same states.) New York and Massachusetts are examples, and California provides a counterpoint. There,
the public sector largely antedates the private, has long played the dominant role in California higher education, and has contributed to amicable
public-private relationships.

5. The overall level of, and public attitudes toward, state support for
higher education also determine the environment in which decisions will
be made. Zero-sum budgetary politics and volatile public-private relations will be more likely in states with low or poorly organized public
support for higher education. Ohio's record of slack funding for state

institutions seems to reflect a real lack of commitment to higher education and a premium on parsimony, whereas in California (at least until
recently) political leaders have usually felt able to seek increased state
appropriations for higher education without fear of recrimination at the
polls.

6. The personal styles and values of higher education leaders in a state
also influence the selection of issues and the setting in which they are debated. That is why Rosenzweig lays the burden of responsibility on
public-sector leaders to help forestall state policies detrimental to private
institutions:

The key to the future lies . . . very largely in the hands of the leaders of the
great public systems of higher education, for their actions and attitudes will
mightily affect the behavior of political leaders. . . . If [public educators] perceive the interests of their systems as lying entirely within the existing bounds
of their systems, we can expect no higher vision from legislatures. If, on the
other hand . . . they are prepared . . . to tolerate the diminution of the empires
over which they preside in the larger interest of education as a whole, then
sensible policies of contraction may prevail.[30]

Nan S. Robinson, vice president for planning of the University of
Massachusetts, believes that responsibility for balanced consideration of
potentially divisive issues lies with the leaders of both sectors:

The fact [is] that popular and legislative disenchantment, inflation, fuel costs,
productivity limits, [and] poor student preparation threaten both public and
private institutions. . . . The essential truth of "hanging together or hanging
separately" should provide the glue for public/private interaction and cooperation. More carnivorous alternatives may leave us all wounded.[31]

There will be greater likelihood of divisive conflict in states where
leaders of the public or the private sector (or both) behave aggressively
or defensively and where they tend to think more in terms of short-run
problems than long-term values. To be sure, conditions may sometimes
require forceful leadership, and there is nothing intrinsically wrong with
an escalation of political tensions in a democracy where the time-
honored method of solving important policy disagreements is through
the political process. One should not always look for compromisers in
positions of leadership.

7. The formal structures and informal dynamics of state government
count for much, too. Is it a "strong governor" state or one where the
senior legislative leadership plays a dominant role? Are executive and

30. Ibid., p. 11.
31. Personal communication to the author, December 1976.

legislative offices increasingly using professional policy staffs, relying more on planning and perhaps less on ad hoc decisions? Does the state have some type of statewide board of higher education and, if so, is it responsible only for coordination or for governance as well? The latter type has a direct relationship with its public institutions and may find it more difficult to provide elected officials with dispassionate advice about higher education policies for the private sector than a coordinating board that ostensibly acts as an umbrella agency for *all* state postsecondary education, public and private.

8. Generally, I anticipate less public-private conflict in states where increasing reliance is placed on capable staffers or on statewide board planning for higher education. But the evidence is mixed. In California and Ohio, public-private relations have been improved by the efforts of their statewide coordinating boards; in New York this may be less true because of the reputation, deserved or not, of private-sector bias by the Board of Regents.

9. Perhaps the strongest set of variables is the personal style, political ideology, and dominant values of a state's political leaders. Historical and demographic conditions, public opinion, higher education leadership, and state structures of government are not to be discounted, but increasingly the dominant forces in higher education policy will be those relating to elected officials. This may please some and frighten others, but it cannot be ignored. Neither is it a recent phenomenon. In the past quarter-century, more than one governor has built his reputation in part on his stance—supportive or critical—on higher education. And as appropriations for institutional and student support have come to claim an ever larger share of state budgets, decisions about higher education policy have come to claim an ever larger share of attention. Even the tough choices forced by a period of retrenchment, while unlikely to win support from the higher education community for those obligated to make them, will certainly affect an official's future prospects at the polls. What remains to be seen is whether firm support for private colleges and universities, even at the cost of diminished support for the state institutions, is a recipe for political success in any jurisdiction.

David Adamany has recently noted an interesting ambivalence in some of the "new liberal" governors that could be important in the resolution of private-sector issues in their respective states.

> Governors like Brown (California), Dukakis (Massachusetts) and Lucey (Wisconsin) want both less government and greater accountability. . . . Even

though their vision of politics may be wrong, nonetheless it is a vision likely to have real force in the coming years.

So the politics of higher education might well be influenced to a significant extent by how elected officials sort out conflicting values in their own ideologies. If they prefer accountability, they may emphasize allocations to public institutions. If they give greater weight to curbing the size of government, they might well develop funding systems (especially student choice systems) which allow private institutions to survive.[32]

One can anticipate more public-private conflict in states where fiscally conservative political leaders act to hold down state expenditures in general and higher education appropriations in particular, or where the values of the state political leaders cause them to take a strong stand for one sector or the other.

The evidence to support this hypothesis is mixed. At one level, I have merely stated the obvious: if leadership is tight-fisted, budget fights will be more common. An important question is whether the fiscal conservativism inheres in the situation (as it now must for Governor Carey in New York, whatever his personal preferences) or whether it lies deeper in the makeup of those temporarily dominant in that state (as seems to be the case with Governor Brown in California). As for favoritism, it will be harder to please both groups during a time of retrenchment. While Governor Nelson A. Rockefeller did act in the 1960s to turn the State University of New York system into a vast and high-quality operation, he also moved to start Bundy aid to private institutions. Such evenhandedness grows ever more difficult. But presumably most leaders have arrived where they are by learning how to avoid stands that engender conflict and backlash. It will be interesting in the years ahead to see how the current crop of leaders handles the ambivalence described by Adamany between their preferences for greater accountability and for less government. The fate of private higher education rests in part on that resolution.

32. Private communication to the author, November 1976.

Chapter Eight

State Policy Options

Colin C. Blaydon

EDITED BY DAVID W. BRENEMAN AND CHESTER E. FINN, JR.

COLIN C. BLAYDON is a professor of policy sciences and business administration and acting director of the Institute of Policy Sciences at Duke University.

Tables

Most states have sought to provide access to higher education for their citizens through support of low tuition policies at public institutions. Access for those wishing to attend private colleges has not, so far, been a matter of general state concern, although the recent expansion in student aid programs to include private campuses indicates mounting interest. This chapter examines possible options open to states should they wish to ensure more evenhanded financial treatment of their public and private sectors.[1] It describes some of the choices available to states seeking more balanced financial policies and analyzes the financial burdens—larger budgets for the states or higher tuition for the students—that such choices create.

Any state that does decide to treat its public and private sectors more evenhandedly faces several interrelated questions. First, inasmuch as the difference in tuition rates, caused primarily by the substantial state subsidies for instruction in public institutions, is the main source of the private sector's competitive disadvantage, the state must decide what to do about this tuition gap: stabilize it, reduce it, or help needy students bridge it with student aid.

If the state elects to reduce the gap, it faces the basic choice of whether to "make the private institutions more like the public," or "the public institutions more like the private." The first option would narrow the tuition gap by providing state subsidies directly to private *institutions*, while the second would do so by emphasizing need-based aid to *students* and diminished subsidies to public institutions.

Related to this choice is a budgetary decision: does the state want to hold constant the current share of its resources being devoted to higher education or is it prepared to increase it? While the fixed-share option is obviously less expensive in dollars, the political cost would be higher, since only by removing real resources from the public sector could the private sector be aided. Such a decision practically guarantees that public tuition will rise relative to private tuition. On the other hand, if total state spending for higher education were to rise in real terms, new resources could flow to the private sector without reductions in the public sector and without increased tuition for anyone.

There is no clear-cut answer to these policy questions. If a state ad-

1. It is not the purpose of this chapter to derive a rationale for state support of private higher education—an issue that is discussed in chapters 1 and 10—so much as it is to explore policy alternatives for those already persuaded that the rationale is sound.

dresses the tuition gap problem by trying to reduce the gap for all students, institutional aid appears to be the mechanism it should select. If the state opts instead to focus on increasing choice for needy students, policies of income- or need-based student aid are appropriate.

To design either an institutional or a student aid program that treats public and private sectors more equally, it is important to settle on a definition of equality. The following discussion of institutional aid defines three plausible measures of financial equality and compares the public and private sectors in the 1974–75 academic year in terms of each of them. The analysis then examines the impact of achieving each of these standards of financial equality. This impact is estimated in terms of the changes that might occur in tuition and the shifts or increases that would be required in state resources.

Equal treatment of the two sectors through student aid can usefully be defined either as eliminating the public-private price difference for students of identical income, or as guaranteeing all students a minimum amount of resources to use on higher education. The former definition implies an aid program based on "need"—cost of attendance minus family contribution—while the latter would rely simply on income. Hence, the analysis presents estimates of the costs of meeting the needs of all students under various formulations.

The conclusions of this analysis are straightforward. Those states that contain the bulk of the private campuses will find it hard to provide balanced support of the two sectors through institutional aid programs. Nevertheless, those same states should be able to meet a substantial part of individual need in both sectors through carefully designed student aid programs—particularly if the state program is synchronized with federal assistance schemes. Whichever approach a state adopts, it can readily lighten the financial burden that such changes entail by moving toward greater equality over several years rather than by drastically shifting policy all at once.

Institutional Aid

Operating subsidies for public institutions have been the principal form of state support for higher education. Few jurisdictions, however, provide such support for private colleges; ten give general-purpose aid and thirteen give specialized aid to particular programs or schools.[2] This pattern contrasts with the recent rapid expansion of state aid for students in private institutions; all but nine states now have such programs.

The dollar amounts (per full-time-equivalent student) shown below highlight the disparity between state subsidies given to private and public institutions, and the influence that this has on tuition rates:[3]

	Total educational program revenue	Nontuition revenue per full-time-equivalent student		
		Outside educational program revenue	State subsidies	Tuition
Sector				
Public	2,845	307	1,995	543
Private	3,390	1,062	93	2,235

Nationwide, state subsidies supply 70 percent of total educational revenue of public institutions compared with just 3 percent in private col-

2. Carnegie Foundation for the Advancement of Teaching, *The States and Higher Education: A Proud Past and a Vital Future—Supplement* (Carnegie Foundation for the Advancement of Teaching, 1976), pp. 35–36.

3. Revenue data are taken from the master tape assembled by Kent Weldon of the National Center for Higher Education Management Systems from the U.S. National Center for Education Statistics, Higher Education General Information Survey for the academic year 1974–75. The definitions are:

Total educational program revenue = outside educational program revenue + state subsidies + tuition (not comparable to "educational and general revenue").

Outside educational program revenue = federal appropriations + restricted endowments + unrestricted endowments + unrestricted gifts + sales and services of educational departments + other.

State subsidies = state appropriations + local appropriations.

Nontuition revenue = outside educational program revenue + state subsidies.

Tuition = gross tuition revenue.

The figures are national averages calculated by weighting state averages by full-time-equivalent enrollment. The numbers in the first three columns include some student aid funds that are channeled through the budgets of the institutions rather than delivered directly to the students.

The analysis focuses on those revenues that support the current operating budget of an institution's educational program. There is no way to obtain from the source a completely satisfactory definition of "educational program revenue." As an approximation the following HEGIS categories are included: tuition and fees; government appropriations; unrestricted private gifts, grants, and contracts; endowment incomes; sales and services of educational activities; and other sources. Excluded are categories dealing largely with research, hospitals, and auxiliary services. Unfortunately, a widely used general category known in earlier surveys as "educational and general revenue" cannot be calculated from the 1974–75 survey.

leges and universities. Tuition provides 66 percent of the educational program revenue of private institutions with the remainder coming from endowments, gifts, federal grants, and other institutionally generated sources. Private institutions have more than three times as much outside revenue per student from the latter sources as the public campuses, which keeps them from being totally reliant on tuition receipts. Without such unrestricted income, private tuition would be even higher than it is today. Thus outside funds tend to narrow the tuition gap between the public and private sectors, although a tradition of higher expenditures per student in many private colleges also generates higher revenue "requirements," which naturally tend to widen the gap.

Equalization of Support between Sectors

In the following analyses, three standards of financial equality are examined: equal state subsidy levels, equal tuition charges, and equal nontuition revenue. The analyses estimate changes that would be necessary to achieve each of these measures of "equality," first, through a reallocation of resources without increased state spending, and, second, through an increase in state spending that is allocated entirely to private campuses.

EQUALIZATION THROUGH REALLOCATION

In this approach to equalizing support for the two sectors, private institutions could be subsidized to offset some or all of the difference between the public and private sectors in terms of a chosen financial measure, subject to the constraint of fixed state spending on higher education.

In its extreme form, equal treatment of the two sectors would mean that the state would provide equal subsidies (per student) to public and private institutions. If each state accomplished this by shifting support from its public to its private institutions, thereby forcing up public tuition charges and permitting private prices to fall (assuming full pass-through of subsidies to student tuition), sizable changes in tuition rates would result, as seen by comparing column 2 of table 8-1 with column 1.[4]

4. The tables in this chapter include national figures (all the states and the District of Columbia) and, also, to display some interstate variations, three groupings of states: New England, because of its large and expensive private sector coupled with its high family incomes; the South, because of its large and relatively lower-cost private sector coupled with its lower family incomes; and a group of selected states chosen for their large higher education systems and large state budgets (California, Illinois, New York, Michigan, Pennsylvania, and Wisconsin).

Table 8-1. *Comparison of Actual Tuition per Full-Time-Equivalent
Student with Tuition under Alternative Equalization Policies,
by Region and Sector, 1974–75*[a]

Tuition in dollars

Region and sector	Actual tuition (1)	Tuition under alternative policies			Percentage change in tuition under alternative policies		
		Equalization of state subsidy (2)	Equalization of tuition (3)	Equalization of nontuition revenue (4)	Equalization of state subsidy (5)	Equalization of tuition (6)	Equalization of nontuition revenue (7)
National							
Public	543	981	900	816	81	66	50
Private	2,235	889	1,135	1,396	−60	−49	−38
South[b]							
Public	544	969	799	801	78	47	47
Private	1,776	177	817	876	−90	−54	−51
New England[c]							
Public	547	1,398	1,551	876	156	184	60
Private	2,621	1,765	1,612	2,290	−33	−38	−13
Selected states[d]							
Public	519	1,022	948	845	97	83	63
Private	2,421	954	1,169	1,470	−61	−52	−39

Source: Column 1, data from U.S. National Center for Education Statistics, Higher Education General Information Survey for the academic year 1974–75, master tape assembled by Kent Weldon of the National Center for Higher Education Management Systems; columns 2, 3, and 4, author's calculations of tuition levels that would have resulted if state subsidies, tuition, and nontuition revenue had been equalized on a state-by-state basis in that same year.

a. National tuition figures are averages weighted by full-time-equivalent enrollment. Regional figures are averages of the states within the respective regions (see notes b, c, and d) also weighted by full-time-equivalent enrollment. This analysis assumes (a) that state spending on higher education remains unchanged, (b) that changes in subsidies would be passed directly on to students in the form of changes in tuition, and (c) that enrollment remains unchanged. In practice, institutions would behave in different ways, but it is entirely possible that with increased enrollment resulting from lower tuition, some colleges would reduce tuition by even more than the increase in subsidy.

b. Alabama, Georgia, Mississippi, North Carolina, South Carolina, Tennessee, and Virginia.

c. Connecticut, Maine, Massachusetts, New Hampshire, Rhode Island, and Vermont.

d. California, Illinois, Michigan, New York, Pennsylvania, and Wisconsin.

Average private tuition rates would actually be lower than public charges ($889 as opposed to $981) because of the larger nontuition revenue available to most private colleges in the form of endowment earnings and gifts.[5] In the South, where private college expenditures per student are less, private schools would offer almost free tuition, whereas

5. Outside revenues are assumed to be unchanged by the advent of large state subsidies, but in fact they might fall, as prospective donors judge their gifts less vital to the institutions' welfare.

tuition in the costlier colleges of New England would only be reduced by one-third.

Alternatively, if each state had eliminated the tuition gap within its borders in 1974–75 by transferring support from the public to the private sector, average private tuition nationwide would have fallen by 49 percent, from $2,235 to $1,135, whereas average public tuition would have risen by 66 percent, from $543 to $900 (as seen in table 8-1, columns 1 and 3).[6]

A third, maybe more realistic, standard for equalizing state treatment of public and private higher education is nontuition revenue. It could be argued that "outside educational program revenue"—mainly gifts and endowment earnings—play a role in financing private institutions comparable to state subsidies for public institutions, and that an appropriate role for the state is to guarantee both sectors the same level of nontuition resources, that is, the sum of state subsidies plus outside educational revenue would be equalized. The tuition gap would then reflect only different levels of spending per student and would lead to a more economically efficient distribution of students between the two sectors. A state subsidy that equalized nontuition revenue would have a less dramatic (though still large) impact on tuition (as seen in table 8-1, columns 1 and 4). Public tuition would rise 50 percent, on average, while private tuition would fall by 38 percent. The resulting tuition rates—$816 in the public and $1,396 in the private sector—would differ chiefly because approximately $580 more is spent per student in private institutions. In the South, public and private prices would be very close, reflecting similar spending levels per student in both sectors. But in New England the tuition differences would remain sizable because of the $1,414 expenditure difference per student between the public and private sectors.

The political costs of achieving any of these three standards of "equality" while maintaining a constant level of state spending on higher education could be reduced if the change were introduced over several years. In that case, for the average state to achieve the 50 percent increase in public tuition needed to equalize nontuition revenue, the requisite increase in public tuition (nationwide) would be almost 8.5 percent

6. Since this policy is designed to equalize public and private tuition, it might seem contradictory that the resulting prices still differ. This seeming anomaly is explained by the larger proportion of private-sector enrollment in states that tend to have higher public rates. Since tuition is equalized only within state boundaries, when the state averages are weighted by the enrollment in each sector, this leads to a higher average private tuition rate nationwide.

a year for five years (or 4 percent a year for ten years).[7] Again, the regional differences are striking. The New England states might well question the value of raising public tuition 9.9 percent a year (in constant dollars) for five years in order to permit private institutions to reduce their prices only 2.5 percent a year.

EQUALIZATION THROUGH HIGHER STATE SPENDING

Wherever there is strong opposition to any increase in public tuition, states seeking to treat their public and private sectors more evenhandedly may only be able to do so by increasing real state spending on higher education. If there had been, for example, a 10 percent increase in each state's institutional support budget in the 1974–75 academic year,[8] and if all of the increment had been devoted to the private sector, the average state subsidy to private institutions would have risen from 5 percent to 36 percent of average public-sector subsidies (see tables 8-2 and 8-3). In terms of dollars per student, the average educational program subsidy to private campuses would have increased almost eightfold, from $93 to $717. If private colleges and universities had passed all of this additional subsidy on to their students in the form of lowered tuition rates, average private-sector charges would have fallen by 28 percent nationwide— to $1,611—thus narrowing the average public-private tuition gap to $1,068.[9] But pronounced regional differences would remain. In New England, where state higher education outlays are small and private-sector enrollment large, a 10 percent increase in spending would translate into an average private-sector tuition reduction of just 7 percent, whereas in the South a similar increase would permit a reduction of private-sector charges of 43 percent. The remaining tuition gaps would be $1,891 in New England and $462 in the South.

However, a 10 percent increase in each state's support is insufficient to equalize the finances of public and private higher education in all states on any of the three measures. To reach parity, state institutional support budgets would have to have risen on average by: (a) 18 percent to equalize nontuition revenue, (b) 27 percent to eliminate the tuition

7. The average annual growth rates are calculated from the total percentage changes in tuition in table 8-1, column 7.

8. Here again, reference is made only to the state subsidy for current operations of an institution's educational program, defined as "state plus local appropriations" in the HEGIS data.

9. Since this option holds public-sector subsidies constant, it is assumed that public-sector tuition would not be affected.

Table 8-2. Impact on Institutions of Higher Education of a 10 Percent Increase in State Program Subsidies, by Region, Academic Year 1974–75

Dollars per full-time-equivalent student

| | Private | | | | | | Public[a] | | | | |
| | State subsidy | | Tuition | | Nontuition revenue | | State subsidy | Tuition | Nontuition revenue | Tuition gap[f] | |
Region[b]	Current[c] (1)	Proposed[c] (2)	Current (3)	Proposed[d] (4)	Current (5)	Proposed[e] (6)	(7)	(8)	(9)	Current (10)	Proposed (11)
National	93	717	2,235	1,611	1,155	1,779	1,995	543	2,302	1,692	1,068
New England	22	205	2,621	2,438	1,265	1,448	1,794	547	2,008	2,074	1,891
South	21	790	1,776	1,006	1,115	1,884	2,037	544	2,310	1,232	462
Selected states	157	808	2,421	1,770	1,141	1,792	2,182	519	2,414	1,902	1,251

Sources: Same as table 8-1, column 1, and author's calculations. National figures are averages of all states and the District of Columbia, weighted by full-time-equivalent enrollment; regional figures are averages of the states within the respective regions, also weighted by full-time-equivalent enrollment.

a. In this proposal, public revenues remain unchanged.

b. See table 8-1 for states included in each region.

c. The institutional subsidy in each state (that is, state appropriations plus local appropriations) is increased by 10 percent and added to the 1974–75 state institutional subsidy for the private sector.

d. Outside educational program revenue, which remains unchanged in each state, and the increased state institutional subsidy mentioned above are subtracted from total educational program revenue, which also remains unchanged in each state. The proposed private tuition assumes that all of the proposed state subsidy is used to reduce private tuition.

e. Sum of the increased state institutional subsidy and private outside educational program revenue.

f. Difference between current or proposed private rates and public tuition rates.

Table 8-3. *Impact on Private Institutions of Higher Education of a 10 Percent Increase in State Program Subsidies, by Region, Academic Year 1974–75*

	Increase in private state subsidy as percent of current private tuition[b] (1)	Private as percent of public					
		State subsidy		Tuition		Nontuition revenue	
Region[a]		Current (2)	Proposed (3)	Current (4)	Proposed (5)	Current (6)	Proposed (7)
National	28	5	36	412	297	50	77
New England	7	1	11	479	446	63	72
South	43	1	39	326	185	48	81
Selected states	27	7	37	466	341	47	74

Source: Calculated from table 8-2, as follows: column 1 = table 8-2 (column 2 — column 1) ÷ column 3; column 2 = table 8-2, columns 1 ÷ 7; column 3 = table 8-2, columns 2 ÷ 7; column 4 = table 8-2, columns 3 ÷ 8; column 5 = table 8-2, columns 4 ÷ 8; column 6 = table 8-2, columns 5 ÷ 9; column 7 = table 8-2, columns 6 ÷ 9.
a. See table 8-1 for states included in each region.
b. The increase in the private state subsidy = the total (public and private) state subsidy increased by the proposed 10 percent, minus the current private state subsidy.

gap in each state, and (c) 30 percent to equalize public and private subsidies per student.[10] These national figures again conceal pronounced state variations; for example, in Nevada a minuscule increase (0.13 percent) would equalize nontuition revenue, whereas at the other extreme in the District of Columbia a 236 percent increase would be required. With increases of no more than 10 percent in institutional support budgets, half of the states could put the two sectors on a roughly equal financial footing in terms of nontuition revenue.[11] But the remaining states, containing two-thirds of total private enrollment, would find it difficult to do this. Included in the latter group are most of the New England and Southern states, and such large private-sector states as Minnesota, New York, Ohio, and Pennsylvania. Not surprisingly, the problem is most difficult to solve in those states where private colleges and their students are concentrated.

10. The necessary percentage increase in each case is calculated by multiplying private enrollment by the difference between the public and private sectors in the per-student revenue measure in each state, then dividing by the state aid budgets. (See table 8-A1 for state detail.)
11. With a 10 percent increase in state institutional aid budgets for educational programs, twenty-five states could bring their private-sector nontuition revenues to within 90 percent of those in the public sector.

A gradual approach to equalization would naturally cut the annual cost increases. A 10 percent increase in real spending is less than 2 percent a year for five years, while an 18 percent increase is about 3 percent annually. Indeed, if the projected "fiscal dividend" for state and local governments materializes in the 1980s,[12] states could provide a higher level of real resources to their private colleges and universities without raising tax rates or reducing other state services, including their support of public higher education.

Designing Institutional Aid

Whether funds are redistributed or budgets increased, and no matter which financial standard is chosen, any state program that attempts to employ institutional aid as the means of equalizing the financial support of public and private colleges must reckon with four major design problems: (1) predicting institutional responses so that the programs will have the desired effects; (2) avoiding undesirable incentives; (3) preserving institutional autonomy; and (4), where applicable, overcoming constitutional barriers to state aid for private and, especially, church-related institutions.

INSTITUTIONAL RESPONSE

Institutional reactions to a new subsidy program are difficult to predict. Colleges have different objectives and face dissimilar situations, and no single economic goal is relevant for all campuses. With the additional money, some may try to increase enrollment, still others may become more selective, or they may simply substitute these additional state subsidies for funds that they had been taking from—or would otherwise have put into—their endowments. In other words, the benefits may not accrue to students in the form of lower tuition.[13]

12. "[In] 1986 the 1973 revenue system will produce 18.3 percent more than is required to maintain 1973 service levels." (Emil M. Sunley, Jr., "State and Local Governments," in Henry Owen and Charles L. Schultze, eds., *Setting National Priorities: The Next Ten Years* [Brookings Institution, 1976], p. 408.)

13. Some college administrators and faculty members may feel, perhaps correctly, that the surest way to increase the "benefits" for their students, and thus to enhance the marketplace position of their institutions, is to use additional revenue to enrich the educational program (or the student aid budget, or faculty salaries) rather than to cut their "posted prices."

UNDESIRABLE INCENTIVES

Another problem relates to the different revenue structures of the two sectors. If a state wishes to make these structures more similar, it could treat each college individually. This is risky because it might unfavorably affect institutional behavior. For example, if a state aid formula took account of income from endowments and gifts and reduced subsidies to institutions that are particularly enterprising in this regard, the latter would have less incentive to seek such private support. Similarly, if the formula took the expenditure structure into account, the incentive to control costs would be diminished, since a greater state subsidy would offset increased spending.

Without considering institutional revenue and cost characteristics, however, it would be impossible to devise sensible measures of financial comparability between the sectors and to redress imbalances. The hazards can be minimized by basing subsidy levels on such information for entire classes of institutions (or programs) rather than on individual campuses. Thus a given amount per private enrollee might be sufficient to put the public and private sectors as a whole on a par with each other. But since the subsidy for a particular campus would not increase if its gift income fell or its costs increased, individual colleges would still have cause to control their expenditures.

INSTITUTIONAL AUTONOMY

A subsidy formula that took account of institutional revenue and expenditure characteristics would lead to greater government involvement in the budget practices of the private campuses. Detailed oversight of financial reporting would be required, and state officials might be tempted to exercise their own judgment about "appropriate" changes in income and outlay.

CONSTITUTIONAL BARRIERS

The prohibition in some state constitutions against aid to private or religiously affiliated institutions might be handled in several ways. Church-related colleges could be excluded from the program, which would worsen their competitive position, or they could alter their religious ties or character sufficiently to be considered legally independent. This solution risks eliminating some of the diversity and special attributes that make private higher education worth supporting. Moreover, it would not solve the problem in those jurisdictions where the constitution prohibits all state aid to institutions that are not publicly controlled.

A preferable way to avoid the constitutional problems (in most cases) while also reducing the likelihood of state intrusion into campus fiscal management is to give the aid directly to private college and university students in the form of a flat grant, sometimes termed a tuition offset. Because the individual student recipient is the immediate beneficiary, this method may be legal where direct aid to institutions is not. Although such tuition offsets are technically student aid, they operate more like institutional aid because they reduce the tuition that all private students face, regardless of family income.[14] The problem of predicting institutional responses would remain. Unless forbidden to do so, some private colleges and universities might boost their tuition rates by the amount of the offset, thus augmenting their revenues without lightening the financial burden on their students.[15] Attempts by the state to prohibit or regulate this behavior would force it to monitor the finances of individual institutions. But the marketplace would assist. When funds are channeled through students a college can "capture" the additional subsidy only by visibly increasing its rates. When payments are made directly to the college itself they can be quietly absorbed without any change in tuition. Hence, if narrowing the tuition gap is itself a primary rationale for increased state support of private higher education, it would seem preferable to adopt a program of tuition offset grants rather than institutional subsidies.

Program Implementation

Because the tuition gap depends equally on public and private prices—and hence on institutional revenue structures—a state that wishes to stabilize or narrow it is well advised to relate its public- and private-sector subsidies to each other. Although it cannot easily (or properly) regulate

---

14. Of course, tuition offsets can also be given directly to the institution, in which case they are indistinguishable from formula aid and, presumably, subject to whatever legal or constitutional impediments there may be to such aid.

15. Presumably those institutions that anticipated no difficulty in recruiting enough students would have the least incentive to cut prices. Others might judge that an improved educational program would make them more attractive to students. Those most vulnerable to price competition by the public sector would presumably avail themselves of tuition offsets by reducing their charges.

private tuition rates, it can readily craft its own subsidy formulas so as
to encourage the type of price changes over time in both sectors that
it judges most desirable.

The institutional aid standards described above have sought greater
financial equality for private and public colleges in order to reduce the
tuition gap. But whether the state's intent is to narrow the gap or simply
to stabilize it in the face of future changes in the higher education environment, the institutional subsidy program that it adopts should link
payments to public and private campuses. In so doing, each state's governmental and educational leaders must reckon with a number of related
variables, since state subsidies are not the only influence on tuition. Any
given formula creates complex incentives and disincentives for institutions and students, and "rewards" and "punishes" them in different ways.
It is immensely difficult to deal wisely with all of these factors, of course,
for a formula that creates a workable incentive for one school may complicate matters for another.

FACTORS AFFECTING TUITION RATES

Four variables in particular warrant consideration. The first is inflation in the cost of goods and services that colleges buy, ranging from
professorial pay to electricity and library books. Does the state want to
underwrite these largely involuntary institutional cost increases in order
to hold down tuition, or does it want them to be passed along to students?
If it is prepared to subsidize them, is it prepared to do so for public and
private institutions alike?

The second is the changing enrollment scene. Should colleges be given
a strong financial incentive to expand, and thus presumably to compete
with one another, in a period when total enrollment is apt to decline in
many jurisdictions? Should they be protected economically from the
consequences of falling enrollment—notably from increases in their costs
per student—or should they be left to curb their expenses (or boost
their tuition) as best they can?

A third variable is the maintenance or enrichment of the educational
program. In the past, most colleges and universities have expanded their
curricular offerings and upgraded their educational quality by obtaining
both more students and more revenue per student. Are all future changes
in one area going to have to be financed by contractions elsewhere or
by tuition increases—or is the state prepared to pay for enrichment,
which means more than keeping pace with inflation?

Fourth is the issue of other institutional income. Should state policy create a continuing incentive for public and private institutions to augment their nonstate, nontuition revenues from such sources as private gifts and federal grants, should it ignore such factors, or should it provide funds that reduce the need for colleges to pursue such outside sources?

Attempts to deal intelligently with these variables cause untold complications for state policymakers, particularly if they endeavor to handle them in ways that ultimately stabilize (or narrow) the difference in tuition rates charged by public and private institutions. Yet there is much to be said for weighing them, and for attempting to forge a link between future public and private institutional subsidies provided by the state. If state support formulas are joined, the competition between public and private institutions for state appropriations will ease—perhaps by being transferred elsewhere, such as to the student marketplace—since adroit lobbying will not increase one particular college's share of the total or reduce another's. By linking support for private institutions to public-sector subsidies, the likelihood of state interference in the finances of individual private colleges is reduced, for it would not be necessary to decide what sorts of costs to "allow" in the private sector, only in the public. Once the state has determined what it is willing to pay for in its own institutions, the formula will automatically determine the subsidy (if any) to private campuses.[16]

TWO OPTIONS

There are many possible formulas for changing public and private subsidies over time and thereby limiting the tuition gap. Two contrasting options sketched below illustrate the range of schemes that states could devise. In the first the state subsidizes additional enrollment in both sectors but requires tuition to rise to cover higher costs, while the second focuses on absorbing cost increases and attempts to be neutral toward changes in enrollment.[17]

Option One. The subsidy per student to public institutions would be

16. Presumably, the state would not want to pay for added costs in the private sector that it is not prepared to cover in the public sector, although this need not be the case if, for example, the state judged its private institutions in greater need of qualitative improvement than its public institutions.

17. Both "formulas" have been greatly oversimplified. They assume, for example, that the state allocates its support to all public institutions according to the same calculations, whereas in fact many jurisdictions employ different formulas for community colleges, four-year colleges, and research universities.

frozen and the total support per institution would be allowed to vary only with enrollment increases or declines. Private institutions would be given the same subsidy per student for each *additional* student. Both sectors would be obliged to raise tuition rates to absorb cost increases.

A formula of this sort treats both sectors equally in that it provides equal rewards for increasing enrollment and incentives for both sectors to control their costs in order to moderate tuition hikes. In addition, to the extent that larger enrollment leads to lower average costs per student and smaller enrollment to higher average costs, this formula also encourages institutions to boost their enrollment as a way of reducing the upward pressure on tuition rates caused by rising costs. Because institutions have to raise their prices to pay for any cost increases they incur, it seems unlikely that this formula would encourage much improvement in program quality unless the campuses are able to tap sources of income other than tuition. Any change in the tuition gap would depend on differential cost increases in the two sectors: if average cost increases were identical, the gap should not change, whereas if private costs rose more per student than public costs, the gap would widen. An obvious defect in this approach, from the public institution's perspective, is that in an era of declining enrollment it could result in less state revenue for public campuses. In those states where continued growth is projected, however, it appears to be a sensible way of strengthening the marketplace and equalizing competition among colleges.

Option Two. State subsidies per student in the public sector would be allowed to rise with increased costs. Private institutions would have subsidies per student equal to the *increase* in those in the public sector. Tuition in both sectors should remain stable in spite of inflation if the private colleges experience the same cost pressures as the public campuses.

In this formula, the state bears the burden of higher costs for both sectors. The incentive for public institutions to control costs imposed by the threat of having to raise tuition is eliminated as state auditors determine allowable increases. The private sector, however, still retains this incentive since its subsidies are independent of its expenses. If private colleges can operate more efficiently than their public counterparts, the state subsidies might actually allow them to improve their competitive position, rather than just maintain it. Since subsidies to the public sector will vary directly with costs, public institutions should be indifferent between enrollment increases and declines. No matter what public enrollment is, the state payment should just cover costs. In the private sector, additional enrollment is encouraged, as in the former option, but less strongly since the marginal subsidy the institution would receive for enrolling an additional student (or that it would lose for enrolling one less student) is only a small part of its total subsidy from the state. A further advantage of this formula is that it would encourage political harmony at the state level between the two sectors of higher education, since both would benefit equally from higher subsidy rates.

It is unlikely that any jurisdiction would wish to adopt the exact terms of either of these oversimplified formulas. A state wishing to address the tuition gap directly through institutional support of public and private campuses would construct one better suited to its individual circumstances and objectives. How much money are its officials prepared to spend? How high are they willing to let public-sector tuition rise, if at all? Have they reason to expect that student demand will or could increase in the 1980s or must they prepare to deal sensibly with shrinking enrollment?

Such questions cannot be answered in the general case or as abstractions, and it will not be easy to agree on answers in particular situations either. Institutional rivalries are already intensifying in many jurisdictions, and a forthright attempt by the state government to revise the rationale and recalibrate the formulas by which it supports colleges and universities is apt to stir further strife. Indeed, state officials may decide that the various "gaps" in institutional revenue patterns and tuition charges between the two sectors do not appropriately explain the problem of private higher education in the 1980s, and that changes in institutional support, however well conceived, may not induce economy, efficiency, social equity, or be politically feasible. They may decide instead to concentrate on the ability of individual students to pay for higher education at the college of their choice, in which case they must grapple directly with the issues of student aid policy.

Student Aid

In seeking more evenhanded treatment of public and private higher education, states could focus on students rather than (or in addition to) institutions. In this case, equal treatment could be defined in any of the following ways: (1) guaranteeing all students a minimum level of resources for higher education (that is, income-based aid); (2) guaranteeing that all students with the same income or family resources would pay the same amount whether they attend public or private colleges (that is, "need-based" aid); or (3) combining a minimum resource guarantee with some sharing of the higher costs of a private education. This section examines the different types of student assistance programs that meet those definitions, looks at costs, problems of program design, and the coordination of state and federal programs.[18]

Income-Based Aid

With income-based student grants, the objective is to bring the resources available to pay college expenses up to some minimum level for all students, without making the grants contingent on the costs of the college attended. Table 8-4 shows the average awards per student that would have been required in 1974–75 to give all students a resource guarantee of $1,400, the ceiling at that time for the federal basic educational opportunity grants.[19] Students attending public institutions or living in the South would have received larger grants because more of them come from low-income families. Students attending college out of state could expect the smallest grants since their families tend to be the most affluent.

From one perspective, student aid based only on income is attractive because it does not distort the institutional price differences that a student faces when choosing between colleges. All students with the same family resources receive the same amount of aid regardless of college attended, and each must bear the full additional cost of attending a more expensive campus. This feature assures that institutions will pay close

18. Before proceeding, a word of caution is needed on the empirical analysis that follows. To estimate the cost of income- or need-based student aid, it is necessary to have state data on family finances by the cost and type of institution attended. (Need is defined as cost of attendance minus family contribution.) Daryl Carlson compiled the available data into a set of state-by-state series that make it possible to estimate family contributions, costs of attendance, and student need by state for the 1974–75 academic year. (Data sources are given in appendix B.) Because of problems with the underlying data series in terms of comprehensiveness and accuracy, it is important to view the results as rough approximations, not as precise estimates. Regional and national figures are presented in this chapter with state-by-state data available from the author upon request.

19. Family contributions are estimated according to the needs-analysis system employed by the basic grant program. However, table 8-4 does not take other federal aid into account in calculating the average grant required by students in each state.

Table 8-4. *Average Awards Required to Meet a Minimum Resource Guarantee of $1,400, by Region and Sector, Academic Year 1974–75*[a]

Dollars per full-time-equivalent student

| | Public | | Private | |
Region[b]	Home state	Out of state	Home state	Out of state
National	320	180	271	143
New England	286	169	245	114
South	459	217	354	168
Selected states	301	160	234	135

Sources: See appendix B. National figures are averages of all states and the District of Columbia weighted by full-time-equivalent enrollment; regional figures are averages of the states within the respective regions, also weighted by full-time-equivalent enrollment. State-by-state figures, on which the averages are based, are available from the author.

a. The minimum resource guarantee is the individual award plus the family contribution, which in this case equals $1,400.

b. See table 8-1 for states included in each region. Students are counted in a state according to residence, and then whether they attend college in their home state or go out of state.

attention to their costs and to the prices of the services they offer. From another perspective, however, this is the least attractive feature of an income-tested grant. If given to students in both sectors, such aid would not compensate for the price distortion already caused by the large state subsidies to public institutions. For this reason, an income-tested program only really makes sense for the purpose here if it is confined to private-sector students.

Need-Based Aid

If the objective is to aid students in both sectors while offsetting some of the price distortion, then a need-tested grant formula is required. A student's award would be a fixed proportion of his need, that is, of the difference between his own resources and the cost of attendance. Average student need in different regions of the country is calculated on this basis in table 8-5. It is apparent that the needs of home-state public students are strikingly uniform across the nation. Although family income patterns vary considerably among the states, this is generally offset by differences in college charges and state subsidy levels.

The needs of students attending home-state private institutions, on the other hand, are greater and vary from state to state. Students enrolled in New England private campuses, for instance, have the most substan-

Table 8-5. *Need for Student Aid, by Region and Sector,*
Academic Year 1974–75[a]

Dollars per full-time-equivalent student

	Public		Private	
Region[b]	Home state	Out of state	Home state	Out of state
National	704	938	1,452	901
New England	700	969	1,853	700
South	760	895	1,196	898
Selected states	708	924	1,631	953

Sources: Same as table 8-4.
a. Need = costs of attendance — family contribution as given in the basic educational opportunity grant schedule.
b. See table 8-1 for states included in each region. Students are counted in a state according to residence, and then whether they attend college in their home state or go out of state.

tial average need, which is 55 percent more than in the South largely because of lower attendance costs at private southern institutions.

Because students who go out of state to college generally have higher family incomes, they have a lower need for aid than their counterparts who attend in the home state. Also, because public colleges and universities impose tuition surcharges on students residing in other states, the need faced by migrating students in the two sectors is roughly equal. In sum, under a program that is to meet 100 percent of student need, out-of-state students in the public and private sectors would receive nearly identical average grants, whereas those attending home-state private schools would receive approximately twice as much as public-sector students.

The disadvantage of such a need-tested program is that while helping to compensate for institutional price differences, it also masks real cost differences among institutions, and thus curbs a desirable feature of the marketplace it seeks to improve. Since a student would receive a larger grant if he attended a more expensive institution he would have little reason to be thrifty and the college would be less inclined to economize. In order to narrow (but not to eliminate) the tuition gap between the public and private sectors, one could devise a dual program (like New York's tuition assistance program) in which grants were based on income (rather than need), but in which the maximum allowable for private students would be considerably higher than it would be for their public counterparts. This would make up for the large price distortion caused by state institutional subsidies while allowing true cost differences among colleges in either sector to affect student choices. But such a scheme raises other questions. What would it mean for out-of-state students in public universities? Would it enhance one form of student choice— between public and private colleges—while curbing other forms, such as the ability to study in another state or to select a more expensive school within the private sector? Would institutions within each sector not be tempted to boost their prices (if not their costs) in order to take full advantage of the maximum grants available to their students?

Sharing the Costs of Aid

Though states are the dominant force in institutional support, the federal government has played the major role in student aid. In 1974–75, the states spent $456 million on student aid compared with $5.8 billion spent by the federal government.[20] Chapter 5 examines the federal programs at length and assumes that the national government will continue to guarantee a minimum level of resources to all those eligible to attend college. If this remains the principal federal role, then the major student aid question for the states is how—if at all—to supplement the federal initiative. Should they wish to do so, the basic choices are:

1. To ignore the federal initiative and provide a flat grant to students at private institutions, thereby narrowing the tuition gap. This procedure most closely resembles current state policies toward public institutions.

2. To raise the minimum resource guarantee above that provided by the federal government. In this case, the ceiling should be raised only for students attending private institutions in order to compensate for the public-private subsidy differential.

3. To undertake a need-based program that supplements federal basic grants. This state program should be available to both public and private students, but its need-based design would narrow the net price gap between the two sectors.

Because it helps low-income students pay for college while simultaneously reducing the tuition gap for those receiving assistance, the third option is the preferred choice.

MEETING STUDENT NEED

Table 8-6 shows the average awards that would have been necessary in 1974–75 to carry out this preferred option and to meet the *full* needs

20. *Special Analyses, Budget of the United States Government, Fiscal Year 1977*, pp. 165 and 167, and table 8-A2. (Federal total includes veterans' and social security payments.)

Table 8-6. *Average State Award Needed to Supplement a Federal Minimum Resource Guarantee of $1,400, by Region and Sector, Academic Year 1974–75*[a]

Dollars per full-time-equivalent student

	Public		Private	
Region[b]	Home state	Out of state	Home state	Out of state
National	384	758	1,181	758
New England	414	800	1,608	586
South	301	678	842	730
Selected states	407	764	1,397	818

Source: Same as table 8-4.
a. Individual award = costs of attendance − family contribution − $1,400;
= need − $1,400;
Average award = averages from table 8-5 − averages from table 8-4.
Family contribution is estimated according to the schedule used for the basic educational opportunity grant program.
b. See table 8-1 for states included in each region. Students are counted in a state according to residence, and then whether they attend college in their home state or go out of state.

of students above the $1,400 minimum resource guarantee then provided by the federal government.[21] (Other percentages can be worked out; for example, 50 percent of the amounts shown in the table would have covered 50 percent of student needs.) The awards for home-state students would have been three times higher for those attending private as opposed to public institutions. Once again the interstate variability is dramatic for private students, but relatively small for those in the public sector. Grants to home-state private students would have been nearly twice as high in New England as in the South. For those who attended out-of-state private colleges, however, the amounts would have been more uniform.

How much would such a program cost? As shown in table 8-7, a program designed to meet the remaining needs of all students above a $1,400 level provided by the federal government would have cost $3.53 billion in 1974–75 and required a 28 percent increase in the higher education budget of the average state. The increases would have ranged from 126 percent in the District of Columbia to 9 percent in Florida.[22] Restricting

21. Because of the half-cost provision, the basic grant program was not an unconditional guarantee of $1,400. For most students, however, particularly in the private sector, it did assure $1,400.

22. Author's calculations based on table 8-A2. A state's higher education budget consists of state and local appropriations (also referred to as state institutional subsidies), state grants and contracts, and state aid that flows directly to the student.

Table 8-7. *Program Cost of Supplemental Need-Based Grants as a Percentage of State Higher Education Budgets, by Region and Sector, Academic Year 1974–75*[a]

	Public need (percent)		Private need (percent)		Total need	
Region[b]	Home state	Out of state	Home state	Out of state	Percent	Amount (millions of dollars)
National	14.1	2.2	8.2	3.1	27.6	3,527
New England	16.4	5.0	20.8	6.6	48.5	248
South	10.8	1.8	5.7	3.1	21.4	317
Selected states	13.7	1.5	9.6	2.4	27.2	1,533

Source: State higher education budgets, table 8-A2; supplemental need-based grants, author's calculations. State higher education budgets are derived by summing state and local appropriations and state grants and contracts as reported by institutions in the 1974–75 HEGIS survey with direct student aid reported in the 1974–75 survey conducted by Joseph Boyd. (Joseph D. Boyd, "National Association of State Scholarship Programs, 6th Annual Survey, 1974–75 Academic Year" [Deerfield, Ill.: NASSP, 1974; processed].) Local government contributions are included within state budgets since this chapter does not deal with the decisions within states regarding the distribution of the burden between state and local taxes.

a. Grants to cover student need above a minimum resource level of $1,400 (presumed to be provided by federal programs).

b. See table 8-1 for states included in each region. Students are counted in a state according to residence, and then whether they attend college in their home state or go out of state.

a program to home-state students would have cut the average budget increase to roughly 22 percent. These sizable figures force one to ask what fraction of need the state should try to cover, whether it is important to assist students going to out-of-state schools, and how quickly a program of aid should be introduced.

INCREASING THE STATE BUDGET

Another way of thinking about cost is to ask what could be achieved with a 10 percent increase in each state's higher education budget if the increment were destined only for student aid. In that case, as shown in table 8-8, a need-tested grant program for home-state students in 1974–75 could have met an average of 45 percent of the students' remaining need (that is, need not met from a federal minimum resource guarantee). A program that included out-of-state students as well could have met 36 percent of such need. Again, if a 10 percent increase (in constant dollars) were phased in so as to cover the 36 or 45 percent of need by the end of five years, the annual budget impact would have been less than 2 percent.

As before, there are substantial regional differences. With its large number of private students, its higher private-sector prices, and its low

Table 8-8. *Effect on Student Need of a 10 Percent Increase in Each State's Higher Education Budget, by Region, Academic Year 1974-75*

Amounts in millions of dollars

Region[a]	Home-state students[b]			All students[c]		
	Total need[d]	Remaining need after increase[e]	Percent of total need met by increase[f]	Total need[d]	Remaining need after increase[e]	Percent of total need met by increase[f]
National	2,850	1,572	45	3,527	2,249	36
New England	190	139	27	248	197	21
South	245	96	61	317	169	47
Selected states	1,313	750	43	1,533	969	37

Sources: Tables 8-7 and 8-A2.
a. See table 8-2 for states included in each region. Students are counted in a state according to residence, and then whether they attend college in their home state or go out of state.
b. Assumes only home-state students are included in the states' student aid programs.
c. Assumes both home-state and out-of-state students are included in the states' student aid programs.
d. Total cost of grants to cover student need above a minimum resource level of $1,400.
e. Need remaining after a 10 percent state higher education budget increase.
f. The difference between total need and remaining need divided by total need.

state expenditures for higher education, New England would have had the most difficulty establishing a program that covered a substantial portion of student need. In fact, a 10 percent increase in higher education budgets would have paid for a grant program that covered on average only 21 percent of student need in New England states but as much as 47 percent in the southern states.

COORDINATING STUDENT AID

Even after a state has decided on its goals for a student aid program, two difficult coordination issues remain. First, how should assistance from other sources be taken into account? And, second, what, if anything, should be done to influence or control scholarship awards made by colleges subsequent to the award of state grants?

The first set of problems deals with those other sources of support for which the amount is known in advance or can readily be estimated, such as veterans' benefits, social security educational benefits, and basic grants. The issue is whether these funds should be counted as part of family income or as aid that can be used by the student to pay directly for the costs of attending college. The distinction is important because the formulas that estimate a family's contribution to the student typically "tax" family income at a fairly low rate, but if these funds are considered student aid, the state grant to the student will be reduced by a like amount—effectively a 100 percent tax rate.

Currently, most states with assistance programs treat basic grants as student aid and reduce their grants accordingly, while veterans' and social security benefits are handled in a variety of ways. The decision to consider these funds as income or as student aid involves a trade-off between a rigid equity standard (that is, treating all such funds as student aid, thereby keeping program costs down) and a more generous standard that views social security and veterans' benefits as rightful income owed to an individual for other reasons and having little to do with need for educational assistance.

The issue of "control" over college student aid funds is subtle and potentially quite sensitive. Individual campuses use their own financial aid resources for a number of purposes, not just to provide assistance to the needy. They may, for example, provide scholarships to individuals or classes of persons whom they wish to attract as students. While no one has recommended that student aid provided by a college from its own resources should be distributed in a manner specified by the state government, the state does have an interest in seeing that its support does not enable institutions to use their own revenues in ways that run counter to the state's objectives. If no "maintenance of effort" or other requirements were imposed, a sudden increase in state student aid would allow colleges either to reduce their expenditures for this purpose or to redirect their student aid outlays to other objectives.[23] A state that does not wish that to happen would find it necessary to attach certain restrictions, but doing so would exact another price in the form of eroded institutional autonomy.

One specific problem in this area is caused by the federal campus-based aid programs (namely, supplemental educational opportunity grants, college work-study, and national direct student loans). Under the current system used to allocate these funds to institutions, any increase in state student aid serves to reduce the aggregate "need" reported by the college and could reduce its federal student aid allocation. If a new state initiative were concentrated on students attending private institutions, then some federal student aid funds would probably shift from the private to the public sector. If the new state program provided student grants to both sectors based on a percentage of need, however,

23. Thus the state could find itself indirectly subsidizing "athletic scholarships," reduced tuition for faculty children, and other forms of student aid that are not linked to individual need or to the goal of equalizing opportunity.

the federal allocations would remain unchanged as long as the state and federal definitions of "need" were the same.

This issue is significant since the federal campus-based aid at 1974–75 program levels can cover about 24 percent of the need for student aid above the $1,400 minimum resource guarantee level.[24] If the federal campus-based programs continue to operate without major changes, therefore, states would be well advised to use the same definition of need as the federal government. If, on the other hand, the campus-based programs were to be modified, then the problem could be resolved by basing federal allocations on need without reference to the amount of grant aid provided by the state.[25] Of course, if major portions of the campus-based programs are to be eliminated and the funds used in other ways, as recommended in chapter 5, then the problem resolves itself.

Summary and Recommendation

For purposes of using student aid programs to treat public and private higher education more evenhandedly, the policy options can be ranked from less to more attractive as follows:

1. Flat, per-student grants, with the amount based on neither income nor need, operate as institutional aid and have the least to commend them.

2. Grants that take differences in family income into account are preferable to flat grants since they direct subsidy funds to those with the lowest incomes.

3. Grants based on "need" are preferable to grants based only on income[26] because they provide more evenhanded treatment of the private sector in the presence of state subsidies to public institutions.

24. Federal campus-based student aid outlays were $844 million in 1974–75. (*Special Analyses, Budget of the United States Government, Fiscal Year 1977*, p. 165.) This is approximately 24 percent of the $3.53 billion of total remaining student aid need in that same year (see table 8-7).

25. The argument for the current (1977–78) practice is that the federal government wishes to target its funds on the areas where the greatest need exists and this requires that state aid funds be taken fully into account. To avoid undermining state support incentives, federal campus-based aid allocations might be reduced by only a specified proportion (for example, 50 percent) of the state contribution.

26. This is true if the grants are made using the same formula for students in both sectors. If grants go only to private students, or if there are different maximum grant levels for each sector, then an "income-tested" grant is preferable in that it will preserve the cost differentials among institutions in each sector in the net price to be paid by students.

Conclusions

If a state's objective is to equalize the institutional financing of both sectors of higher education within its borders, there are essentially only two approaches that can be used. The first is to increase state subsidies to the private sector through direct institutional aid (or by disguising such aid as tuition offsets payable to all private students), and the second is to reduce the subsidies now given to the public institutions. Various combinations of both approaches are, of course, possible.

Large budget increases would be required in many states if the first approach were attempted.[27] These high costs put direct aid strategies beyond the reach of most states, unless they are introduced gradually. Compounding the policy dilemma further, chapter 7 persuasively documents the political constraints that limit the practicality of the second approach.

These considerations suggest that the states are likely to adopt more modest, more feasible, and less divisive intermediate objectives than full and immediate evenhandedness with respect to state financing of public and private higher education. Three such goals are described below.

Goal One. Prevent further widening of the tuition gap in real terms. The states could adopt policies that treat the two sectors evenhandedly in regard to future changes in the higher education environment, particularly any decline in enrollment or inflation in cost. Such a policy would be based on the assumption that the chief problem facing private colleges and universities is not the present financial disparity between the sectors, but rather that current state policies, if continued, will produce an ever-widening financing gap as inflation continues. This gap could worsen if there are sizable enrollment declines in the 1980s.

This initial goal could be accomplished in two ways. If no subsidy is to be given to private campuses, then the subsidy to public institutions should be set to cover only a portion of future cost increases. This should be done in such a way that the tuition gap—while widening in absolute terms—would remain constant relative to the average family's ability to pay. Public tuition would have to rise as costs increase.[28]

27. As noted above it would have required an 18 percent increase in 1974–75 institutional support budgets for higher education in the average state to equalize nontuition revenues in the two sectors, and a 30 percent increase to equalize state subsidies.

28. If family incomes kept pace with college costs, then this policy would mean

If the state sought to keep public tuition very low, however, the goal of restraining the tuition gap could still be accomplished, but only by subsidies for private institutions. Any increase in the subsidy per student given to the public campuses would have to be matched by increases for the private sector sufficient to keep the constant-dollar gap unchanged. Such aid could take the form of either direct institutional payments to private colleges and universities or indirect support via flat grants (or tuition offsets) for all private-sector students.

Goal Two. Narrow the tuition gap in real terms. Two approaches could also be taken to narrow the real tuition gap. First, any of the schemes described above for boosting state support of private institutions—either through increases in total postsecondary spending or through reallocation of existing expenditures—would reduce the price differential between the two sectors. Once such a step toward equalization were taken, the state could then preserve the narrower gap, as in Goal One, by appropriate adjustments in the state subsidy for the private sector whenever public support rose.

Alternatively, the state could simply leave the existing financial base of both sectors unchanged, but agree to match any increase in subsidies per student in the public sector with equal increases in the private sector. For example, consider a state that subsidizes its public and private institutions at $2,000 and $200 per student, respectively. If the public subsidy were increased by 10 percent, or $200, then the private subsidy would also go up by $200, a 100 percent increase. By freezing the present gap in current dollars, inflation will cause the real gap to diminish over time.

Goal Three. Help students to bridge the gap. Regardless of the policy adopted to reduce or stabilize the tuition gap, some differential will remain between prices students face at public and private institutions. Therefore, a reasonable state objective would be to assist needy students in bridging some or all of that gap.

One method noted earlier would have the states supplement the federal basic grants in order to meet a substantial part of remaining student need. In most states outside of New England, I have calculated that it would have taken less than a 10 percent increase in state higher education outlays in 1974–75 to cover one-third of this need. Such a program of state student aid, particularly if interstate portability were permitted, would be compatible with the federal-state student aid effort advocated

---

that public tuition would rise at the same rate as institutional program costs. Again, I assume identical cost increases in public and private institutions.

in chapter 5. Furthermore, if the recommendations of that chapter were adopted, the federal government would help to pay for the state programs, so that more of the remaining student need could be covered with less burden on the states than the analysis in this chapter would suggest.

IN SUMMARY, there is no question that the states have it within their power to prevent further widening of the financial gap between public and private higher education institutions, to narrow it, and to help needy students bridge whatever gap remains. But none of these is a small or costless undertaking, particularly in those jurisdictions where the problem looms largest. A modest percentage increase in current outlays for higher education would enable most states to move a good part of the way toward evenhanded treatment of the two sectors. However, when those percentages are translated into actual dollars and added on to present state budget levels, they may appear so large as to be politically infeasible. Gradually phasing these costs in over several years would lighten the fiscal burden, particularly if state revenues increase, but even then state officials may find it difficult to persuade themselves that increased support of higher education is justified in an era when enrollments will probably be declining in many jurisdictions. Yet the principal alternative, that of transferring resources from the public sector to the private, is no less formidable, albeit for different reasons.

APPENDIX A: STATE STATISTICAL TABLES

Table 8-A1. *Increase in State Subsidy of Institutions of Higher Education Needed to Equalize Treatment of Public and Private Sectors, by State, Academic Year 1974–75*

| | Percent increase needed per full-time-equivalent student | | |
| | To equalize | To equalize | To equalize |
State	state subsidy	tuition	nontuition revenue
Alabama	13.97	6.99	3.94
Alaska	10.00	1.67	2.54
Arizona	5.17	3.62	0.42
Arkansas	15.26	4.94	6.64
California	17.16	15.18	11.06
Colorado	10.13	14.35	a
Connecticut	52.24	61.06	50.57
Delaware	13.44	5.99	a
District of Columbia	476.11	376.15	235.75
Florida	18.58	16.90	4.21
Georgia	25.20	15.05	13.55
Hawaii	8.09	4.32	3.52
Idaho	28.59	7.23	3.89
Illinois	34.26	28.85	13.99
Indiana	36.52	20.25	3.77
Iowa	47.52	28.57	a
Kansas	13.66	7.50	5.35
Kentucky	20.45	5.48	9.02
Louisiana	16.17	14.07	8.44
Maine	37.10	41.75	18.17
Maryland	17.78	14.25	7.58
Massachusetts	124.86	160.94	70.80
Michigan	15.19	8.94	5.80
Minnesota	28.11	22.29	5.19
Mississippi	10.89	4.97	3.87

(Continued)

Table 8-A1 (*Continued*)

	Percent increase needed per full-time-equivalent student		
State	To equalize state subsidy	To equalize tuition	To equalize nontuition revenue
Missouri	39.48	30.98	30.53
Montana	9.90	5.94	0.83
Nebraska	26.96	15.59	6.79
Nevada	0.59	0.36	0.13
New Hampshire	69.78	79.48	64.93
New Jersey	24.69	25.22	12.94
New Mexico	8.32	5.69	0.38
New York	45.07	41.27	13.99
North Carolina	32.73	18.32	11.39
North Dakota	6.75	3.66	2.83
Ohio	29.40	25.23	9.48
Oklahoma	19.26	14.44	10.27
Oregon	12.99	13.05	4.24
Pennsylvania	43.91	36.89	17.05
Rhode Island	92.35	68.25	28.18
South Carolina	28.31	12.72	4.57
South Dakota	30.73	25.31	4.98
Tennessee	36.93	26.53	17.76
Texas	16.40	14.61	9.88
Utah	54.83	6.69	30.24
Vermont	67.91	68.97	a
Virginia	20.13	16.30	11.13
Washington	14.31	13.57	1.57
West Virginia	18.46	15.82	3.74
Wisconsin	15.12	9.88	4.72
Wyoming[b]	...	...	...
National average	30.48	27.12	18.38

Source: U.S. National Center for Education Statistics, Higher Education General Information Survey for the academic year 1974–75, master tape assembled by Kent Weldon of the National Center for Higher Education Management Systems.

a. Private nontuition revenue per full-time-equivalent student is greater than public nontuition revenue per full-time-equivalent student.

b. Wyoming has no students in private institutions.

Table 8-A2. *State and Local Higher Education Budgets,*
Fiscal Year 1974–75

Millions of dollars

State	Total state and local appropriations (1)	Grants (2)	Direct student aid (3)	Total higher education budget (4)
Alabama	164.955	11.454	n.a.	176.409
Alaska	35.226	20.705	n.a.	55.931
Arizona	179.488	4.250	n.a.	183.738
Arkansas	95.331	3.050	n.a.	98.381
California	1,809.614	103.030	41.057	1,953.701
Colorado	157.811	8.384	7.043	173.238
Connecticut	131.589	8.920	2.667	143.176
Delaware	34.438	1.129	0.080	35.647
District of Columbia	28.424	0.761	n.a.	29.185
Florida	389.282	51.692	4.864	445.838
Georgia	221.818	12.300	1.186	235.304
Hawaii	63.657	0.589	n.a.	64.246
Idaho	49.712	3.820	0.040	53.572
Illinois	620.721	27.747	63.220	711.688
Indiana	235.967	12.160	11.800	259.927
Iowa	164.511	2.669	6.573	173.753
Kansas	139.263	5.189	2.884	147.336
Kentucky	169.438	12.703	0.555	182.696
Louisiana	183.568	8.911	n.a.	192.479
Maine	38.345	1.723	0.384	40.452
Maryland	207.282	9.118	0.321	216.721
Massachusetts	211.634	7.331	11.198	230.163
Michigan	548.976	15.844	18.568	583.388
Minnesota	194.026	8.748	8.526	211.300
Mississippi	119.286	9.249	n.a.	128.535
Missouri	211.467	4.349	3.875	219.691
Montana	35.635	1.959	n.a.	37.594
Nebraska	88.276	3.919	0.286	92.481
Nevada	26.274	2.128	n.a.	28.402
New Hampshire	22.918	1.797	n.a.	24.715
New Jersey	279.781	20.384	27.579	327.744
New Mexico	57.848	3.017	n.a.	60.865
New York	1,209.157	130.000	108.450	1,447.607
North Carolina	344.205	12.299	n.a.	356.504
North Dakota	36.097	0.437	0.256	36.790

(*Continued*)

Table 8-A2 (*Continued*)

State	Total state and local appropriations (1)	Grants (2)	Direct student aid (3)	Total higher education budget (4)
Ohio	359.244	30.913	17.540	407.697
Oklahoma	105.436	3.009	0.540	108.985
Oregon	150.466	6.698	2.334	159.498
Pennsylvania	429.467	44.747	73.191	547.405
Rhode Island	48.176	2.160	1.984	52.320
South Carolina	169.052	8.141	6.080	183.273
South Dakota	30.731	1.072	0.213	32.016
Tennessee	165.800	9.436	3.618	178.854
Texas	614.398	21.742	7.500	643.640
Utah	74.399	5.330	n.a.	79.729
Vermont	17.064	1.094	2.804	20.962
Virginia	215.974	6.474	0.800	223.248
Washington	265.729	7.818	3.196	276.743
West Virginia	77.215	3.325	1.500	82.040
Wisconsin	367.763	11.713	13.669	393.145
Wyoming	29.509	0.424	n.a.	29.933

Sources: Local and state data, same as table 8-A1; student aid data, Joseph D. Boyd, "National Association of State Scholarship Programs, 6th Annual Survey, 1974–75 Academic Year" (Deerfield, Ill.: NASSP, 1974; processed).

n.a. Not available.

APPENDIX B: STUDENT NEED DATA
SOURCES

The estimates of student financial need used in this chapter are based on data prepared by Daryl Carlson for the U.S. Office of Education. The main features of this data base are as follows:

1. Income distribution data are from the annual survey of entering freshmen conducted by the Cooperative Institutional Research Program (CIRP) of the American Council on Education and the University of California at Los Angeles. These data were not available for certain institutional categories in certain states, in which cases national average distributions were used.

2. Cost of attendance data are from the annual survey of college costs by the College Scholarship Service. The budget for out-migrating students equals the home-state budget for the relevant institutional category plus the national average out-of-state charges for that category. Again, for states and institutional sectors with no student budget data, national average costs were substituted.

3. Estimated parental contributions were developed from basic educational opportunity grant summary data with adjustments for state-by-state variations in assets and family size. For each income class, a distribution of family contributions was used, rather than a simple average.

4. The enrollment data refer to full-time-equivalent undergraduates from the HEGIS Opening Fall Enrollment Survey for 1974–75 as part of the U.S. National Center for Education Statistics, Higher Education General Information Survey (HEGIS).

5. To determine the distribution of enrollment between home-state and out-of-state institutions, the HEGIS residence and migration surveys for fall 1968 and fall 1972 were used as the base, with similar data from the CIRP annual surveys used to fill in for states and institutional categories where HEGIS data were not available.

6. Data apply to the state of the student's residence, not, in the case of out-migrating students, to the state in which they were enrolled.

State-by-state estimates of student financial need are available from the author. Because national averages had to be substituted for missing data in various categories, as mentioned above, the national and regional figures used in the text are the most useful and reliable for the purposes of this study.

Chapter Nine

A View from the Campus

David G. Brown and Thomas E. Wenzlau

EDITED BY DAVID W. BRENEMAN AND CHESTER E. FINN, JR.

DAVID G. BROWN, executive vice president for academic affairs and professor of economics at Miami University, was previously provost at Drake University. THOMAS E. WENZLAU, president of Ohio Wesleyan University, was a professor of economics at Lawrence University.

Tables

ALL college and university presidents worry about public policy—now more than ever before. Today, the government is rule maker and referee, provider and contractor, owner and competitor. Almost imperceptibly its scores of regulations and variegated programs of support have penetrated nearly every facet of college life so that virtually all institutions are inextricably linked to public policy.

And, while current policies—developed for a growing market now past—were not designed to harm higher education's private sector, the changing circumstances in which they will be applied could lead to its decay as assuredly as if by design. If private higher education were to absorb all the projected enrollment contraction from today to 1985 (one result of a strategy to preserve public institutions), it could shrink into insignificance—not defunct, to be sure, but little more than a remnant of the once vibrant enterprise that enrolled half the nation's college students.

Private college presidents view the status quo as a clear and present danger to all of them. And yet no two are agreed on a public policy agenda that would favor the private sector, nor on how to present such an agenda to the people who make policy decisions at the state and federal levels. There are many views from the campus.

However, there *is* widespread agreement on what the key issues are (even if there is none on the solutions), and the purpose of this chapter is to concentrate on those discussed in this book, viewing them from the campus perspective: how the college president evaluates government strategy and how he acts—and reacts—in the public arena.

Our investigation of the college scene is necessarily limited in scope; we rely heavily on our own exposure to state and national politics and on our own academic experiences. We also interviewed presidents of several midwestern private colleges and universities and sent brief questionnaires to presidents of Ohio institutions.[1]

1. We did not attempt a random sample of American private campus leaders, but rather elicited selected opinions on the issues introduced in this book. In the main we focused on the four-year liberal arts college. The presidents of six private colleges and universities generously granted us long personal interviews, and we are grateful to each of them. In addition, special thanks are due John D. Millett of the Academy for Educational Development (and former chancellor of the Ohio Board of Regents) and James A. Norton, the present chancellor. We sent questionnaires (dealing chiefly with student aid issues) to thirty-eight presidents of Ohio private campuses and have drawn upon the twenty-nine responses.

Three Criteria for Judging Public Policy

Government involvement takes many forms, some more welcome than others. Good policy from the presidents' standpoint achieves public ends while it respects and preserves the independence of the institution, augments or safeguards the financial resources of the institution, and favors neither the public nor the private campus at the expense of the other.

Independence

A margin of sovereignty is clearly a critical factor for the private institution. More specifically this means the freedom to reach its own judgments about what to teach, how to teach, to whom, and by whom.

No private institution can be wholly independent. All are constrained by general rules (such as commercial law) and subject to general regulations (such as those governing radiation safety). The further erosion of independence caused by social legislation (unemployment compensation, fair labor standards, truth in advertising, and the like) is a necessary and appropriate cost of a better society. Furthermore, private universities that bid on government "jobs" are appropriately obligated to do the job (say, testing the quality of water) according to agreed means (with no polluting effluent) known by all at the time of bidding.

From the private campus standpoint, one test of good government is its commitment to future policies that achieve public goals via means that minimize erosion of independence and that allow diverse institutions to deviate from some public norms in order to preserve other social values.

Financial Impact

High-quality education—whether public or private—is costly. For most private institutions, high costs must be met by tuition levels that limit the number of students able to pay their way. Historically, philanthropists and governments have helped to keep college tuition within bounds by subsidizing the institutions. In the 1973–74 academic year only 36 percent of private college and university revenues came from unassisted student tuition and fees; another 22 percent came from governmental appropriations, grants, and contracts; and about 10 percent more from government-supported student aid, some of it channeled through the institutions and some given directly to the student.[2]

Thus the withdrawal of all government support could result in a decline of up to 32 percent in private college and university income. While the net impact might not seem that large (with fewer students and research contracts, costs would also decline), the precarious financial condition of private campuses means that the disappearance of government funding would jeopardize the economic survival of some institutions as well as the quality of education offered by many.

Justice

Though still genteel, competition among colleges is lively and increasing. All seek students and most seek government contracts. Nothing is more troubling to a private college president than to see students flock to a nearby public college only as a result of low tuition, not because educational quality is necessarily better there, nor because the state institution necessarily spends more per student. Rather, its subsidy from the state (for which the private campus is ordinarily ineligible) allows the public college to charge less, even if it spends the same or more per student as the private institution. When private-sector officials call for equal or just treatment, they mean a public policy that favors neither private nor public campuses, policies that award student subsidies and institutional grants on performance criteria alone and that are blind to the sponsorship of the college.

This intensity of concern for justice is admittedly new. During the 1950s and 1960s, policies to expand public higher education buffered many private colleges from unwanted pressures to expand. The market for students was so vibrant that private institutions could grow or not, as they chose. There was comparatively little stressful competition between public and private institutions.

As leaders of private colleges contemplate a more volatile and menacing future marketplace, they hope that the system will provide for the survival of the best institutions—not just those with heavily subsidized prices. Private colleges and universities are prepared to compete but they

2. Table 2-8. The percentages are based on educational and general revenue.

understandably prefer to do so in an environment that is not economically prejudiced against them.[3]

College Presidents' Views on Government Actions

These three criteria color a campus president's reactions to specific legislative proposals and government actions. Whether the issue is a proposed revision of tax exemptions, a change in state subsidy policy, or new rules regarding eligibility for financial aid, the president normally expresses an institutional opinion.

On the basis of our own knowledge, the interviews we conducted, and the questionnaire responses, we have been able to develop what we consider to be the typical reactions of private college presidents to five different types of public policies that most strongly affect their institutions' well-being: tax policies, student aid (direct and campus-based), federal grants for research and the like, state and local subsidies, and regulatory activities. Table 9-1 indicates what we judge to be the relative importance of these issues to the typical college and university president. We believe, for example, that student aid is the chief concern of the four-year college president whereas federal grants and tax exemptions preoccupy the university president.

Tax Exemptions

Exemptions and other tax expenditures by government on behalf of private campuses elicited uneven responses from college and university presidents.[4] Indirect exemptions, especially the tax treatment of contributors,[5] were emphasized as an important—some said crucial—form of government support. The financial impact of eliminating or substantially limiting these tax preferences is generally thought to be catastrophic for a number of private campuses. The estimates in table 2-7 indicate that gifts from living persons to private colleges and universities would be

3. We speak here primarily of price competition. As McPherson points out in chapter 3, nonprice competition is also important, but less immediately susceptible to public policy.

4. See chapter 6 for a comprehensive discussion of all tax issues from the government's perspective.

5. These include income tax deductions for contributions, exemption of capital gains on donated assets, and exemptions applicable to bequests.

Table 9-1. *Public Policy Issues Confronting Private Institutions of Higher Education, by Major Category, and Relative Concern of Private College and University Presidents: A Subjective Estimate*

Category	Units of concern (total = 100 for each president)	
	Typical four-year college president	Typical university president
Taxation[a]	25	25
Student aid (direct and campus based)[b]	35	20
Federal grants[c]	5	25
State and local grants[d]	15	10
Regulations[e]	20	20
Total units of concern	100	100

Sources: Authors' estimates, based on interviews, questionnaires, and experience.

a. Examples are deductions for donors; exemptions; credits; and local, state, and federal taxes.

b. Examples are veterans' benefits; social security; basic educational opportunity grants; local, state, and federal assistance; national direct student loans; college work-study programs; supplemental educational opportunity grants; loan subsidies; and assistantships.

c. Examples are research contracts, general institutional grants, program support, and capitation grants.

d. Examples are subsidies, research contracts, general institutional grants, program support, and capitation grants.

e. Examples are affirmative action, occupational safety, and patent and report requirements.

cut by more than one-third if revisions to the Internal Revenue Code no longer permitted tax deductions for contributions. Campus spokesmen feel strongly that government must not impair their institutions' access to private income and wealth, nor should it remove existing incentives for individuals (and corporations) to support the college of their choice.

Unfortunately, because many prospective donors tend to have high income and substantial wealth, tax provisions that treat these persons favorably are politically vulnerable. Virtually every congressional effort at tax reform has questioned the charitable deduction. In response to attacks against something they deem a basic right, presidents of private colleges have been active in Washington. However crisis-oriented their defense, it also has a rational basis, for these policies are demonstrably effective in generating private resources for higher education.

In contrast, institutional tax exemptions[6] (as distinct from those to donors or to students) have become so solidly taken for granted that presidents often forget that these are also a part of their government support structure. In interviews, few presidents spontaneously mentioned insti-

6. Exemption from property taxes and frequently from payment of sales and excise taxes on institutional purchases.

Table 9-2. *Impact on Students of Various Tax Exemption Policies at a Representative Private Liberal Arts College*[a]

Dollars per student per year

	Impact	
Type of exemption	Immediate	Long run
Institutional		
Property tax	205	205
Sales and excise taxes on purchases	34	34
Total	239	239
Donor		
Current annual support	155	155
Capital-account gifts	...	155
Total	155	310
Student		
Sales tax on tuition, room, and board	197	197
Total exemptions affecting tuition	591	746
Income tax on earnings and scholarships of students	250	250
Total tax exemption benefits per student	841	996

a. This representative liberal arts college is coeducational with 2,200 students and 165 full-time-equivalent faculty. It had a total budget of $12.5 million in 1975–76 of which $9.4 million represented educational and general expenditures. Tuition and student fees generated $7.2 million, or 77 percent of the total; with $1 million in gifts, $0.3 million in endowment earnings, and $0.9 million from other sources supplying the remaining 23 percent of educational and general spending.

tutional tax exemptions as an important form of aid. When prompted, all recognized their significance but still saw them as basically different from direct dollar support of either institutions or students and appealing in part because they were *not* direct. Even those institutions whose leaders make a moral issue out of rejecting direct government aid aggressively support (or certainly do not reject) tax expenditures made on their behalf. Many presidents perceive a significantly greater distance from government where tax provisions are concerned, a distance that helps insulate their treasured independence. In addition, the imprecision of estimates of the value of tax benefits further lessens the feeling of institutional dependence on government.

Some presidents have little appreciation of the millions of dollars in tax expenditures that support private higher education.[7] Nor have we found that students (and their families) comprehend the value *to them* of tax exemptions to donors, to the institution, and to themselves. In table 9-2 we attempt to translate those large sums into "tuition dollars" for a student attending a representative liberal arts college.

7. Tables 2-7 and 2-8.

In terms of gross dollar impact, the property tax exemption is probably the most important. Measuring its impact is difficult but we assume that the institution is located in a relatively low-tax state and community, that it has a physical plant valued at approximately $42 million, and that it would otherwise pay in excess of $450,000 a year in property taxes. Hence, this exemption saves each student about $205 annually. The university is also exempt from federal excise and state sales taxes on its purchases. These taxes would otherwise be passed on to students in the form of higher tuition. This exemption saves each student an estimated $34 more.

If we accept the conclusion in chapter 2 that about one-third of total giving from living individuals would disappear without donor exemptions, and if we assume that eliminating the deduction from corporate and estate taxes would cause comparable reductions, the institution would lose an additional $340,000 in operating income, or $155 per student. Over the long run, the reduction in capital gifts (for endowment, buildings, and equipment) could be replaced by an additional tuition charge of $155 per student a year.

While not affecting student charges as such, the exemption of tuition, room, and board payments from state and local sales taxes saves the student (or his family) up to 7 percent of the total charge (depending upon the jurisdiction in which the institution is located). At our representative institution, this saving amounts to $197 a year, which the college would otherwise collect for the state.[8]

When all these provisions are added up, the typical student may be benefiting annually from tax expenditures equivalent to as much as $750 in tuition plus perhaps $250 in other exemptions. This constitutes a very substantial government subsidy.

Still another form of tax advantage for higher education—an income tax credit for college costs—is regularly proposed in Congress. It evokes disparate responses from presidents. Some welcome it for their middle-income students who cannot qualify for government student aid programs. Some favor any tax expenditure over any appropriated expenditure program because it is indirect. Others worry that a medium-sized

8. The student (or his family) also benefits from favorable tax treatment of his earnings while a student, his veterans' educational benefits, social security survivor benefits, and sundry scholarships, fellowships, and tuition remissions. The precise value of these benefits is impossible to estimate except for a particular individual or in the aggregate. Nevertheless, their value is not inconsequential and could easily amount to $200 to $300 annually for a typical student. (See table 6-1.)

credit would offset a larger fraction of public college attendance costs, thus worsening the public-private tuition ratio (though not the actual gap). Even those who do not favor a tuition tax credit are reluctant to oppose the idea openly for fear of alienating congressmen and others who view it as beneficial to the private sector. On balance, the tax credit idea does not appear likely to generate ardent or unified political support from private college leaders.

Student Financial Aid Programs

Private college presidents judge student aid to be the most consequential form of federal assistance for their institutions. For one thing, it can provide a partial bridge over the gap in tuition rates between private and public institutions.[9] It reduces the net price to the students concerned and—depending on the provisions—encourages competition. Student choice is further improved when the college supplements government-supplied subsidies with its own funds.

Student aid also makes it possible for institutions to recruit a student population that is more diverse racially, economically, socially, and academically. More recently, as competition for students has intensified, some presidents view these aid programs as critical to their institutional efforts to maintain enrollment.[10]

A further advantage of such programs is that the substitution of government funds for institutional funds releases resources that can often be reallocated to curriculum development and program enhancement. Thus the government indirectly supports improvements in educational quality.

THE STUDENT AID DEFICIT

Although government student aid lightens the institutional burden, such programs also tend to increase the campus "student aid deficit," the

9. See Howard R. Bowen and W. John Minter, *Private Higher Education, Second Annual Report on Financial and Educational Trends in the Private Sector of American Higher Education* (Association of American Colleges, 1976), pp. 80–86, and chapter 3 of this book.

10. It is impossible to determine what would happen in the absence of government student aid programs. Would private institutions have offered a lower net price (tuition) using institutional resources to encourage student heterogeneity? Clearly, they would have made some effort to foster equal opportunity and to avoid declining enrollments, but rather less than with federal aid available.

amount by which total aid awards made by an institution exceed the funds received for that purpose.[11] If a student receives an assistance package consisting of both government and campus funds, the aid deficit obviously is larger by the amount of institutional funds in the package than it would have been if the student had not enrolled. This deficit is ordinarily covered by allocating unrestricted income to student aid.

Many presidents expressed genuine concern about the student aid deficit but their anxiety may not be well founded. They fear that if the deficit grows relative to total educational and general revenues, either tuition will have to be increased or a smaller share of income will remain to purchase educational resources, and neither option is desirable. A rise in the student aid deficit (or in the deficit relative to income), however, does not necessarily worsen the financial situation of the institution. It is necessary to know the cause before reaching that conclusion.

If the deficit increases because additional students are enrolled, the financial pressure will lessen as long as the students bring in sufficient marginal revenues (tuition net of any "discount" of institutional student aid) to cover the marginal costs (incremental operating costs) they impose on the college. If marginal costs exceed marginal revenue, though, the college's financial situation would worsen, straining the resources available for education.[12] In the latter instance, from a financial standpoint, such students should not be admitted.

Higher operating costs that cause increased student aid deficits are a source of concern. With stable enrollment, the college can respond either by raising tuition (and probably the student aid deficit too), or by cutting back in another area of the budget and sacrificing educational quality. Increased aid deficits indicate that the student market in which the college can compete effectively is shrinking, while reduced quality will eventually impair the institution's nonprice competitive position.[13]

11. Hans H. Jenny and G. Richard Wynn, *The Golden Years: A Study of Income and Expenditure Growth and Distribution of 48 Private Four-Year Liberal Arts Colleges, 1960–1968* (College of Wooster, 1970), pp. 97–110. Jenny and Wynn use the term student aid subsidy gap for what we have named the student aid deficit.

12. Marginal costs bear no necessary relation to tuition, depending instead on an institution's current enrollment and operating conditions. If excess capacity exists, marginal costs could indeed be zero.

13. Hans H. Jenny and G. Richard Wynn, *The Turning Point: A Study of Income and Expenditure Growth and Distribution of 48 Private Four-Year Liberal Arts Colleges 1960–1970* (College of Wooster, 1972), pp. 26–31. The trend of an increasing proportion of liberal arts college resources flowing into financial aid evident in the 1960s continued into the 1970s. (See table 2-A4.)

Regardless of the cause of the increased aid deficit, state and federal student aid programs invariably improve the financial picture of the institution. When the aid deficit rises due to higher operating costs, government aid programs that increase with educational costs permit the institution to raise its tuition without as much impact on the students with the least ability to absorb it. Even if government aid remains constant in the face of higher tuition rates—or if the additional aid deficit is attributable to the enrollment of government-aided students who also receive institutional support—it is still financially profitable to have government aid, as long as the aid plus whatever tuition the students can pay cover the added costs the students impose on the college.

The two available alternatives lead to less desirable results. If the college, for instance, chooses not to enroll a particular student who is eligible for government assistance, the student aid deficit might be reduced (compared to accepting him with government aid) but any operating deficit—certainly a more critical financial indicator—would be increased. The difference between the revenues lost from the outside funds the student would have brought with him and the costs avoided because he was not enrolled measures the amount of change. Alternatively, if the institution decides to enroll a student and, instead of government aid, substitutes assistance money from its own resources, the student aid deficit would become even larger than with such aid, and the overall operating deficit would be increased (compared to accepting the aid) by the amount of the forgone government funds. In either case the institution's overall financial position is less satisfactory than it would have been with government student aid.[14]

PREFERENCES AMONG AID PROGRAMS

Elsewhere in this book, the distinction is clearly drawn between direct government aid to students (such as basic educational opportunity grants) and indirect assistance programs where funds flow first to the institution for distribution in accordance with government guidelines

14. This point is discussed further in chapter 2. It may be noted that the only instance when an institution is unmistakably "burdened" is if it accepts a student receiving both institutional and government student aid rather than one who needs no aid whatever. This situation was more important in the past than today. Institutions sought heterogeneity and paid for it with student aid. As the applicant pool has shrunk, substituting a full-paying student for an aided student has become harder, save for the more prestigious schools.

(such as supplemental educational opportunity grants). Many states have aid schemes resembling one or both types of these federal programs. Some presidents make much of this difference. A few refuse (with great public protestation) to accept government funds from the latter programs. Others, less adamant, still prefer direct aid to students because it affords the institution substantially greater insulation from government interference. Presidents taking this position argue that direct government aid to students is more compatible with the goal of maintaining institutional independence.

Other presidents favor college-based aid programs because the funds are more responsive to student and institutional needs. Under the federal supplemental grants program, for example, the financial aid officer has wide discretion in allocating government funds. He is able to use them to pursue the institution's own goals in the student aid arena and can respond to the financial situations of individual students. These presidents believe that, where student aid personnel are capable, the efficiency of a student aid dollar paid to the institution is higher than the same dollar paid directly to students.

The twenty-nine Ohio presidents who responded to our brief questionnaire ranked government student aid programs according to their "preferences." We did not supply criteria. The average ranking for these programs, from most preferred to least, is as follows:

Program	Rank (average based on scale of one to seven)
Ohio instructional grants[15]	2.3
Basic educational opportunity grants	2.8
Supplemental educational opportunity grants	2.8
National direct student loans	4.0
College work-study	4.5
Guaranteed student loans	5.6
Veterans' educational benefits	6.5

The presidents strongly (but not unanimously) favored need-based grant programs rather than loans, work, or veterans' benefits; the latter received a low rating from virtually every respondent.

Our analysis of funds flowing to these same institutions from the vari-

15. A state direct student aid program similar to the federal basic educational opportunity grants.

ous government student aid programs in 1975–76 showed that the Ohio instructional grants were not only the presidents' favorite, but also the largest single source of student assistance funds for these institutions. We doubt that that is entirely coincidental.

The college presidents saw the differences between direct and indirect aid less clearly than most analyses would suggest. One commented, for example, that "OIG, BEOG, and SEOG are grant programs which obviously help directly to reduce the cost differential between public and private institutions." It evidently mattered little to him that one of these programs is state and two are federal, or that two deal directly with students whereas one is college-based. The presidents were evenly divided when asked whether they would prefer an increase in basic or supplemental grants, and their preferences do not appear to be related to the amounts yielded by the two programs.

Among other comments made by the presidents to explain their preference for direct student aid were: "BEOG is more flexible and available to part-time students"; "BEOG has very stringent eligibility . . . requirements"; "BEOG—reaches more students, portable, simplest application for students"; and "SEOG—need for these funds is diminishing as BEOG is more fully funded."

Those of their colleagues favoring indirect student aid wrote: "SEOG need-based grant funds awarded by the institution can provide the student with a wider range of schools to choose from by narrowing the cost difference between public and private institutions"; "The SEOG program is listed first because it is national in scope and because it is administered by the institution, allowing some discretion within federal guidelines."

Amid the general applause for student aid programs emerged one frequently voiced criticism: presidents often find that such programs are not funded for a sufficiently long period or early enough in the year to permit adequate campus planning and good management. Most colleges and universities accept a moral obligation to maintain aid to an eligible student throughout his college career. These obligations are undertaken with the expectation that government programs will continue and will be adequately funded. This too often proves unwarranted. While it may be unreasonable to expect government to provide four years' advance notice of elimination or reduced funding for student aid programs, the seemingly casual way in which Congress and state legislatures change objectives generates vexing financial problems for colleges and universities.

AID PORTABILITY

A current concern among some private college presidents is the "localizing" effect of most state student aid programs. Support that can only be used in the home state imposes an undesirable constraint on student choice and ultimately has a negative impact on the quality of educational experiences of students everywhere. The provision of geographic heterogeneity in a student population helps broaden the experience and horizon of students.

But portability is a mixed blessing for private higher education, and the presidents range from strong support to indifference in their attitude toward it, generally following their institutional interests. We heard little actual opposition even from those presidents whose campuses could be somewhat harmed by greater interstate movement of students, while heads of institutions with regional or national student bodies see portable grants as an important feature of federal or state student aid. The following comments from Ohio presidents are typical:

"This would be a step toward making 'choice' a reality. Many of our students who come from the northern Kentucky area would be eligible for a state grant but cannot receive assistance if they attend a college in Ohio."

"Certainly this would give us greater flexibility with our own dollars. With only about 30 percent of our students from Ohio, we would stand to pick up substantial support as out-of-state students with such grants offset university dollars in the financial aid package."

Others, reflecting an opposite self-interest, were equally candid:

"The majority of our students are Ohio residents. We would not want to encourage a migration of students outside the state."

"Portable OIG could well mean a further out-migration of Ohio students; simple portability may not be the answer, for obviously state legislators are going to want to know where Ohio dollars are winding up and why."

But some had a more detached and balanced view. One observed that such a program "would probably not add a measurably large increase in net in-migration to Ohio, since it would afford the opportunity for Ohio students themselves to go out of state. The concept is a healthy one, however, which if it received sufficient funding on a continuing basis and sufficient publicity with a minimum of bureaucratic circumlocution would benefit private institutions all over the country."

Like so many issues in higher education, portability generates no unanimity. Differing institutional self-interests preclude unified action even when the welfare of students seems clearly to indicate the broadest possible choice of colleges. At the same time, because student welfare is involved, opposition, where it develops, will be subtle and perhaps less effective than support for portable grants. Nevertheless, this division in the ranks of higher education leaders will do little to overcome the parochialism of elected officials ill-disposed to send their state's tax dollars into other jurisdictions.

Categorical Programs

The federal government is a vital partner in virtually all doctoral training, research, and professional programs. Without federal dollars the quality and extent of institutional effort would be greatly diminished in areas such as health, engineering, and the natural sciences. This dependence on government participation has obvious drawbacks. But however oppressive government requirements and regulations may become, few universities, public or private, can afford to risk the loss of federal funds.

Access to research contracts carries a price tag and, while almost all university presidents pay the price, they also urge that some of the undesirable consequences of categorical funding be carefully examined. From the campus perspective, four such potential problems deserve attention: erratic timing of appropriations, changing governmental priorities, rigid contract specifications, and the complicated processes of accountability.

TIMING

Political assemblies and government agencies work on different timetables from faculty senates and research laboratories. Universities are slow-moving and contemplative. Most tasks require long periods of preparation. Faculty must be contracted a year ahead. Scientific equipment must be ordered for delivery six months later. Space must be renovated for special purposes. Sequential experiments, such as moving through twenty-five generations of guinea pigs, must be painstakingly performed.

In contrast, government appropriations are erratic and susceptible to changes in public sentiments. Monies allocated in November often must be spent by the end of the fiscal year. Contract renewals may not be confirmed until a few days before contract expiration.

If the partnership between government and university is to be effective, these differences must be accommodated. Public policy should take account of the university's singular metabolism. Longer-term contracts, earlier assurances of renewal, and phase-out awards must become standard practice.

SHIFTING PRIORITIES

At each crisis—whether the teacher shortage of the 1960s, the Sputnik of the 1950s, or the energy quandaries of today—governments rush for solutions and universities have responded.

Yet urgency raises false hopes and fresh problems. Washington typically pays only for immediate research projects while encouraging the university to move strongly into the chosen field of inquiry. In time, the campus is left to sustain ongoing research and training activities that were originally stimulated by special government grants, while society moves on to other priorities.

To expect fee-paying students or private philanthropists to maintain research and training activity that has lost its power to attract public dollars is simply not realistic. To require universities to promise a "continuation of effort" is neither honest nor practical. It is time to acknowledge that government will get quality research from universities only for whatever period it wishes to pay.

OVERPRESCRIPTION

Money means power. Kingman Brewster laments that all too often the government philosophy is: "Now that I have bought the button, I have a right to design the coat."[16] One precious academic attribute is the ability to generate new and creative solutions. Yet too often institutions are asked to implement ready-made solutions in prescribed ways.

Take, for instance, medical education. Congress recently approved legislation intended to procure more doctors for rural and other shortage areas. One proposal would have required six weeks of training in an underserved area as a compulsory part of the medical school curriculum; noncompliance would have meant no funds. If the legislation had passed with that proviso, most universities would have complied. But one must question the cost and effectiveness of actions that intrude into curriculum decisions, albeit in pursuit of laudable goals, without a full examination of alternative remedies and the feasibility of voluntary rather than coercive

16. Cited in Derek C. Bok, *The President's Report, 1974–1975* (Harvard University, 1976), p. 4 (reprinted in *Harvard Today*, vol. 18, no. 4 [Winter 1976]).

programs. Perhaps changing medical schools is not the wisest way to improve the geographic distribution of physicians.

Each college president had his repertoire of horror stories: public broadcasting grants would be continued only if station wattage is increased and a new person hired in the promotion department; nursing school grants would be continued only if the curriculum were restructured to accommodate "later learners."

The government, according to college presidents, should specify only what is to be done, not how it is to be done. They favor monetary awards granted on a competitive basis by a professional bureaucracy admonished not to impose extraneous requirements on the recipients. However, they recognize that, from the government's standpoint, it is much more efficient to specify exactly what the recipients are to do rather than waiting for them to stumble upon it themselves.

ACCOUNTABILITY

Like other government contractors and grantees, universities must report fully and openly on their use of all tax monies. The issue is how: by completing forms? by being audited? by being visited by a panel of experts? The bureaucracy must account for its stewardship of public funds, but too often it tends to emphasize written reports, mechanistic quotas, and technicalities. Because the institution receiving $5,000 usually has to complete the same form as the one receiving $3 million, proposals from smaller campuses are discouraged. The burden of responding to government requests for information saps the energy of researchers, teachers, and administrators. Streamlined reporting must be joined by a search for less intrusive methods of accountability.

Direct State Support

The problems at the federal level tend to be aggravated at the state level. The presidents we interviewed clearly implied that direct state subsidies and capitation payments are undesirable forms of support. From a public policy point of view, subsidies are a quick and effective way to lure institutions into specific actions—training more nurses, starting a new social welfare program, developing an interdisciplinary project on alternative energy sources. But from an institutional standpoint, the power of unilateral withdrawal or reduction in subsidy forces a dependency relationship that undermines the independence of all universities and their ability to determine the best means of accomplishing desired ends. Several years ago, for example, one large private university found itself unable to sustain its medical school without assistance. Eventually the state agreed to subsidize its operating expenses, and today that support amounts to $8 million a year. State agencies have become actively involved in the discussion of curriculum and have stipulated that at least half the students must come from within the state. Now they are talking about requiring a general practice internship. Individual legislators have threatened hostile votes unless their candidates are admitted to medical school. The administrators in that university say that if they had only known the true conditions of the grant they would never have requested it.

State agency officials and legislators seem to be more prone than federal officials to making threats and placing post hoc conditions upon grants. The state-federal difference appears to be at least in part a function of the greater professionalism of the federal bureaucracy and of the geographic proximity of state officials to the college.

A second worrisome aspect of state subsidies relates directly to the public sector but has a powerful indirect effect on the private as well. During the 1950s, enrollment-based formulas became the normal mode of channeling state dollars into public universities. By placing a bounty on each new head, state governments induced a rapid expansion of institutional capacity, an expansion that was needed if the enrollment bulge were to be accommodated.

The needs of the 1950s were very different from those of the 1980s, but subsidies based on enrollment prevail in most jurisdictions. Public colleges and universities are still being tempted to expand, even though most enrollment forecasts point downward. New mechanisms, reflecting contemporary social needs, must be devised so that public institutions are given the incentive to improve their offerings rather than further eroding the private sector's share of the market.

Regulatory Policies and Activities

By definition this category of government policies should be most threatening to the independence of private institutions. It is no secret that the past several years have brought a pronounced deepening of concern over government regulation. Dissatisfaction with federal "social" legislation has not been confined to academic circles.[17]

No one likes to be regulated, but in the realm of "social" regulations it is awkward if not intellectually dishonest for campus leaders to seek exemption from requirements aimed at praiseworthy objectives and generally levied on myriad other institutions. Typical comments were: "We should be examples. Institutions of higher education should be leading the society in programs beneficial to the society." "We should be embarrassed, even ashamed, to be forced by legislation to pursue courses of action which we should have initiated on our own."

Hence, when presidents protest government regulation, they usually confine their grievances to enforcement and compliance procedures rather than the substance of policies that spawn them. This may be disingenuous, for bureaucracies can seldom tailor their practices to particular classes of institutions, and it might well turn out that no procedures true to the spirit of the legislation could honor all the sensitivities of the academic community.

Presidents were troubled by four different aspects of the problem: first, the draconian nature of regulations that threaten the cut-off of all government monies to a campus failing to comply with a small provision affecting only part of the institution; second, the insistence that educational institutions use forms and procedures designed for commercial establishments; third, the duplication of reporting requirements and oversight by numerous agencies; and, fourth, the cost in money, energy, and inconvenience of retooling portions of the academic enterprise, be they staircases or faculty selection procedures, in uncompensated obedience to government dictates.

Recommendations for Policymakers

Campus leaders want public policy to recognize private colleges and universities as a valuable alternative to government sponsorship of higher

17. See, for example, Bok, *The President's Report 1974–1975;* Charles B. Saunders, Jr., "Is Regulation Strangulation?" *College Board Review,* no. 100 (Summer 1976), pp. 2–5; Carol Van Alstyne and Sharon L. Coldren, *The Costs of Implementing Federally Mandated Social Programs at Colleges and Universities* (American Council on Education, 1976); Ralph Kinney Bennett, "Colleges under the Federal Gun," *Reader's Digest,* vol. 108 (May 1976), pp. 126–30; Karen J. Winkler, "Proliferating Federal Regulations: Is Government Now 'The Enemy'?" *Chronicle of Higher Education,* vol. 13 (December 13, 1976), p. 3.

education, to see them as different from a manufacturing company as well as from a large public university, and to view them as able and willing to serve the public interest. We make the following specific suggestions to state and federal policymakers.

1. *Adopt a wide variety of programs, not a single program.* Public support of private higher education should take many forms, involve different levels of government, scatter administrative responsibility over many agencies. Such variety will reduce the dependency of a private college upon a single source of funds and thereby foster greater autonomy.

2. *Continue favorable tax treatments for higher education, notably the charitable deduction.* These benefits are of great value financially and encroach least upon independence.

3. *Avoid unyielding rules.* Instead, whenever possible, incentives should be provided for those institutions that wish to participate in programs while the right of others not to participate should be maintained.

4. *Seek advice from campus leaders when formulating and administering public policy.* The government could conduct well-publicized hearings before framing legislation, form academic advisory committees, extend peer review procedures, arrange "visiting appointments" in legislative and agency offices, and encourage visits to the campus by agency officials.

5. *Design programs with forward funding and a reasonable phaseout period.* Government programs should provide a stable planning base for colleges and universities. Mindful of institutional commitments to students and faculty, agencies should allot funds at least a year in advance and should maintain some minimal support during a phaseout period.

6. *Continue student financial aid programs by making most payments to students, not institutions.* This policy offers the best insulation from government interference in matters where continued independence is important for the institution.

7. *Establish federal incentives for the portability of state student aid grants.* Such a policy would encourage both access and choice for students, heighten healthy competition among colleges, and reduce the pressure to increase public enrollment.

8. *Cancel the expansionary incentives of the enrollment-based subsidy.* Since the need to expand capacity in higher education has generally ended, we would favor substituting a sliding scale that would subsidize new students at marginal rather than average cost. We also favor states imposing enrollment limits on individual campuses.

9. *Enable private colleges and universities to qualify for all categories of public support, including an extension of state subsidies.* No private college or university should be prohibited from meeting reasonable conditions for obtaining student subsidies or research contracts merely because of its orientation. Public universities should be forced to face competition in all programs.[18]

10. *Relate the amount paid for enrollment subsidies to private colleges to the subsidy paid to public institutions.* Clearly, the payment of higher subsidies for students attending private colleges (because they must pay a higher tuition) is unjustified. Conceptually, the *upper* limit for private subsidy should be the amount actually saved by the state by not supporting the same student at a public university. A fair and feasible amount will normally be lower.

THE YEAR 1978 finds private campus leaders seeking wider recognition of the social benefit of their institutions. They do not ask for direct subsidy or equal support. Rather, they seek the right to bid competitively. They ask not to be burdened by regulation when other means can achieve the same purpose.

Already public policy has catapulted private colleges into a quasi-public arena. The challenge for tomorrow is to devise still more ways to continue the unique contributions of private campuses to public ends.

18. When private colleges are granted the "right to bid," *all* conditions of the contract must be recognized. The state should not discriminate against its own institutions by placing constraints that are not applied to private contractors. Private colleges must agree to the same reporting requirements, the same continuity of effort, the same patent and copyright policies and disclosure agreements. Often these requirements will curtail independence, and private colleges may voluntarily choose not to bid. Having the right to bid against reasonable specifications is the most that can be asked for them.

Chapter Ten

An Agenda for the Eighties

David W. Breneman and Chester E. Finn, Jr.

DAVID W. BRENEMAN is a senior fellow in the Brookings Economic Studies program. CHESTER E. FINN, JR., currently senior legislative assistant to Senator Daniel P. Moynihan, is a former research associate in the Brookings Governmental Studies program.

THERE IS a strong public interest in the future well-being of private higher education in the United States, but it does not coincide with the welfare of individual colleges and universities, widespread as that perception may be, nor can it be adequately understood from the analytic perspective of the private sector alone. The educational, economic, and political complexities discussed in the preceding chapters suggest that any attempt to address policy issues affecting private higher education piecemeal will prove unsatisfactory in the absence of a clear and defensible statement of public objectives. Policy should be responsive to society's overall interests in the nature, scope, and purposes of higher education as it approaches a decade or more of limited growth or retrenchment.

The Public Interest in Higher Education for the 1980s

The remarkable expansion in enrollment and public financial support that has occurred during the last twenty-five years is evidence of the wide range of benefits—public and private, pecuniary and nonpecuniary —that have popularly been considered to flow from higher education. While demographic factors have accounted for much of this growth, even more important have been the increases in high school completion rates and college attendance rates within successive age cohorts.[1] Equality of educational opportunity, although loosely defined and imperfectly attained, became (and remains) a well-established goal for education policy.

Higher education evolved during this period from an elite to a mass phenomenon, and a parallel change occurred in its social role. As the number and proportion of eighteen- to twenty-two-year-olds attending college increased, higher education became the principal institution for aiding young people to make the transition from adolescence to independence. The alternatives to college are essentially limited to military service, crafts and trades, unskilled employment, job training, or unemployment. American society has come perilously close, therefore, to mandating college for everyone—and to branding as failures all who

1. Allan M. Cartter, *Ph.D.'s and the Academic Labor Market* (McGraw-Hill, 1976), p. 50.

413

elude that mandate.[2] Furthermore, by subsidizing a portion of college costs, the state tips the balance in favor of one particular form of human capital development, since those who forgo college are seldom provided with an equivalent subsidy for other forms of skill acquisition. Much of the recent popular criticism of college is, in part, a reaction to the limited options for youth and the pressures for universal college education.[3]

Consequently, one prudent step toward developing a sound higher education policy for the 1980s would be the planning of a coherent human resource program for young people that would integrate higher education with various skill-development programs. Although the purpose of this book is not to prescribe or evaluate specific types of noncollegiate postsecondary training, nor to discuss the types of program reorganization required to produce a comprehensive youth policy, sound educational policy must go beyond college choices.[4]

The Marketplace for Undergraduates

In regard to higher education, the factor that dominates most policy debates is the projected shrinkage of the traditional college-age population in the 1980s and early 1990s. Whether enrollment stabilizes or de-

---

2. We do not mean to dismiss the wide array of other postsecondary educational experiences already available in many types of institutions—from public "technical-vocational" schools to apprenticeships to proprietary schools specializing in flight training, cosmetology, computer programming, and the like. There is an obvious demand for such offerings, and many of them are well conceived and effectively run. But at neither the state nor the national level have they been integrated into a set of systematic policies for the education of young people.

3. See, for example, Caroline Bird, *The Case Against College* (David McKay, 1975).

4. In commenting on a draft of this chapter, Howard R. Bowen, R. Stanton Avery Professor of Economics and Education at the Claremont Graduate School, criticized this argument:

> I can agree with you that higher education is not the only possible transition from dependent youth to independent adulthood, or that it is a desirable or feasible experience for all people. But I would argue that the burden of proof is on those who argue that others are better transitional institutions. What are they? What evidence is there that such institutions will be put in place before the end of the century? Even if such institutions were created (I assume they would be work or apprenticeships), they would probably only delay education until a later stage in life and not permanently reduce the need for higher education. The nation would surely still want to work toward providing education up to the reasonable capacity of its people and this calls for a lot more education than we are now offering. (Correspondence with the authors.)

clines significantly from current levels, there is a strong presumption that the nation currently has sufficient places for full-time undergraduate study to accommodate student demand for a decade or more. Continued growth in the number of institutions or of college faculty seems unlikely. Hence, the challenge is to make efficient use of current facilities and personnel. If substantial enrollment shrinkage should occur, the issue will become one of managing retrenchment in a way that preserves and enhances the capacity of higher education to meet society's demands upon it.

Some thoughtful observers do not accept enrollment stabilization or decline in the 1980s as a given. Howard R. Bowen writes:

> My main point relates to the underlying assumption that enrollments will, and should, decline. My arithmetic tells me that if women attended college at the same rate as men, if poor people attended at the same rate as middle- and upper-income people, if people in Alabama attended at the same rate as those in Arizona, and if adults attended in larger numbers, enrollments could double by the end of the century. I would not argue that this is likely to happen but I would contend that a basic question for public policy—one that is not settled—is: what level of enrollment is desirable? The answer is not necessarily that enrollments should merely follow demographic trends. (Correspondence with the authors.)

Bowen is clearly correct in arguing that enrollment levels respond in part to policy choices and need not simply follow demographic or labor market trends.[5] It is also a fact, however, that Allan M. Cartter's projections of declining academic demand for PhDs in the 1970s and 1980s were disregarded for several critical years during the 1960s while graduate programs continued to expand as if no end were in sight. Many of the problems currently facing graduate education could have been avoided if those projections had been taken seriously. We are reluctant therefore to base our policy discussion for the 1980s on the possibility that enrollment might expand markedly, rather than stabilize or decline.

THE NEED FOR DIVERSITY

The overriding goal for higher education policy is to ensure that whatever resources are available are used efficiently to accomplish society's educational objectives.[6] Any truly efficient policy must consider the value of diverse settings, attuned to the varied needs, abilities, and in-

5. These issues are discussed in greater detail in chapter 3.
6. "Efficiency" is used here in the broad economic sense that includes concern for both resource use (costs), and outcomes produced (benefits).

terests of the college population. Some students thrive, for instance, in large universities, others in small colleges; some like competitive settings, others prefer nurturing environments; some want to live away from home, others must commute; some desire technical and vocational preparation, others favor the liberal arts; some want a secure, in loco parentis institution that inculcates values and tells them what to study, others want one offering a vast smorgasbord of electives; some seek schools with high academic standards giving entry to postgraduate study, while others prefer to test the water in an open admission institution; and there are always those who want schools with a tradition of serving a particular race, sex, or denomination.

The United States is fortunate to have colleges and universities that are capable of supplying educational offerings to meet this wide range of preferences. Such variety is a tribute to the absence of centralized planning, the stress on local initiative, the concern for institutional autonomy, and the presence of a large and thriving nongovernmental sector within higher education.

The need for diversity, then, provides a first rationale for a public interest in private higher education. The public sector could supply such heterogeneity only through expansion or radical change (for example, by converting community colleges or comprehensive universities into small, four-year colleges), but either course would be wasteful in a period of limited growth. Furthermore, public institutions cannot be affiliated with religious denominations and are unlikely to serve a single race or sex.

Inasmuch as the private colleges and universities are already well established, simple parsimony suggests that society should strive to use their resources rather than continue to expand its public sector. If the rationale above is accepted, however, policymakers will have to adopt a national perspective toward higher education. Few states currently offer within their borders a complete assortment of postsecondary programs, and since there is no need (nationally) to increase the number of full-time undergraduate places, greater student mobility across state lines should have a high priority for the 1980s. Students should be matched with colleges that meet their requirements wherever the colleges are located. During the years of higher education's expansion, it made sense to build new campuses near the potential clientele, but for at least the next decade, the focus should be on moving students, not creating new institutions.

DEVELOPING A NATIONAL "SYSTEM"

Viewing the 3,000-odd colleges and universities within the United States as a national "system" requires fundamental changes in outlook and policy. Higher education planning for public institutions is currently an activity of the individual campuses (or of multicampus systems) and of statewide agencies. In recent years, private institutions within each state have been integrated into state planning activities with varying degrees of involvement and success. Regional compacts, such as the Western Interstate Commission on Higher Education, the New England Board of Higher Education, and the Southern Regional Education Board provide some interstate planning capability and a means for encouraging the sharing of educational resources, but the effectiveness of such agencies is limited by the autonomy and budgetary powers of the individual states. The latter have understandably focused on their own institutions and until recently have largely ignored the private colleges within their borders, as well as out-of-state universities. Financing policies naturally reflect this attitude: state residents are provided with subsidized tuition at state institutions, nonresidents are charged higher rates, and residents who attend private or out-of-state public institutions receive little, if any, subsidy from their home states. Not only do prices charged bear little relation to costs, but interstate mobility is discouraged. While many students are perfectly content to attend college near home, for some these "tariff barriers" cause serious financial and educational inconvenience.

Students should not be driven to enter particular colleges simply because of the vagaries of the ways in which public subsidies are administered. The allocation of resources to institutions, and the related decisions regarding which campuses and programs should thrive and which fail in the 1980s, can best be determined in response to student choice.[7] Reasonable accommodation of student interests will call for some programs to change, for new ones to be developed, and for others to be dropped; for some schools to expand and for others to shrink. A decen-

7. One reader of an earlier draft points out that this is "a terribly expensive mandate." We certainly do not expect public policy to accommodate every passing educational fancy or incidental student preference. Higher education cannot afford to be tyrannized by its consumers any more than by its benefactors. But this argues even more strongly for a national marketplace, so that a student wishing to study Sanskrit can be directed to a university already providing it rather than demand that it be offered by the nearest campus.

418   DAVID W. BRENEMAN AND CHESTER E. FINN, JR.

tralized process based on informed student choice is society's surest mechanism for guiding such evolution. This *is* a marketplace, and should be helped to work as such, rather than be impeded by public policy. If the nature and terms of fair competition can be established, society would have some reason to believe that the institutions and programs that survive would be the "right" ones.[8]

Institutional "survival" per se is *not* our primary concern, of course, nor do we regard it as a satisfactory criterion for public policy. If the supply of higher education has outstripped future demand, and if policies geared to reasonable social objectives such as equal opportunity do not stimulate enough demand to match the supply, it follows that the supply must shrink. No public interest is served by artificially stimulating demand or supporting superfluous programs and institutions, save where other (nonteaching) considerations are compelling.[9] But disparities in college prices caused by uneven institutional subsidies are not themselves a valuable form of diversity and impede rather than enhance the optimal working of the student marketplace.[10] (Price variation caused by true differences in program costs or institutional outlays is another matter.) Private and public campuses should have an equal opportunity to survive and prosper and should be equally liable to shrinkage and, in extreme circumstances, to closure.

THREE PROVISOS

Encouraging interstate portability of subsidies appears to be one logical means of developing a national system of colleges and universities and of diversifying educational offerings open to students. However, three limitations should be borne in mind.

8. An effective national marketplace requires ready student access to information about educational offerings (and prices) around the country, and it also requires at least a modicum of national planning wherein someone is courageous enough to say that college *A* is not very good, despite its claims. We hope that the higher education community—the national associations, the accrediting bodies, groups of respected scholars, and the like—will take seriously this responsibility for "consumer protection" and planning, for if it does not the pressures will increase for government to do so, the inevitable result being further regulation.

9. It may, for example, be important to support the work of productive scholars in disciplines that do not attract enough students to gain their support through the undergraduate marketplace.

10. While the familiar argument about the "social" versus "private" benefits of higher education cannot be settled, whatever social benefits are produced from enrollment at a state-supported college are also generated from attendance in an independent university, no matter where it is located (and vice versa).

First, the resistance of legislators ought not to be underestimated. Many object to underwriting the cost of students from other states and to supplying tuition income via student aid to colleges and universities located in other jurisdictions. Those states—Pennsylvania is a notable example—that have allowed their student aid grants to be used elsewhere are outnumbered by those that confine their subsidies to their own citizens and their own institutions, and in many places these barriers are rising, not falling.

Second, the number of persons affected is relatively small. Out-of-state students account for just 14 percent of total enrollment,[11] and there is no reason to presume that this figure will rise dramatically; attending college in another state is generally an elite rather than a mass educational ambition. Moreover, it is usually a realistic one only for full-time students without other responsibilities.

Third, enrollment of part-time and older students has grown in recent years. Many are employed and have families; they are therefore not mobile and can only be served if opportunities are provided locally. Service to this new student population does not, however, necessarily dictate the expansion of public campuses. Opportunities for teaching them in existing private institutions should be fully explored; tuition subsidies to enable part-time students to attend private universities are likely to be more efficient than expanding public institutions or building new ones.

Two More "Marketplaces"

The nation's higher education system performs another function—the creation of new knowledge through basic research and scholarship—that is related to, but distinct from, the transmission of knowledge from one generation to the next. Herein lies an additional rationale for a public interest in private higher education, an interest reasonably well served by a second type of "marketplace," the peer review system for allocating research grants. Yet a third "marketplace" is provided by the idiosyncratic world of private philanthropy, which in higher education is capable of fostering pedagogical excellence, of encouraging bold innovation, of underwriting outright experimentation, of succoring odd

11. Fall 1972 resident degree-credit enrollment. (W. Vance Grant and C. George Lind, *Digest of Education Statistics, 1975 Edition*, National Center for Education Statistics [Government Printing Office, 1976], p. 77.)

institutions, of sustaining schools with "viewpoints" and "values" and even theologies.

RESEARCH

Although demographic fluctuations and changing labor market requirements may shrink the demand for full-time undergraduate and graduate education in the 1980s, society's appetite for scientific and technical research and for humanistic scholarship is not determined by the same forces. It is entirely possible that the demand for research will increase while the demand for education declines. This country has heavily relied upon its universities for basic research and scholarship, and there is no evidence that this reliance is diminishing.[12] Government (and private) agencies interested in research and kindred activities ordinarily adopt peer review and other quality-based procedures to direct funds into universities best able to perform particular projects and carry out defined activities. The number of institutions used for this purpose is now adequate; therefore, public policy should be concerned not with adding to the supply of research universities, but with sustaining quality. This is quintessentially a *national* undertaking, and the nation will require public policies—mostly federal—to promote it. At present the private universities conduct a substantial proportion of the nation's scientific research and are also preeminent in humanistic scholarship and many of the professions. Hence, policies that sustain this "marketplace" are apt to benefit the private sector also.

The dilemmas of undergraduate finance and pricing policy caused by a dual system of higher education do not have their obvious counterparts in the realm of research. Most policy issues that concern universities in this area have not typically been posed along public-private lines. However, any discussion of society's interest in higher education for the 1980s would be incomplete without a few observations on the importance of university-based research and scholarship and the need for a national strategy to sustain it.[13]

12. See Bruce L. R. Smith and Joseph J. Karlesky, *The State of Academic Science: The Universities in the Nation's Research Effort* (Change Magazine Press, 1977), particularly chapter 3, "The Changing Relationships: Universities and Other R&D Performers."

13. In emphasizing "excellence" at the level of graduate training and research, we do not mean to slight the equal opportunity goals that energize our discussion of undergraduate education. Disadvantaged students need access to graduate and professional schools, too, although it is to be hoped that solid undergraduate education will equip them to compete on equal terms. (For further discussion of this issue, see

It should go without saying that the more heavily the managers of governmental research and other categorical programs rely on academic excellence and scholarly merit in their funding decisions, the better they will serve the long-term interests of the nation's leading universities, public as well as private. That axiom smacks of elitism, but it bears repeating because the academic community is not always as forthright as it might be in favoring excellence over democracy in funding decisions, and government agencies are under heavy pressure to distribute their funds more evenly.[14] With few exceptions (for example, Title III of the Higher Education Act of 1965, the "strengthening developing institutions" program) the categorical federal programs help to reinforce already strong universities, and not to bolster those that are faltering. On those terms, the major private universities can hold their own, and federal policy should continually challenge them to do so.

The axiom has four corollaries.[15] First, while government agencies are always tempted to concentrate on applied research and development activities with visible results, and while universities can often assist with these, it is the support of basic research that replenishes the nation's intellectual capital and invigorates scholarly institutions. Second, the research faculties must renew themselves, and the primary way they do this is by training graduate students; it is shortsighted to regard the current "PhD surplus" as justification for eliminating support for graduate programs.[16] Third, although public policy should never encourage them to be inflexible, universities are ponderous creatures that depend on stable funding patterns and are vulnerable to sudden shifts in government support. Finally, while Washington agencies understandably want the most research mileage for their money, universities have a valid point when they assert that without adequate support for overhead expenses they cannot long continue to do the nation's work. This is especially true of

National Board on Graduate Education, *Minority Group Participation in Graduate Education* [NBGE, 1976; available from National Academy of Sciences].)

14. A recent report from the academic community that does argue strongly and persuasively for resource allocation based on merit is *Research Universities and the National Interest: A Report from Fifteen University Presidents* (Ford Foundation, 1978).

15. These and related concerns are examined more closely from the perspective of college and university presidents in chapter 9.

16. Detailed discussions can be found in two reports of the National Board on Graduate Education: *Federal Policy Alternatives toward Graduate Education* (NBGE, 1974), and *Outlook and Opportunities for Graduate Education* (NBGE, 1975), and also in *Research Universities and the National Interest*.

private campuses, which lack the basic institutional subsidies that the states provide for their public counterparts, and which are correspondingly more dependent on the federal government. No one wants to encourage profligacy, but it is simply a fact that myriad university operations, from the power plant to the research library to the provost's office, must function smoothly or the institution cannot properly assist with more specific national missions.

PHILANTHROPY

A related danger for higher education as it enters a prolonged period of limited growth and stable (or diminished) resources is the onset of rigidity—a loss of vitality and of the ability or willingness to innovate. Avoiding this problem will be particularly difficult for an educational system that has been accustomed to experimenting through growth and changing by addition—not substitution—of resources. Resisting tendencies toward stagnation is primarily an institutional task, but one that should be of concern to educational policymakers. Improving the student marketplace as discussed above will encourage campus responsiveness, but there is another "marketplace" fairly well attuned to the problem, and hence worth noting and preserving, even at some cost in public resources: the world of the private donor.

Flexibility and the capacity for innovation are not the exclusive preserves of higher education's private sector, which receives three-fourths of these resources, but they are often found there. "Many of the most interesting educational reforms that . . . I have studied," David Riesman concludes from his decades of observation, "have been easiest to undertake in private colleges, which remain small (and recruit a distinctive constituency) by choice, and which do not need to fear direct legislative or other political reprisal if the experiment turns sour."[17] Public subsidies cannot reliably (or constitutionally) assure these characteristics, whether they are fed through the student marketplace or the "marketplace" of high-quality research and professional training. Nor are outright public subsidies needed, or even additional public policies. All that is needed is to continue doing something that is already being done, which is making it attractive (chiefly through the tax laws) for private donors to use their money for purposes that the nation wants to advance but that the government cannot readily finance in any other way.

17. Personal communication to the authors.

Emil Sunley's analysis of the charitable deduction in chapter 6 sets forth the policy dilemmas posed by these controversial tax provisions. While modest refinements may be tolerable (for example, some change in the tax treatment of appreciated gifts), eliminating or limiting these provisions would be detrimental to higher education, particularly to its private sector, unless accompanied by new and—in our judgment—unlikely forms of direct support. Although the "marketplace" of private philanthropy confers markedly uneven benefits on colleges and universities, those that gain the most from it would be hard pressed to hold their own without the quarter-billion dollars induced by the charitable deduction.[18] We are therefore wary of otherwise laudable tax "reforms" that might erode donors' incentives to support higher education. We are not unconcerned with the equity, progressivity, and uniformity of the tax structure, nor do we contend that the financial well-being of private colleges is more important than these goals. But we do ask lawmakers to recognize that hundreds of the nation's private colleges and universities, including many of its most eminent and some of its most unusual, depend heavily for their income on their prowess in the "philanthropic marketplace," and that the charitable deduction is commensurately important to them.

THE NEED FOR PRIVATE INSTITUTIONS

Our emphasis on this trio of marketplaces—for students, for research, and for philanthropy—bespeaks a judgment that centrally planned and administered higher education "systems" by definition cannot adequately safeguard institutional autonomy and academic freedom. Pluralistic governance and independence are intrinsically important to untrammeled inquiry, scholarly excellence, and educational diversity. With the best will in the world, the fifty state governments are unlikely to emphasize adequately such subtle, vulnerable, and inherently "private" values. While we do not anticipate a surge of neo-McCarthyism in the statehouses, the fashions of good government today stress public values—accountability, equality, uniformity—that cannot alone sustain the type of academic enterprise the nation requires in its third century. Although the existence of a dual system of higher education causes unending headaches for policymakers and accounts for the bulk and complexity of analyses such as this one, we nevertheless conclude that society cannot

18. The estimate is for 1973–74 and refers only to gifts from living individuals to private colleges and universities. (See table 2-7.)

satisfactorily attain its educational objectives by relying on public institutions alone. If higher education's private sector did not already exist, it would be necessary to create it. Since it does exist, it is necessary to find appropriate means of sustaining it.

A Policy of Drift?

Before embarking on an examination of new policies, it is necessary to speculate briefly on the probable direction higher education would take should it simply drift on current policy tides. Inertia, too, represents a policy option.

No wholesale disaster will befall the private sector. Scores of strong institutions will continue to attract students, teach them well, add to human knowledge and, somehow, contrive to find the necessary resources. If 300 campuses close, 1,200 will endure. If enrollment falls by 20 percent, four-fifths of today's impressive numbers will remain. If average tuition rises above $5,000, many families will still pay it.

Nonetheless, serious problems will lie ahead if this course is adopted, hampering society's overall ability to gain what it seeks from higher education.

First, the states will define their interest in higher education in parochial terms and erect barriers to student mobility. Educational quality may suffer, as uniform (and politically defensible) financing formulas fail to differentiate functions, and as each state's impulse toward self-sufficiency dictates that six mediocre programs shall remain in a six-state region that needs perhaps two or three that are strong. The leading public research universities may be particularly hard pressed to maintain their competitive advantage in the struggle for state appropriations.

Second, shrinking enrollment within a state will intensify competition for students and resources. The political dynamics of the legislature will make it all but impossible to close down extraneous public campuses, or to perform radical surgery on them. Instead, a number of state institutions will fall victim to a wasting disease. Seeking to cure themselves by minimizing competition and resource diversion, they will oppose measures to bolster the state's private colleges or to ease student access to them. Similarly, some private campuses will succeed in getting increased state support on grounds that are more political than educational.

Third, while many states will continue their modest programs of aid to private higher education, the private sector will bear the brunt of whatever retrenchment takes place. Fearful about the future viability of their institutions, professors may leave for more secure berths on public campuses. More vulnerable than their public counterparts to enrollment fluctuations, the second- and third-tier private colleges will have trouble sustaining themselves with fewer students. A widening tuition gap, coupled with the public sector's determination to maintain its own enrollment, will set in motion a painful cycle wherein fewer students will lead to shrunken resources followed by educational decay, which in turn will make it harder to attract students. The allure of elite private campuses, combined with their greater ability to cut the "net price" through student aid, means that they too will draw students away from their less prestigious brethren.

Fourth, the federal government will maintain its strong commitment to access symbolized by the basic educational opportunity grants, but that program's appetite for funds will consume most of the resources available for need-based student aid. The cumbersome and controversial campus-based programs will not hold their own in real terms and may in time vanish, as Washington determines that, if it cannot afford to do everything, it should at least do one thing well. To keep its promise of equal educational opportunity, it will provide access through subsidies for low-income students, leaving it to the states to cover instructional costs, whether through low tuition or more student aid, and also leaving the states with the costlier and more ambiguous task of providing choice.

Fifth, a middle-class society faced with mounting educational costs will persist in its efforts to find ways of lightening the burden on the middle-income family. Since it is hard to make a convincing case for direct aid to such students, this quest will take three forms: continued pressures to reduce tuition in state institutions, to raise the ceiling on student aid to cover higher-income groups, and to renew the campaign for indirect federal subsidies in the form of tuition tax credits or deductions. Some hard-pressed private colleges will join in this tax credit campaign, finding tax relief the most salable way to cut the "net cost" burden borne by the students they wish to enroll. Some public institutions will not object, so long as they are not asked to give up the state subsidies that hold down their tuition rates.[19]

19. While tax credits for higher education are dubious public policy, it would not be irrational for state colleges and universities to favor them. Because public-sector costs of attendance are lower than those in the private sector, a modest tax credit—say $250—would compensate families for a larger fraction of those costs. The net tuition gap would not be affected, but the ratio would shift in favor of public institutions.

Sixth, with its emphasis on access and possibly on tax breaks for those who do not qualify for basic grants, Washington will continue to turn a blind eye to the actual composition of the higher education industry, to the welfare of individual colleges and types of institution, and to such attractive but politically unrewarding proposals as interstate mobility and student choice. In the state capitals, educational planners and co-ordinating boards will endeavor to include the private sector in their plans, but planning processes developed too late to mold the higher edu-cation industry in an era of growth will not be effective in shaping its retrenchment. Institutional self-interest will generate strong political pressures, generally favorable to the public sector, that will swamp the efforts of the planners, whose only weapon will be persuasion in nego-tiating with the governor and legislature. Once the private institutions realize that statewide planning can do little for them, they too will defect to the statehouse, where campuses that are lucky or well connected will win ad hoc subsidies that will buttress them while further vitiating the work of the planners.

Seventh, as a few jurisdictions do provide fresh institutional subsidies for some of their private campuses, these schools will tend to lose their private character and become indistinguishable from traditionally public colleges. Perversely, those private institutions that fare best in the state policy arena are the most likely to lose the characteristics that made them private and worth preserving. They will trade independence for new forms of dependency on the state.

Admittedly, this is a gloomy vision, and not every feature of it will touch every state, let alone every campus. Differences among jurisdic-tions and institutions will persist, and some will enter the 1990s with few scars from the battles of the 1980s. There is no reason to expect the proven resilience and inventiveness of American higher education to vanish, just because some of its analysts are apprehensive.

But there is no reason to be sanguine, either, when the stakes are high, the risks considerable, and when each month brings more accounts of internecine warfare in academic ranks. Indeed, with tensions mounting so fast during a period of larger-than-anticipated enrollment (1974–77), one can reasonably expect much greater animosity a few years hence. Problems that look merely stubborn in 1978 are apt to seem insoluble in 1985.

Therefore this is an opportune time to chart alternatives to a policy of drift. But as veteran voyagers well know, it will not be easy. National higher education policy poses one conundrum after another, except for those willing to presuppose boundless resources and goodwill. Parsimonious solutions tend to ease one problem by exacerbating another. Clear-cut choices pit one academic faction against another. The buttressing of one group of institutions or students is generally a menace to another.

Preferred Policy: A National Student Marketplace

A policy of drift will not achieve the goals for higher education in the 1980s discussed earlier, nor can state or federal policies alone be expected to achieve them. Left to their own devices, the states will concentrate on their own residents and institutions, which is perfectly rational behavior from each state's standpoint.

Furthermore, no single set of policies can address all concerns. Hence, the general policy framework that we advocate below is neither a "comprehensive solution," nor a detailed set of formulas. Instead, it is a way of thinking about the financing of full-time undergraduate education and the respective roles of federal and state governments in establishing a workable national marketplace that serves the public interest.

The federal government could produce an effective national marketplace, even given current state behavior, if it were willing to subsidize the additional costs that students incur when they attend a private or out-of-state public college in preference to a home-state public campus. But the potential cost of such a program rules it out as a serious option.

Over two million students currently attend private campuses or migrate to other states, and a national program of tuition offsets could not distinguish those students who would migrate or attend private campuses without the subsidy from those whose college choice would be altered by it. Consequently, tuition offsets could not be limited to just those students whose behavior it would change, but would also have to include many for whom the subsidy would simply be a windfall. The program would be very expensive. Hartman estimates that an additional outlay of approximately $4.4 billion would have been required in 1973–74 to provide private college students and out-migrants with the same level of subsidy they would have received if enrolled at a home-state public campus.[20] While no one seriously proposes that Washington undertake

20. See table 5-A4.

such an expenditure in order to equalize the subsidies available to students, some versions of the tuition offset proposal would go a considerable distance toward closing the tuition gap.[21] Moreover, we share the skepticism of Gladieux and Wolanin (in chapter 4) that federal lawmakers would be willing to "solve" the private college financing problem in this manner. Thus only through the purposeful linking of state and federal financing policies can the goal of a national marketplace for higher education become a reality.

Further, we believe that Washington will (and should) continue to concentrate its money on need-based student aid[22] as opposed to direct institutional support. Our stress on the desirability of a national student marketplace and our assumption that the public interest does not require the survival of all 3,000-odd colleges and universities through the 1980s rule against direct federal institutional support.

The states' principal concern should be the tuition gap between public and private sectors and how to narrow (or at least stabilize) it. As noted in chapter 1 and elaborated by Colin Blaydon in chapter 8, states that wish to freeze or narrow the tuition gap have two basic options, with vastly different budgetary and political implications: (1) subsidies for state institutions can be reduced and the funds redirected into need-based student aid, forcing public colleges and universities to raise their tuition (or lower their quality); or (2) states can increase support for private institutions and their students through direct institutional grants or tuition offsets, thereby enabling private campuses to stabilize or lower their charges.

The first option—making the public sector more like the private—entails low budget outlays but high political costs, whereas the reverse strategy—making the private sector more like the public—minimizes confrontation at the cost of enlarged expenditures. Although leaders in each state may grope toward an equilibrium position somewhere along this fiscal-political continuum, the trade-off between political and budgetary costs is real, and promises to become more vexing in the next decade.

21. The National Council of Independent Colleges and Universities advocated a joint federal-state tuition offset program limited to students attending private colleges. This was estimated to cost between $500 million and $2.5 billion, depending upon the portion of average public subsidy covered. (See discussion in chapter 5.)

22. The current campus-based student aid programs take into account both family income and college costs, while the basic grants program is income-tested and responsive to college costs over a more limited range. See chapter 5 for a critical evaluation of these programs.

The argument for a national student marketplace for undergraduate education can therefore be translated into the following four operational requirements:

1. State and federal financing policies should be purposefully linked.

2. Price barriers to interstate mobility of students should be reduced.

3. Federal programs should continue their emphasis on need-based student aid rather than direct institutional aid.

4. Tuition differentials between public and private sectors should be stabilized or narrowed.

Perfecting the Marketplace

Among the various policy options discussed in this book, the one that comes closest to meeting these requirements is Robert Hartman's proposal in chapter 5, which calls for an explicit attempt by Washington to change state financing practices by providing the states with an incentive to increase significantly their direct student aid programs. The mechanism for effecting this change would be federal matching grants to states that establish (or expand) portable, need-based scholarship programs usable in both private and public institutions. The federal government would offer to pay x percent of each additional dollar spent on portable state scholarships, so that a dollar for scholarships would cost the state (100 minus x) percent, whereas a dollar for institutional support would cost the state a full dollar. The federal government would thus use the pricing system to encourage states to help finance an effective national marketplace for higher education. Hartman assumes the states would respond to this incentive by shifting support away from public campuses and into student aid programs, leaving public institutions with little recourse but to raise tuition, thereby tending to rationalize higher education prices.[23] With prices more nearly reflecting costs, and with low-income students aided by federal basic grants and by portable, federal-state scholarship grants, the higher education marketplace could be left to work without interference on the fate of programs and institutions. Although many private colleges would benefit from expanded, and portable, state scholarship programs,[24] it is clear that Hartman's main interest

23. Some campuses may resist tuition increases, opting instead for lower prices and lower quality. Whether this form of "diversity" would be desirable is an open question.

24. Private colleges that serve primarily home-state residents might lose under this scheme and might benefit more from nonportable state scholarship programs. See discussion of this point in chapter 9.

lies in increasing public tuition levels and rationalizing prices. Thus he unabashedly sides with those who would make the public sector more like the private.

In large measure, his reasoning is prompted by the assumption that federal and state higher education expenditures are unlikely to increase in real terms in the near future. True to this view, he also argues that the federal contribution to state scholarship programs should be paid for by reduced budgets in the federal campus-based student aid programs. Similarly, his assumption of relatively fixed state expenditures for higher education accounts for his belief that states will (and should) redirect money from institutional support into student support. His basic proposal can be separated from these budget assumptions, however, and we consider other possibilities below. First, it is necessary to evaluate the proposal on economic and political grounds.

Although Hartman does not commit himself unequivocally in chapter 5, his preferred policy of diverting subsidies from institutional support is shared by those economists who urge elimination of all subsidies on the grounds that subsidizing higher education for those who can afford to pay the full cost is inequitable and inefficient. This more extreme position denies the presence of external benefits worthy of—or requiring—general subsidy and concentrates exclusively on subsidies as a method for redistributing income and opportunity. Hartman's position—not directly confronting the full cost question, but "tilting" that way—is apparently based on his conclusion that evidence on the nature, magnitude, and value of social benefits is inconclusive.[25] Precise identification, measurement, and evaluation of external benefits produced by higher education have proven to be analytically intractable tasks, and promise to remain so; consequently, the optimal levels and types of public subsidy for higher education are necessarily—and properly—political decisions. We reject the view that social benefits are negligible—indeed, our intuition and experience suggest that they are considerable. But we do agree with Hartman's basic proposition that the present policy of subsidizing such benefits by state grants to just one set of institutions is not defensible analytically—though it has a strong historical foundation—and that it distorts student choice among colleges.

25. See Robert W. Hartman, "The Rationale for Federal Support for Higher Education," in Lewis C. Solmon and Paul J. Taubman, eds., *Does College Matter? Some Evidence on the Impact of Higher Education* (Academic Press, 1973), pp. 271–92. For another view, see Howard R. Bowen, *Investment in Learning* (Jossey-Bass, 1977).

Even if one believes there are important external benefits from higher education, there is still a strong argument for using income-tested subsidies to generate those benefits because, as McPherson argues in chapter 3, the enrollment decisions of low-income students are more sensitive to price than those of high-income students. Hence, a given quantity of public subsidy will "buy" more additional students (and more social benefit) if focused on persons with limited private resources.

If the analytical case for Hartman's proposal (or some variant thereof) is strong, as measured by the four criteria above, its political prospects are considerably weaker. In its pure version, that is, with fixed state and federal expenditures assumed, the proposal would be opposed by three potent groups. First, middle- and upper-income families would lose the option of sending their children to heavily subsidized state campuses and would instead have to pay more for education themselves. Because such families would not normally qualify for need-based aid, they can be expected to oppose any sharp increase in public tuition. Second, most public campuses would resist vehemently any proposal that threatened their claim on direct state support, forcing them to compete for students without the advantage of heavily subsidized tuition, a move that would particularly threaten those public institutions with the least nonprice appeal to students. Third, the smaller and less attractive private campuses might expect to lose from the portability feature and would probably support expansion of nonportable student aid programs instead. In sum, current financing methods that limit student choice and inhibit the working of a national student marketplace benefit several powerful constituencies that can be expected actively to resist changes of the type proposed by Hartman.

Support for his proposal might come from the stronger private colleges and universities,[26] from some state legislatures and governors, and possibly from the executive and legislative branches of the federal government.[27] We are not sanguine about the proposal's political prospects,

26. We are uncertain whether the plan would be actively supported, if it came to a vote, within the National Association of Independent Colleges and Universities. Also, it is conceivable that some of the stronger public universities would see merit in the portability feature, for it would help them attract a more diverse group of students. Moreover, the "flagship" campuses in the various state systems may fear the leveling effect of institutional support policies within their states. Nonetheless, unbending commitments to low tuition might prevent these universities from breaking ranks with their lesser public brethren.

27. Since the plan requires federal initiative, without such support the discussion is moot.

however, partly because of the opposition's strength and partly because Washington has shown little willingness to accept a leadership role in shaping the structure of higher education as the enterprise heads into a no-growth phase. It is possible, however, that when the reality of retrenchment hits home, perhaps with the closing of one or more highly visible private colleges, federal officials will be jolted into action. Thus the probability that some version of this proposal may eventually find favor cannot be ruled out.

A More Gradual Approach

Our preferred version departs from Hartman's in several important particulars. Whereas he clearly emphasizes increased public tuition (forced by reduced institutional support), we see a more important issue to be the portability and adequacy of student aid grants, which will require (as in Hartman's proposal) an explicit national policy and adequate financial incentives to the states. But, unlike Hartman, we neither assume nor hope that state governments will respond to this inducement by rapidly shifting the bulk of their higher education outlays from institutional to student aid.[28] We foresee (and favor) a more gradual change of emphasis, as experience with the new policy grows. In its first years, the new federal program might exercise its effect on incremental state expenditures, that is, support to state campuses would remain roughly constant, with increased outlays devoted to student aid. In some states, the federal stimulus might induce a larger increase in total higher education budgets. Over time, an equilibrium might be reached in which states provide a substantial (but lower) percentage of public-sector institutional support, public tuition is higher but still below private tuition, and a greater percentage of state aid flows through need-based grants to students. Such a balance would take into account the fact that state colleges and universities provide valuable services to the states apart from undergraduate instruction. Meanwhile, student choice among colleges will have been enhanced, the higher education marketplace will have become a more reliable guide to resource allocation, and those private colleges that compete successfully for students will have received public aid in a manner that minimizes the threat to their autonomy.[29]

28. Indeed, the findings reported by Susan Nelson in chapter 2 suggest that increased state support for student aid has generally not been at the expense of appropriations for public institutions.

29. See the discussion on this point in chapters 7 and 9.

We do not attempt to estimate the net financial costs of this proposal because a wide range of discretionary state and federal behavior is possible. Hartman argues that the net cost could be negligible if the federal component were entirely financed with funds now consumed by the campus-based programs and if the state components were simply a dollar-for-dollar displacement of institutional aid by student aid. Both more and less costly versions of his basic plan are possible, depending primarily upon state decisions regarding the amounts of subsidy to be provided to public institutions and through student aid.[30] But the central feature of most variants is a substantial redistribution of current outlays, both among students and existing government programs, which would limit the potential costs to government.

Nonetheless, the redistribution of benefits and burdens that makes such a program financially feasible may render it politically unworkable, even with our modifications. We turn, therefore, to other policy options that could be pursued if our preferred policy is not supported.

"Second-Best" Policies

Inasmuch as we have argued that the best policy for financing undergraduate education requires a purposeful linking of federal and state strategies, it is not surprising that we regard as second-best any proposal confined to one level of government or the other. Nevertheless, the difficulty of forging such a link between Washington and the fifty state capitals, and the proven resistance of higher education policy to complex reform schemes, means that this prescription may not be followed.

Federal Options

Even limiting possible options to measures dealing with undergraduate financing specifically intended to bolster the private sector, one must still reckon with dozens of different formulations. Instead of probing the details of particular plans, therefore, we map four approaches below that, although not mutually exclusive, lend themselves to separate examination.

30. Also, see Hartman's discussion of the federal budget implications in chapter 5. It may be noted that early 1978 brought unexpected signs of a possible loosening of the federal pursestrings controlling aid to higher education, and evidence also of new surpluses in many state treasuries. Should these trends persist, some budgetary "trade-offs" sketched in this chapter will be far less vexing.

AMENDING THE PRESENT GRANT PROGRAMS

Hartman in chapter 5 postulates the continuation of the basic educational opportunity grants (BEOG) as the foundation of need-based federal aid to students. Gladieux and Wolanin in chapter 4 do not question this, although they caution that BEOG is apt to remain an "access" program and thus not wholly satisfactory to private colleges and their students.

Because direct subsidies to needy students will remain the cornerstone of federal policy for undergraduate education, and because the basic grants program is generally well conceived and widely accepted, we see no point in reexamining its rationale. However, the present structure of the federal student aid system tends to pit BEOG against the three campus-based subsidy programs in the competition for funds, thereby making rivals of what should be complementary goals of access and choice.

From the private sector's standpoint, the BEOG program has two major defects. Its needs-analysis system confines aid to students from low-income families, and the ceiling on individual grants[31] means that those lacking other resources find it far easier to enroll in a public institution in their own state than to pay the higher prices of a private or out-of-state public university. Boosting the maximum basic grant to $1,800, as authorized by Congress in 1976, would ease both conditions, but not enough to have a significant impact on student choice or on the competitive position of private higher education.

Yet the campus-based programs, particularly supplemental education opportunity grants (SEOG), offer a peg on which to hang a heavier federal commitment to choice if only they were meshed with basic grants in a unified subsidy strategy. This could be done either by replacing SEOG with a second tier added to the basic grants program or by leaving SEOG in place but focusing it more specifically on students attending high-priced colleges.[32] These schemes share three common

31. The Carter administration's budget proposal for fiscal 1978 requested increased funding for BEOG to support maximum grants of $1,600 and extend coverage to families in the $13,000 to $17,000 income range. (*Higher Education Daily*, vol. 5 [February 23, 1977], p. 1.)

32. As examples, see (1) the testimony and recommendations of the American Council on Education in *Higher Education Legislation, 1975*, Hearings before the Subcommittee on Education of the Senate Committee on Labor and Public Welfare, 94:1 (GPO, 1975), pt. 1, pp. 518–97; (2) Consortium on Financing Higher Education, "A Synopsis of Federal Student Assistance: A Review of Title IV of the Higher

characteristics: they allow Washington to continue skirting the sensitive issue of college pricing policy; they provide a larger federal subsidy to a student choosing a high-priced campus than the same student would receive at a lower-priced institution; and, by giving the prospective matriculant greater foreknowledge of the federal aid he can anticipate, they enhance the student's ability to incorporate net price considerations into his enrollment decision.[33]

But there are two drawbacks. First, by giving larger subsidies to those attending high-priced colleges, any such scheme invites the states to boost their public-sector tuition for the wrong reasons. They can harvest a fiscal windfall by passing some of their higher education costs on to the federal government, whereas states (and institutions) that struggle to keep college prices low are "penalized." The other drawback is cost. While Washington's actual budgetary burden will depend on a program's specific construction, any scheme that seeks to underwrite choice without cutting back on access is sure to be expensive.[34]

Although a conscious link between federal and state financing policies is to be preferred, even if no such link is forged, the federal government should search for a better fit between its access and choice programs, and SEOG should be seen as a complement to BEOG rather than as an atavism of the 1960s that competes with basic grants for funds.

With respect to the present BEOG program, it is imperative to stress one troubling flaw and one emergent problem, both of which should be dealt with even if no other changes take place.[35]

The provision limiting individual stipends to no more than half the

Education Act," in *The Student Financial Aid Act of 1975,* Hearings before the Subcommittee on Postsecondary Education of the House Committee on Education and Labor, 94:1 (GPO, 1975), pp. 612–19; and (3) Chester E. Finn, Jr., *Scholars, Dollars, and Bureaucrats* (Brookings, 1978). The last of these reviews the virtues and drawbacks of embracing access and choice within a single two-tiered basic grants program.

33. Because the campus-based programs presently provide little such foreknowledge, additional changes would be required to make them do so. A two-tiered basic grants program would serve this purpose more directly.

34. Reliable cost estimates are impossible because there is no way to forecast the induced effects of such a program. Finn in *Scholars, Dollars, and Bureaucrats* estimates that the gross cost of a "super-BEOG" program would range up to $5.0 billion. Of course, the net cost would depend on the assumptions one makes about expenditures for present programs that would be supplanted.

35. We raise them here not to advance the interests of private higher education but to strengthen the national government's central program of aid to needy students.

recipient's cost of attendance has superficial appeal—no one should have a free ride—and it also helps to contain the program's cost; but it takes a painful toll on the neediest students enrolling at the lowest priced colleges and thus impedes attainment of the federal goal of access. The arguments to preserve it advanced by some private college spokesmen should be seen for what they are—entirely selfish. Insofar as student choice is a valid national objective, it should be encouraged by measures attuned to high-priced institutions, not by making postsecondary access harder for those in greatest need of assistance. Some state education officials give a more legitimate reason for retaining the half-cost limit: if Washington covered all of a needy student's costs of access and the states' role in student aid were reduced to fostering choice, the legislatures might become uneasy about the rationale for such outlays. A shrewder strategy, they contend, would call for a federal-state student aid partnership at all levels, whether the recipient opts for a low-tuition community college or a high-priced private university. The counter-argument, of course, is that if any state does not hold up its end of that arrangement, its needy students may not be able to afford college anywhere.

A problem that did not surface during the early years of BEOG has begun to be troublesome as the program becomes better established and participation rates soar. Although technically not an "entitlement" plan,[36] from the student's standpoint, BEOG must work as if it were or the financial foundation it was meant to provide is undermined. If the formula says that a student with family contribution x matriculating at college Y is due a basic grant of amount z, then every similarly situated student must also receive z, not just in the freshman year but for as long as he remains

36. A true entitlement scheme, such as social security benefits, is not subject to the budget and appropriations cycle. Whatever funds are required to honor the government's legal commitment are automatically paid out. Two other federal student aid programs—veterans' education benefits and guaranteed student loans—may be termed semientitlements, in that their outlays, while appropriated, are determined by program demand rather than budget constraints. (The student is not entitled to obtain a loan, but once he gets it he—and his lender—become entitled to a variety of nondiscretionary federal subsidies, guarantees, and the like.) By contrast, the campus-based programs (and many others) are discretionary outlays, with a fixed appropriation meted out to as many students as it will cover. The basic grants program falls within this spectrum in that it establishes an entitlement (really a maximum) but specifies procedures to be followed (a reduced payment schedule) when appropriations are too small to honor the full entitlement. Once the payment schedule is set for a given year, for all intents and purposes the program operates like an entitlement to that schedule.

eligible. This approach makes program costs difficult to contain. Outlays of $2.1 billion in fiscal 1978 (school year 1978–79) are anticipated to assist 2.4 million participants with subsidies ranging up to $1,600.[37] The authorized ceiling of $1,800 would boost the price tag further, and so would ending the half-cost limitation.[38] Yet the cost of college has risen even faster in the years since BEOG was enacted, and if grant levels lag too far behind, access will be impeded. Awards should keep pace with real increases in college costs and individual grants must be made reliable and not subject to annual debate if the BEOG program is to function successfully as the nation's foundation program of student assistance.

STUDENT LOANS

Loans will still play an important role in federal student aid. No one relishes debt, but it is apparent that many people cannot pay for college out of current income, and there is little prospect that additional subsidies will be large enough to reduce dramatically the costs borne by students and their families. Hence, for many students at various income levels, college attendance will continue to hinge in part on the ability to borrow. Washington should continue to moderate the risks for borrower and lender alike.

From time to time it has been suggested that the federal government should make heavier and more imaginative use of the loan mechanism, perhaps expanding it into a full-scale educational opportunity bank. Under this scheme, young people could borrow the money that they need to pay for whatever kind of postsecondary educational experience they deem most suitable.[39] A particularly engaging formulation of this idea would make the size and terms of the repayments contingent on the borrower's later income and would designate the Internal Revenue Service as the government's collection agent. The present Student Loan

37. U.S. Office of Education estimate.

38. Although the maximum grants may be increased to $1,800 in fiscal 1979, the number of currently eligible students may decline, resulting in little change in total costs. Proposed changes in the family contribution schedule to extend coverage to higher-income families could raise costs appreciably, however. The elimination of the half-cost provision from an $1,800 BEOG program would add $250 million to $400 million more to the outlays required to fully fund it. (Calculated by Alan Wagner, College Entrance Examination Board, Washington office.)

39. *Educational Opportunity Bank*, A Report of the Panel on Educational Innovation (GPO, 1967); Robert W. Hartman, "The National Bank Approach to Solutions," in Lois D. Rice, ed., *Student Loans: Problems and Policy Alternatives* (College Entrance Examination Board, 1977), pp. 74–89.

Marketing Association (SLMA) could evolve into the direct lending agency.

The idea has considerable appeal and lends itself to a number of interesting variations. Instead of relying on current income, as the grant programs do, it would treat everyone alike during the student phase, differentiating later according to ability to pay. Those who seek a high-priced education could obtain the funds for it without asking the taxpayer to subsidize their aspirations or their tastes. If some segments of the population needed extra help, or if certain career specialities were to be emphasized, subsidies or loan forgiveness features could be built into the program.[40]

College and university leaders have long been divided, however, in their attitude toward loans. Spokesmen for public higher education generally oppose heavy reliance on student borrowing because of its implication that the individual rather than society should pay for postsecondary schooling, and because it thus flies in the face of the low-tuition doctrine. In 1970, for example, the two major associations of state universities vigorously denounced the opportunity bank idea, asserting that it ". . . asked [the student] to enter into a special Federal income-tax indenture for most of his working life in order to permit colleges and universities to recapture approximately the full cost of educational services through sharp increases in required charges. Its most glaring defect from the standpoint of public policy is that it proposes to shift to the student the cost, at an escalating rate, of higher education."[41] There is no evidence that these associations have changed their stance, and even less reason to underestimate their political effectiveness should Congress again give serious consideration to the idea. Nor is there any way of knowing precisely what effect an educational opportunity bank would have on private colleges and universities, for despite the income contingent repayment feature, most students would still have to borrow a great deal more to enroll in a high-priced institution.

40. See D. Bruce Johnstone, *New Patterns for College Lending: Income Contingent Loans* (Columbia University Press, 1972); and Robert W. Hartman, *Credit for College: Public Policy for Student Loans* (McGraw-Hill, 1971).

41. American Association of State Colleges and Universities and National Association of State Universities and Land-Grant Colleges, "Recommendations for National Action Affecting Higher Education," reprinted in *Higher Education Amendments of 1970,* Hearings before the Subcommittee on Education of the Senate Committee on Labor and Public Welfare, 91:2 (GPO, 1971) pt. 2, pp. 1218–33 (quotation, p. 1224).

Even if no such grand reform is attempted, the present federal student loan programs need attention. The two major programs—national direct student loans (NDSL) and guaranteed student loans (GSL)—pose knotty issues that call for more extended scrutiny than we can give them here.[42] Many analysts argue that the two loan programs should be rationalized (or consolidated), for there seems little justification for the different subsidy rates and forgiveness features. Indeed, interest subsidies may have little educational or social justification at all, although once on the statute books they are difficult to remove. We suspect that what matters most to prospective student borrowers (and the colleges they are struggling to pay for) is that the capital be available in the first place and that students be able to repay in reasonable installments over a long period of time once out of school. What matters to banks and other lenders is that the government backstop the student borrowers, guaranteeing that loans will be repaid, and that suitable arrangements be made (such as those through SLMA) for selling the loan paper and recycling the capital. The few dollars that federal interest subsidies trim from the monthly repayments probably have little effect on student access or choice, while costing the government hundreds of millions each year, money that could better be used to expand grant programs. Student loans are especially important for the private colleges, and Washington should continue to do its part, but this calls for a stable, efficient, and easily understood program of guarantees or insurance, not for interest subsidies.[43]

INSTITUTIONAL SUBSIDIES

The federal government has thus far resisted the academic community's pleas for unrestricted institutional support. To be sure, a "cost-of-education" allowance scheme was authorized in 1972,[44] but it is linked to student aid and, in any case, has never been funded. A handful of small programs such as the annual payments to land-grant universities and the developing institutions program provide modest amounts of more or less unrestricted income to selected campuses, but Washington has de-

42. The topic receives thorough treatment in Lois D. Rice, ed., *Student Loans: Problems and Policy Alternatives.*

43. Needy students who are poor credit risks may have difficulty obtaining loans from private lenders, and the presence of federal guarantees has not solved this problem of capital availability. Hence, we would not recommend phasing out the NDSL program until an alternative method is developed to ensure that all students can borrow the necessary funds.

44. Education Amendments of 1972 (86 Stat. 375).

clined to take the broad hint dropped by the American Council on Education in 1969 (and by many others since) that "the principal unfinished business of the Federal Government in the field of higher education is the necessity to provide support for general institutional purposes."[45] Congress and the executive branch have also turned deaf ears to the private sector's special pleading for tuition offsets or similar forms of institutional support confined to its own members.

Federal institutional support can take one of two forms, but neither of them makes a persuasive claim on the limited revenues available for higher education in the next decade. Washington could subsidize *all* colleges and universities, or it could support selected campuses, such as those judged to be on the financial brink. The first would cost a lot of money, do little or nothing to improve the competitive position of private institutions, unburden the states of a responsibility that historically is theirs, and do less to foster equal educational opportunity than channeling the same resources into need-based student aid. The second is a political minefield, pitting the self-interest of some segments of higher education against others, calling for impossible choices between the maintenance of strong campuses and the resuscitation of weak ones, and implying a criterion for federal policy—the viability of individual colleges and universities—that flies in the face of a marketplace strategy. While postsecondary institutions can scarcely be blamed for wanting more money, or for looking to Washington as a source, first priority should be given to student aid. Insofar as institutions providing undergraduate education warrant direct subsidies, that responsibility properly remains in state and private hands. And, even if politically feasible, federally funded tuition offsets and other schemes designed to create for private campuses a subsidy structure akin to the one that the states have provided for their public institutions are not appealing. Two well-meaning policies do not make for a rational, equitable, or efficient system of postsecondary finance, and private higher education would surrender much of its distinctive value if it became dependent on Washington for ordinary operating income.

TAX BENEFITS FOR STUDENTS

Emil Sunley in chapter 6 has described the range of existing tax benefits aimed at students and their parents, and we are not aware of any

45. American Council on Education, *Federal Programs for Higher Education: Needed Next Steps* (ACE, 1969), p. 17.

serious proposals to do away with them. In the immediate future the main debate over federal tax benefits for undergraduate education is apt to center on a popular idea not yet enacted, that is, a tuition tax credit or kindred forms of relief for students and their families.

Despite its appeal, the main impulse behind this proposal seems to be tax relief for middle-income families, not improvement in the system by which society pays for higher education. Certainly there is no evidence that credits (or deductions) on the modest scale likely to be enacted would either draw more students into higher education or significantly bolster the financial condition of shaky colleges and universities. Their principal effect would be either to substitute federal tax expenditures for a portion of tuition outlays or to lead to increased tuition charges. The lost revenue could be better used to strengthen the need-based student aid programs, perhaps allowing the definition of "need" to envelop more middle-income families and enlarging payments so that private colleges would become more accessible.[46] If the middle class is to gain fiscal relief through the tax system, that should take the form of alterations in the basic rate structure, not through something disguised as a higher education program.

State Options

Analyses of state policies and politics, such as those offered in chapters 7 and 8, describe the remarkable variations from one jurisdiction to the next. Consequently, it is difficult even to speak intelligently about "the states," let alone to formulate policy guidance applicable to more than one of them.

With respect to the financing of undergraduate education, Blaydon adduces a trio of "goals" that might be adopted by a state wishing to buttress the competitive position of its private sector. The available means to achieve any of these three goals are straightforward and familiar: adjusting the pattern of institutional subsidies, the pattern of student subsidies, or some combination of the two. Alternative blends of ends and means yield various costs and imply differing answers to the basic strategic question that underlies much of what is discussed in this

46. In early 1978, congressional opponents of tax credit legislation were devising "alternatives" along these lines within the framework of student aid programs. It is important to bear in mind that in discussion of tuition tax relief "middle income" is often construed to include families earning more than $30,000, a group that would not be touched by need-based grant aid unless the student assistance programs were enlarged by unjustifiably large amounts.

book: whether the private sector should be made more like the public, or the public more like the private.[47] We comment briefly on each of Blaydon's goals, shading our observations with some of the political "realities" set forth by Berdahl in chapter 7.

GOAL 1: STABILIZE THE TUITION GAP

The state may endeavor to stabilize in real terms the current tuition gap between its public and private colleges so that the private sector does not face ever tougher price competition during a period when declining enrollment and nonprice contests will pose hardship enough. The simplest ways to do this are to provide direct subsidies to private institutions sufficient to offset rising educational costs and to limit future increases in public-sector subsidies to similarly indexed amounts. While the gap between "posted prices" in public and private colleges would probably continue to widen, in real terms (and presumably in relation to the incomes of students and families seeking to pay those prices) it would hold constant.[48] Since the state's main interest lies in fostering educational access and choice for its residents rather than adding to the disposable income of its private campuses, the colleges and universities would have to agree to use these state subsidies to hold down tuition, not to augment (real) expenditures per student.[49]

47. Although we pose the basic policy choice in its starkest—and most simplified—terms, less extreme versions of this theme are possible, even likely. One can easily imagine, for example, that the weaker private campuses will become increasingly dependent on state support, and hence more public in nature, while the stronger public institutions resort to higher tuition to offset diminished state support, hence becoming more private in character. Under this scenario, the state would provide a base level of support for higher education, public and private, while private dollars would pay for higher quality above this base, in both public and private institutions. The result would be a blurring of the traditional distinction between public and private campuses, as "hybrid" institutions of differing degrees of quality became more common.

48. In the past fifteen years real incomes have risen a little faster than college prices. If that trend continues, stabilizing the real tuition gap would diminish the income-deflated gap. This would mean gradual improvement over time in the market position of the private sector, although not enough to offset the effects of a shrinking college-age population.

49. Of course, if the private institutions in a state persuade the legislature that their educational quality is as important to the public interest as their net price to the student, they may obtain permission to use subsidies for other purposes. Indeed, a state seriously interested in the well-being of its private colleges and universities would do well to heed McPherson's comments in chapter 3 about the importance of nonprice variables in the competition for students.

From the state's perspective, the chief advantage of adopting this modest goal is that costs would be similarly modest. But there are several obvious drawbacks. Because such a program does not actually narrow the tuition gap, it does not guarantee any improvement in the private sector's marketplace position. Like any other institutional subvention meant to contain posted prices for all students, it has the effect of subsidizing the education of the wealthy as well as the needy and of spreading available funds across a large number of persons rather than concentrating them on the smaller number facing sizable economic barriers to college attendance. By providing across-the-board subsidies to private postsecondary institutions, it treats them more like public campuses, eroding that fundamental distinction between the two and threatening detailed state supervision of university balance sheets. Such subsidies, keyed to educational costs and presumably allotted according to an enrollment-based formula, also force the issue of how a state deals with out-of-state students and whether it is prepared to pay for their education in private institutions when it ordinarily declines to do so on public campuses.[50] Finally, any scheme of this sort raises a host of political and constitutional questions. Some states are prohibited from subsidizing the ordinary costs of private, especially church-related, colleges, and Berdahl shows that even where such payments are constitutional they tend to cause considerable friction between the two sectors.

GOAL 2: NARROW THE TUITION GAP

The state may attempt to narrow the public-private price gap in real terms. It could, for example, do that (in a period of continuing inflation) by stabilizing the current-dollar gap. Rather than simply keeping pace with inflation, the state might match every increase in public-sector institutional subsidies with a dollar-for-dollar increase in its support for private campuses. This would have the long-run effect of freezing the nominal tuition gap while bringing the ratio in real terms closer to parity. Of course, a large initial outlay for private institutional subsidies would permit an actual reduction in private-campus tuition, just as a reduction in support for the public colleges and universities would force an increase in *their* charges with essentially the same effect on the gap.

One can easily be so beguiled by the pros and cons of innumerable

50. This problem could be solved in the private sector much as it is in the public by confining the per-student subsidy to the number of state residents enrolled. But that solution runs counter to our goal of increased interstate mobility.

policy combinations as to lose sight of the fundamental shortcomings of *any* scheme that sets as its goal the equalizing of public- and private-sector prices. Policymakers can "equalize downward," subsidizing private campuses at enormous cost to the taxpayer; "equalize upward," withdrawing subsidies from state schools at enormous political cost; or compromise by partially subsidizing some private schools and withdrawing some funds from public institutions. Besides all the drawbacks noted above in connection with Blaydon's first goal, strategies for harmonizing a state's treatment of public and private colleges turn out, not surprisingly, to be most difficult for precisely those jurisdictions where the private sector looms largest and where improving its lot may seem most important. Nationwide, Blaydon estimates that a 10 percent increase in state higher education budgets directed to private institutions could be translated into a 28 percent reduction in private tuition, but this reduction varies from a modest 7 percent in New England to a substantial 43 percent in the South (table 8-3). Alternatively, reallocating present state postsecondary outlays from public to private institutions in amounts sufficient to equalize their tuition charges would mean a 66 percent boost in public-sector prices and a 49 percent reduction in private-sector rates (table 8-1). We cannot identify a single state with a large enough revenue surplus and an amicable enough political climate to give us any confidence in the feasibility of wholesale strategies of this sort. Some jurisdictions may gradually move toward more equal subsidies and a narrower tuition gap, but what effect that has depends on how "gradually" is interpreted: 1990 may be too late for a number of private campuses.

State officials may also wonder why they should boost their overall investment in higher education at a time when total enrollment is shrinking and excess capacity emerges as a real problem. From the analyst's perspective that may be a good reason for rerouting public-sector revenue into the private sector, rather than increasing total outlays, but the political peril of such a step may be more compelling to those who must face the voters.

GOAL 3: HELP STUDENTS BRIDGE THE TUITION GAP

Whether the tuition gap is stable, narrowing, or growing, the states have a third clear option, which is to help more students bridge it. Although one can devise various ways of doing this, we join Blaydon in favoring need-based grants to individual students for use on both public and private campuses.[51] The tough questions for the state are (a) how much of the population to aid, (b) what portion of each person's "need" to underwrite, (c) whether to make the grants portable, (d) how to synchronize them with the various federal programs, and (e) how to restrain the colleges from exploiting them by recklessly boosting their outlays and their prices.

Each state must answer these and similar questions for itself, constrained by its available resources, by its ability (or willingness) to convert institutional subsidies into student assistance, and by the presence or absence of a federal incentive program. As with the institutional strategies, the central dilemma is the obvious one: states with (relatively or absolutely) small private sectors will find it easier to design and pay for generous aid programs for their students than others where the private sector is much larger. Nevertheless, the rapid increase in need-based state student aid programs in recent years augurs well for the feasibility of this general strategy, which also has much to commend it in providing equal educational opportunity. Assisting a middle-income student to pay the added costs of attending a high-priced university may not serve quite the same social purpose as helping an impoverished individual to enroll in an inexpensive community college, but the advantage of need-based aid is that both goals are served by the same program; in neither case is the taxpayer subsidizing educational outlays that the individual could easily have made for himself. Moreover, channeling resources to students strengthens the higher education marketplace and relates the fiscal health of an institution to its ability to provide a sought-after service rather than to the influence of its friends in the state capital.

RECOMMENDATIONS

Our reading of state political dynamics yields little reason for either confidence or despair about the prospects for large-scale state student aid programs keyed to individual need. Although their accessibility to

51. Flat grants amount to institutional subsidies or tuition offsets, and should be analyzed that way, although certain political and constitutional hurdles may be cleared by channeling them through the students. Of course, flat grants serve to bridge the tuition gap only if they are confined to students attending private institutions. As for income-tested student subsidies, there is much to be said for them on grounds of access and equal educational opportunity, but they do nothing to reduce the disparity in net price of public and private colleges unless limited to students attending the latter. "Need," however, allows for simultaneous attention to both individual circumstance and differing college prices.

both public and private college students should make them attractive to leaders of both sectors—few would openly oppose assistance to impoverished freshmen—the details of a particular aid scheme may generate considerable strife. Overall constraints on a state's budget heighten the trade-off between student and institutional support, with the private sector favoring the former and the public campuses preferring the latter. But on balance, we still favor the student aid strategy as a serviceable mechanism. The optimal program would be need-based and portable,[52] erected atop the major federal aid programs, sufficiently generous to bring a large part of the college-going population within financial range of the private sector, and yet not so lavish as to tempt public or private institutions into a fresh round of tuition increases. We would also favor each state's stabilizing the public-private price gap, at least in real terms, as discussed in goal 1 above, but if a choice must be made between student aid and the institutional subsidies needed to stabilize that gap, our clear preference would be for the former.

Paralleling these beneficial measures for the private sector is the touchy problem of how a state should handle its public postsecondary system in a time of retrenchment. Any decision to mothball an entire publicly supported institution is sure to be hard-fought and bloody, for jobs, hopes, and tradition are all deeply involved. Yet a clear-eyed look into the future must face the possibility that the public interest in some jurisdictions will best be served by drastic actions of that sort. In other states, Berdahl suggests, well-planned surgical procedures that spare the institutions while forcibly shrinking them may be more sensible, and certainly more palatable politically. Almost everywhere, state higher education planners and elected officials will be well advised to think twice before encouraging further *expansion* of the public sector. Circumstances could well dictate judicious growth of some campuses and fresh formulations of the educational missions of others, but expansion in one locale may need to be offset by contraction elsewhere, and it is healthier if both are planned rather than inadvertent. The difficulties of performing surgery

52. While fully probable grants would be ideal, state officials may look more kindly upon reciprocity pacts whereby student aid from state *A* can be used in state *B* provided *B* also allows its grants to be carried into *A*. Such bilateral agreements, perhaps encouraged by regional compacts, could even provide for an annual accounting and settlement between the participants. While this approach ostensibly calls for each state to negotiate arrangements with all forty-nine others, in practice most migrating students could be accommodated by a smaller number of reciprocal agreements.

on educational institutions ought not be underestimated, but allowing them to deteriorate and waste away will ultimately prove more damaging and expensive. Moreover, where an existing campus, public or private, has excess capacity, a careful rearrangement of institutional roles and responsibilities may take up that slack while avoiding costly expansion.

We are mindful of the seeming contradiction between our advocacy of the student marketplace as the soundest molder of institutional destinies and our emphasis on comprehensive state planning that embraces public and private campuses alike. When demand was mounting and enrollment swelling in the 1950s and 1960s, untrammeled competition was an efficient, speedy, and responsive way to build a diverse educational system. Hence, few states developed strong planning mechanisms, and most will enter the 1980s with the "political marketplace" as the chief alternative to the student marketplace. While the private sector's growing political sophistication means that statehouse battles will be fierce, the public interest will best be served if elected officials seek the counsel of disinterested educational planners before adopting ad hoc solutions to the problems of individual campuses. Such professional advice may help them judiciously to shape the terms of competition in the educational marketplace rather than to intrude on behalf of failing institutions. Only a brave or foolhardy state official will allow himself to enter the fray without the protection that an intelligent planning process can provide.

Statesmanship amidst Retrenchment

This volume presupposes that private higher education is important to American society. Although we have dealt but briefly with the conventional rationale for that belief, the first part of this chapter paints in broad strokes a vision of higher education for the 1980s and beyond in which the characteristics we ascribe to private colleges and universities are indispensable. It is not our place to argue the case for private higher education, but rather to appraise the efforts of its advocates. We take for granted that they will unabashedly present their brief as best they can in the state and national capitals, and chapters 4 and 7 indicate that they are generally strengthening their abilities to do just that.

It would be a mistake, however, to take an altogether sanguine view of the private sector's political prospects. Its case for itself is made with conviction, but based on "soft" ideas about the nature of a free, diverse, and pluralistic society, rather than the "hard," quantifiable cost-benefit terms that lend themselves to policy analysis. Moreover, while private college presidents, such as those whose views are reflected in chapter 9, and their state and national representatives, are intelligent, sincere, and often eloquent, their policy agendas are hard to differentiate from those of many other claimants. We find no fault with the three criteria that Brown and Wenzlau adduce for "good" policy—independence, financial stability, and evenhandedness—but are hard-pressed to name any group whose desires cannot be reduced to the same essentials.

What is more, the central distinction of private higher education—the fact that it is not *public* higher education—poses its overriding political dilemma. It exists side by side with a large and well-established network of institutions that government already has a vested interest in maintaining, and insofar as the private sector's well-being is threatened by competition from those institutions, it finds itself turning for solutions to the source of its problems.[53] Nor will the public colleges and universities sit quietly by as the private schools seek more favorable treatment. While chapters 4 and 7 document their growing political prowess, they also depict parallel increases in public higher education's performance in government arenas and the seemingly intractable conflict between the two sectors with respect to some (but not all) policy issues. When public and private oppose one another and, for good and sufficient reasons of self-interest, fail to present a common front to perplexed officials, all too often the result is a stalemate that may preserve the status quo but hardly makes for inspired social policy.

In Washington, the fragmented nature of the higher education policy-making process itself discourages government officials from pursuing such overarching concerns as the "fate of the private sector," and leaves institutional spokesmen puzzled as to where in the confusion they should lodge their complaints and their requests. They cannot identify anyone in the federal establishment who is really "in charge" of higher education policy and must therefore resort to piecemeal measures that may cancel each other out or induce unfortunate side effects. It is not to be

---

53. Here we use "government" in a generic sense. Obviously, the federal government has no stake in the maintenance of state-sponsored colleges and universities, but neither has it shown much inclination to assert an interest in the welfare of private campuses.

wondered that by 1978 many Washington higher education spokesman had overcome their traditional reluctance to see the enterprise rationalized and were prepared to gamble that the benefits of a cabinet-level department of education or some similar structural reform would exceed the costs.[54]

In the state capitals, one encounters fewer agencies and decision-making points, but the disarray surrounding higher education policy may be almost as great, with tangled goals, overlapping jurisdictions, and jealous constituencies. One cannot read Berdahl's account in chapter 7 without noting the endless series of state study commissions and special task forces that sometimes seem to substitute for hard choices.[55] Here, too, private-sector spokesmen face most directly the aforementioned conundrum, that their audience ordinarily consists of officials with a proprietary interest in the welfare of their rivals. In few states does a single official or governmental unit combine responsibility for the well-being of *all* higher education with the authority to do much to foster it. With rare exceptions, the most eloquent and powerful figures in the postsecondary political arena at the state level are the presidents of individual universities and their protectors in the legislature rather than persons with a distinterested overview of the entire enterprise.

In advancing its case for beneficent public policy, private higher education cannot escape the fundamental paradox that the more successful it is in garnering public support, the more dependent it becomes on that support, and the more its autonomy—its major raison d'être and its rationale for succor—is sapped by the terms of the support. As higher

54. President Carter's expressed willingness during the 1976 campaign to establish a department of education contributed to this development, but the academic community's interest antedated it. In the summer of 1975, the American Council on Education urged the Senate to recognize that one major reason for "the continuing lack of leadership and support for education from the Executive Branch is the low status of the bureaus and programs of the Education Division in the Department of Health, Education and Welfare." *Higher Education Legislation, 1975,* Hearings, pt. 1, p. 556. (For general discussion, see Rufus E. Miles, Jr., *A Cabinet Department of Education* [American Council on Education, 1976], and the Carnegie Council on Policy Studies in Higher Education, *Federal Reorganization: Education and Scholarship* [Carnegie Foundation for the Advancement of Teaching, 1977; available from the Council].)

55. See also *The States and Higher Education: A Proud Past and a Vital Future,* A Commentary of the Carnegie Foundation for the Advancement of Teaching (Jossey-Bass, 1976), and *Coordination or Chaos?* Report of the Task Force on Coordination, Governance, and Structure of Postsecondary Education (Education Commission of the States, 1973).

education heads into the 1980s, the issue of government regulation has begun to rival the issue of government assistance, and the two appear destined to remain firmly linked. But the debate over regulation transcends even the arguments about financing, for in many instances the government controls that threaten to compromise the freedom of educational institutions are tied loosely if at all to public funding. Liberal impulses that motivate society toward an enhanced concern for the values symbolized by private higher education also lead it toward greater "social" regulation of its various institutions. While this dilemma reaches far beyond the interests of colleges and universities, and while the latter may have no claim to exemption or preferential treatment, one cannot deny the potentially damaging impact of external regulation on educational institutions whose value to society depends so much on their sovereignty.

By now it is clear that making wise public policy in the field of higher education is going to get harder, not easier. On the one hand, government officials will face Solomon-like decisions with respect to the very existence of entire colleges and universities. On the other hand, they will have to resist strong pressure to make such decisions, instead leaving these matters to the vagaries of the marketplace, ill-structured as it may be.

One hopes the academic community will produce its own statesmen, persons whose understanding of the role of higher learning in American society and whose vision of the higher education system as a whole will make them valued counselors to perplexed government officials at the state and national levels. Economic pressures suggest, however, that parochialism will infest the political arenas in which higher education policy will be made. One cannot wish it away, nor can one anticipate the vast infusion of resources that might "buy" it away. Yet the strength and quality of the nation's higher education system in 1990 will depend in no small part on the ability of state and federal officials to overcome such parochialism. And that alone is reason enough for the academic community to help them.

Glossary

Abbreviations

AAC: Association of American Colleges
AACJC: American Association of Community and Junior Colleges
AASCU: American Association of State Colleges and Universities
AAU: Association of American Universities
ACE: American Council on Education
ACT: American College Testing Program
ACUSNY: Association of Colleges and Universities of the State of
    New York
AICCU: Association of Independent California Colleges and Universities
CEEB: College Entrance Examination Board
CFAE: Council on Financial Aid to Education
CICU: Commission on Independent Colleges and Universities
    (New York state)
COFHE: Consortium on Financing Higher Education
CSS: College Scholarship Service
CTA: California Teachers Association
ERIC: Educational Resources Information Center
FIPSE: Fund for the Improvement of Postsecondary Education[1]
HEGIS: Higher Education General Information Survey[2]
NAICU: National Association of Independent Colleges and Universities
NASFAA: National Association of Student Finanical Aid Administrators
NASULGC: National Association of State Universities and Land-Grant
    Colleges
NCES: National Center for Education Statistics[2]
NCFPE: National Commission on the Financing of Postsecondary
    Education[1]
NCICU: National Council of Independent Colleges and Universities
NIE: National Institute of Education[1,2]
NSL: National Student Lobby
SLMA: Student Loan Marketing Association (Sallie Mae)[1]

1. Created by the Education Amendments of 1972.
2. Under the Education Division of the U.S. Department of Health, Education,
and Welfare.

Carnegie Classification System

The Carnegie Commission Classification System of Colleges and Universities is one that was developed by the Carnegie Commission on Higher Education in 1973; it has never been updated. Each of the 2,565 colleges and universities included in U.S. Office of Education, *Advance Report on Opening Fall Enrollment in Higher Education: Institutional Data, 1970* (National Center for Educational Statistics, 1970) was classified in five main and eighteen subcategories. These are fully described, and the institutions listed, in *A Classification of Institutions of Higher Education,* A Technical Report Sponsored by the Carnegie Commission on Higher Education (Carnegie Foundation for the Advancement of Teaching, 1973). The most important categories are summarized below.

DOCTORAL-GRANTING INSTITUTIONS

Research universities I: the fifty leading universities in terms of federal financial support of academic science in at least two of the three academic years, 1968–69, 1969–70, and 1970–71, provided that they also awarded at least fifty doctoral degrees in 1969–70.

Research universities II: other universities selected from the one hundred institutions with the most federal financial support in two academic years between 1968–69 and 1970–71 and awarding at least fifty doctoral degrees in 1969–70, or universities selected from the fifty institutions awarding the largest number of doctoral degrees between 1960–61 and 1969–70.

Doctoral-granting universities I: universities awarding forty or more doctoral degrees in 1969–70, or those receiving at least $3 million in total federal financial support in either 1969–70 or 1970–71 and awarding twenty or more doctoral degrees.

Doctoral-granting universities II: universities awarding at least ten doctoral degrees in 1969–70 and a few new universities that were expected to increase the number of degrees they awarded.

COMPREHENSIVE INSTITUTIONS

Comprehensive universities and colleges I: schools offering liberal arts and at least two professional or occupational programs and enrolling 2,000 or more students.

Comprehensive universities and colleges II: schools offering liberal arts and at least one professional or occupational program and enrolling, if private, at least 1,500, or, if public, at least 1,000 students.

LIBERAL ARTS COLLEGES

Liberal arts colleges I: colleges whose graduates scored well in national merit scholarship qualifying tests or that were among the two hundred whose graduates later received doctorates at the forty leading doctoral-granting institutions between 1920 and 1966.

Liberal arts colleges II: all liberal arts colleges not included in category I.

TWO-YEAR INSTITUTIONS

All two-year colleges and institutes, including those that offer professional education.

SPECIALIZED INSTITUTIONS

Professional and specialized institutions, such as theological seminaries, bible colleges, and institutions offering degrees in religion (but not offering a liberal arts program); medical schools and other separate health professional schools (listed as separate campuses in *Advance Report on Opening Fall Enrollment in Higher Education*); schools of engineering and technology and business and management offering limited programs and awarding bachelor's degrees; schools of art, music, and design; law schools; teachers colleges; and other specialized institutions, such as graduate centers, maritime academies, and military institutes (not offering a liberal arts program).

Federal Student Aid Programs and Authorizing Legislation

Basic educational opportunity grants (BEOG): the largest of the direct federal student aid programs, administered by the U.S. Office of Education. Grants of up to $1,400 a year (authorized to rise to $1,800 a year in 1978–79, although the effective ceiling is $1,600 in fiscal 1978), or half the cost of attendance at the student's institution, are awarded on the basis of financial need. Students must be enrolled at least half time. With a $1,600 ceiling, grants are generally available only to students with adjusted family incomes of roughly $15,000 or less (for a family of four with one child in college). The program was established by the Education Amendments of 1972 (86 Stat. 235) and authorized through fiscal 1979 by the Education Amendments of 1976 (90 Stat. 2081).

College work-study (CWS): provides 80 percent of the minimum wage for part-time employment of low-income students, up to twenty hours a week during the academic year and forty hours during vacations. The awards are made by the college or university. Students must be employed by academic institutions, government agencies, or nonprofit organizations, which pay the remaining 20 percent. They must be enrolled full time to qualify. The CWS program was established by the Economic Opportunity Act of 1964 (78 Stat. 508) and extended through fiscal 1982 by the Education Amendments of 1976 (90 Stat. 2081).

Education Amendments of 1972 (86 Stat. 235): among other provisions, established basic educational opportunity grants and state student incentive grants; reauthorized (with amendments) the college work-study program, guaranteed student loans, and national direct student loans; converted educational opportunity grants into supplemental educational opportunity grants; created the Student Loan Marketing Association, a government-sponsored private corporation, financed by private capital, to provide liquidity and facilitate transactions involving insured student loans; established the National Institute of Education, the Fund for the Improvement of Postsecondary Education, and the National Commission on the Financing of Postsecondary Education (see separate listings for individual programs).

Education Amendments of 1976 (90 Stat. 2081): reauthorized (with amendments) existing student aid programs (BEOG, SEOG, CWS, NDSL, SSIG, GSL—see separate listings) and created, modified, or extended a number of federal education programs and agencies.

Educational opportunity grants (EOG): the original federal campus-based student aid program, established by the Higher Education Act of 1965 (79 Stat. 1219) to aid students with "exceptional financial need." Institutions made grants to full-time students of up to $1,000 per academic year for a maximum of four years. These grants were authorized as supplemental educational opportunity grants (SEOG) by the Education Amendments of 1972 (86 Stat. 235).

GI bill (veterans' education benefits, veterans' educational assistance): provides a flat monthly allowance for up to forty-five months for schooling undertaken within ten years of discharge, out of which the veteran must pay tuition, books, and living expenses. This is one of the largest federal student aid programs ($5.23 billion in 1976, of which $4.3 billion went to higher education); payment is not based on financial need. Payments to veterans with no dependents were $270 for each month enrolled in full-time study in fiscal 1976. The program was changed for men and women entering the Armed Forces after January 1, 1977. Those who want education benefits must contribute to a fund for a minimum of twelve months, which entitles them to matching support from the Veterans Administration at the rate of $2 for every $1 contributed. Individual contributions are limited to $2,700, and benefits may be paid for a maximum of thirty-six months. Education benefits were enacted under the Serviceman's Readjustment Act of 1944 (58 Stat. 284); the present aid program was authorized by the Veterans' Readjustment Benefits Act of 1966 (80 Stat. 12) and amended by the Veterans' Education and Employment Assistance Act of 1976 (90 Stat. 2383).

Guaranteed student loans (GSL): a program to insure and subsidize loans to students made by banks, other commercial lenders, and colleges and universities. The government pays the interest on loans to students from families with adjusted gross income of $25,000 or less while the student is attending school and interest charges in excess of 7 percent while the loan is being repaid. To qualify, students must be enrolled at least half time in an eligible institution; they may borrow up to $2,500 a year, or a total of $7,500, for undergraduate study. Borrowers have ten years to repay, beginning nine months to a year after they leave school. The program was established by the Higher

Education Act of 1965 (79 Stat. 1219) and extended through fiscal 1981 by the Education Amendments of 1976 (90 Stat. 2081).

Higher Education Act of 1965 (79 Stat. 1219): established the educational opportunity grants program (original version of present SEOG program), the guaranteed student loan program, and many other federal programs in higher education, including community service, college library assistance, aid to "developing institutions," and the National Teacher Corps.

National direct student loans (NDSL): a federal campus-based student aid program that funnels federal capital to institutions for direct lending to students at an interest rate of 3 percent, with full federal interest subsidy during student years. Students who are enrolled at least half time and have financial need may borrow up to $2,500 during the first two years of undergraduate study and $5,000 during the last two years. Repayment terms are similar to the GSL program, although the subsidized interest rates differ. The program was established by the National Defense Education Act of 1958 (72 Stat. 1580) (originally designated as national defense student loans) and extended through fiscal 1979 by the Education Amendments of 1976 (90 Stat. 2081).

Social security benefits (old-age, survivors, and disability insurance): dependents of social security beneficiaries who are unmarried, full-time students are entitled to continue receiving child insurance benefits until the end of the academic term in which they turn twenty-two. This is the second largest federal program of direct aid to students; average monthly payments during fiscal 1976 were $143, with $1.3 billion distributed overall. A dependent's benefits are based on the parent's entitlement, calculated at one-half the parent's if the latter is retired or disabled, three-quarters if the parent is dead. After the age of eighteen, the child's benefits are deducted from the parent's check and paid directly to the dependent. Benefits were continued for students aged eighteen to twenty-two by the Social Security Amendments of 1965 (79 Stat. 286).

State student incentive grants (SSIG): a program set up by the Education Amendments of 1972 (86 Stat. 235) to encourage states to establish their own student aid programs. The federal government matches state allocations up to a predetermined level for need-based grants to individual students. The law provides that scholarships, which are limited to $1,500 a year per full-time student, be available only to students with "considerable financial need." The Education Amendments of 1976 require that state programs matched by SSIG funds be open to students in both public and private nonprofit schools. The grants are authorized through fiscal 1979 by the Education Amendments of 1976 (90 Stat. 2081).

Supplemental educational opportunity grants (SEOG): provides federal funds for campus-based student aid grants in addition to amounts distributed under the basic grants program. The college or university administers annual awards of up to $1,500, or half the total amount of financial aid provided to the individual; there is a maximum of $4,000 for four years of undergraduate study. Originally designated as educational opportunity grants (EOG) by the Higher Education Act of 1965 (79 Stat. 1219), this program was authorized through fiscal 1979 by the Education Amendments of 1976 (90 Stat. 2081).

Frequently Used Terms

Access: policies guaranteeing a student admission to, and ability to afford, at least one college or university. In recent debates over student aid programs, the term has become a code word signifying policies thought to favor low-tuition public institutions.

Campus-based programs: federal student aid programs in which individual recipients and the amounts of their assistance are determined by the college or university. Although based on need, these programs use a relatively flexible definition and are therefore much liked by institutional financial aid officers, particularly in the private sector. The three main programs are supplemental educational opportunity grants, college work-study, and national direct student loans (see *Federal Student Aid Programs* above).

Choice: policies guaranteeing a student admission to, and ability to afford, colleges and universities with a wide range of prices. In recent student aid debates, the term has become a code word signifying policies thought to favor private institutions. While "access" and "choice" were once deemed complementary, in a period when shrinking enrollment is anticipated, the two words connote rival policy objectives.

Direct student aid: programs in which the state or federal government, rather than the educational institution, determines an individual's eligibility for assistance and the amount to be provided (see basic educational opportunity grants, GI bill, social security benefits, and the guaranteed student loan program).

Discounting: the policy of reducing tuition at an institution's discretion in order to attract particular applicants; generally administered as a full or partial tuition scholarship.

Educational and general (E and G) revenue: income received by institutions for educational purposes; equals total current revenue minus revenue from auxiliary enterprises (such as student centers and dormitories) and major service programs (such as hospitals), and revenues designated for student aid. (This measure derives from the HEGIS surveys of financial statistics of instituitions, but after the 1974–75 survey revision, E and G revenue can no longer be calculated from the reports.)

Full-time-equivalent (FTE) enrollment: a measure used for determining comparable enrollment (and subsidies keyed to enrollment) at institutions with part-time students. For budgetary purposes, for example, three part-time students may be treated as equivalent to one full-time student (that is, as one FTE student).

Half-cost limitation: a limit built into the basic educational opportunity grants program that confines individual stipends to no more than half the cost of attendance at a given college or university, with cost defined to include tuition plus room, board, and other expenses.

Indirect student aid: state and federal student assistance money channeled to recipients through, and administered by, the institution (see *Campus-Based Programs*).

Need: in student aid parlance, measures the difference between the annual cost of attending a given college and the amount of private (that is, personal and family) resources that a student can contribute.

Portability: a policy that allows students to use financial aid provided by their state of residence at a college or university located in another state.

Student aid deficit or student aid gap: the difference between an institution's student aid expenditures and student aid revenue; an institution's unrestricted or general funds devoted to student assistance.

Tuition offset grants: a term referring to any of a number of programs providing per capita government payments to private colleges and universities or their students. The purpose is to reduce the tuition differential between private and public sectors. (See NCICU, *A National Policy for Private Higher Education* [Association of American Colleges, 1974], chap. 5, for discussion of numerous versions of this type of aid.)

Conference Participants

with their affiliations at the time of the conference

HENRY J. AARON *Brookings Institution*
DAVID ADAMANY *University of Wisconsin, Madison*
ROBERT C. ANDRINGA *Committee on Education and Labor, U.S. House of Representatives*
STEPHEN K. BAILEY *American Council on Education*
ROBERT O. BERDAHL *State University of New York, Buffalo*
COLIN C. BLAYDON *Duke University*
DAVID W. BRENEMAN *Brookings Institution*
DAVID G. BROWN *Miami University, Oxford, Ohio*
J. MARTIN CAROVANO *Hamilton College*
RICHARD M. CYERT *Carnegie-Mellon University*
CHESTER E. FINN, JR. *Brookings Institution*
LAWRENCE E. GLADIEUX *College Entrance Examination Board*
NATHAN GLAZER *Harvard University*
ROBERT W. HARTMAN *Brookings Institution*
ROGER W. HEYNS *American Council on Education*
T. EDWARD HOLLANDER *New York State Education Department*
JOHN C. HONEY *Syracuse University*
HANS H. JENNY *College of Wooster*
HERBERT KAUFMAN *Brookings Institution*
CARL KAYSEN *Massachusetts Institute of Technology*
STEVEN MULLER *Johns Hopkins University*
SUSAN C. NELSON *Brookings Institution*
BARBARA W. NEWELL *Wellesley College*
JOSEPH A. PECHMAN *Brookings Institution*
MICHAEL S. MCPHERSON *Williams College*
JOHN D. PHILLIPS *National Association of Independent Colleges and Universities*

459

ROY RADNER *University of California, Berkeley*
LOIS D. RICE *College Entrance Examination Board*
NAN S. ROBINSON *University of Massachusetts*
EMIL M. SUNLEY, JR. *Brookings Institution*
G. FREDERICK THOMPSON *University of British Columbia and California Postsecondary Education Commission*
THOMAS E. WENZLAU *Ohio Wesleyan University*
THOMAS R. WOLANIN *Committee on Education and Labor, U.S. House of Representatives*

Index